D1442773

The Principal's Legal Handbook

Editors

William E. Camp, California State University, San Bernardino
Julie K. Underwood, University of Wisconsin - Madison
Mary Jane Connelly, University of Tennessee, Knoxville
Kenneth E. Lane, California State University, San Bernardino

National Organization on Legal Problems of Education

1993

DISCLAIMER

The National Organization on Legal Problems of Education (NOLPE) is a private, nonadvocacy, and nonprofit association of educators and attorneys. The opinions expressed in this publication are those of the authors and do not represent official views of the Organization.

Copyright © 1993

by

National Organization on Legal Problems of Education

All Rights Reserved

ISBN 1-56534-056-6

Published by

NATIONAL ORGANIZATION ON LEGAL PROBLEMS OF EDUCATION
3601 S.W. 29th Street, Suite 223
Topeka, Kansas 66614
(913) 273-3550

Table of Contents

Schools and the Law

Students And The Law

1

Search and Seizure in the Public Schools

Gail Paulus Sorenson, Nelda H. Cambron-McCabe, and Stephen B. Thomas

Introduction

A Justice Department study released in 1991 showed that nine percent of secondary school students were the victims of battery, robbery, and rape during a six month period in the late 1980s.[1] Also in 1991, Florida reported that assault (defined as bodily harm or threat of harm), weapons possession, and drug or alcohol possession ranked at the top of a year-long, statewide study of serious school offenses.[2] While assault/battery made up 43% of the offenses, there were nearly 3,000 instances of weapons possession and almost 2,500 cases of drug or alcohol possession. These studies, taken together, suggest that the issue of search and seizure may be even more important to educational administrators and policymakers in the 1990s than it was in the 1980s.

Search policies and procedures may entail personal searches and/or searches of personal possessions, as well as the use of metal detectors, scent dogs, two-way mirrors, and drug tests (e.g., urinalysis). Depending upon the particulars of each policy and the procedures followed, students may be able successfully to claim that their right to be free from unreasonable search and seizure under the fourth amendment has been violated. Sometimes the claim is couched in more general terms: that school personnel have invaded a student's right of privacy, a right that the Supreme Court has held to be implicit in the United States Constitution, and a right that most certainly implicates fourth amendment values and concerns. Where rights are violated, evidence of wrong-doing may be suppressed in juvenile or criminal proceedings against the students (the "exclusionary rule"), and the potential exists for school district and/or individual liability for violating students' constitutional rights.[3]

Legal Issues

The original intention of the fourth amendment—and other provisions of the Bill of Rights—was to prohibit the federal government from violating certain fundamental rights of individuals. The restriction on government power was extended to state governments in the mid-twentieth century and has now been applied to public school officials as well.[4] The amendment states that individuals have a right "to be secure in their persons, houses, papers, and effects, against unreasonable searches and seizures...," and that probable cause is required for a warrant. A legally enforceable warrant must describe the place to be searched and the persons or things to be seized. Not all searches by government officials are constrained by the probable cause and warrant requirements. For example, a search may be conducted incident to a lawful arrest, even though a warrant has not been acquired. Search and seizure is also legal if evidence or contraband is in plain view of an officer, assuming the officer is lawfully on the premises. Additionally, reasonable searches by school officials that are justified at inception and are reasonably related in scope to the circumstances that prompted the search also are permissible. The standards affecting educators were advanced by the Supreme Court in *New Jersey v. T.L.O.*, in 1985, and are the focus of this chapter.[5]

Standards for Conducting A Search

Two primary standards have evolved under the fourth amendment: "probable cause" and "reasonableness" under all circumstances. Probable cause is the standard explicit in the amendment and exists where the facts and circumstances within the searcher's knowledge, and received from trustworthy sources, are sufficient to warrant a person of reasonable caution to believe that a particular offense has been committed.[6] However, the Supreme Court has noted that the probable cause standard is not an "irreducible requirement of a valid search."[7] Rather, the fundamental command of the fourth amendment is that searches be reasonable and, although probable cause and a warrant "bear on the reasonableness of a search," at times neither is required. The Court argued that where "a careful balancing of governmental and private interests suggests that the public interest is best served by a fourth amendment standard of reasonableness that stops short of probable cause, we have not hesitated to adopt such a standard."[8]

The reasonableness standard was applied in *New Jersey v. T.L.O.*, the only school search and seizure case decided by the Supreme Court to date. In that case, a teacher saw T.L.O. and a companion smoking in a lavatory in violation of school rules. The students were questioned by the vice principal. The first student admitted to smoking, but T.L.O. denied smoking as well as being a smoker. The administrator then asked to see T.L.O.'s purse, which she reluctantly provided. After opening her purse, the vice principal immediately saw a pack of cigarettes. Possession of cigarettes was not a violation of school rules, but possession did support the eye witness testimony that T.L.O. had been smoking. Once the administrator removed the cigarettes, he noticed rolling papers, which he associated with marijuana use. He then conducted a thorough search of the purse and discovered a small quantity of marijuana, a pipe, numerous one dollar bills, plastic bags, a list of people who owed T.L.O. money, and two letters implicating her in drug sales. The evidence was turned over to the police and delinquency charges were filed. Although T.L.O. at first confessed to selling drugs, she later claimed that all the evidence provided by school officials should be suppressed because the items were seized in violation of her fourth amendment rights.[9]

In deciding the case, the Supreme Court held that the fourth amendment applies to searches conducted by public school officials but that the probable cause standard is not required. Instead, to meet constitutional scrutiny, such searches need to be reasonable. In examining the events leading to a search, the Court ruled that a search would be reasonable if it were:

- justified at its inception, i.e., there were reasonable grounds for suspecting that the search would turn up evidence that the student had violated either the law or a school rule
- reasonably related in scope to the circumstances that justified the search in the first place, i.e., the measures adopted were reasonably related to the objectives of the search and not excessively intrusive in light of the age and sex of the student and the nature of the infraction.[10]

In *T.L.O.*, both searches were held reasonable. The report that she was smoking justified the first search for cigarettes, while the discovery of rolling papers prompted a reasonable suspicion that the purse contained marijuana.

The reasonableness standard advanced by the Supreme Court was not new in the school setting; most lower courts had previously applied this standard to the search of students. However, the post-*T.L.O.* cases indicate that, at a minimum, searches of students must be based on objective facts.[11] Factors that have been considered in determining reasonableness include:

> the child's age, history, and record in the school; prevalence and seriousness of the problem in the school to which the search is directed; exigency to make the search without delay and further investigation; probative value and reliability of the information used as a justification for the search; the school officials' experience with the student and with the type of problem to which the search was directed; and the type of search.[12]

Concomitant with the necessity to show articulable facts to establish reasonable grounds to search, most courts have required individualized suspicion; that is, searches by school officials must be based on facts that support a reasonable belief that the individual student is engaged in a proscribed activity or possesses certain contraband.[13] In circumstances of grave danger, however, it may be sufficient that suspicion focus on a small group of students, as suggested by a case where one of five or six students in a group was suspected of having a weapon.[14]

According to the Supreme Court, the reasonableness of a search is assessed in terms of all the circumstances surrounding the search. Recent cases are instructive in understanding what factors establish reasonable grounds to conduct a search. In a Washington state case, a student challenged the search of his locker in which school officials discovered hallucinogenic mushrooms.[15] Among the facts found to establish reasonable grounds were information from a student that the suspected student was selling marijuana, the administrator's belief that the student was a drug user based on several reports from teachers and on her own observations, and the student's frequent presence at a location known for drug trafficking among students. The search was upheld.[16]

Similarly, information from a student informant in another case, along with prior reports of drug selling, was held sufficient to justify the search of a student's person, locker, and car.[17] A California appellate court also held the search of a student's pockets permissible when he was found in a restroom during class time without a pass.[18] The student's nervous appearance and failure to produce a pass coupled with frequent drug incidents in the restrooms established a reasonable basis for the search.[19]

In contrast, the Supreme Court of California found that the search of a student who hid a calculator behind his back was not reasonable.[20] An assistant principal stopped several students as they walked through campus to inquire as to why they were late for class. When one student attempted to conceal a calculator case, the school official requested to see the case and, upon the student's refusal to relinquish the case, escorted him to the school office to be searched. In the absence of any prior knowledge of possession, use, or sale of drugs, the court concluded that lateness for class did not establish a reasonable suspicion that the student was engaged in prohibited conduct. Likewise, a Michigan federal district court held that the search of a student who was hiding behind cars in a parking lot when she should have been in class did not establish a reasonable suspicion that she possessed illegal drugs.[21] The court noted that the student's actions created a suspicion that she had violated "some rule or law," but the burden is on administrators to show that the conduct establishes a reasonable suspicion that a specific rule or law has been violated and that the search will produce evidence of that violation.

Clearly, courts view previous experience of administrators as an important element in establishing reasonable suspicion. In recent cases, the suspicious behavior of a student augmented by an administrator's knowledge of the student's history and an understanding of the seriousness of the problem in the school has led courts to support searches based on general suspicious conduct. The reasonableness standard, however, may be inadequate in the school setting if police are involved in a search. Depending on the nature and extent of police involvement, probable cause may be required.

The Supreme Court noted in *T.L.O.* that it was not addressing what standard would be required when school officials conduct searches "in conjunction with or at the behest of law enforcement agencies."[22] Subsequent cases suggest that reasonable suspicion will be applicable if police officers assume a narrow, limited role.[23] For example, the officers do not develop the facts that prompt a search or direct school officials to search a student.

Scope of the Search

After a search is found to be justified at its inception, the scope of the search must be assessed. According to the Supreme Court, the search must be reasonably related in scope to the circumstances that justified the interference initially. A number of courts have found the right to inspect lockers to be inherent in school officials' authority to manage the schools. The Supreme Court of Kansas stated that "it [is] a proper function of school authorities to inspect the lockers under their control and to prevent their use...for illegal purposes."[24] The Tenth Circuit Court of Appeals asserted that there is a duty to inspect where possible violations of the law may exist.[25]

Many courts have found that the joint control of lockers by students and school officials lowers students' expectation of privacy. In some cases where searches have been upheld, students had prior notice that school officials maintained a list of combinations or a master key and that lockers would be inspected on a regular basis.[26] While the authority to inspect lockers is broad, the search of selected lockers must be based on a reasonable suspicion that specific contraband will be found since some expectation of privacy has been violated.

The search of personal property involves a greater expectation of privacy than the search of a school locker, but such searches are not considered excessively intrusive when reasonable grounds exist to conduct the search. As shown in *T.L.O.*, the search of a student's purse based on the belief that it contained cigarettes was justified.[27] Other searches that have been upheld based on reasonable suspicion involved jackets, books, storage containers, and cars.[28]

The use of drug-detecting dogs in searching property raises several issues regarding the reasonableness of the extent of the search, as well as the justification for the search. The Supreme Court has not addressed the use of canines in schools, but along with the vast majority of lower courts, has held that the use of dogs to sniff objects is not a search and involves a very limited investigation.[29] The Fifth Circuit Court of Appeals specifically held that the "sniffing" of student cars and lockers is not a search. However, if a search of the property is later conducted on the basis of a dog's alert, reasonable suspicion can only be shown by establishing that the dogs are reliable in detecting drugs.[30]

The Fifth Circuit Court of Appeals stated that "the fourth amendment applies with its fullest vigor against any intrusion on the human body."[31] Because of the intrusiveness of a search of a student's person, the circumstances must adequately justify such an interference. Where searches at their inception have been based upon reasonable suspicion, courts have generally upheld the search of students' pockets.[32] Pat-down searches also have been found to be reasonable when an initial search of a student's clothing or possessions revealed physical evidence of the violation of a school rule or criminal law.[33]

Strip searches, however, have required substantial evidence and probable cause. While the Supreme Court has not addressed this level of intrusion, other courts have made strong pronouncements. The Second Circuit Court of Appeals stated that "as the intrusiveness of the search intensifies, the standard of fourth amendment reasonableness approaches probable cause, even in the school context."[34] The Seventh Circuit Court of Appeals noted that "it does not require a constitutional scholar to conclude that a nude search of a thirteen-year-old child is an invasion of constitutional rights of some magnitude. More than that: it is a violation of any known principle of human decency."[35] Courts have not prohibited strip searches, but litigation indicates that circumstances will be carefully weighed to substantiate the necessity for such an invasion of privacy. While the use of canines to "sniff" objects is not a search, the sniffing of persons has been held to be a significant invasion of privacy and thus to constitute a search. As such, courts have generally required that school officials have individualized suspicion that a student possesses drugs prior to the use of dogs in a search.[36] However, if individualized suspicion exists, other less intrusive methods to search are preferable.

The final case in this section concerns the rare charge that school officials have violated a student's fourth amendment right to be free from unreasonable seizure. Not surprisingly, the Tenth Circuit Court of Appeals made clear that a vice principal's twenty-minute questioning of a student accused by two others of a bomb threat was "reasonably related in scope to determining whether he had indeed called in the...threat."[37]

Recent Developments

There is little question that drug use is a serious problem in some districts; however, many questions surround the legality of school-initiated drug testing of large numbers of students. Drug-testing policies not only implicate fourth amendment search and seizure provisions, but, depending on how they are structured, also may implicate the fourteenth amendment's equal protection and due process clauses which prohibit discrimination and arbitrary invasions of personal privacy, respectively. It is possible that such policies may implicate state constitutional and statutory provisions as well.

Although there are few reported cases, a federal district court ruled in 1989 that a urinalysis program applicable to all secondary-school students participating in extracurricular activities was an unconstitutional violation of students' privacy rights under the fourth amendment.[38] Applying two 1989 Supreme Court cases from outside education,[39] the court found that the "global goal of prevention" did not provide the "compelling interest" necessary to justify the program: "[E]very court that has considered urine testing of the general student body in a public school has found it unconstitutional."[40] The court also opined that a 1988 Seventh Circuit case approving the random drug testing of interscholastic athletes and cheerleaders[41] would not survive the 1989 Supreme Court precedent, thus casting doubt on the one major case where limited, school-sponsored drug testing had been previously approved.

An even more problematic issue, because of the paucity of judicial guidance, involves the use of metal detectors to screen for dangerous weapons and to deter potential school violence. Although metal detectors have reportedly been used or approved for use in Detroit, Chicago, New York City, and in counties in Pennsylvania and Florida[42] (with the earliest use in the Detroit schools in 1985);[43] the legality of the systematic or random use of metal detectors is not known. In early legal skirmishes involving the Detroit public schools, however, newspapers reported a judicial order limiting the use of detectors to situations where reasonable cause suggested a violation of law or school rules—thus following the Supreme Court's guidance in *T.L.O.*[44] Whether the numbers of weapons involved and the potential danger, along with assertions of the limited intrusiveness of metal-detector screening, will lead to an exception to the general rule requiring particularized suspicion is left for future decision.

As a final note, it may be worth assuring educators, who are compelled by state law to report suspected child abuse and/or suspected drug and alcohol abuse, that the defense of qualified immunity is available for investigatory searches. Although there are few cases, it appears that immunity may provide a successful defense for otherwise reasonable searches conducted pursuant to an investigation of abuse.[45]

Recommendations For Practice

- The Supreme Court held that the fourth amendment applies to public schools but recognized that the stringent warrant requirement based on probable cause is not appropriate. School administrators can conduct searches if there are reasonable grounds for concluding that the search will produce evidence that a student is violating or has violated the law or a school rule.
- Reasonableness is not established solely by objective facts but also by the personal knowledge and experience of the administrator.
- In addition to reasonable grounds, the scope of the search must not be excessively intrusive in light of the age and sex of the child and the nature of the infraction. Accordingly, the methods employed in a search must be balanced against the necessity or purpose of a search. If credible information indi-

cates that a student possesses a weapon, a more intrusive search might be more justified than if a student is suspected of possessing cigarettes.

- The intrusiveness of the search also will determine the degree of certainty required to make the search reasonable. Thus, the search of a student's purse requires an administrator to have a reasonable suspicion that evidence of a violation of a school rule or statute may be found. But to conduct a strip search, the higher standard of probable cause generally will be required, in addition to greater necessity.

- Policies that involve the drug testing of groups of students by urinalysis should be avoided unless it is clear that a compelling justification exists.

- The development of metal-detector screening policies should be examined as judicial clarification of the legality of such policies continues to advance.

- While school administrators have been given significant discretion to search students to ensure a safe school environment, students' rights to be free from unreasonable searches also has been affirmed. It is advisable for school officials to enact policies addressing when searches will be conducted, what establishes reasonable grounds to search, what types of searches will be conducted, and who will initiate searches. Parents and students should be informed each year of the school's procedures for conducting searches.

References

[1] Education Wk., Oct. 9, 1991, at 12, col. 2.

[2] Education Wk., Oct. 2, 1991, at 2, col. 4.

[3] Liability under section 1983 of the Civil Rights Act of 1871 (42 U.S.C. § 1983) is beyond the scope of this chapter. For more information see Monell v. Department of Social Servs. 436 U.S. 658 (1978).

[4] See Wolf v. Colorado, 338 U.S. 25 (1949); Elkins v. United States, 364 U.S. 206 (1960); Mapp v. Ohio, 367 U.S. 643 (1961).

[5] 469 U.S. 325 (1985). For additional general information on search and seizure, see L. FISCHER & G. SORENSON, SCHOOL LAW FOR COUNSELORS, PSYCHOLOGISTS & SOCIAL WORKERS at 139-145 (1991).

[6] Carroll v. United States, 267 U.S. 132 (1925).

[7] New Jersey v. T.L.O., 469 U.S. 325, 340 (1985).

[8] Id at 341.

[9] In 1914, the United States Supreme Court, in Weeks v. United States, 232 U.S. 383 (1914), adopted the "exclusionary rule" for federal criminal trials; that rule was extended to state criminal trials in 1961 in Mapp v. Ohio, 367 U.S. 643 (1961).

[10] T.L.O., 469 U.S. 325, 341-342 (1985).

[11] This is consistent with the Supreme Court's ruling in the law enforcement area. In recognizing an exception of the warrant requirement for police officers, the Court held that searches must be supported by "specific and articulable facts." Terry v. Ohio, 392 U.S. 1, 21 (1968).

[12] M. MCCARTHY & N. CAMBRON-MCCABE, PUBLIC SCHOOL LAW: TEACHERS' AND STUDENTS' RIGHTS 219 (1987).

[13]*See In re* William G., 709 P.2d 1287 (Cal. 1985); Kuehn v. Renton School Dist. No. 403, 694 P.2d 1078 (Wash. 1985).

[14]*In re* Alexander B, 270 Cal. Rptr. 342 (Ct. App. 1990).

[15]State v. Brooks, 718 P.2d 837 (Wash. Ct. App. 1986).

[16]*See also,* Commonwealth v. Carey, 554 N.E.2d 1199 (Mass. 1990); (teacher informant provided information justifying reasonable-suspicion search).

[17]State v. Slattery, 787 P.2d 932 (Wash. Ct. App. 1990).

[18]*In re* Bobby B., 218 Cal. Rptr. 253 (Ct. App. 1985).

[19]*See also,* Wynn v. Board of Educ. of Vestavia Hills, 508 So. 2d 1170 (Ala. 1987), *In re* Frederick B., 237 Cal. Rptr. 338 (Ct. App. 1987); R.D.L. v. State, 499 So. 2d 31 (Fla. Dist. Ct. App. 1986); *In re* Robert B., 218 Cal. Rptr. 337 (Ct. App. 1985).

[20]*William G.,* 709 P.2d 1287.

[21]Cales v. Howell Pub. Schools, 635 F. Supp. 454 (E.D. Mich. 1985). *See also, In re* Pima County Juvenile Action, 733 P.2d 316 (Ariz. Ct. Appt. 1987).

[22]*T.L.O.,* 469 U.S. 325, 341 (1985).

[23]Cason v. Cook, 810 F.2d 188 (8th Cir. 1987), *cert. denied,* 482 U.S. 930 (1987); Martens v. District No. 220, 620 F. Supp. 29 (N.D. Ill. 1985). *See also, In re* Alexander B., 270 Cal. Rptr. 342 (Ct. App. 1990) (police officer's search held "reasonable" based on order from dean who had reasonable cause to believe student had gun).

[24]State v. Stein, 456 P.2d 1 (Kan. 1969), *cert. denied,* 397 U.S. 947 (1970). But *see* S.C. v. State, 583 So. 2d 188 (Miss. 1991) (*T.L.O.* standards applied to locker search).

[25]Zamora v. Pomeroy, 639 F.2d 662 (10th Cir. 1981).

[26]*See* State v. Stein, 456 P.2d 1 (Kan. 1969); *In re* Donaldson, 75 Cal. Rptr. 220 (Ct. App. 1969).

[27]*T.L.O.,* 469 U.S. 325, 341. *See also,* Cason v. Cook, 810 F.2d 188 (8th Cir. 1987), *cert. denied,* 482 U.S. 930 (1987). But *cf.* T.J. v. State, 538 So. 2d 1320 (Fla. Ct. App. 1989) (search of zippered pocket in purse too broad when only knife was sought).

[28]*See* Wynn v. Board of Educ., 508 So. 2d 1170 (Ala. 1987); State v. D.T.W., 425 So. 2d 1383 (Fla. Ct. App. 1983).

[29]United States v. Place, 462 U.S. 696 (1983); Another court has held that a school official also may sniff for the scent of marijuana and that such action is not a search. Burnham v. West, 681 F. Supp. 1160 (E.D. Va. 1987), *supplemented* 681 F. Supp. 1169 (E.D. Va. 1988).

[30]Horton v. Goose Creek Indep. School Dist., 690 F.2d 470 (5th Cir. 1982), *clarified* 693 F.2d 524 (5th Cir. 1982), *cert. denied,* 463 U.S. 1207 (1983).

[31]*Id.*

[32]*See* Martens v. District No. 220, Bd. of Educ., 620 F. Supp. 29 (N.D. Ill. 1985); *In re* Bobby B., 218 Cal. Rptr. 253 (Ct. App. 1985).

[33]*See Cason,* 810 F.2d 188.

[34]M.M. v. Anker, 607 F.2d 588, 589 (2d Cir. 1979).

[35]Doe v. Renfrow, 631 F.2d 91, 92-93 (7th Cir. 1980), *cert. denied,* 451 U.S. 1022 (1981).

[36]*See* Horton v. Goose Creek Indep. School Dist., 690 F.2d 470 (5th Cir. 1982), *clarified,* 693 F.2d 524 (5th Cir. 1982)., *cert. denied,* 463 U.S. 1207 (1983). *See* Doe v. Renfrow, 631 F.2d 91 (dog's sniff of person not a search).

[37]Edwards v. Rees, 883 F.2d 882, 884 (10th Cir. 1989).

[38]Brooks v. East Chambers Consol. Indep. School Dist., 730 F. Supp. 759 (S.D. Tex. 1989), *aff'd mem. sub. nom.,* Brooks v. East Chambers County School, 930 F.2d 915 (5th Cir. 1991). *See also,* Patchogue-Medford Congress of Teachers v. Board of Educ., 517 N.Y.S.2d 456 (1987) (drug testing of probationary teachers prior to tenure held unconstitutional) and Georgia Assoc. of Educators v. Harris, 749 F. Supp. 1110 (N.D. Ga. 1990) (drug screening of all applicants for state employment violated search and seizure provision).

[39]Skinner v. Railway Labor Executives' Ass'n, 109 S. Ct. 1402 (1989) and National Treasury Employees Union v. Von Raab 109 S. Ct. 1384 (1989).

[40]*Brooks,* 730 F. Supp. at 765.

[41]Schaill v. Tippecanoe School Corp., 864 F.2d 1309 (7th Cir. 1988).

[42]Education Week, Mar. 16, 1988, at 7 col. 1; Education Week, Mar. 27, 1991, at 3, col. 1; Education Week, April 10, 1991, at 2, col. 4.

[43]Education Week, Mar. 16, 1988, at 7, col. 1.

[44]*Id.*

[45]*See* Landstrom v. Illinois Dep't of Child and Family Servs., 699 F. Supp. 1270 (N.D. Ill. 1988).

2
Freedom of Expression
David Schimmel

Introduction

For more than 175 years, it was assumed the United States Constitution did not protect student freedom of speech or press. If students challenged school censorship during those years, courts presumed that the school's policy or disciplinary action was valid, and students had the burden of proving that the censorship was unreasonable. The task was nearly impossible, and the rare student who went to court almost always lost. In effect, the first amendment applied to adults in the community but not to students in the schools.

In the 1969 landmark case of *Tinker v. Des Moines*,[1] the United States Supreme Court held that the first amendment did protect freedom of expression in the public schools. Most administrators have come to accept the *Tinker* ruling and have shaped their school policies accordingly. However, in a 1986 case on student speech[2] and a 1988 controversy concerning student newspapers,[3] the Supreme Court ruled in favor of administrative limitation on student expression. In view of these apparently conflicting rulings, this chapter clarifies the scope and limits of student freedom of expression in the public schools.

Legal Issues

Student Expression

In *Tinker v. Des Moines*, the Supreme Court ruled that students do not "shed their Constitutional rights to freedom of speech or expression at the schoolhouse gate."[4] In hundreds of cases since then, every state and federal court has reaffirmed this basic principle. Clearly, the first amendment still protects a student's personal opinions, even controversial ones.

According to the Supreme Court, "Students in school as well as out of school are...possessed of fundamental rights which the State must respect, just as they themselves must respect their obligations to the State."[5] Since schools are "educating the young for citizenship," they should protect the "Constitutional freedoms of the individual, if we are not to strangle the free mind at its source and teach youth to discount important principles of our government as mere platitudes."[6] Thus, in *Tinker* the Court ruled that students had the constitutional right to wear black armbands to public schools and to publicize their opposition to American involvement in the Vietnam War.

The Court realized that protecting controversial speech might cause problems in schools. In fact, it recognized that "any word spoken, in class, in the lunchroom, or on the campus, that deviates from the views of another person may start an argument or cause a disturbance."[7] According to the Court, "our Constitution says we must take this risk; and our history says that it is this sort of hazardous freedom—this kind of openness—that is the basis of our national strength...independence and vigor."[8]

Disruptive Speech

Despite the breadth of the *Tinker* decision, it also recognized that schools can legally limit student expression. In *Tinker*, the Court identified that limit when it wrote that any student conduct which "materially disrupts classwork or involves substantial disorder or invasion of the rights of others" is not protected by the constitutional guarantee of freedom of speech.[9] Thus, a federal appeals court allowed administrators to enforce a "no-button" rule in a Cleveland high school because evidence indicated that such symbols led to serious fighting between black and white students and substantially disrupted the educational process.[10]

Symbolic speech, however, cannot be prohibited merely because administrators are fearful or concerned about possible disruptions. As the Supreme Court stated: "Undifferentiated fear or apprehension of disturbance is not enough to overcome the right to freedom of expression."[11] To restrict such expression, administrators must justify their actions based on evidence, not just intuition, that the forbidden expression would substantially interfere with the work of the school. They cannot prohibit a particular opinion merely "to avoid the discomfort and unpleasantness that always accompany an unpopular view."[12]

Principals do not have to wait until a disruption takes place to limit speech. In a case concerning a student demonstration inside a school, a judge explained that a school official may restrict student expression when there is significant evidence of a "reasonable likelihood of substantial disorder."[13] A similar result was reached in an Indiana case in which several students were suspended for distributing leaflets calling for a "school walkout." Since only four students walked out, the suspended students claimed that their leaflets did not cause a substantial disorder. But the judge ruled that student expression is not protected where administrators "can demonstrate any facts" which lead them to reasonably "forecast" substantial disruption.[14] Since dozens of students disrupted classes when they walked out the day before, the administrators had adequate evidence to believe the leaflets would prompt a similar disruption.[15]

Obscene or Vulgar Speech

Courts have never protected student speech or writing that is obscene. Language is not legally obscene merely because it contains offensive, vulgar, or "dirty" words. To be legally obscene, material must violate three tests developed by the Supreme Court: (1) it must appeal to the "prurient" or lustful interest; (2) it must describe sexual conduct in a way that is "patently offensive" to community standards; and (3) taken as a whole, it "must lack serious literary, artistic, political, or scientific value."[16]

Until recently, it was not clear when school administrators could prohibit and punish vulgar and offensive speech that was not legally obscene or disruptive. In 1986, the Supreme Court partially clarified this issue in the case of *Bethel v. Fraser*. The case involved a high school senior, Matthew Fraser, who was punished for giving a nominating speech at a school assembly that referred to his candidate using "an elaborate, graphic, and explicit sexual metaphor."[17] In *Bethel*, the Court ruled that school officials have broad authority to punish students for using "offensively lewd and indecent speech" in classrooms, assemblies, and other school-sponsored educational activities—even if the speech did not cause disruption and was not legally obscene. In addition, *Bethel* held that administrators have discretion to define and determine what constitutes vulgar and offensive speech.

It is not clear whether *Bethel* gives school officials discretion to punish vulgar speech among students that occurs in hallways, cafeterias, or other noneducational settings. In any case, *Bethel* does not mean that administrators can punish students for expressing personal views merely because they are controversial, unpopular, or offend majority opinion.[18]

School-sponsored Curricular Publications

The first amendment gives very little protection to student free-dom of the press in school-sponsored, curricular publications. This decision was the ruling of the Supreme Court in the 1988 case of *Hazelwood v. Kuhlmeier*. The case involved a St. Louis high school principal who objected to two stories about pregnancy and divorce in a student newspaper that were written and published as part of a regular journalism course. The Court ruled that a curricular newspaper was not a "public forum" and that "school officials were entitled to regulate the contents...in any reasonable manner."[19] The Court explained that when a student expresses personal, contro-versial views on school grounds, such views are protected by the first amendment and the principles of *Tinker* apply. In school-spon-sored publications or theatrical productions that are part of the school curriculum, educators may exercise greater control and set higher standards for student speech. Thus, the Court wrote that in a curricular publication, educators have broad discretion to pro-hibit articles that are "ungrammatical, poorly written, inadequately researched, biased or prejudiced, vulgar or profane, or unsuitable for immature audiences."[20] In short, the Court held that neither teachers nor administrators violate the first amendment by "exer-cising editorial control over the style and content of student speech in school-sponsored expressive activities so long as their actions are reasonably related to legitimate pedagogical concerns."[21] The Court concluded that the principal in *Hazelwood* acted "reasonably" in de-leting the controversial articles because of his concern that the ar-ticles were not sensitive to the privacy interests of the students, boyfriends, or parents who were mentioned.[22]

Student-sponsored Underground Publications.

The Supreme Court decision in *Hazelwood* does not give school officials control over the style and content of underground student periodicals which are published without school sponsorship or sup-port and are not part of the curriculum. Instead, *Tinker* governs such publications, and their distribution usually cannot be prohib-ited unless administrators have evidence to forecast that they will cause substantial disruption, interfere with the rights of others, or promote illegal activities. Thus, underground publications cannot be banned for discussing unpopular, sensitive, or controversial topics, and students cannot be punished merely for criticizing school of-ficials or administrative policies in such publications.

Students may be required to submit their publications to admin-istrators for review before distribution. The justification for allowing prior review, explained one judge, is "to prevent disruption and not to stifle expression."[23] Most courts have prohibited schools from censoring publications through prior restraint without clear, objective standards and procedural safeguards.[24]

Recent Developments

Since 1988, school officials have relied on the *Hazelwood* decision to justify policies restricting student expression. This decision has led to a variety of interpretations in state and federal courts. Some judges have interpreted *Hazelwood* broadly and supported restrictions on school-sponsored expression that was not related to the curriculum. For example, a divided federal appeals court ruled in favor of the Nevada principals who refused to print an advertisement by Planned Parenthood not only in the school newspaper and yearbook, which were published as part of the curriculum, but also in the athletic programs, which were not.[25] According to the court, schools retain the right to disapprove of ads that might carry a school-sponsored message to readers and put their imprimatur on one side of a controversial issue. Furthermore, some judges have interpreted *Hazelwood* to grant administrators broader control over curricular decisions than they had in the past.[26]

Other judges have interpreted *Hazelwood* more narrowly. One example is a case concerning restrictions on a peace group's participation in Career Day in Atlanta schools. Administrators argued that *Hazelwood* permitted them to control the content of the curricular programs and ban any group that criticized opportunities presented by other participants. However, a federal appeals court struck down the ban. It acknowledged that schools could decline to discuss military careers. If such a topic is discussed, the *Hazelwood* decision does not justify "allowing educators to discriminate" against a particular viewpoint.[27] Another federal decision that interpreted *Hazelwood* narrowly concerned a controversial student-written piece in a school-sponsored noncurricular newspaper. The School argued that their authority to control the curriculum should include extracurricular or co-curricular activities such as the student paper, but the court disagreed. The judge declined to interpret *Hazelwood* broadly because it "opens the door to significant curtailment of cherished first amendment rights." The court concluded that "educators may exercise greater editorial control over what students write for class than what they voluntarily submit to an extracurricular, albeit school funded, publication."[28]

A number of recent controversies involved student distribution of religious or political publications. Policies prohibiting distribution of such materials have been struck down. A Colorado case involved students who were suspended for giving out a Christian newspaper, *Issues and Answers*, in violation of a policy prohibiting distribution of "material that proselytizes a particular religious or political belief." The administrators argued that *Hazelwood* allowed them to prohibit distribution of such controversial publications, but the judge disagreed and explained: "Because students have a right to engage in political and religious speech," school policies that completely ban such publications "do not advance any legitimate government interest." Instead, by preventing students from discussing issues they feel are important, the policies inhibit their individual development and "defeat the very purpose of public education in secondary schools."[29] In a similar 1991 Pennsylvania case that also concerned a school policy prohibiting distribution of all proselytizing materials, a federal judge "categorically rejected" the school's argument that such a prohibition was "necessary to an educational environment."[30]

On the other hand, content-neutral policies that simply regulate the time, place, and manner in which students can distribute publications are usually upheld. In a recent Colorado case that also concerned *Issues and Answers*, students challenged school rules that prohibited distribution of newspapers in hallways. Since distribution was allowed in other school locations, and the restrictions were applied equally to all students, the restrictions were designed to maintain order, and the restrictions were not based on the viewpoint of the publication; the court concluded that the policy did not violate student freedom of expression.[31] In another case challenging a policy that banned distribution of publications in school hallways (but allowed them elsewhere), a federal court ruled that reasonable restrictions "on the time, place, and manner of communicating nonschool speech" did not violate the first amendment.[32]

In a related Supreme Court decision concerning the recognition of religious clubs, the Court upheld the Federal Equal Access Act, which prohibits public secondary schools that maintain a "limited open forum" from denying equal access to students who wish to meet on the basis of the "religious, political, philosophical, or other content" of the speech at such meetings. Concerning their fear that by permitting controversial speech, a school will appear to endorse it, the Court wrote: "We think that secondary students are mature enough and are likely to understand that a school does not endorse or support student speech that it merely permits...."[33]

Although no public school in any state can provide less protection for student speech than required by the United States Supreme Court, individual states or school districts can provide more than this minimum. Thus, in the aftermath of *Hazelwood*, a number of states—through statute or judicial interpretation—now have greater protection for student expression. In New Jersey, a state superior court ruled in favor of a student whose movie reviews for the school-funded extracurricular newspaper were censored because they reviewed R-rated films that the principal considered "inappropriate for junior high students." Judge Francis stated that, if he were to decide the case under the United States Constitution, he would be "compelled to declare," that the school's action was not constitutional under "the test laid down by the United States Supreme Court in *Hazelwood*." He ruled that the school violated the student's rights under the New Jersey Constitution, which is "more expansive than the first amendment" and "indicates that free speech is an affirmative right."[34]

In other states, student expression is protected by statute. For example, the California Education Code states: "Students of the public schools shall have the right to exercise freedom of speech and of the press...whether or not such publications...are supported financially by the school...."[35] As a result, a California court ruled in favor of a student who wrote a controversial article in a school newspaper. In explaining his decision, the judge wrote: "The broad power to censor expression in school-sponsored publications for pedagogical purposes recognized in [*Hazelwood* v.] *Kuhlmeier* is not available to this state's educators."[36] In Massachusetts, the law states: "The right of students to freedom of expression in the public schools of the Commonwealth shall not be abridged provided that such right shall not cause any disruption or disorder...."[37] Colorado law protects freedom of expression and prohibits prior restraint in student publications "whether or not such publication is school sponsored."[38]

"Hate Speech" Codes

Many schools have codes of conduct that prohibit threatening, harassing or offensive expressions directed at individuals based on their race, religion, or gender. A 1992 Supreme Court decision, *R.A.V. v. St. Paul*, led some lawyers to question whether all "hate speech" codes are now unconstitutional.[39] The case concerned a teenager who was charged with cross-burning under a St. Paul Bias-motivated Crime Ordinance which prohibited symbols or expressions that arouse "anger, alarm, or resentment on the basis of race, color, creed, religion or gender." The Supreme Court held the ordinance unconstitutional because it was a "content-based" restriction which outlawed some hostile expressions (e.g., based on race or religion) but not others (e.g., based on political or union affili-ation or homosexuality). According to the Court, cities can achieve the same positive results by prohibiting all threats, intimidation and "fighting words" (those words that "by their very utterance" inflict injury or incite violence) and not just speech directed at cer-tain groups. It is uncertain whether the decision would also outlaw similar speech codes at elementary and secondary schools since ad-ministrators have greater flexibility and discretion in regulating vulgar and offensive speech at their campuses.

Recommendations for Practice

Three Supreme Court decisions—*Tinker*, *Bethel*, and *Hazel-wood*—have summarized and explained the constitutional principles that apply to student expression in the public schools. What emerges from these more recent rulings is a sense that the first amendment applies broadly to a student's personal views and nar-rowly in areas that are considered part of the curriculum.

- When a student speaks or writes as an individual, such ex-pression is protected by the first amendment and cannot be restricted unless it causes substantial disruption or interferes with the rights of others. Students may not be punished for expressing their personal opinions about controversial politi-cal, social, or educational issues—even if their views are un-popular and in conflict with the ideas of most students, teach-ers, and administrators.

- Administrators have always had broad discretion in regulat-ing student speech or writing that was part of the school cur-riculum. Recent Supreme Court decisions have clarified the scope of such control. In *Bethel*, the Court ruled that educa-tors can define and punish "vulgar and offensive" language in classrooms, assemblies, and probably in any other required educational activity. In *Hazelwood*, the Court held that educa-tors may exercise broad "editorial control" over curricular publications and plays when there are legitimate educational reasons for doing so. In addition, educators probably can con-trol student publications that are not part of the formal cur-riculum if they are school-sponsored, teacher-supervised, edu-cational activities.

- Administrators have much broader discretion in controlling student speech in school-sponsored curricular activities—even if the student's views are not disruptive or obscene and do not interfere with the rights of others. In such cases, courts will tend to presume that administrative control is valid, and it will probably be upheld unless students can prove that the school's control or punishment of their views was unreasonable, arbitrary, or unrelated to legitimate educational goals.

- It is not yet clear to what extent courts will apply the principles of *Hazelwood* or *Tinker* to school-sponsored extra-curricular activities. Therefore, to be constitutionally safe, cautious administrators should follow *Tinker* more than *Hazelwood* in establishing policies governing school-sponsored publications that are not part of the curriculum.

- Since some states provide greater protection for students' rights than *Hazelwood* requires, principals should check relevant state statutes and regulations, judicial opinion, and district policies before developing school rules or imposing punishments that restrict student expression.

- Schools cannot ban student distribution of publications because they advocate a particular religious, political, or social view. However, administrators can establish policies that regulate the time, place, and manner for distributing materials in the schools. Such rules must be viewpoint neutral and cannot be so restrictive that they prevent the dissemination of student opinions.

- Administrators should distinguish between what they have authority to do legally and what it is wise to do educationally. *Hazelwood* probably allows schools to censor all articles on sensitive topics in curricular publications. But is censorship the best way to train students to exercise their first amendment rights in a mature manner? Or would it be wiser for schools to set high standards of journalism and teach students to be fair and responsible in the way they write about controversial or sensitive topics?

- It is not yet clear whether the recent *St. Paul* decision outlaws "hate speech" codes at public schools. Administrators would be less likely to have their speech code challenged if it applied to all students.

- The *Hazelwood* and *Bethel* decisions suggest that the current Supreme Court is likely to give greater deference to administrative discretion than to student expression in school-sponsored educational activities. The Court still holds that students have the constitutional right to express controversial personal opinions in the public schools.

References

[1] 393 U.S. 503 (1969).

[2] Bethel School Dist. No. 403 v. Fraser, 106 S. Ct. 3159 (1986).

[3] Hazelwood School Dist. v. Kuhlmeier, 108 S. Ct. 562 (1988).

[4] 393 U.S. 503, 506 (1969).

[5] *Id.* at 511.

[6] *Id.* at 507.

[7] *Id.* at 508.

[8] *Id.* at 508-509.

[9] *Id.* at 513.

[10] Guzick v. Drebus, 431 F.2d 594 (6th Cir. 1970), *cert. denied*, 401 U.S. 948 (1971).

[11] 393 U.S. 503, 508 (1969).

[12] *Id.* at 509.

[13] Karp v. Becken, 477 F.2d 171 (9th Cir. 1973).

[14] Dodd v. Rambis, 535 F. Supp. 23 (S.D. Ind. 1981).

[15] The above discussion is based on material from FISCHER, SCHIMMEL, and KELLY, TEACHERS AND THE LAW. Ch. 8 (3d ed. 1991).

[16] Miller v. California, 413 U.S. 15 (1973).

[17] Bethel School Dist. No. 403 v. Fraser, 106 S. Ct. 3159, 3160 (1986).

[18] For more on *Bethel, see* D. Schimmel, *Lewd Language not Protected: Bethel School District v. Fraser*, 33 ED LAW REP. 999 (1986).

[19] Hazelwood School Dist. v. Kuhlmeier, 108 S. Ct. 562, 569 (1988).

[20] *Id.* at 570.

[21] *Id.* at 571.

[22] Comments about *Hazelwood* in this chapter are based on D. Schimmel, *Censorship of School-Sponsored Publications: An Analysis of Hazelwood v. Kuhlmeier*, 45 ED LAW REP. 941 (1988).

[23] Shanley v. Northeast Indep. School Dist., 462 F.2d 960 (5th Cir. 1972).

[24] In *Hazelwood*, the Supreme Court ruled that school officials could control school-sponsored publications without specific written regulations. But it declined to decide whether such regulations "are required before school officials may censor publications not sponsored by the school" (*Hazelwood* at 571). Since several federal appeals courts have required that schools have written due process safeguards in reviewing underground publications, such regulations continue to be required in the absence of a Supreme Court ruling to the contrary.

[25] Planned Parenthood v. Clark County School Dist., 941 F.2d 817 (9th Cir. 1991).

[26] Virgil v. School Bd. of Columbia County, Fla., 862 F.2d 1517 (11th Cir. 1989).

[27] Searcey v. Harris, 888 F.2d 1314, 1324 (11th Cir. 1989).

[28] Romano v. Harrington, 725 F. Supp. 687 (E.D.N.Y. 1989).

[29] Rivera v. East Otero School Dist., R-1, 721 F. Supp. 1189, 1194 (D. Colo. 1989).

[30] Slotterback v. Interboro School Dist., 766 F. Supp. 280 (E.D. Pa. 1991).

[31] Hemry by Hemry v. School Bd. of Colorado Springs, 760 F. Supp. 856 (D. Colo. 1991).

[32] Nelson v. Moline School Dist. No. 40, 725 F. Supp. 965 (C.D. Ill. 1989)

[33] Board of Educ. of Westside Community Schools v. Mergens, 110 S. Ct. 2356, 2360 (1990).

[34] Desilets v. Clearview Regional Bd. of Educ., Superior Court of New Jersey, Gloucester County No. C-23-90, May 7, 1991. Article I, Paragraph 5 of the New Jersey Constitution states: "Every person may freely speak, write, and publish his sentiments."

[35] California Education Code, § 48907 (1991).

[36] Leeb v. DeLong, 243 Cal. Rptr. 494, 498 (Cal. App. 1988).

[37] General Laws of Mass., Chpt. 71, § 82 (1991)

[38] Colorado Revised Statutes 22-1-120 (1) (1990).

[39] R.A.V. v. St. Paul, 60 L.W. 4667 (1992).

3

Student Dress Codes

Kenneth E. Lane and David O. Stine

Introduction

There exists a fundamental conflict between the first amendment rights of students and the inherent responsibility of school administrators to maintain a safe learning environment. This conflict is never more apparent than when confronting the issues of student dress and association. The courts consistently have reinforced student constitutional rights and yet at the same time have substantiated the authority of school personnel to discipline students and to maintain a reasonable, safe atmosphere in which all students can be educated.

The tenth amendment to the United States Constitution by omission reserves education to the states. The legislatures in every state have set policies, regulations, and laws to govern how local schools are to be operated. The local school boards in turn make additional policies to govern the operation of the schools. The premise of local control is a strong factor as each local community elects its trustees to determine policy for its district and its schools. Among these policies are issues concerning what is appropriate student dress. The responsibility to insure a proper learning environment is weighed against the individual rights of students.

Legal Issues

The United States Supreme Court case, *Tinker v. Des Moines*,[1] set the stage for debates regarding dress codes and associations by declaring unconstitutional the disciplining of students for symbolic expression of opinion unless it can be shown that there is substantial disruption of the school's routine. Additionally, the first amendment rights of students may be infringed upon when student expression would materially interfere with the operation of the school and the rights of other students to learn.

Is a restriction on dress codes or student association an infringement of the protected rights of students? In answering this question, two main points will be considered. First, does the need for a safe school override the individual's right to express oneself in one's dress? Second, does gang attire constitute a threat to the safety of students in the school, thus allowing restriction by the school?

Safe Schools

What is involved in the creation of a safe school? One concept is that the authority for the administration of the public schools is clearly the responsibility of local school districts. Zirkel clarifies this relationship between the courts and the local school stating that:

> Traditionally, the U.S. Supreme Court has been reluctant to interfere in school matters related to the rights and responsibilities of students. A number of reasons explain this orientation, with perhaps the major one being the strong belief of the judiciary in the American tradition of local control over the schools."[2]

The California Department of Justice states that teachers and administrators must enforce school rules and the law in order to control and eliminate harmful behavior. It goes on to say that "student violators must receive consistent consequences via school discipline measures."[3]

The National Commission on Excellence in Education reaffirms the need for the development of firm and fair codes of conduct in its report, *A Nation At Risk*.[4] It further states that the burden teachers face in maintaining discipline could be reduced by clear rules and regulations of student behavior. This recognition mandates the need for school authorities to spell out their expectations for student dress and behavior in such a way that students will understand exactly what is expected from them. The federal courts have also upheld the school district's right to establish regulations for the day-to-day operations of its schools and "to demand conduct that is conducive to the fulfillment of its responsibility to educate."[5]

The courts are not clear in giving administrators the authority to control the school environment to protect all students and to protect themselves from litigation. The California Supreme Court has stated that the law imposes on school authorities a duty to supervise the conduct of children necessary to their protection because of the tendency of students to participate in aggressive and impulsive behavior.[6]

Dress Codes

Community involvement in the process of establishing dress codes is invaluable. While there is no legal requirement that they be involved, political and economic factors suggest that the involvement of the community is crucial. In Henry County, Georgia, 3200 parents signed a petition against the dress codes adopted by the school board; while $50,000 in legal fees were spent by the school board in Saugerties, N.Y. to defend itself against a lawsuit filed by a student suspended for wearing a shirt with a vulgar message.[7] The authority to establish dress codes is delineated in *King v. Saddleback* and the *Olff v. East Side Union* cases where it was determined that the districts' rights included that of governing student dress as well as hair length and conduct.[8] In many districts, the length of hair and wearing of badges are included in dress code policies.

A key issue in upholding dress codes involves the establishment of a relationship between the specific regulation and a legitimate school objective.[9] The rulings of the courts have been inconsistent regarding several aspects of acceptable school dress. In *Breen v. Kahl*,[10] the right of students to wear their hair at any length or in any manner was declared an ingredient of personal freedom protected by the Constitution. However, in *Karr v. Schmidt*,[11] the ruling was that student choice of hair length is not constitutionally protected. In *Scott v. Board of Education, Union Free School District #17*,[12] prohibiting girls from wearing slacks to school was found to be in violation of students' rights because it was considered only an issue of taste and style; not of safety, order, or discipline. In *Bannister v. Paradis*,[13] the court ruled it unconstitutional to prohibit students from wearing dungarees since wearing them did not pose a danger to the health and safety of others and did not cause a disturbance or incite disciplinary problems. If attire is immodest such as short skirts more than six inches above the knees, the courts have upheld school regulation.[14]

Association

In addition to the implications of dress code, the right of association is also a consideration. The National School Safety Center states that "rights of association must be subordinated to the orderly conduct of classes and other curricular affairs on campus."[15] Regulation of association most commonly revolves around the issue of gang activity and the dress associated with gangs. The rationale for addressing the issue of association rests with the concern that all activities that endanger students on the way to, while at, and on the way home from school be eliminated. If a student's manner of dress has the potential of causing violence on campus, that clothing must be eliminated. A clear example of this responsibility was demonstrated in *Biggers v. Sacramento City Unified School District*[16] where a high school student was attacked by a group of gang members and seriously injured. The court found that the school was liable for damages because it was aware of the gang problem and had neglected to take any action to protect the students, the least of which would be to restrict outward displays of gang affiliations.

The issue of association and gang attire becomes confusing when reviewing school board policies. In southern California, many school boards have passed policies which specifically address gang attire. Some of those policies address the issue by stating that certain styles of clothing are not permissible. Some school districts have gone beyond this limit by specifically naming certain professional sports team clothing as being impermissible because gangs identify themselves with them. The question then becomes: is it constitutional to outlaw specific organizational clothing? Some school districts have chosen to bypass the issue by declaring all sports organization related clothing impermissible.

The key factor for school administrators is to consider the difference between behavior which is disruptive and appearance which may be "fashionable" or unusual. School-aged young people have always had strong ties with their peer groups, a teenage peer subculture. This normal association has manifested itself in the poodle skirts and crew-cuts of the 1950s, mini-skirts and tie dyed shirts of the 1960s, long hair and rock music of the 1970s, and the designer clothes and MTV of the 1980s. Every decade brings in new and different fads and the teen culture often makes its own unique statement in the form of dress. Teenagers seem to seek identity by looking alike. School administrators must determine the difference between normal self-grouping of teens and negative or violent behavior of individuals or groups which detracts from their formal education. There is no doubt that local school boards can control student dress and the California Department of Justice emphasizes the magnitude of this concern when it states that "dress codes are highly controversial: few areas of student conduct have stirred up more litigation than alleged 'dress code' violations. Courts do support reasonable and clear school regulations governing the appearance of students."[17]

Recommendations for Practice

As a general rule, school districts need to adhere to the *Tinker* guidelines in designing regulations pertaining to student dress. If specific attire can be related to a disruption in the educational process, then restrictions will be upheld by the courts. General guidelines for schools to follow in establishing dress codes should be able to withstand judicial scrutiny include:[18]

- A nexus between the regulations and the maintenance of school discipline and prevention of interference with the educational environment should exist. The school must demonstrate what health or safety threats are being prevented by grooming standards designed to avoid such danger.
- School dress and grooming standards should be specific and precise.
- Apply rules uniformly to all individuals.
- More narrow guidelines may be drawn for specific activities including band and athletics.
- Minimum due process procedures must be provided before suspending or dismissing students.
- The dress code should address those items of clothing that are not worn by the student population in general.
- Reference to specific professional sports teams clothing such as the Los Angeles Raiders and the Los Angeles Kings should not be included in the dress codes.

References

[1] Tinker v. Des Moines Indep. Community School Dist., 393 U.S. 503, 89 S. Ct. 733 (1969).
[2] P. Zirkel & S. Nalvonr. *A Digest of Supreme Court Decisions Affecting Education*. PHI DELTA KAPPA 32 (1988).
[3] California Department of Justice. LAW IN THE SCHOOL. Sacramento: State of California 19 (1990).
[4] A NATION AT RISK: THE IMPERATIVE FOR EDUCTIONAL. National Commission on Excellence in Education. Washington D. C.: U.S. Department of Education, U.S. Printing Office 29 (1983).
[5] STUDENTS' RIGHTS AND RESPONSIBILITIES HANDBOOK. CALIFORNIA STATE DEPARTMENT OF EDUCATION: Sacramento, CA (1986).
[6] Totsiello v. Oakland Unified School Dist., 242 Cal. Rptr. 752 (Cal. App. Ct. 1987).
[7] Stover, D. *The Dress Mess*. AMERICAN SCHOOL BD. J., 177 (6), 26-29 (1990).
[8] King v. Saddleback, 445 F. 2d 932 (9th Cir. 1971); Olff v. East Side Union (305 F. Supp. 557 (N.D. Cal. 1969)
[9] Wallace v. Ford, 346 F. Supp. 156 (E.D. Ark. 1972).
[10] Breen v. Kahl, 419 F.2d 1034 (7th Cir. 1969).
[11] Karr v. Schmidt, 460 F.2d 609 (5th Cir. 1972).
[12] Scott v. Board of Educ., Union Free School Dist. #17, 305 N.Y.S.2d 601 (1969).
[13] Bannister v. Paradis, 316 F. Supp 185 (1970).
[14] Wallace v. Ford, 346 F. Supp. 156.

[15]NATIONAL SCHOOL SAFETY CENTER. SCHOOL DISCIPLINE NOTEBOOK. Malibu, CA.: Pepperdine University Press(1987).

[16]Biggers v. Sacramento City Unified School Dist., 25 Cal. Ct. App. 3d 269 (1972).

[17]CALIFORNIA DEPARTMENT OF JUSTICE, 82.

[18]See, Gee, E. G. & Sperry, D. J. EDUCATION LAW AND THE PUBLIC SCHOOLS: A COMPENDIUM. (1978).

4
Student Discipline

Richard S. Vacca

Introduction

Most of today's public school systems have formal policies and rules specifically covering student discipline. Generally, such documents, often referred to as "Student Codes of Conduct," specify the nature and severity of the student offense and include the alternatives of punishment available for each. Carefully written to avoid vagueness, these documents typically enumerate the procedures to be followed in dealing with student offenders and often designate the person(s) responsible for enforcing each rule and implementing each procedure.

In enforcing a public school system's disciplinary code, the severity of the punishment of a student is an important factor to consider.[1] Generally, the more serious the punishment—an expulsion from school rather than a one-day suspension—the more formalized and extensive are the requirements of procedural due process. For example, the Seventh Circuit Court of Appeals held that a high school senior who had been suspended from school because of drinking for three days and subsequently missed final exams and did not graduate, was not entitled to the same level of due process as was a student being expelled from school.[2] Courts have consistently held that confrontation and cross-examination of witnesses against a student, and a student's representation by counsel may not be mandatory though "desirable when the possible discipline of a student is severe."[3]

The age of the student or student group will affect the formality of the procedural due process to be afforded.[4] In addition, whether or not a student is a diabled child will impact on the nature of the process.[5]

Legal Issues

Basic fairness is the rationale of contemporary procedural due process. Fairness should undergird every decision made by a governmental entity, especially public schools. Over the past 30 years, courts have been very active in extending to public school students due process rights under the United States Constitution when they are involved in disciplinary situations.

Corporal Punishment

An age-worn mode of student punishment available in public schools is corporal punishment, the affliction of physical pain upon a student for misconduct. The legal justification for using corporal punishment is found in state statutes. Some states specifically allow it, some states forbid it, while others do not mention it but by implication authorize or allow its use. The law on corporal punishment has not changed significantly in recent years, and both federal and state courts have consistently upheld its reasonable use where the state law allows. However, a growing number of states and localities now forbid its use.

Where corporal punishment is used, it must conform to the laws of the state, to local school board policy, and to the common law standard of reasonableness. Courts have, over the years, spelled out nine general guidelines as to what constitutes reasonable corporal punishment. These guidelines suggest that corporal punishment:

- Must be allowed by state statute (either directly or by inference).
- Must be implemented consistent with state statutory requirements.
- Must be used as a method of correction.
- Must not be cruel or excessive.
- Must not involve anger or malice.
- Must suit the age, sex, and physical condition of the child.
- Must involve use of an appropriate instrument.
- Must not leave permanent or lasting injuries.
- Must be appropriate for the offense.[6]

Baker v. Owen[7] was the first case in this area to come before the United States Supreme Court. It allowed teachers to administer corporal punishment and did not require prior parent approval for such punishment. The following four procedural guidelines were approved in the decision: students were warned in advance of the specific kinds of behavior that could result in their being corporally punished, corporal punishment was not to be the "first-line" of punishment, when corporal punishment was administered to a student a second school official was present to witness the act, and parents of a punished student were furnished a written statement on request about the act including reasons for it and the names of the witnesses.

In *Ingraham v. Wright*[8] the United States Supreme Court decided that the use of corporal punishment in a public school does not fall within the eighth amendment's prohibition regarding cruel and unusual punishment. The eighth amendment applies only to situations involving criminal punishments. The Court held further that a student is not entitled to notice and a hearing prior to corporal punishment. In the Court's opinion, if children are subjected to unreasonable applications of corporal punishment they may obtain remedy by filing a civil suit.[9]

Hall v. Tawney[10] was a post-*Ingraham* case decided by the Fourth Circuit Court of Appeals. The court in *Hall* faced three basic issues: the legality of corporal punishment, the procedural due process guarantee of a hearing prior to the punishment, and the student's constitutional right to ultimate body security. To the Fourth Circuit, corporal punishment does not violate a child's protected rights. However, the force used by a disciplinarian must not be disproportionate to maintaining order and discipline in the school, nor should it be the product of malice, sadism, or brutality. The court believed that not every violation of state tort law or criminal assault law amounts to a violation of a constitutional right. In *Hall*, the court did treat the substantive due process issue of a student's right to ultimate body security, and held that this right applies to situations of corporal punishment.

Two years later, the Supreme Court of West Virginia addressed the procedural guarantees available to students in that state prior to the administration of corporal punishment. According to the court, the following minimal due process procedures should be utilized: a student should be given an opportunity to explain his version of the disruptive event "as such an explanation may convince a fair-minded person that corporal punishment is not warranted," and absent some extraordinary factor, the administration of corporal punishment should be done in the presence of another adult, "to protect both the student and the person administering corporal punishment by providing a neutral observer."[11]

Exclusion From School

Generally, state statutes grant school administrators the legal duty to establish, maintain, and protect the school's learning environment. It is a basic tenet of school law that school authorities may exclude from school any student whose conduct interferes with or in any way disrupts the operation of the school; or who openly defies school rules, or whose conduct is willfully insubordinate; or who poses a threat of harm to himself, to other persons, or to school property.[12]

The terms used to characterize exclusion of students from school are suspension and expulsion. Generally, suspension denotes a temporary exclusion from school with a presumption that return to school is possible. Typically, by state code provision, school authorities possess the legal prerogative to suspend students from classes and from school.[13] Expulsion denotes a longer term of exclusion from school with a presumption of finality regarding the termination of one's status as a student. Considered the most severe student punishment available to school authorities, state statutes and local policies usually provide that only a local school board has the prerogative to expel a student.[14]

In recent years, litigation has involved both the right of school authorities to suspend or expel, and the minimal procedural due process rights of students prior to suspension or expulsion. Following the landmark decision in *Gault*,[15] in which the Supreme Court held that minor juvenile offenders in juvenile court were entitled to certain procedural due process protections, several lower courts began to clarify the procedural due process rights of students facing exclusion from school. The matter was ultimately treated by the United States Supreme Court in *Goss v. Lopez*.[16]

Observing that a student possesses a property right to a public education, protected by the guarantees of the fourteenth amendment, the Supreme Court overturned an Ohio statute which allowed summary suspensions for up to ten days. In the Court's opinion, minimum procedures must be followed prior to exclusion from school. The Court held that in suspensions of ten days or less, notice of the charges and the right to be heard are required. And, if the student denies the charges, he or she must be informed of the evidence against him or her and be given the opportunity to present his or her side of the story.[17] However, this requirement can be done informally and immediately after the incident. In *Goss*, the Supreme Court did not require that a public school system allow students to be represented by counsel, to present witnesses, or to confront and cross-examine witnesses. Nor did the Court rule on the elements of due process for suspensions of longer than ten days. The Court did observe that more procedural due process may be needed for longer suspensions.[18]

Of major importance to the daily practice of school administrators is the Court's attitudes toward due process and school discipline, often missed by those who analyze this landmark case. First, the Court reemphasized the notion that procedural due process is a flexible legal standard, determined by the nature of the misconduct and the severity of the penalty. Second, the Court held that school officials are free to remove a student from school prior to a suspension if his or her presence is a danger to persons or property and/or is disruptive to teaching and learning.[19]

Beyond the guidelines of the Supreme Court, a local school administrator is also bound by state statutory mandates and state court decisions, and these requirements vary. However, the following guidelines are generally accepted nationally and serve as excellent guidelines for school administrators:

- students must know in advance what standards of behavior are proscribed in their school and what modes of behavior are expected;
- they must know what specific disciplinary actions and punishments attach to violations of the rules;
- they must receive immediate and informed notice when they are accused of an infraction and an opportunity to present his or her side of the story; and
- students must have an opportunity to appeal the decision to another administrative level within the school system.

The administrator is reminded that these general elements become more formalized and technical when an expulsion is in process.[20]

Two other student exclusion decisions from the United States Supreme Court should be briefly mentioned at this point because of their bearing on student procedural due process entitlements. The cases are *Wood v. Strickland*,[21] and *Carey v. Piphus*.[22] *Wood* involved the issue of students being allowed to sue local school board members for damages under section 1983 for a denial of procedural due process in an expulsion hearing. In upholding the school board's actions, the Supreme Court held that individual board members could be sued if they knew or reasonably should have known that they denied students their constitutional rights or if board members acted with malicious intent.[23]

Carey was a consolidation of two cases, both involving the suspension of a student from school. One student had violated a rule prohibiting the use of drugs at school, while the other student violated a rule against males wearing earrings at school. In rendering its decision in *Carey*, the Supreme Court held that students suspended from school without procedural due process are entitled to recover nominal damages of $1.00 and possibly extensive lawyers' fees. However, before any compensatory damages are awarded, a student must first submit proof of actual injury caused by the denial of due process. Punitive damages may be possible where a student can establish that school officials acted with the malicious intent to deprive him/her of his/her rights.[24]

The Relevance of a Miranda-type Warning

Currently, other possible elements of procedural due process are being clarified in the courts. One such element concerns whether or not a student is entitled to a *Miranda* warning prior to being questioned by school authorities. This element would require school authorities to advise a student of his or her rights as a police officer must do prior to arresting a criminal suspect. In *Boynton v. Casey*,[25] a high school student was subjected to questioning by his school principal and vice-principal concerning the use of marijuana on school premises. During the one-hour questioning session, the student was denied permission to leave and was not informed of his right not to answer questions, nor was he allowed to have his parents present at the questioning. Admitting that he used marijuana on school property, Boynton was immediately suspended.

Subsequently, in federal district court, Boynton and his parents alleged that by refusing their son permission to leave the initial questioning session, failing to advise him of his right to remain silent, failing to notify him that he had a right to have his parents present during questioning, and failing to notify his parents of the questioning; school officials denied him procedural due process. In dismissing the complaint for failure to state a federal constitutional claim upon which relief can be granted, the court held: the student was not entitled to *Miranda* warnings to being questioned by school authorities, and there was no requirement that the authorities notify the student and his parents of a right to have the parents present during questioning.[26]

Suspension and Expulsion of Exceptional Children

In 1988 the United States Supreme Court held, among other things, that the "stay put" provision of the Education of All Handicapped Children Act, now retitled the Individuals with Disabilities Educational Act (IDEA), prohibits state and local school authorities from *unilaterally* excluding disabled children from the classroom for dangerous or disruptive conduct growing out of their disabilities during the pendency of a review proceeding.[27] The Court stated that school authorities may use procedures (including a suspension for up to ten school days) to deal with students who pose immediate danger to themselves or others, or who cause substantial disruption of classrooms or the school.[28]

Recommendations for Practice

Contemporary public school administrators would be wise to adhere to the following guidelines from case law as they carry out their daily disciplinary routines:

- The legal duty to control a school must be balanced with the procedural due process entitlements of students.
- Due process is neither a fixed nor stagnant concept since it changes from situation to situation and is dependent upon a continuum of factors.
- Fairness is the rationale of contemporary procedural due process in public schools.
- The technicalities of criminal procedure including *Miranda*-type warning, presence of an attorney, and confrontation and cross-examination of witnesses do not automatically transfer into school disciplinary procedures.
- Timely and adequate notice, an explanation of the charges against the student, and a chance to be heard are the minimal elements of procedural due process in student disciplinary episodes.
- Procedural due process requires school administrators to be predictable and consistent and to exercise caution, thoughtful restraint, and common sense when disciplining students.
- Student discipline must incorporate several alternative sanctions for misbehavior which were previously announced to students and directly linked to modes of misbehavior, and it must follow the dictates of reasonableness.
- Students who represent an imminent threat of harm to themselves or others or who disrupt the school or its classrooms should be dealt with immediately with appropriate sanctions.
- Students who are covered by the Individuals with Disabilities Education Act, and whose misbehavior is directly related to their disability, are not under a school system's regular suspension and/or expulsion process.
- Suits for damages may result if administrators knew or should have known that their actions violate the procedural due process entitlements of their students.

References

[1]"In school discipline cases the nature of the sanction affects the validity of the procedure used in imposing it,..." *Schools*, 68 Am. Jur. 2d § 269, at 593. The reader is reminded that matters of academic discipline are treated different from matters of discipline for misbehavior. *See, e.g.,* Moore v. Hyche, 761 F. Supp. 112 (N.D. Ala. 1991).

(The court saw no due process violation in the denial of a student to membership in the Beta Club at a public high school).

[2]Lamb v. Panhandle Community Unit School Dist. No. 2, 826 F.2d 526 (7th Cir. 1987). For another case concerning the issue of the severity of the expulsion as an "unfair punishment" see, Adams v. City of Dothan Bd., 485 So. 2d 757 (Ala. Ct. Civ. App. 1986).

[3]Schools, supra note 1, at 597. In Newsome v. Batavia, 842 F.2d 920 (6th Cir. 1988), it was held that an expelled student was not entitled, as a matter of right, to the names of student accusers; nor was he entitled to cross-examine the administrators who investigated his situation.

[4]Id. at 593.

[5]Honig v. Doe, 108 S. Ct. 592 (1988).

[6]Portions of this chapter are adapted from H. C. HUDGINS and R. S. VACCA, LAW AND EDUCATION: COMTEMPORARY ISSUES AND COURT DECISIONS, 311-345 (rev. third ed. 1991).

[7]395 F. Supp. 294 (M.D. N.C. 1975), aff'd 423 U.S. 907 (1975).

[8]430 U.S. 651 (1977).

[9]Id.

[10]621 F.2d 607 (4th Cir. 1980). For a recent case showing the criminal prosecution of a private school principal for excessive paddling of a student see Commonwealth v. Douglas, 588 A.2d 53 (Pa. Super. 1991).

[11]Smith v. West Virginia State Bd., 295 S.E.2d 680 (W. Va. 1982). For a more recent case see Wise v. Pea Ridge School Dist., 855 F.2d 560 (8th Cir. 1988).

[12]HUDGINS and VACCA, supra note 6, at 289-90. School administrators must be cautious when dealing with a student who is covered by special education law who has been mainstreamed into the school, Honig, supra, note 5.

[13]Id.

[14]Id.

[15]In re Gault, 387 U.S. 1 (1967).

[16]419 U.S. 565 (1975). For a recent case involving minimal procedural requirements necessary in an expulsion proceeding see Carey on behalf of Carey v. Maine School Admin. Dist., 754 F. Supp. 906 (D. Me. 1990).

[17]See also, Newsome, 842 F.2d 920.

[18]Id.

[19]Id.

[20]See, e.g., New Braunfels Indep. School Dist. v. Armke, 658 S.W.2d 330 (Tex. Ct. App. 1983). School officials are warned that a court of law will nullify a policy or rule if its wording is vague, Claiborne v. Beebe, 687 F. Supp. 1358 (E.D. Ark. 1988); and, it should be reemphasized that students covered by special education law may create an exception to this rule. Honig, 108 S. Ct. 592 (1988).

[21]420 U.S. 308 (1975).

[22]435 U.S. 247 (1978).

[23]Wood, 420 U.S. 308. For a comprehensive look at the liability of public school administrators under 42 U.S.C. § 1983, see, R. S. VACCA and H. C. HUDGINS, JR., LIABILITY OF SCHOOL OFFICIALS AND ADMINISTRATORS FOR CIVIL RIGHTS TORTS (1982).

[24]Carey, 435 U.S. 247. For an article demonstrating an example (the use of corporal punishment) of the growing number of litigants bringing civil rights tort suits in federal court see, Henderson, Constitutional Implications Involving the Use of Corporal Punishment in the Public Schools: A Comprehensive Review, 15 J. OF LAW AND EDUC. 255 (Summer 1986).

[25]543 F. Supp. 995, (D. Me. 1982).

[26]Id. For additional cases see: Keough v. Tate, 748 F.2d 1077 (5th Cir. 1984), involving the issue of pre-suspension due process; Pollnow v. Glennon, 594 F. Supp. 220, aff'd 757 F.2d 496 (2d Cir. 1985), involving the issue of whether a student would be advised that he can call his mother; Brewer by Dreyfus v. Austin Indep. School Dist., 779 F.2d 260 (5th Cir. 1985), involving the issue of whether or not criminal procedure is transferred into school procedure; New Jersey v. T.L.O., 105 S. Ct. 733 (1985) where the Supreme Court held that a standard of reasonable suspicion applied to school searches of students and their belongings, and not the police standard of probable cause; see State v. Moore, 603 A.2d 513 (N.J. Super. A.D. 1992) for a recent case showing the reasonable suspicion standard as being a lesser standard than that of probable cause; and Davis v. Churchill County School Bd., 616 F. Supp. 1310 (D. Nev. 1985) concerning whether suspension hearing may be closed to the public.

[27]See Honig, 108 S. Ct. 592; involving procedural issues in possible suspension or expulsion of mainstreamed disabled students in public schools.

[28]Id. at 605. See also, Kaelin v. Grubbs, 682 F.2d 595 (6th Cir. 1982).

5
Disciplinary Hearings and Due Process

Jeffrey J. Horner

Introduction

Discipline in public schools has proven to be a matter of paramount importance in present day education. Courts have attempted to balance the students' constitutional protections from arbitrary and excessive discipline against the need for school officials to maintain order and discipline in the school setting. For the most part, courts have been tolerant of school officials who give advance notice of prohibited behavior and administer punishment in a reasonable manner consistent with the due process rights enjoyed by the student.

An important element in discipline is recognizing the difference courts have delineated between severe and minor disciplinary actions. Courts continually recognize that more expansive due process is required for students subject to expulsion or long-term suspension (usually eleven days or more), as opposed to those students receiving lesser punishment. The need for school districts to recognize and satisfy these legal requirements is imperative to ensure that due process is provided.

Legal Issues

In general, students have the right to freedom from bodily restraint cognizable under the fourteenth amendment of the United States Constitution.[1] This right does not extend so far as to implicate the eighth amendment prohibition on cruel and unusual punishment.[2] The courts have held that the eighth amendment applies only in the criminal context, not student discipline proceedings.[3] With respect to the fourteenth amendment concern, courts have recognized the rights of students to be informed of prohibited behavior and afforded certain procedural safeguards prior to the imposition of punishment. The extent of these procedural rights is the primary focus of *Goss v. Lopez*.[4] Decided in 1975, *Goss* has been the leading case in the student due process area for over fifteen years. *Goss* holds that, in the event of minor disciplinary infractions calling for suspensions of ten days or less, a student must only be afforded the opportunity to tell one's side of the story before punishment is imposed. This opportunity is the "hearing" envisioned under *Goss* for minor disciplinary infractions. The scenario changes significantly for long-term suspensions of eleven days or more and expulsions. More thorough due process is required before imposing these punishments. The procedures for expulsions vary between states and an administrator should consult the state statutes for precise requirements.

Gathering of Information Concerning the Infraction

Generally, the first step in a student discipline case involves securing information about the infraction. Most often a complaint of student misconduct comes from a teacher, school administrator, or student. A teacher may see students fighting on the playground. The teacher would then report this incident to the proper authority. Any information gathered about a possible infraction should be communicated to the person in charge of discipline at that school, usually a principal or assistant principal. It then becomes incumbent upon that administrator to move forward with an investigation.

Completing the Investigation of the Allegations

After receiving a report of a possible disciplinary infraction, it is usually standard procedure for an administrator to conduct a further investigation. One of the first parts of this investigation should be to talk to the accused student and to determine if he or she committed the acts in question. The student should always be given the opportunity to relate his or her account of the allegations. The student may agree with the facts stated by the administrator, thereby essentially confessing to the wrongdoing. If this occurs, the administrator is in a position to immediately recommend the appropriate punishment for the infraction. In most cases, a student will disagree with the facts related by the administrator. In this case, the administrator should make further inquiry of other witnesses to ascertain the facts concerning the event. If two views exist of the incident in question, the administrator may believe whomever he or she feels is the most credible.

Ascertaining Whether the Misconduct Warrants Severe or Minor Punishment

Perhaps the most important step in the disciplinary process from a due process perspective is for the administrator to determine the nature of the punishment. If it is determined the incident warrants short-term suspension or other minor punishment, then such punishment can be immediately imposed by the administrator. The process of affording a student the opportunity to tell his or her side of the story is the only "hearing" contemplated in *Goss* for minor disciplinary infractions. Written notice should be sent to the student and the student's parents or guardians, describing the nature of the misconduct and the punishment to be imposed. Absent applicable state statutes or administrative regulations, a further appeals process is not legally required; however, in order to be fair to all involved, many school districts allow an appeal to a higher level, such as the superintendent's office. In some instances, however, the investigation may reveal a more serious violation of school policy. If the proposed punishment for an infraction is expulsion or suspension for eleven days or more, a student is entitled to more thorough due process. The punishment cannot be immediately imposed. First, a letter should be sent to the student's parents, outlining the charges against the student and informing them of the student's rights under the appropriate school policies and law. Copies of all applicable policies should be attached. Next, it must be determined whether the student or parents desire a hearing on the charges. If such hearing is requested, a letter notifying them of the hearing date, the administration's witnesses, and the nature of the witnesses' testimony in sufficient detail to prepare a defense should be sent to the parents and student. All letters should be hand delivered or sent by certified mail to make certain that the notice is received.

Preparing for the Hearing—Cases Involving Possible Expulsion or Long-Term Suspension

Many state statutes require that expulsion or long-term suspension hearings be held before a school board. Statutes in other states allow designees of the school board, usually school administrators such as principals, to hear these cases. All parties are generally best served if the school principal or other administrator conducts the initial hearing. Several benefits are attained by having the initial hearing before a building administrator. First, such hearings are appropriate administrative functions. Second, holding the hearing before the administrator provides due process at the earliest time and at the lowest possible administrative level.

Because a student is entitled to an impartial hearing, the administrator acting as "the judge" should avoid becoming overly involved in investigating the case prior to the hearing. If the administrator acting as a hearing officer becomes actively involved in the investigation, he or she should request that the school district superintendent appoint another administrator to hear the matter because the administrator could become a witness in the case.

Conducting the Hearing

At the expulsion or long-term suspension hearing, the administration has the burden of going forward and proving its case by a preponderance of the evidence. Because student disciplinary cases are not criminal actions, the higher burden of proof associated with criminal actions (beyond a reasonable doubt) does not apply. The administration must prove that the student violated a school rule which warrants expulsion or long-term suspension. Generally, it is not necessary for a school district attorney to be present unless the student has an attorney. Also, the hearing should be tape recorded or transcribed by a court reporter in order to maintain a record for future use. Court reporters are much more expensive than tape recorders. In most instances, a good tape system will suffice to preserve a record of the hearing. A court reporter should be used only if the case is particularly complex and is likely to be appealed.

The first step of the hearing process is for the hearing officer to state the ground rules. He or she may read an outline of the proceedings, which should be provided to all in attendance so that everyone is apprised of the rules. The administration will begin the proceedings by presenting its case. The student or representative may be allowed to cross-examine witnesses presented by the administration. Time limits on cross-examination generally are not a good idea. Such limitations simply raise the specter of unfair treatment and violation of due process. The hearing officer may, however, require that the testimony be relevant and not repetitive or cumulative. Both the administration and the student may seek to sequester witnesses. This option simply means that each witness, other than parties to the case, may be required to remain outside of the hearing room until testimony is given.

After the administration has presented its witnesses and documentary evidence, the student should then present his/her case. Again, time limits should not be placed on the student's presentation. After the student has presented his/her case, the hearing officer should allow rebuttal evidence and closing arguments. After the presentation of arguments, the administrator may render a decision at that time or may reserve the right to render the decision at a future date. The decision should have two parts. The first finding should state whether the student engaged in prohibited behavior, and the second finding (if necessary) should specify the appropriate punishment. Any decision made by the administrator should be confirmed in writing. This notification letter should inform the parents or guardians of the decision and the right to appeal to the next administrative level.

The Processing of the Initial Decision

After a student has been afforded a hearing, generally no further appeals process is legally required. However, many states require that such an appeals process be afforded to students. It is probably a good idea to allow an appeal so that the concept of fundamental fairness is observed. In most cases, an appeal of an expulsion or long-term suspension is directed to the local school district board. An appeal to the board can be based on either the record made before the school administrator or new evidence presented to the board. In order to save time, expense, and repetitive testimony; an appeal based on the record is preferable. The board may then either listen to the tape recordings or read the transcript of the initial proceedings and review any documents. Each side should be given an equal amount of time to present arguments based on the record.

Based on a review of the record and the arguments of both parties, the board should make its ruling. The board should adopt specific findings of fact and conclusions of law similar to those made by the school administrator. It may make its decision either at the time of the hearing or at a later date. Any decision should be confirmed in writing and sent to the student and parents. The board should also pass a motion confirming its decision.

Further Appeal Outside the School District—Consideration by the Courts or a Central Education Agency

If the punishment imposed by the board is an expulsion or long-term suspension, the student or parents may have the right of appeal to a body outside of the school district. This determination is normally dictated by state law. Some states afford an appeals route to the state education agency. Other states allow appeal directly to the state or federal court system. If a particular state allows appeal beyond the school board level, the student and parents should be informed of this right in the letter notifying the student of the expulsion or long-term suspension.

Recommendations for Practice

Courts have recognized the rights of students to be informed of prohibited behavior and afforded certain procedural safeguards prior to the imposition of punishment.

- The administrator should move forward with an investigation by gathering additional information on any disciplinary infractions reported. Administrators should make further inquiry of other witnesses to ascertain the facts concerning the event.
- The administrator must determine the nature of the punishment as the necessary steps will be modified with increasing severity. The scenario changes significantly for long-term suspensions of eleven days or more and expulsions. More thorough due process is required before imposing these punishments.
- A letter should be sent to the student's parents, outlining the charges against the student and informing them of the student's rights under the appropriate school policies and law for more severe punishments.
- If the administrator acting as a hearing officer becomes actively involved in the investigation, he/she should request that the school district superintendent appoint another administrator to hear the matter.

References

[1]Ingraham v. Wright, 430 U.S. 651 (1977).
[2]Id.
[3]Id.
[4]Goss v. Lopez, 419 U.S. 565 (1975).

6

Academic Sanctions

Patricia F. First

Introduction

In attempting to fashion penalties for misbehavior related to academic work, administrators have sometimes turned to grade reductions and other academic sanctions. Academic sanctions have also been used as questionable penalties in discipline cases such as unexcused absences and drinking a glass of wine. An academic sanction such as a grade reduction is definitely an acceptable disciplinary tool for school authorities to use when poor academic performance is the issue. There is less agreement regarding the use of academic sanctions when student misbehavior and/or absences are the issues and even less agreement when academic sanctions are used as punishment for nonacademic reasons. In some cases, an academic sanction is designed to take away from a student something he or she has otherwise earned. School officials are not always upheld by the courts in applying such sanctions. There is strong reasoning in the argument that what a student has already earned he or she is entitled to, even if the student later engages in unacceptable behavior. But not all school officials would agree, especially when the student's unacceptable act is particularly offensive to the values or the person of the educator. The court must see the relationship between the offense and the punishment, and the court must see the punishment as contributing to the attainment of the desirable educational goals of the school system.[1]

Legal Issues

The legal issues of academic sanctions, including rationality, liberty and property interests, and substantive due process, may exist separately or all of them may be involved and intertwined. These factors create many legal complexities surrounding the issue of academic sanctions. It is important to note that all of the older cases on academic sanctions were evaluated in light of decisions by the United States Supreme Court.[2] The older cases blend alternative constitutional arguments, such as academic penalties implicate property rights, the stigmatization academic penalties may cause a student may violate a liberty interest, or that particular sanctions are so lacking in rationality, i.e. a connection between the behavior and the penalty, they may violate substantive due process. Since school deprivations may implicate fourteenth amendment property interests,[3] it is not always clear if the imposition of academic sanctions implicates a student's property rights. "Though the state-created right to public school admission implicates a constitutionally protected property interest, expulsions and suspensions which hold that interest must normally be preceded by fourteenth amendment due process."[4] Where the academic sanctions involve speech-related conduct, due process claims may be brought under first amendment liberty interests. When considering a sanction such as a grade reduction, the school administrator is considering a penalty with possible long-term consequences for the student. The seriousness of such a penalty calls into question a profound attitude of fairness, the very heart of due process. To ensure the student due process, the academic sanctions must be rationally related to a valid educational purpose, i.e. they must be reasonable.

Automatic Penalties

Where the penalty lacks a rational connection to educational objectives or is irrationally severe, it may be violating substantive due process. Some schools provide uniform, automatic penalties for some specified acts or omissions. It can be argued that automatic penalties deprive the individual student of the means to assure that a rational relationship exists between the act and the punishment. In the case of academic penalties, this action may be a problem because such a penalty, as opposed for example to the denial of attendance at a social event, could affect the student's entire academic career. It could also be argued that such a penalty is detrimental to the school's goal of educating the student and/or keeping the student in school. There is also a difference of opinion on the assessment of automatic penalties. If an academic penalty is automatically activated for nonacademic rule breaking, without a prior hearing, some courts have objected.[5] On the other hand, automatic suspensions and expulsions under established school rules have been upheld.[6] Some of these cases illustrate the disagreements between local boards of education and state government over the scope of authority of the boards. Grade penalties may be reversed if such penalties are not authorized by that state's education statutes, or if their use constitutes an abuse of the school board's discretion.[7]

Absenteeism and Truancy

It has been an accepted "truth" in education that students must attend class to benefit from the educational program and so most courts have found that academic penalties for absenteeism have served a valid educational goal. Given, however, the stress on outcomes based education that is part of our national policy consciousness in the 1990s, this "truth" may be increasingly hard to justify. Questions about the propriety of academic sanctions rest on questions of rationality. "If the questioned sanction bears no rational relationship to legitimate school interests, that fact alone is grounds to invalidate the challenged punishment."[8]

When considering an academic sanctions policy, it is necessary to consult the relevant state laws in order to determine the scope of school board power in this area. When the problem is truancy, state laws may come into play. A Colorado court found that academic sanctions for absenteeism were impermissible under that state's statutory provisions.[9] The school board policy stated that any student who missed more than seven days during a semester would not receive academic credit for the courses taken. It was irrelevant whether the absences were because of illness, family problems, or any other reasons. The court invalidated the school board's policy, holding that the board had exceeded its authority since the policy conflicted with the state law that required attendance for 172 days excluding absences for illness and disciplinary suspensions.

Under an Arkansas state law, a similar policy was upheld by that state's Supreme Court, which held that the policy in question fell under the board's power to make reasonable rules and regulations for the administration of the schools.[10] This board policy disallowed course credit and permitted expulsion of students who accumulated more than twelve absences.

In general, loss of credits as a result of loss of study time because of misconduct, s likely to be sustained.[11] In a 1988 Michigan case, a grade reduction was upheld for failure to make up lost class time.[12] When grade reductions or credit penalties are imposed solely for unauthorized absences, there is division of opinion on whether constitutional rights are implicated and whether due process hearings are required.[13] In 1976, an Illinois court upheld a school board policy that reduced students' grades as punishment for unexcused absences.[14] One letter grade was dropped for each class missed. The court's reasoning was that the sanction was helpful in discouraging truancy, which the court saw as an indication of a lack of effort. The court saw as acceptable that good grades would be dependent on effort, including class attendance. The student argued that grades should reflect only academic achievement, but the court was not persuaded. In 1978, an Illinois court invalidated a school board policy that automatically lowered a student's grades for unexcused absences.[15] This court expressed the view that the school board could enact a policy for treating disciplinary infractions, but the board lacked the power to employ academic sanctions for student misbehavior.

In a current case, the American Civil Liberties Union has taken up the cause of a man who is fighting the grade reduction given his son for missing a history class.[16] The ACLU filed an *amicus* brief in this appeal with the State Board of Regents. It argues that the policy of reducing a student's grade because of an absence from class "works an arbitrary disciplinary sanction on student academic performance." If a student has done good work and attended the bulk of the classes, does it make sense to lower the evaluation of this long-term effort due to a short-term lapse in attendance? Such actions are punitive, not educational.

One is cautioned against generalizations because the cases reviewed are specific to the board policies under consideration and, for another, the decisions may be swayed by variable state laws dealing with the specific powers of school boards within a state. In Kentucky, the court declared invalid a policy providing for a five-point reduction of a grade for each unexcused absence during a nine-month period.[17] The court held that the board was without power to authorize this punishment since it was not provided for in the state statutes governing student conduct. "When a school board adopts a policy that is beyond the scope of its authority or conflicts with statutes or administrative regulations adopted by the state agency, that policy will be ruled *ultra vires* by the courts."[18] The Supreme Court of Connecticut also upheld a board's view that academic grades should reflect more than examinations and papers.[19] The court upheld the school board's policy that provided for a five-point reduction in the course grade for each unapproved absence and denied course credit for absences in excess of twenty-four.

In a recent Michigan case involving absences, the father of the student brought action, challenging the board's attendance policy which permitted letter grade reductions of students who, having a certain number of absences, failed to attend mandatory after-hours study sessions.[20] The Court of Appeals held that the attendance policy was within the board's authority; the policy did not implicate a liberty or property interest of the student deserving of constitutional protection; and, even assuming the student had a constitutionally protected liberty or property interest, the attendance policy did not violate the student's right to substantive or procedural due process. Heavy academic penalties, such as long suspensions or expulsion, may be nullified by a state's truancy laws. They are generally disapproved by the courts. A school board may have difficulty justifying loss of class credits for excessive absence caused by suspension.[21]

Violations Unrelated to Academic Work

The imposition of academic sanctions for disciplinary violations unrelated to academic work that could inhibit promotion to the next grade may be considered an irrational means of maintaining discipline. As in most issues surrounding academic sanctions, the law is not uniform.[22] In the setting of any school policies, the board and administrators must take care not to interfere with students' rights which may seem to be unrelated to the issue at hand. An example is an academic sanctions policy which interfered with the free exercise of religion. In *Church of God v. Amarillo Independent School District*,[23] the court found violations of the first amendment's free exercise clause. The district's policy imposed a grade reduction for unexcused absences while limiting students to two excused absences per year for religious reasons. The court agreed that this policy interfered with the students' right to free exercise of religion under the first amendment.

Similarly, academic sanctions for behavioral problems may violate provisions of the Individuals with Disabilities Education Act.[24] In a 1987 Mississippi case, where the court found for the student, the school board imposed the academic penalty of no credits for an entire school year on a learning disabled tenth grader who had been caught possessing marijuana and knives.[25] The student had been receiving services under the IDEA.

Cases concerning alcohol and drugs seem to incite school officials to impose penalties which may seem excessive in the long-run when compared to the nature of the offense. The circumstances and procedures impact the courts' decisions. Use of marijuana and beer brought a ten-day academic suspension to a high school student in 1989. The Appeals Court decided that the student had received all the process that was due and that the disciplinary action taken by the school was rationally related to a valid state interest.[26]

Particularly when sanctions interfere with learning and grading, for instance in preventing a student from taking examinations, the penalty may scar the student's life. Mary Angela Myre filed a complaint alleging that her rights to substantive due process had been violated when she was improperly subjected to in-school suspension and, as a consequence, missed certain examinations related to college admission.[27] The discipline measure resulted from Mary's having been found in possession of beer at an out-of-town football game. Mary, a high school senior at the time, admitted the offense and was given a choice as to which form her discipline would take—in-school or out-of-school suspension. After discussing the matter with her parents, Mary chose in-school suspension for a five-day period. During the suspension, she missed examinations and sought and obtained injunctive relief. The court found that the rule under which Mary had been disciplined was a valid one; but that, as applied to these circumstances, it constituted a deprivation of her rights to substantive due process.

In a case which surely must get the prize for disciplinary zeal, an eleventh grade student, while on a field trip to New York City with her humanities class, joined four other students in ordering and drinking a glass of wine in a restaurant. When questioned later by school authorities, she admitted the incident whereupon she was suspended for five days, excluded from classes, expelled from the cheerleading squad, prohibited from taking part in school activities during the five days suspension period and was later permanently expelled from the National Honor Society. Under the district's disciplinary policy, a further penalty of grade reduction was imposed, so that her grades in each subject for the entire second grading period would be reduced by ten points.[28] The court, noted that, grades are not merely of fleeting interest. They become a permanent record upon which all future educational opportunities are based and the court overturned the school's actions.

Recommendations for Practice

The relationship between the punishment of the student and the furtherance of the goal of the school to educate the child seems to be an important consideration during policy deliberations on the use of academic sanctions. In the 1990s, the dropout problem and the questions about how to best serve children at risk are high on the nation's social policy agenda. Though the use of academic sanctions has sometimes been upheld,the administrator might consider whether it is appropriate to use academic sanctions where they might further discourage already discouraged and troubled children.

In the 1990s, our educational system is moving rapidly to an outcomes-based mode. District, state, national and even international assessment is a reality. Though there have been cases where the courts have upheld grade reductions for such reasons as excessive absences on the grounds that if the student was not there, the student could not be participating and learning; outcomes based evaluations may make "seat time" arguments obsolete. From a policy point of view and the point of view of the goals of the schools, this reasoning may also apply eventually to the need for outcomes testing provisions for those students who are denied grades because of suspensions or expulsions.

- Proposed policies on academic sanctions, if imposed for nonacademic reasons, need to be examined to be sure that they contain the elements of procedure that courts associate with basic constitutional fairness: fair and timely notice of the charges to the affected party; the hearing on those charges; fair opportunity to prepare for the hearing; hearing and decision by an impartial tribunal; the right to present evidence and testimony; and the right to confront and challenge adverse witnesses and evidence.
- The content and timing of notice and hearing may vary depending upon the specifics of the incident involved and the particular state laws and school board policies since state statutes often accord greater substantive and procedural due process than the minimum protections under the fourteenth amendment. Varying student and school interests may make the use of elements beyond the minimum requirements desirable in particular circumstances.[29]
- Where grade reductions are part of academic evaluation, courts do not generally require additional procedural safeguards beyond notice.[30]
- Exceptions need to be allowed within valid rules and policies. The specific circumstances always need to be taken into consideration. Clearly, a five-day suspension when no examinations will be missed is qualitatively different from a five-day suspension during which the student misses three examinations.
- The school's use of academic sanctions should clearly reflect the school's philosophy and goals.

References

[1]Ladson v. Board of Educ., 323 N.Y.S.2d 545 (N.Y. 1971).
[2]Goss v. Lopez, 419 U.S. 565 (1975) and Board of Curators v. Horowitz, 435 U.S. 78 (1978)
[3]Id.
[4]W. D. VALENTE, EDUCATION LAW: PUBLIC AND PRIVATE, Vol 1, 545, (1985).
[5]Braesch v. DePasquale, 265 N.W.2d 842 (Neb. 1978); Jones v. Latexo Indep. School Dist., 499 F. Supp. 223, (E.D. Tex. 1980).

[6]Mitchell v. Board of Trustees, 625 F.2d 660 (5th Cir. 1980); Fisher v. Burkburnett Indep. School Dist., 419 F. Supp. 1200 (N.D. Tex. 1976); Dunn v. Tyler Indep. School Dist., 460 F. 2d 137 (5th Cir. 1972)

[7]Hamer v. Board of Educ. Twp. High School Dist. No. 113, 383 N.E.2d 231 (Ill. App. 1978); Gutierrez v. School Dist., R-1, 585 P.2d 935 (Colo. 1978); Dorsey v. Bale, 521 S.W.2d 76 (Ky. 1975); Campbell v. Board of Educ. of New Milford, 475 A.2d 289 (Conn. 1984)

[8]Id.

[9]Gutierrez, 585 P.2d 935.

[10]Williams v. Board of Educ. of the Marianna School Dist., 626 S.W.2d 361 (Ark, 1982).

[11]R.J.J. by Johnson v. Shineman, 658 S.W.2d 910 (Mo. Ct. App. 1983); Williams, 626 S.W.2d 361; Fisher, 419 F. Supp. 1200.

[12]Slocum v. Holton Bd. of Educ., 429 N.W.2d 607 (Mich. Ct. App. 1988).

[13]Campbell, 475 A.2d 289; Hamer, 383 N.E.2d 231; Knight, 348 N.E.2d 299 (1976); Williams, 626 S.W.2d 361.

[14]Knight, Id.

[15]Hamer, 383 N.E.2d 231.

[16]United Press International, Rhode Island Man Fights Son's Grade Reduction, (March 8, 1991).

[17]Dorsey, 521 S.W.2d 76.

[18]B. Fraser and E. Grumbach, Imposition of Academic Sanctions, PRINCIPAL'S HANDBOOK: CURRENT ISSUES IN SCHOOL LAW, 35-40 (W. E. CAMP, et. al., eds., 1989).

[19]Campbell, 475 A.2d 289.

[20]Slocum, 429 N.W.2d 607.

[21]King v. Farmer, 424 N.Y.S.2d 86 (Sup. Ct. 1979).

[22]Jones, 499 F. Supp. 223; Donaldson v. Bd. of Educ., 424 N.E.2d 737 (Ill. App. Ct. 1981).

[23]511 F. Supp. 613 (1981).

[24]20 U.S.C., § 1401.

[25]The Board of Trustees of the Pascagoula Municipal Separate School District v. Doe, 508 So.2d 1081 (1987).

[26]Palmer v. Merluzzi, 868 F.2d 90 (3d Cir. 1989).

[27]Myre v. The Board of Educ. of Seneca Township High School Dist. No. 160, 439 N.E.2d 74 (Ill. App. Ct.1982).

[28]Katzman v. Cumberland Valley School Dist., 479 A.2d 671 (1984).

[29]Goss, 419 U.S. 565.

[30]M. McCARTHY and N. CAMBRON-McCABE, PUBLIC SCHOOL LAW: TEACHERS' AND STUDENTS' RIGHTS, 2d ed. (1987).

7

Child Abuse

Joan L. Curcio and Amy C. Milford

Introduction

Concurrent with two 1990 United States Supreme Court decisions concerning victims of child abuse[1] was a report delivered to the Secretary of Health and Human Services from the United States Advisory Board on Child Abuse and Neglect. In the report, the Board described a national "child protection emergency" and recommended numerous improvements in the prevention, identification, and treatment of abuse and neglect.[2] Schools were included in the "complex web" of agencies that had a responsibility to respond appropriately to this emergency.[3] Child abuse is an immediate as well as future concern to educators; first, because state statutory requirements place them in the role of assisting the state by taking positive action to protect children. Second, the legal issues surrounding child abuse and schools are rapidly becoming more complex. Teachers and administrators themselves are being named in suits of alleged abuse; plaintiff students and parents are claiming federal, as well as state, violations by schools; school board actions regarding personnel practices and training related to child abuse are being scrutinized. Expectations for school officials to participate in solving child abuse problems have gone far beyond mandated reporting.

The state's concern for a child's welfare and the child's right particularly to be free from harm grows out of the legal concept of the state as "father" to all persons. This legal authority to protect individuals who are not legally competent quite naturally has been extended to minor children, who due to age are unable to take care of themselves. In exercising this intent to provide protection to children, the state sometimes conflicts with parental or other interests. However, a state's authority to provide for a child's welfare is "superior to that of the parent when the parent's natural right is improperly exercised."[4] Under some circumstances, parental rights are forfeited by acts of commission or omission which are not in the best interests of the child.[5] This forfeiture may occur when parental actions jeopardize the health and/or safety of their children.[6] Educators share in a part of the duty to protect the health and welfare of children under their supervision.

Legal Issues

Characteristics of Child Abuse

The National Center on Child Abuse and Neglect identifies four types of abuse and neglect.[7] Physical abuse is physical assault and battery with, for example, a knife or strap, and includes burns, fractures, multiple bruises, and other actions that lead to physical harm to a child. Emotional abuse includes verbal or emotional assault, close confinement, inadequate nutrition, denial of necessary medical care for diagnosed emotional problems, and permitting or abetting delinquent behavior. Sexual abuse involves molestation, incest, and sexual exploitation. Neglect includes abandonment, denial of medical care, nutritional deprivation, lack of proper clothing or hygiene, exposure to health hazards, and permitting chronic truancy or failure to enroll a child in school.

The perpetrators of child abuse come from every walk of life. They are of all ages and all socioeconomic levels; of every religious persuasion; as likely to be city dwellers as rural residents; and rarely sociopathic or psychotic. They do not have readily identifiable characteristics that make it easy for a school administrator to recognize. They do tend, however, to repeat their abusive actions and to increase them in frequency and severity until intervention occurs.[8]

Child Abuse Reporting Requirements

In response to the "hidden epidemic" of child abuse,[9] federal and state legislatures have moved to provide protection. In 1974, Congress passed the Child Abuse Prevention and Treatment Act, giving financial assistance to states which had programs for identifying, preventing, and treating cases of child abuse and neglect. The National Center of Child Abuse and Neglect was created as a part of that act.[10]

Individual states have each enacted child abuse and neglect statutes which require educators, sometimes specifically named, to report suspected child abuse. Every educator, acting in a professional capacity, who suspects child abuse or neglect, must report that suspicion to appropriate authorities in the state. Proof of abuse is not required, and to facilitate reports, state reporting laws generally include a provision of immunity from civil and criminal liability for the reporter when the report has been made in good faith.[11]

The Failure to Report

Most states provide for penalties (fines, jail terms, or both) assessed against mandatory reporters who fail to report suspected abuse or neglect. Nevertheless, school personnel still are not fully complying with the statutory requirement. Reasons that educators offer for reluctance to comply with the law include: not knowing what circumstances "clearly" give rise to a suspicion of child abuse; the lack of diagnostic experience; the possibility of being sued for defamation or other reasons; fear of impeding a teacher/student relationship; prior lack of response from the authority to which the report was made; unwillingness to implicate suspected colleagues (where an abuser is a school official) without clear proof.[12] Since the failure to report can incur civil or criminal liability (or both) under state laws, and potential liability under federal laws, this reluctance renders educators clearly vulnerable to legal action. Not surprising then, they have been subject to suits in the past and will continue to be in the future.

Immunity

State statutes grant immunity to those individuals who report suspected abuse or neglect in good faith. The immunity protection afforded those who are mandated to report suspected child abuse was tested in North Carolina in *Davis v. Durham City Schools*.[13] A substitute teacher brought an action against the school system alleging malicious prosecution, defamation, intentional infliction of emotional distress, and negligence. The suit arose out of a principal's report to the Department of Social Services of complaints by students of physical abuse from the teacher. The court held that the teacher's claims were barred by the state's statute granting immunity from civil and criminal liability for those making suspected abuse reports. In any proceeding involving liability, good faith is presumed.[14]

Violations of Federal Law: Section 1983

When a school district or school official is deliberately indifferent to the rights of students to be kept safe from harm, there is the potential for civil rights liability. Most of the recent child abuse cases[15] have their arguments grounded as a violation of 42 U.S.C. section 1983. This law provides redress to an injured party who has suffered the deprivation of rights, guaranteed under the federal constitution or federal statutes; at the hands of a person acting "under color" of state law. According to the United States Supreme Court, when the execution of a governmental agency's policy or custom (such as a school district's) inflicts the injury, then the agency as a body or individuals as agents are responsible under section 1983, and subject to liability.[16] For instance, should a school board or its agents customarily ignore reporting laws that mandate specific behavior from them, or customarily fail to investigate or act upon information concerning student abuse complaints concerning employees, there may be a basis for a section 1983 suit. Plaintiffs choose such a civil rights tort action because school defendants usually do not have the same extensive immunity from this federal protection of constitutional rights as is available to them under state tort laws.[17] However, the burden of proof resting on the plaintiff in a section 1983 action is a heavy one.

The mother of a profoundly battered child, Joshua DeShaney, attempted recently to recover damages in a section 1983 action against a social services department for failing to protect the child from his father's violence, depriving him of liberty without due process. The Supreme Court denied relief, because the state's failure to protect a person against private violence does not violate the due process clause.[18] Despite the plaintiff's inability to recover damages in this case, it still has considerable significance for schools because of the plaintiff's attempt to show that the state had an affirmative duty to protect the child against harm, alleging a special relationship had been created between them.

In the same year that the Supreme Court found that the state did not owe a duty to Joshua, it sent a school abuse case back to a lower court to be resolved in light of the *DeShaney* decision. In that remanded suit, *Stoneking v. Bradford Area School District*, a circuit court saw a distinction between the two situations that puts school officials on notice. In *Stoneking*, a female band member brought a section 1983 action against a school district, principal, assistant principal, and superintendent for injuries arising out of the band director's sexual assaults upon the student. On remand from the Supreme Court, the U.S. Circuit Court chose not to rest its decision on the affirmative duty issue, but moved instead to whether or not a school district custom or practice that appeared to condone or authorize sexual assault was being maintained; such actions could be construed as encouraging a climate "where innocent girls were victimized."[19] Since the school district and its officials were acting under color of state law when supervising the band director and the band director was a school district employee subject to their immediate control, it was possible the court reasoned, that an affirmative link between Stoneking's injury and the school's policies and practices could be proved. The court sent it back for a jury's consideration.[20] Meanwhile, the district settled the case with the plaintiff.

There are a number of behaviors which can cause school officials to be seen as showing callous or "deliberate indifference" toward potential harm for section 1983 purposes. Specifically, the courts have pointed to a school district's failure to provide proper training; failure to train employees to identify abused children and to execute their duties regarding abuse; and failure to handle complaints of abuse on the part of state employees appropriately. Such practices, if seen as grossly negligent or deliberately indifferent, could be the basis for school liability in a section 1983 claim.[21]

Abuse Within Schools

Sexual abuse is an issue increasingly the subject of litigation for schools. John Crewdson, in his book on child sexual abuse, says that one of the best ways for potential abusers to gain access to children is to be a caretaker, a teacher, or to work in the schools.[22] Cases of sexual assault and abuse in recent years would support the fact that school employees in various positions are having to defend themselves against sexual abuse charges. In sexual assault cases, as the *Stoneking* case discussed above, supervisors may be vulnerable not only to a section 1983 suit as a result of their own behaviors regarding assault complaints; they may have liability hiring an abusive employee. Therefore, attention to the selection process and the need to follow acceptable, sometimes statutory, means of screening personnel becomes important.

Sometimes the accusation of abuse against a school employee is related to physical abuse resulting from corporal punishment. Under the doctrine of *in loco parentis*, school officials generally have the right to use corporal punishment as a means of discipline if not prohibited by state statute or local policy. However, when that punishment becomes excessive or abusive, the child and his/her parent may bring legal action against the teacher or administrator. Interestingly, parents and others who are seeking to eliminate the use of corporal punishment in schools are making use of the child abuse and neglect statutes.[23] As an example, in the state of Florida, when a report that a school employee abused a child by use of excessive corporal punishment, and it was confirmed by the Department of Health and Rehabilitative Services,[24] the school administrator's name was entered on a state abuse registry as an abuser.

Although this classification could disqualify the employee from continuing to work with children, a Florida court upheld the statutory provision since its legitimate purpose was to protect children from abuse.[24]

Title IX As Protection Against Abuse/Harassment

An important victory in the lives of women and girls was won with the case of *Franklin v. Gwinnett County Public Schools*[25] which strengthen the protections of Title IX of the Education Amendments of 1972 by finding that a monetary remedy is available for sex discrimination cases filed pursuant to Title IX. Title IX provides that schools which receive federal funding shall not engage in the practice of sex discrimination.[26] Despite the law, the lack of a remedy in the form of monetary damages has kept it from being a major deterrent to sex discrimination.[27]

In her complaint, Franklin alleged that beginning in her sophomore year, Mr. Hill, a coach and teacher, harassed her through conduct ranging from sexually-oriented discussions to calling her out of classes to take her to a private office in order to have forcible sex with her.[28] Franklin filed the Title IX action against the school district seeking monetary damages for sex discrimination in connection with the sexual harassment and abuse by Hill while she was in high school.[29] The complaint further stated that even after Franklin spoke to school officials concerning Hill's repeated harassment, teachers and administrators took no steps to halt the improper/criminal conduct and even discouraged Franklin from pressing charges against Hill.[30]

The school district argued that when Congress passed the law there was no specification of remedies available to the victim and damages should be limited to injunctive relief.[31] The Court reasoned that this remedy would not help Franklin since she was a student at the time of the alleged repeated harassment and Hill had already resigned from the school district when charges were brought.[32] The Court concluded that if a right of action exists to enforce a federal right, and Congress is silent on the question of remedies, a court may order any appropriate relief.[33] The Court's unanimous ruling was important because it provides the victims of sex discrimination with a remedy that will spur school boards and administrators to guard against such misconduct.[34]

Recommendations for Practice

Case law on child abuse involving schools is on the rise. The issues include failure to report suspected abuse, failure to act on the basis of complaints, sexual assaults on children by school employees, physical assaults as a result of corporal punishment, and policies and practices regarding abuse in schools that demonstrate deliberate indifference to the potential harm of children. Often the failure to report or investigate an abuse complaint in schools is tied to an administrative decision to delay or ignore action out of concern for confidentiality or loyalty to an employee. However, it is clear that school districts and school officials do have responsibilities and liabilities to these issues. There are specific procedures and useful behaviors to use in maintaining a safe environment for children, with side benefits of less litigation and expense.

- Know the indicators of abuse and train others who have a duty to report suspected abuse. While no one sign may mean that abuse is occurring, a closer look should be taken when indicators occur repeatedly and/or in combination with each other.[35]
- Have a clear policy on the principal's role and the teacher's role in reporting; teachers express uncertainty about the expectations of the principal regarding procedures (particularly beginning teachers).
- Include among school procedures directions for how to proceed when an abuse investigator comes to school.
- Inform parents of the school's policy regarding child abuse and the procedures followed by the school in the event of potential child abuse allegations.
- Follow up directly on suspicions shared by others that staff members are involved in abuse. Investigate and document such complaints; take necessary action; keep appropriate school officials informed. Statutory reporting requirements place the responsibility on school personnel to act as a safety valve in abusive situations. The responsibility to protect children cannot be weighed against the chance that a school employee might lose a job; a child's physical and emotional health outweighs that chance.
- Publish a handbook and provide inservice training on abuse and neglect for staff use and be aware of any customs which may smack of callous indifference toward the safety of children; they may appear to be the official policy of the school or school district.

- Provide training for parents so that they too can recognize the signs of abuse and know where to go or who to contact for assistance.
- Encourage cooperative efforts with local child protective services; use them to train staff and to work with high-risk children.
- Use legal screening methods to keep abusers out of the schools through the hiring process.

References

[1] *See* Maryland v. Craig, 110 S. Ct. 3157 (1990) and Idaho v. Wright, 110 S. Ct. 3139 (1990).

[2] Education Wk., Aug. 1, 1990, at 7.

[3] N.Y. Times, June 28, 1990, at A13.

[4] K. ALEXANDER and M. D. ALEXANDER, AMERICAN PUBLIC SCHOOL LAW, 216 (2d ed. 1985).

[5] *Id.* at 217.

[6] Wisconsin v. Yoder, 406 U.S. 205 (1972).

[7] A. FEAD, THE CHILD ABUSE CRISIS: IMPACT ON THE SCHOOLS, 2 (1985).

[8] D. BROADHURST, EDUCATORS, SCHOOLS, AND CHILD ABUSE. National Committee for Prevention of Child Abuse, 2-3 (1986).

[9] P. Zirkel, *Child Abuse and the Law*, Updating School Board Policies, National School Boards Association, (vol. 17, no. 3) 4 (March, 1986).

[10] R. Salmon and M. D. Alexander, *Child Abuse and Neglect: Implications for Educators*, ED. L. REP. at 11, (1986). *See* Public Law 93-247, 88 Stat. 4 (1974) codified as amended at 42 U.S.C. §§ 5101-5107 (1975 & Supp. IV 1980).

[11] D. BROADHURST, *supra*, note 8 at 8.

[12] R. Salmon and M. D. Alexander, *supra*, note 10 at 2.

[13] Davis v. Durham City Schools, 372 S.E.2d 318 (N.C. App. 1988).

[14] *Id* at 320.

[15] *See* Doe v. Douglas County School Dist., WL 156568 (D Colo. 1991); Thelma D. v. Board of Educ. of the City of St. Louis, 934 F.2d 929 (8th Cir. 1991); J. O. v. Alton Community Unit School Dist. 11, 909 F.2d 267 (7th Cir 1990); Landstrom v. Barrington School Dist. 220, 739 F. Supp. 441 (N.D. Ill. 1990).

[16] Monell v. Department of Social Services of the City of New York, 436 U.S. 658 (1978).

[17] J. T. Horner, *The Anatomy of a Constitutional Tort*, 47 ED. L. REP. 1 (1989)

[18] DeShaney v. Winnebago County Dep't. of Social Servs., 109 S. Ct. 998 (1989), at 1004.

[19] Stoneking v. Bradford Area School Dist., 882 F.2d 720 (3d Cir. 1989), at 730.

[20] *Id.* at 731.

[21] *Id.* at 725.

[22] J. Crewdson, BY SILENCE BETAYER, SEXUAL ABUSE OF CHILDREN IN AMERICA, 115 (1988).

[23] R. Salmon and M. D. Alexander, *supra*, note 7 at 17-18.

[24] W. M. v. Department of Health and Rehabilitation Services, 553 So. 2d 274 (1989).

[25] Franklin v. Gwinnett County Public Schools, 112 S. Ct. 1028 (1992).

[26] 20 U.S.C. § 1681 (a).

[27] P. First and L. Rossow, *An Enormous Victory for Women and Girls*, SCHOOL L. REP., May 1992, at 1, 2.

[28] *Franklin*, 112 S. Ct. 1028 at 1031.

[29] *Id.* at 1028.

[30] *Id.* at 1031.

[31] P. First, *supra*, note 27 at 2.

[32] *Id.*

[33] *Franklin*, 112 S. Ct. 1028 at 1033.

[34] P. First, *supra*, note 27 at 2.

[35] D. BROADHURST, *supra*, note 8 at 6.

Special Education
And The Law

8

Rights, Entitlements, and Responsibilities of Parents of Disabled Children

Carol A. Denzinger and Stephen B. Thomas

Introduction

Over the past two decades there has been growing awareness that students with diverse needs must be viewed as unique individuals and provided education accordingly. While the primary aim of related legislation has been to help children with disabilities receive benefit from their educational experiences, Congress also has given to their parents the opportunity to play an important role in the educational process. Legislation and related case law not only have provided parents with procedural safeguards to ensure an appropriate education for their handicapped children but have entitled them to specific school services and benefits. Since courts have allowed aggrieved parents to sue in their own name under these acts,[1] principals and other school officials are advised to remember that parents have rights.

Legal Issues

The Individuals with Disabilities Education Act[2] (IDEA—the Education for All Handicapped Children Act as amended in 1990) provides grants to states that meet guidelines ensuring a free appropriate public education (FAPE) to all children with disabilities. The concept of "appropriate education" is ambiguous and little guidance as to its substance is provided within the Act. In reviewing this dilemma, the Supreme Court[3] asserted that in most cases an individual child will be provided an appropriate education if the extensive procedural safeguards[4] within the Act are followed. Such safeguards help guarantee that each eligible child receives an education provided in the least restrictive environment and that the program is designed so they receive "some educational benefit." To ensure the development and delivery of an appropriate program, federal law requires recipients of assistance under the Act to involve the parent in the entire process, from original evaluation to exit (either graduation or age twenty-one).

Determining the Responsible Parent

Prior to examining provisions of the law that establish parent rights, it is necessary to determine who qualifies as the responsible parent or surrogate under IDEA and related federal statutes (i.e., section 504 of the Rehabilitation Act of 1973 and the Family Educational Rights and Privacy Act—FERPA). While the answer to this question may appear obvious (i.e., the natural parent), consider how the changing family has complicated the issue. As recently as 1988, 61% of the children under age seventeen lived with both their natural mother and father, 32% lived with only one natural parent, and 7% lived with neither. During that same year, females age seventeen and under gave birth to 95,869 children while females under age fifteen gave birth to 10,588 children.[5] Although many of these underage youth are parents, they remain minors under state contract law, thereby further complicating the process.

Given the above, school districts are often faced with a variety of problems when determining which parent, family member, or surrogate has the right to represent the child, approve the IEP, request a hearing, provide access to school records, or personally gain access to such records. In order to resolve this initial problem, school officials will need to determine who has guardianship over the child, whether related court orders direct the involvement of individuals in addition to the guardian, and whether the child is capable of representing himself once he has reached the age of majority.

For the purpose of IDEA, a "parent" includes not only the child's natural parent, but also may be a legal guardian, a surrogate parent,[6] or other persons acting in place of a parent such as a grandmother or stepparent with whom the child lives. The term does not include the state if the child is a ward of the state.[7] In cases where the parents are divorced or separated, the parent receiving custody of the child will generally be the responsible party for IDEA purposes, unless a divorce decree or court order stipulates otherwise.[8] In the case of joint custody, districts have the responsibility to involve both parents and provide them with the same rights and responsibilities as if they remained a single family unit.

Where parents are divorced, both often maintain the right to inspect their child's educational records. In one case, the court ruled that the code interpreting FERPA "allow[s] inspection by either parent, without regard to custody, unless such access is barred by state law, court order, or legally binding instrument."[9] In a second case where the parents had joint custody, the mother refused to provide the father with information regarding their child's schooling. The school district was not only required to allow the father access to the child's educational records, but also had to provide copies of all information mailed or carried home to families in the district. The court reasoned, however, that mailing correspondence was merely for the father's convenience, and that he must pay related expenses.[10]

Even where one parent has custody, financial responsibility for the child may be an issue. In a Massachusetts case, the noncustodial father had financial responsibility for his child's educational expenses and desired reimbursement for privately attained related expenses. The court found that, barring court order, a parent has a basic right to participate in planning despite marital status, and it was imprudent to permit the development of an educational plan without consulting the party responsible for the child's overall education. The court found that the father had the right to disapprove the IEP which had been developed by the school district and accepted by the mother.[11]

Where minor parents are involved in the IEP process, it is generally true that they retain parental rights barring the determination of incompetence or the removal of guardianship rights.[12] On occasion, districts involve both the minor parent and grandparent to help ensure the participation of at least one family member, particularly if both the minor parent and the child reside with the grandparent. In case of disagreement between the parent and grandparent, district decisions should generally be made in collaboration with the minor parent. It is important to note that the child's right to a FAPE is in no way impaired by the fact that the parent is a minor, even where it might be argued that under state law the minor parent did not have the right to enter into a legally binding contract.[13]

Since educational services may be appropriate through the student's twenty-first birthday, another related issue involves parent rights under IDEA after the child becomes his own guardian. The Act has remained silent in this regard;[14] however, the Second Circuit Court of Appeals recently addressed the issue. That court allowed the cessation of services where a child over eighteen gave his consent, but required the district to provide the parent with written notice of its actions. In support of its decision to provide parental notice, the court noted that the statute and relevant regulations contemplate that IDEA procedural safeguards apply to an eighteen to twenty-one year old where there has been no adjudication of incompetency.[15] Accordingly, while they must receive notice, parents do not have the right to force services for a child of legal age where the student is unwilling to provide consent.

Parent Rights

Once the district has determined who has the responsibility to represent the child (e.g., the natural parent, relative, surrogate, or the child), it then must involve that person or persons in virtually all activities that help shape the child's educational program. In providing each eligible child with an appropriate program, the district is required to involve the parents in evaluation, IEP development, and placement.[16] The district must:

- communicate in the parent's native language or other mode of understandable communication, unless it is clearly not feasible to do so;
- allow the parents to involve other individuals of their choosing in the process;[17]
- ensure that parents have access to records, yet retain such records in confidence from unauthorized parties;
- ensure that parents are fully informed about the hearing process and its related appeals (i.e., mediation where available, impartial hearing, and the courts).

Written notice must be provided to the parents whenever the district proposes to initiate or to change the identification, evaluation, or educational placement or program of the child or when the district refuses to change the above notwithstanding parental request. Under IDEA, written notice includes:

- a description of the proposed school district action or inaction;
- an explanation of the reasons for the proposed action or inaction;
- a summary of alternatives considered by the district prior to its decision including the reasons each was rejected;
- a description of testing and evaluations used to make the decision;
- a description of other relevant factors; and
- a notice of due process rights and procedures.[18]

Where consent is required, parents must be fully informed about that which they are signing. Educational jargon is to be explained or replaced by everyday language, and appropriate interpreters must be provided at board expense for parents whose primary language is not English, including those who are deaf.[19] Additionally, correspondence in braille may be necessary for blind parents if such action is considered a moderate accommodation.[20] Where written communication is used and the parents are functionally illiterate, the district must keep a record of verbal communications to document its good faith in providing active parent participation.

Note that communications must be in the parents' native language or other form of communication if it is feasible to do so. This statement indicates that there may be circumstances where communication would not be feasible, but no clear guidance is provided. Possible examples may be where the district is attempting to communicate with an individual who is deaf and blind and does not possess the ability to speak, or speaks a rare tribal dialect. In such instances, it may prove impractical to fully involve the parent or to acquire anything resembling "informed consent." Accordingly, where possible, it may be necessary to appoint a surrogate.

Written notice and informed parental consent are required prior to initiating a specialized evaluation to determine the child's need for special education and related services.[21] If parents disagree with the results of the evaluation, they may obtain a second evaluation which must be considered when planning the child's individualized education. The second evaluation will generally be at school district expense unless the district initiates a hearing to contest the expense and substantiates that its initial evaluation was adequate.[22] While informed parental consent is necessary for initial evaluation, it is not required for reevaluations, even when the district did not properly secure permission for the initial placement.[23] Furthermore, generalized screening done en masse requires notice to parents but does not require written consent.

After evaluation, the school district initiates a placement meeting to determine what, if any, special education and related services are appropriate to meet the unique needs of the child. Districts must take steps to ensure that one or both parents are present at each meeting or are afforded the opportunity to participate. Ensuring participation includes timely notification of the meeting which is to occur at a mutually agreeable time and place. If parents are unable to attend the meeting, participation through individual meetings or telephone calls with the parent is required.[24]

Participation goes beyond physical presence, however. School officials and parents should work as equal partners in the process. Parents have the right to offer suggestions regarding the child's placement to be considered equally with those of other team members. A district has no obligation to provide a specific program or methodology, notwithstanding parental request, provided the district placement is also appropriate for the child. For example in a related case, the parents of a deaf child desired a cued speech program while the school district recommended one of total communication. The court found the total communication program was adequate to meet the child's needs and ruled for the district.[25]

Two courts have interpreted that "participation" also allows parents to tape record the proceedings of IEP meetings.[26] In the first case, the parent was unable to take notes because of a disabling condition in her hand.[27] In a second case, the mother whose primary language was Danish wished to review tapes at home with a dictionary in hand.[28] Both courts reasoned that tape recording would allow the parents greater participation in the process, thereby fulfilling the spirit of the statute.

Throughout the process, parents and their representatives have the right to inspect and review any information used to plan the child's education including records related to identification, evaluation, and placement of the child. The school district must accommodate reasonable requests for explanation and interpretation of the records and provide copies free or at nominal cost.[29] One court ruled that a parent's right to inspect records extends to raw psychological data (e.g., Rorschach ink blot test results) which were part of the child's temporary evaluation file.[30]

When parents disagree with the content of a file, they can request that records be removed or amended, or they can attach an addendum to the record explaining their concerns. Any attached addendum must be maintained with the original record and may not be removed or gleaned from the files unless the controversial material also is removed. Additionally, parental consent or eligible student consent is required before information is released to individuals who are not exempt from the Act's provisions.[31] If the school district opts to tape record IEP meetings, these recordings also are considered to be part of the child's educational record and are subject to the same confidentiality requirements.[32]

At any stage of the process, (e.g., before initial evaluation, before placement, or after placement), parents may contest a proposed or current decision they feel does not appropriately meet their child's needs.[33] The statute establishes a system of hearings and appeals[34] which may address specific aspects of the child's evaluation or program; the appropriateness of the placement; the access to records and how they are used; or the failure to meet procedural safeguards. The school district also has the right to initiate the hearing process. Related disputes often involve the parents' refusal to permit evaluation of their child; payment of a second or third evaluation; maintenance of the child in the "then current placement"; and reimbursement for parentally acquired placements.

During hearings, parents have the right to present evidence, compel the attendance of witnesses, and cross-examine witnesses. They also have the right to receive written findings of fact and decisions and a written or electronic verbatim record of hearings.[35] One court found that either a written or electronic record satisfied the intention of the law, and the district had no obligation to grant parent requests for a particular form. In this case, the parents argued that a written record would be more beneficial in proceeding with due process.[36]

Generally, prevailing parents have the right to receive attorney fees from the school district.[37] The law does not provide appointment of an attorney for parents wishing to pursue litigation under the Act, nor does failure to provide such attorney create a constitutional or statutory violation.[38] Additionally, nonattorney parents may not legally represent their child's interests during court action and recover fees.[39]

Parent Entitlements

In addition to "parent rights" specified above, parents often claim that they have specific entitlements. As part of the child's individualized education, related services may be required to help the child benefit from special education. Listed among the related services is "parent counseling and training" defined as "assisting parents in understanding the special needs of their child and providing parents with information about child development."[40] Such services were intended by Congress to bolster the educational process in the home.[41] The obligation to provide counseling and training to parents has been in the courts on several occasions. Taken in the aggregate, these cases support the following conclusions:

- the district is required to provide training for the parents if such training will enable the child to benefit from his IEP or help the parents deal with the emotional stress of dealing with the child in the home;[42]
- it is not enough to suggest that the parents attain the service or to provide information where this service may be obtained—the district is directly responsible for arranging the service for the parents;[43]
- but the district is not mandated to plan meetings completely "around the schedules of the parents," particularly where good faith efforts are made to identify mutually agreeable times and locations.[44]

The courts have further ruled that inservice training is intended for support personnel including teachers and specialists who work in the school system and need not be provided to parents.[45]

A second related service often contested by parents is transportation. Under IDEA, transportation includes travel to and from school and between schools, travel in and around school buildings, and specialized equipment (such as special or adapted buses, lifts, and ramps) if required to provide special transportation for a handicapped child.[46] On two occasions, parents have argued that this related service extends to them. The parents in the first case sought reimbursement for summer programming and transportation expenses they incurred during this placement. The court reasoned that neither federal nor state law required reimbursement for the parents' transportation costs, but rather such laws created an entitlement only for the child.[47] In a second case, the child was placed in a residential facility in Florida while the parents lived in Georgia. Parent counseling and training was written into the IEP to aid family interaction. The parents requested that the school district provide transportation, in addition to hotel accommodations for the family of four, for frequent visits between the residential facility and home for both the child and his family. The court limited the number of visits between home and school to three round trips for the child. Additionally, although both transportation and parent counseling and training were related services in the child's IEP, the district was ruled not to have an obligation to provide transportation or lodging for the family to visit a Georgia facility where parent training was to be provided. According to the court, the purpose of transportation is to allow the child to receive an education, not to provide therapeutic benefits.[48]

While IDEA provides parents of children with disabilities a myriad rights, section 504 of the Rehabilitation Act[49] may provide additional rights to parents who are also handicapped. A recent case out of the Second Circuit involved the hearing impaired parents of hearing children.[50] The parents wished to participate in school functions such as parent conferences but could not benefit from these meetings without the assistance of a sign language interpreter. The court ruled on the parents' behalf, finding that the district must make moderate accommodation to handicapped parents as well as children. It is important to note that while the court required the school to make reasonable accommodations to allow the handicapped parents the opportunity to participate in school initiated parent activities, it did not require accommodation for extracurricular events (i.e., the court did not believe the child's graduation ceremony was a school initiated activity for the purposes of its ruling).

Part H of IDEA provides additional financial assistance to states that implement a statewide, comprehensive, interagency program to provide services to infants and toddlers—aged two and under—and their families.[51] While school districts are not solely responsible for providing services under this section, their partial responsibility deserves attention. Under this section, states accepting grants must ensure that appropriate early intervention services will be available to all infants and toddlers needing the services no later than the fifth year of the state's participation under this part.[52]

Many of the provisions discussed in previous sections of this paper also apply to this age group. Parent participation is to be an essential component to the process;[53] involvement of others at parent discretion is required;[54] notice must be provided[55] with parental consent prior to initial evaluation and placement;[56] access to student records is provided;[57] and communication must be in the parents' native language or other form of communication, if feasible to do so.[58] Due process proceedings are nearly identical to those outlined above, but may be somewhat less formal at the state's discretion.[59]

Children who qualify[60] are to receive an evaluation of both their unique needs and the family's strengths and needs related to the development of the child. Family assessments are voluntary on the part of the family.[61] After evaluation, the Individualized Family Service Plan (IFSP)[62] is written to include both child and family goals. Parents are to receive family training and counseling as appropriate to enhance their ability related to their child's development.[63] Case management services are to be included to aid the family in receiving the rights, procedural safeguards, and services under the law.[64] Finally, unlike the provisions of Part B affecting older children, Part H specifically provides transportation services to the child's family where this will be necessary to attain specified services.[65]

Parent Responsibilities

Many educators feel that if schools are ever to succeed, parents must become active participants in the educational process. Federal law, however, does not make the quality of a disabled child's education dependant on parental participation. The closest IDEA comes to imposing any kind of "responsibility" on the parent is through the development and implementation of an IFSP. Theoretically, the role the parent plays is far greater at this level than it is at the elementary and secondary levels. Notwithstanding the aforementioned, the school district cannot require parent participation as part of the educational program. In a related case, a child was placed in a private facility by the public school with the mother's reluctant agreement. The private facility subsequently conditioned the child's continued attendance upon the mother's attendance in psychotherapy. The court concluded that the mother had a right to refuse psychotherapy without negatively impacting her child's education.[66] In a second case, a child with spina bifida had been excluded from regular education and filed suit under the Rehabilitation Act. The court ordered the district to admit the child and concluded that admission could not be conditioned on the mother's presence in the classroom.[67]

The introduction of case management, while assisting in the provision of services to children, may further remove responsibility from parents. With limited interpretation other than the expansive description in the regulations, it appears that the case manager could take responsibility for even the most routine tasks, such as arranging for "well child" visits to the family physician or clinic and completing insurance claims to secure reimbursement for medical expenses.[68]

As the above indicates, parents have a number of rights and entitlements under federal law, but have few actual responsibilities. In fact, the Seventh Circuit Court of Appeals recently ruled that parents need be neither justified nor cooperative to gain a desired placement for their child. In this case, the district made numerous attempts to address parental concerns but met continued opposition from the family. A divided court suggested that the parents were so hostile toward an appropriate school district placement as to "poison" this option in the mind of the child. Such conduct appeared to tie the hands of the court since the proposed placement was no longer capable of meeting the child's needs. As a result, the court directed the district to fund a private school placement.[69]

Recommendations for Practice

Although federal law requires a partnership between school officials and parents when providing an education for disabled children, actual practice suggests that the term "partnership" may all too often be a misnomer. At times, school officials and parents work together as equal partners in the process; however, the relationship may be dominated by the district with communications being selected and limited and involvement opportunities being restricted. When this action occurs, parents are generally poorly informed and reluctantly involved. All too often, a parent's first meeting with the IEP committee is called so that a signature can be acquired on a completed IEP. Parents may not be fully informed of their own and their child's rights and entitlements. Many districts have improved in this area and now provide more "understandable" literature and devote more time and resources to informing and educating parents. Other districts, however, may have to adjust their procedures significantly if they are to even minimally comply with IDEA regulations.

When parent rights are disregarded, there is a greater likelihood that disgruntled parents will file for impartial hearing and will claim a violation of their rights under federal law. Once parents initiate formal due process, districts have the financial responsibility of the hearing officer, transcripts, and their own legal fees. Under the worst of circumstances, the process could extend through the courts and these costs could increase significantly and include compensatory education, reimbursement for private programs, and plaintiff's attorney fees.

It is time for districts to reexamine their policies related to parent involvement and rights considering recent changes in the law. The law guarantees certain parent rights and entitlements; however, it is the local school district that can increase parent responsibilities as well by making them equal partners in the education of their children by completing the following checklist:

- Identify a parent or provide a surrogate for each child.
- Allow estranged, separated, or divorced parents to review records and receive notices unless restricted by a divorce decree or court order.
- Involve both parents where joint custody has been established.
- Inform each parent of all the rights and entitlements due him/her under federal and state law.
- Receive informed consent from the appropriate parent (even if the parent is a minor) or an adult special need student between the ages of eighteen and twenty-one.
- Involve the parent in all phases of evaluation, IEP development, and placement.
- Communicate with the parents in their native language or other form of communication.
- Devise a system allowing inspection and amendment of educational records.
- Allow parents to tape record meetings.

- Provide parent counseling and training as needed and include as part of this training information about attaining other services that may benefit the child and family.
- Involve the parents in all ways possible and insure their active participation where appropriate.

References

[1]Tschanneral v. District of Columbia Bd. of Educ., 594 F. Supp. 407 (D.D.C. 1984). *See also* Rothschild v. Grottenthaler, 907 F.2d 286 (2d Cir. 1990) where the court ruled that parents may sue the school district under section 504 when the district fails to provide moderate accommodation to the parent's handicap.

[2]20 U.S.C. § 1400 *et seq.*

[3]Board of Educ. of Hendrick Hudson Cent. School Dist. Bd. of Educ. v. Rowley, 102 S. Ct. 3034, 3050 (1982).

[4]20 U.S.C. § 1415.

[5]National Center for Health Statistics Family Structures and Children's Health: U.S. 1988 (June 1991); 1 Vital Statistics of the United States 1988, Natility.

[6]34 C.F.R. § 300.514. Once a nonparent has appropriately acquired surrogate status, that individual possesses rights comparable to those of the natural parent. *See* Abney *ex rel.* Kantor v. District of Columbia, 849 F.2d 1491 (D.C. Cir. 1988).

[7]34 C.F.R. § 300.10.

[8]Henderson, v. Morristown Memorial Hosp., 487 A.2d 742 (N.J. Super. Ct. 1985).

[9]Page v. Rotterdam-Mohonasen Cent. School Dist., 441 N.Y.S.2d 323, 325 (Sup. Ct. 1981).

[10]Fay v. South Colonie Cent. School Dist., 802 F.2d 21 (2d Cir. 1986).

[11]Doe v. Anrig, 651 F. Supp. 424 (D. Mass 1987).

[12]R. V. MacKay, The Law Of Guardianship (3d ed. 1980).

[13]Under certain conditions, minors may have the right to contract. While their contracts are not void, they are voidable. Some authors suggest that minors over twelve may enter into legally valid contracts with the permission of their parents. *See* 42 Sattinger, O.C. (ed.), Am Jur 2d. *Infants* (IV)(A) § 58 (1969) and Institute of Judicial Administration, American Bar Association, Standards Related to Rights of Minors (1980) at 111.

[14]34 C.F.R. § 300, appendix C., question 22.

[15]Mrs. C. v. Wheaton, 916 F.2d 69, 73 (2d Cir. 1990). The court based its reasoning on 34 C.F.R. § 300.300(b)(4) which addresses students age 3-5 and 18-21 and states that "[i]f a public agency provides education to a handicapped child in any of these age groups, it must make a free appropriate public education available to that child and provide that child and his or her parents all the rights under Part B of the Act and this part."

[16]Louis M. *ex rel.* Velma M. v. Ambach, 714 F. Supp. 1276 (N.D.N.Y. 1989); Honig v. Doe 108 S. Ct. 592, 604 (1988).

[17]34 C.F.R. §§ 300.562(b)(3), 300.344(a)(5). In Medford v. District of Columbia, 691 F. Supp. 1473 (D.D.C. 1988), the court ruled that the EHA regulations neither require nor prohibit the attendance of counsel at the IEP meetings. The court points out that occasionally hearing officers may even require the presence of an attorney at a child's IEP meeting to protect the child's substantive rights and the parents' right to meaningful participation.

[18]34 C.F.R. §§ 300.504; 300.505.

[19]34 C.F.R. § 300.505.

[20]34 C.F.R. § 300.9.

[21]34 C.F.R. § 300.504.

[22]34 C.F.R. § 300.503(a),(c); Evans v. District No. 17 of Douglas County, 841 F.2d 824 (8th Cir. 1988).

[23]Carroll v. Capalbo, 563 F. Supp. 1053 (D.R.I. 1983).

[24]34 C.F.R. § 300.345(a),(c).

[25]Lachman v. Illinois State Bd. of Educ., 852 F.2d 290 (7th Cir. 1988).

[26]IDEA does not directly address this issue, however the Department of Education suggests that tape recording IEP meetings is permissible at the option of either party. 34 C.F.R. § 300 appendix C, question 12.

[27]V.W. v. Favolise, 131 F.R.D. 654 (D. Conn. 1990).

[28]E.H. v. Tirozzi, 735 F. Supp. 53 (D. Conn. 1990).

[29]34 C.F.R. §§ 300.562; 300.566(a)

[30]John K. v. Board of Educ. for School Dist. #65, 504 N.E.2d 797 (Ill. App. Ct. 1987).

[31]34 C.F.R. §§ 300.567; 300.569(b); 300.571.

[32]34 C.F.R. § 300 appendix C, question 12.

[33]Whether the parents are married or simply have joint custody does not appear to affect their individual right to participate or to request due process. However, parents who relinquish guardianship may also surrender due process rights. See Susan R.M. ex rel. Charles L.M. v. Northeast Indep. School Dist., 818 F.2d 455 (5th Cir. 1987).

[34]The statute allows states some latitude in establishing due process systems. Mediation, where available, is an initial option. One tier systems provide only one administrative hearing, that being at the state level; while two tier systems provide two administrative hearings—the first at the local level and an appeal at the state level (20 U.S.C. § 1415(b)(2); 34 C.F.R. §§ 300.506, 300.510). Where a state has elected to establish a two tier system, the initial hearing may take up to forty-five days from the time of initial filing to the date a written decision is provided. The administrative appeal to the state can take an additional thirty days. Administrative appeals generally are completed at this point, although further appeal through a court of appropriate jurisdiction is possible (20 U.S.C.§ 1415(b)(2); 34 C.F.R. § 300.511).

[35]20 U.S.C. § 1415(d); 34 C.F.R. § 300.508(a)(4).

[36]Edward B. v. Paul, 814 F.2d 52 (1st Cir. 1987).

[37]20 U.S.C. § 1415(e)(4).

[38]Daniel B. v. Wisconsin Dep't of Pub. Instruction, 581 F. Supp. 585 (E.D. Wis. 1984).

[39]Lawson v. Edwardsburg Pub. School, 751 F. Supp. 1257 (W.D. Mich. 1990). The court held that 28 U.S.C.A. § 1654 allows litigants to act as their own counsel, but does not extend to parents wishing to represent minor children. See also Meeker v. Kercher, 782 F.2d 153, 154 (10th Cir. 1986).

[40]34 C.F.R. § 300.13(b).

[41]U.S. Code Congressional and Administrative News, 94th Congress First Session (1975) at 1435.

[42]Stacey G. ex rel. William and Jane G. v. Pasadena Indep. School Dist., 547 F. Supp. 61 (S.D. Tex. 1982).

[43]Chris D. v. Montgomery County Bd. of Educ., 753 F. Supp. 922, 933 (M.D. Ala. 1990).

[44]Max M. v. Illinois State Bd. of Educ., 629 F. Supp. 1504, 1517 (N.D. Ill. 1986).

[45]Rettig v. Kent City School Dist., 720 F.2d 463 (6th Cir. 1983).

[46]34 C.F.R. § 300.13(b)(13).

[47]Bales v. Clarke, 523 F. Supp. 1366 (E.D. Va. 1981).

[48]Cohen v. School Bd. of Dade County Fla., 450 So. 2d 1238 (Fla. Dist. Ct. App. 1984).

[49]29 U.S.C. § 794.

[50]Rothschild, at 907 F.2d 286.

[51]20 U.S.C. § 1471(b).

[52]34 C.F.R. § 303.302.

[53]34 C.F.R. § 303.343(a).

[54]34 C.F.R. §§ 303.402, 303.422, 303.343(a)(iii).

[55]34 C.F.R. § 303.403.

[56]34 C.F.R. § 303.404.

[57]34 C.F.R. § 303.402.

[58]34 C.F.R. § 303.403(c).

[59]34 C.F.R. § 303.420.

[60]Under 34 C.F.R. § 300.16, handicapped infants and toddlers are those who require early intervention services because they experience a developmental delay as specified by state law, in the areas of cognitive development, physical development, language and speech development, psychosocial development or self help skills; have a diagnosed physical or mental condition that has a high probability of resulting in developmental disability—such as the infant with Down's Syndrome; or, at the state's discretion, children who are at substantial risk of developmental delay if not provided early intervention services.

[61]34 C.F.R. § 303.322(b)(d).

[62]The Individualized Family Service Plan (IFSP) is provided in lieu of the IEP for older children. See 34 C.F.R. § 303.340 for IFSP requirements.

[63]34 C.F.R. § 303.12(c)(2); § 303.12(d)(3).

[64]34 C.F.R. § 303.6. The Department suggests that it is also appropriate for the case manager to assist the family in securing certain nonrequired services as discussed in note 2.

[65] 34 C.F.R. § 303.23.

[66] Teresa Diane P. *ex rel.* Marilyn J.P. v. Alief Indep. School Dist., 744 F.2d 484 (5th Cir. 1984).

[67] Hairston v. Drosick, 423 F. Supp. 180 (S.D. W. Va. 1976).

[68] 34 C.F.R. § 303.6(2).

[69] Board of Educ. of Community Consol. School Dist. #21, Cook County, Ill. v. Illinois State Bd. of Educ., 938 F.2d 712, 718 (7th Cir. 1991).

9
Eligibility and the Appropriate Education

Julie K. Underwood

Introduction

In 1990, what had previously been known as the Education for All Handicapped Children Act, became the Individuals with Disabilities Education Act.[1] Even with a new title, the law is basically the same. Each state that accepts funding (all fifty states have) must assure that all children with disabilities receive a free appropriate public education.[2] This section will cover two areas of concern within this field: eligibility and the definition of an appropriate education.

Legal Issues

Eligibility

There exists a problem of determining who is to be served under IDEA. The statute defines "children with disabilities" as children "with mental retardation, hearing impairments including deafness, speech or language impairments, visual impairments including blindness, serious emotional disturbance, orthopedic impairments, autism, traumatic brain injury, other health impairments, or specific learning disabilities; and who, by reason thereof, need special education and related services."[3] It should be noted that in order to qualify for services under IDEA children must not only fit into one of these categories but also must require special education because of the handicapping condition.[4] For example, the child who may be health impaired by virtue of diabetes but needs only injections of insulin may be disabled but is not qualified or eligible under IDEA because that handicapping condition does not require him/her to have special education. Conversely, there is the problem of the child who may need services that other children receive under IDEA, such as counseling or residential treatment, but who may not fall within one of the categories of handicapping conditions. This problem usually arises in the context of a child who is drug dependent.[5] These children are not necessarily always IDEA eligible but are still protected by and may receive services under section 504.

Another question regarding eligibility is whether the child must show that he or she is able to benefit from the special education in order to be eligible for services under IDEA.[6] This issue was presented in *Timothy W. v. Rochester School District*.[7] In this case, a child who was severely handicapped was denied services by the school district under a claim that the child was allegedly unable to benefit from the special education. The court determined that educability was not an eligibility requirement under IDEA. In essence, it followed the zero-reject principle, that is, that Congress intended every child to be served under the Act and, in fact, that Congress gave first priority to the severely and profoundly handicapped.

Although the holding in *Timothy W.* seems to indicate that no child with disabilities could be excluded from the benefits of IDEA, the nagging question of whether some child may be found too severely disabled to be covered by the Act remains. Timothy W. was very severely handicapped and profoundly mentally retarded. However, the court noted that there was considerable evidence that he "is aware of his surrounding environment, makes or attempts to make purposeful movements, responds to tactile stimulation, responds to his mother's voice and touch, recognizes familiar voices, responds to noises, and parts his lips when spoon fed."[8] There is a question of how a court would react to a child who is nonresponsive or not aware of his or her surroundings. This situation was presented to an Illinois hearing panel before *Timothy W.* In *Parks v. Pavkovic*,[9] the court speculated about a hypothetical case of a child who was in a coma and unresponsive. The hypothetical child was in a comatose or semicomatose state and had only reflexive responses. The state level review panel determined that the child was not eligible for special education. The district's decision to discontinue evaluative procedures was found to be justified in light of the continued prolonged static condition. The panel found that the services required were not educational in nature since the child was nonresponsive.[10] Thus, here the court found that responsiveness was an eligibility requirement.

Massachusetts courts determined that, when in doubt, schools should err on the side of providing a child services. In *Christopher C. v. Weston Public Schools*, the state level review officer determined that since the testimony concerning residual brain activity and purposeful behavior was inconclusive, the doubt must be resolved in favor of the student. The district was ordered to provide special education for one year with comprehensive monitoring, reporting and assessment procedures.[11]

Appropriate Education

IDEA requires that a free appropriate education be provided to every child with disabilities. Superficially, this mandate appears relatively straightforward. The simplicity of the mandate, however, has caused confusion among educators and often conflict between educators and parents. In fact, the vast majority of due process procedures initiated concern a determination of what is an "appropriate education." What is "appropriate," of course, will differ with respect to each child, since appropriateness requires attention to the unique needs of each individual.

The statute defines an appropriate education in very general terms.[12] The vital aspects of the definition in the statutes and regulations include: specially designed in conformity with an individual education plan; education as suitable as that offered the nonhandicapped, based on proper evaluation; attention to the educational setting; and proper procedural safeguards.

These phrases have not eliminated confusion in the schools and the courts. Before 1982, many interpretations of the appropriate requirement were offered, and the extent of services required to be provided to handicapped students varied widely. The Supreme Court ended some of this uncertainty when it decided *Board of Hendrick Hudson v. Rowley*.[13] The Court found that if an individualized program of instruction was being provided, with sufficient supportive services to permit the child to benefit from the instruction, the child was receiving the level of services required to be appropriate under the Act.

The Court described the proper judicial review process as a simple two-step process. "First, has the state complied with the procedures set forth in the Act? And second, is the individualized educational program developed through the Act's procedures reasonably calculated to enable the child to receive educational benefits?"[14] This review is more procedural than substantive. Although it may seem that the Court found no substantive standard prescribing the level of education in the Act, it did set a vague substantive standard—the child must be receiving those services necessary for him/her to receive education benefits.

The Court's definition of an appropriate education includes the requirement that the special education and related services provided must meet the standards of the state. As long as a state meets the minimal requirement of the Act in its statute, it is free to impose higher standards on itself.[15] In a number of states, statutes have been interpreted to impose higher substantive standards.[16]

The courts since *Rowley* have been reviewing appropriateness of placements to determine only if instruction is provided with enough support services to permit a child to receive educational benefits.[17] A program which is reasonably calculated to provide educational benefits was fairly easy for the Court to determine in *Rowley*. This standard, however, provides minimal information and does little to help an IEP team to devise an IEP and agree on the appropriate type and amount of services to be provided to a particular student.[18] Nonetheless, the team must undertake this task—probably its most difficult. Some general considerations to guide this decision can be gleaned from the cases.

In considering program and placement options for a particular student, one must be aware that in nearly every situation more than one program or placement may be appropriate for the student. These options range from some that are minimally appropriate to clearly superb placement/program options. The courts have stated clearly that the team does not have to select the best option, or select only from options that maximize the student's potential.[19] The problem then becomes one of selecting from this array. Other considerations also enter into the selection of an option, including the least restrictive environment, mainstreaming, the best interests of the child, and the cost to the district.

The key consideration when selecting from the array of appropriate program or placement options is that the determination of appropriateness be made on an individualized basis.[20] This requirement is one of the cornerstones of the Act. Individualized determination of services is implied by the use of the term IEP. It is implicit in the procedural safeguards, the evaluation requirements and the review cycles contained in the Act. In addition, the Act even states that instruction must be "specially designed to meet the unique needs of a child with a disability."[21] This language implies that individual determinations of appropriateness need to be made to ascertain and meet the particular needs of each student.

To be appropriate, the program must address each of the student's handicapping conditions,[22] and he/she should be making progress in these areas.[23] Programs which have led to regression or stagnation have been determined to be inappropriate.[24] The evaluation of an appropriate IEP should reveal that the student has made meaningful progress under the program.[25] Where there has been no experience with a proposed program; teacher qualification, quality of IEP, and progress of other similar students can be used to assess appropriateness.[26]

The Act does not require that a district provide an unlimited commitment of resources to meet the needs of a handicapped student. It must be emphasized, however, that cost can be a determinant only when more than one possible appropriate placement option exists. Neither low nor high cost can make an inappropriate placement appropriate. Courts have recognized that "cost can be a legitimate consideration when devising an appropriate program for individual students. Nevertheless, cost considerations are only relevant when choosing between several options, all of which offer an "appropriate" education."[27]

Recommendations for Practice

The determination of appropriateness must be made on an individualized basis.

- In essence, the IEP team is to develop a list of possible programs or placements from which the particular student would derive educational benefits.
- The team must narrow this list to those which are the least restrictive,[28] mainstreamed to the maximum extent appropriate, and in the best interests of the child. From this narrowed list, the team may select any option.
- In making this final determination, many things may be taken into consideration, including availability and cost.

References

[1] P.L. 101-476; 20 U.S.C. § 1400 *et. seq.*
[2] 20 U.S.C. § 1401.
[3] 20 U.S.C. § 1401(a)(1).
[4] Many states have resolved the problem of having to categorize special education students who have more than one disability by classifying the student according to the primary disabling handicap. Maine-Endwell Central School Dist., 502 ELHR 228 (SEA 1981). *See also* Garrick B. v. Curwensville Area School Dist., 669 F. Supp. 705 (M.D. Pa. 1987).
[5] For example, in a California case, a student was determined not to be seriously emotionally disturbed but instead only socially maladjusted, and thus not qualified for services under IDEA. The student was a "punker" who demonstrated a problem with authority and social norms, had a low toleration for frustration, and was impulsive and manipulative. It was determined that his academic problems were due to truancy and substance abuse and not emotional disturbance. Sequoia Union High School Dist., 559 EHLR 133 (N.D. Cal. 1987). *See also* Doe v. Belleville Public School Dist., 672 F. Supp. 342 (S.D. Ill. 1987).

[6]The argument here is that since the district must provide services from which the child can benefit, Board of Hendrick Hudson v. Rowley, 458 U.S. 176 (1982), if the child cannot benefit from services, none are required.

[7]875 F.2d 954 (1st Cir. 1989).

[8]Id. at 962.

[9]753 F.2d 1397 (7th Cir. 1985).

[10]Case No. SE-53-81, 506 EHLR 240 (1984).

[11]Christopher C. v. Weston Public Schools, Case No. 86-0531, 509 EHLR 154 (Mass. 1987).

[12]The term "free appropriate public education" means special education and related services which (a) have been provided at public expense, under public supervision and direction, and without charge, (b) meet the standards of the state educational agency, (c) include an appropriate preschool, elementary, or secondary school education in the state involved, and (d) are provided in conformity with the individualized education program required.   20 U.S.C. § 1401 (a)(18).

[13]458 U.S. 176, 102 S. Ct. 3034 (1982).

[14]Rowley, 102 S. Ct. at 3051.

[15]In Rowley the Court emphasized that this standard constitutes a federal floor of opportunity, not a ceiling on the right to educational services. Id. at 3047-48.

[16]For example: New Jersey—Board of Educ. of East Windsor v. Diamond, 808 F.2d 987 (3d Cir. 1986); Michigan—Barwacz v. Michigan Dep't of Educ., 674 F. Supp. 1296 (W.D. Mich. 1987); California—Pink v. Mt. Diablo Unified School Dist., 16 EHLR 1026 (N.D. Cal. 1990).

[17]The term "education" is broadly defined under the Act. For severely disabled or emotionally disturbed students, education is often largely nonacademic. In these situations "educational benefit" is a very broad concept. See Jefferson County Bd. of Educ. v. Breen, 853 F.2d 853 (11th Cir. 1988); Timothy W. v. Rochester, 875 F.2d 954 (1st Cir. 1989).

[18]Several cases have addressed the issue of whether the regular school day or calendar must be extended for particular handicapped students. The courts have unanimously held that when an extended program is necessary for the child to benefit, one must be provided. These cases have typically hinged on whether the child has a regression-recoupment problem. This problem is when a child suffers a disproportionate degree of regression during that time when s/he is not receiving services and it takes an unacceptable length of time for the child to recoup those skills that have been lost. This analysis has been applied to academic as well as nonacademic skills. E.g., Alamo Heights Indep. School Dist. v. State Bd. of Educ., 790 F.2d 1153 (5th Cir. 1986); see also Yaris v. Special School Dist. of St. Louis County, 728 F.2d 1055 (8th Cir. 1984).

[19]The concept that an appropriate education is not necessarily the best possible education, but is one that provides the handicapped child with needed functional skills, was reiterated in Rettig v. Kent City School Dist., 788 F.2d 328 (6th Cir. 1986).

[20]An OSEP ruling stated that the district's practice of labeling handicapped children must be limited to eligibility requirements and could not be used for determination of services and programs for children with similar disabilities. Richards, 211 EHLR 440 (OSEP 1987). This practice is difficult sometimes to conceptualize, since in determinations of eligibility the district must attach a label to a child.

[21]20 U.S.C. § 1401 (16).

[22]Russell v. Jefferson School Dist., 609 F. Supp. 605 (N.D. Cal. 1985)

[23]A student's promotion from grade to grade does not automatically mean that a program is appropriate. Hall v. Vance County Bd. of Educ., 774 F.2d 629 (4th Cir. 1985); In re Van Overeem, 555 EHLR 182 (1983).

[24]Kruelle v. New Castle County School Dist., 642 F.2d 687 (3d Cir. 1981); Colin K. v. Schmidt, 536 F. Supp. 1375 (D.R.I. 1982).

[25]Polk v. Central Susquehanna Intermediate Unit 16, 853 F.2d 171 (3d Cir. 1988).

[26]The courts have generally limited their review of a state's choice of instructional methods. Where a student is making progress with the selected method, the court will not question whether another method might work better. Evans v. Dist. No. 17, 841 F.2d 824 (8th Cir. 1988). Bertolucci v. San Carlos Elementary School Dist., 721 F. Supp 1150 (N.D. Cal. 1989).

[27]Clevenger v. Oak Ridge School Bd., 744 F.2d 514, at 517 (6th Cir. 1984); see also A.W. v. Northwest R-1 School Dist., 813 F.2d 158 (8th Cir. 1987).

[28]If it is determined that only one placement option is appropriate for a particular child, that placement is, by definition, the least restrictive environment for that child. In Johnston v. Ann Arbor Public Schools, 569 F. Supp. 1502 (E.D. Mich. 1983), the court upheld the placement of a cerebral palsied child in a special school, since it had been determined that an appropriate education could not be provided in a less restrictive environment even with the addition of supplemental aids and services.

10
Transition for Individuals with Disabilities

Stanley L. Swartz, Jeff McNair, and Joseph O. Turpin

Introduction

The Individuals with Disabilities Education Act extended mandatory public education to include planning and programs to ensure a successful transition from K-12 educational experiences to community integration including meaningful employment. Transition services are defined as a "coordinated set of activities for a student, designed within an outcome-oriented process, which promotes movement from school to post-school activities, including post-secondary education, vocational training, integrated employment (including supported employment), continuing and adult education, adult services, independent living, or community participation."[1] The emphasis of current legislative authority has developed from a growing research base indicating the need for coordination of agencies serving individuals with disabilities. The National Council on Disability[2] summarized these findings in making recommendations for the development of a national policy. The recommendations issued by this group included many of the elements that had gained recognition as needs that must be addressed to impact the transition from school to adult life. Their findings included:

- that upon leaving school, students with disabilities and their families have a difficult time accessing appropriate adult services;
- effective transition planning for high school students with disabilities can facilitate their success in adult life;
- graduates with disabilities are more likely to be employed following school if comprehensive vocational training is a primary component of their high school programs and they have jobs secured at the time of graduation;

- there are insufficient partnerships between the business community and schools for the purpose of enhancing employment opportunities for students with disabilities; and
- parent participation during high school facilitates the successful transition of students with disabilities from school to adult life.

Support for the transition process can be provided on three different levels. First, there may not be any need for specific support. This lack of support would be the case for most students with mild disabilities. Second, students may need time-limited services including specific training such as on-the-job support or support in finding independent living arrangements. However, the assumption is that this support will only be needed for a specific period of time. Third, some individuals will need a specific type of support on an ongoing basis including specialized services permitting the individual to live normally within the community. Individuals with severe disabilities might be expected to need various levels of support throughout their lifetimes including ongoing support of an extensive nature. The outcome for each of these types of support is different. For individuals needing no support, time-limited support, or specific ongoing support, the outcomes are typically competitive employment and independent living. For individuals with severe disabilities that need ongoing support of an extensive nature, the expected outcomes are usually supported employment and supported living arrangements. Although in some cases, individuals with severe disabilities who need extensive and ongoing support may live independently and work in competitive employment.

Legal Issues

Transition Program

A successful school transition program can be conceptualized as a four step procedure: (1) foundation, (2) process, (3) culmination, and (4) follow-up. The transition foundation includes all education, training, and experiences which prepare an individual for adult life. An educational program is designed to develop functional skills, or skills that have a high probability of being required of someone as an adult. A foundation for students with mild educational disabilities will include academic skills that can be built upon with post-secondary vocational training or college training. For individuals with more severe educational disabilities, the curriculum will be more basic and include functional or survival types of academic skills. For all students, however, the curriculum should include training in social and vocational survival skills.

Survival skills are those that generalize across social and vocational settings. For example, social survival skills include behaviors such as responding appropriately to questions, appropriately expressing needs such as the location of a restroom, and appropriately interacting with others in social settings. Vocational survival skills include reporting to work on time, working at one's workstation for a continuous period of time, and asking for clarification if an instruction is not understood. The need for these types of skills is not specific to individuals with disabilities but rather are expected of all adults.

The formal transition process begins at age 14 when the schools are expected to begin transition planning with the development of an individualized transition program (ITP). Similar to the individualized education plan (IEP), the ITP details efforts designed to prepare the student for the transition to adult life. ITP meetings should be attended by the student, parent, teacher, and adult service providers representing agencies that might assist the student with transition. The ITP includes a statement of the student's current levels of functioning, objectives relative to skill areas still in need of development, activities important to a successful transition, and who will perform the activities. The types of issues that might be addressed on an ITP are postsecondary education, employment, living arrangements, recreation and leisure activities, health issues, and transportation. Discussion takes place in each of these areas regarding what the student hopes to do as an adult and how these goals can be facilitated by the transition team.

Transition culmination occurs with the actual movement from secondary school to adult life. The transition team is charged with the responsibility of ensuring a smooth change from school to community service agencies and the provision of the activities described in the ITP. Finally, transition follow-up is the last step. By evaluating outcomes, school administrators can adjust the program and the process to ensure the most appropriate outcomes.

Special Education Legislation

The importance of the transition from public school educational programs to appropriate postsecondary experiences for individuals with disabilities and the necessary support services to successfully accomplish this transition has a history that can be traced through public policy reflected in legislation and the resultant changing professional practices. That the individualized education program must now include a specific statement of the needed transition services is a result of a process that has included a research base demonstrating that the absence of such planning diminishes the likelihood of student success.[3] Additionally, political activism directed toward establishing the need for a follow-along plan for all children with disabilities has resulted in legislation that ensures a continuum of services for individuals with disabilities throughout their lives.[4]

The need for transition services has been addressed in special education, vocational education, and rehabilitation legislation. Culminating in P.L. 94-142, the Carl Perkins Vocational Education Act, and the Rehabilitation Act of 1973, and refined in the Individuals with Disabilities Education Act and the Americans with Disabilities Act, a summary of this history is instructive to the understanding of changing public attitudes and awareness and changing public policy.

The Education of All Handicapped Children Act of 1975 (P.L. 94-142) required that children with disabilities have available to them a free, appropriate public education, and protected the rights of children with disabilities and their parents to procedural due process and safeguards in the evaluation and placement process. Central to this legislation was making increased federal funds available to the states for the purposes of assuring the implementation of this law. Key to the eventual recognition of the need for transition services was the provision that the effectiveness of these programs be evaluated.

P.L. 94-142 marked the first consideration that special education programs for children with disabilities were a right and therefore mandated. Two key provisions of the law, the individualized education program (IEP) provided in the least restrictive environment (LRE) paved the way for the provision of transition services. The IEP is a planning document that assures an appropriate education that is outcome-based. LRE is a requirement that children with disabilities be integrated with their nonhandicapped peers. The law also targeted a nontraditional population for service: the 18-21 age group. This group is the primary focus of transition programs.

Further legislation in 1983[5] addressed the need to coordinate the education and training of youth with disabilities to assist in the transitional process from school to employment and postsecondary education. Major emphases included the design of vocational programs to increase the potential of youth with disabilities for competitive employment and to encourage the development of cooperative training models between educational agencies and adult service agencies. This law marked the emergence of the transition process as a major focus in programs for children with disabilities.

A number of important revisions in secondary education and transitional services were included in 1986.[6] Programs were expanded not only for whom can be served but also the nature of the services to be provided. Services could now be provided to children recently graduated or exited from the public schools. Transition was reconceptualized as a theme of programming throughout a child's school career even though it has as its purpose the transition to adult life. The Individuals with Disabilities Education Act expanded the concept of transition to include independent living and full participation of youth with disabilities in community programs as appropriate goals.[7] This change represents a movement from education as a means to competitive employment to a broader goal of full community integration. Requirements for IEP development include a statement of needed transition services by age 16, or age 14 when appropriate, and any necessary interagency responsibilities after school exit. Programs are expanded to address the development of job skills for transition to the workplace and social skills to enable youth to participate fully in community life.

Vocational Education

The Carl Perkins Vocational Education Act allocated federal funds for equipment, staff, and buildings.[8] Ten percent of funds available under this act were earmarked for students with disabilities and 22 percent for the disadvantaged. This act provided for assessment of interests and abilities related to vocational education programs; special services, including adaptation of curriculum, instruction, equipment, and facilities; guidance, counseling, and career development activities conducted by professionally trained counselors; and counseling services designed to facilitate the transition from school to postschool employment opportunities. By its very inclusion in Carl Perkins, vocational education for students with disabilities was legitimized. The focus of programming from education in the traditional academic sense to programs that emphasize employment and necessary functioning for adult life was made possible with the requirement that a portion of the funds authorized under this act be reserved for use by programs designed to benefit individuals with disabilities.

Rehabilitation Legislation

Building on a long history of the progressive expansion of services to individuals with disabilities, the Rehabilitation Amendments marked the major entry into training for competitive employment.[9] Though earlier establishment of sheltered workshops had employment as a goal, this legislation placed efforts in integrated community settings. The Rehabilitation Act of 1973[10] provided the statutory foundation for the Rehabilitation Services Administration and established priority for rehabilitation services to those with the most severe disabilities; initiated and expanded programs for individuals previously being underserved, including homebound and institutionalized clients; expanded employment opportunities for individuals with disabilities; included section 503 which eliminated architectural and transportation barriers impeding citizens with disabilities in public governmental buildings; required an individualized written rehabilitation plan (IWRP) with an annual review which outlines, in the form of a contract developed in conjunction with the client, the conditions and responsibilities under which services will be provided; funded research and demonstration projects concerned with the rehabilitation of individuals with severe disabilities; and included section 504 which prohibits discrimination in any program or activity receiving substantive federal funds for an individual solely by reason of the disability.[11]

Important to the eventual emphasis on transition for school-aged children was the inclusion of education for children with disabilities as one of the major features of the Rehabilitation Act. Children to be served by the public schools were guaranteed similar protections as adults served by rehabilitation and other service agencies. P.L. 94-142 was specifically referenced in the language of the law. This inclusion of school-aged children in the language of the act set the stage for the eventual coordination of services of various agencies because of the wide authority of this act.

Rehabilitation, Comprehensive Services, and Developmental Disabilities Amendments of 1978[12] continued and enlarged the three main trends of the history of rehabilitation legislation: it increased the commitment to rehabilitation research by expanding its research provisions and by stipulating the need and the means for ensuring coordination in the research enterprise; it continued the movement from a focus on preparation for employment to a focus on preparation plus affirmative action for enlarging opportunities for competitive employment for individuals with disabilities; it continued the attempt to provide services to underserved populations, especially the individuals with developmental disabilities and other severe disabilities;[13] it authorized the expansion of rehabilitation to include independent living as an objective for individuals served under the act; and it provided employer incentives for training and hiring individuals with disabilities.[14] Programs that required an affirmative action-type push were encouraged by this act. Transition at its inception was this type of an effort. This act authorized the use of funds to provide a variety of support mechanisms that allowed transition programs to be mounted.

The Vocational Rehabilitation Amendments of 1986[15] made notable changes to include the use of supported employment (defined as employment in an integrated setting with ongoing support services) as an acceptable outcome for the rehabilitation program.[16] Much of the historical emphasis of the state/federal rehabilitation agencies had been in rehabilitation that resulted in almost total independence of functioning for clients. This had the obvious effect of excluding serious efforts on behalf of individuals with moderate and severe disabilities. This act legitimized and authorized funding for services which were supportive in nature and expected to be ongoing. Much of what is provided as transition programming is authorized in this act.

The Americans with Disabilities Act[17] is federal civil rights legislation that bars job discrimination against individuals with physical or mental disabilities. Access for individuals with disabilities to mass transportation, public buildings and transportation (defined as commonly used by the public), and governmental services has also been assured.[18] This act is considered an important extension of the Rehabilitation Act of 1973 because of the dramatically increased number of employers (those employing more than 15) that are affected. This act is seen as a last step in a process designed to ensure the integration of individuals with disabilities into the mainstream of American society. Any effort or program that could assist in the integration is authorized under this act. The recognition that many individuals with disabilities will need support throughout their lives is carefully included in the provisions of the law. Transition that is initiated under laws governing special education in the public schools has as its goal the support for programs in keeping with the provisions of this initiative.

Employment Related Legislation

The Job Training Partnership Act of 1982[19] was designed to shift training away from the public sector to the private sector. Individuals with disabilities are targeted as a special population for services under this act. Incentives were made available to employers to accommodate individuals with disabilities in community-based employment settings. The Supplemental Security Income Improvement Act of 1986 removed work disincentives by allowing recipients to work without loss of benefits.[20] It allowed participation in a variety of training programs, including supported employment, while still receiving income assistance.

Taken together, these pieces of legislation chart the evolution of programming for individuals with disabilities from regular education programs to programs and services that ensure a continuum beginning in the public schools and extending to community integration. Such a movement was a public recognition of the need to coordinate efforts on behalf of individuals with disabilities as various governmental agencies assumed responsibility for service provision. It is important to remember that new initiatives built into legislation do not develop in isolation. Research demonstrating program efficacy and professional practice that evolves because of field-based experience and research are important to the ultimate recognition that change is needed. One good example of this influence can be seen in the review of the Education for the Handicapped Act implementation mandated by Congress. In both the Eleventh[21] and Twelfth[22] Annual Reports to Congress, the need and importance of transition to the eventual success of students as adults are highlighted.

Recommendations for Practice

The focus on transition represents an important milestone in the history of efforts to serve individuals with disabilities. Past efforts were basically designed to guarantee access. Current efforts focus on the outcomes of special education. There has been a clear recognition that children with disabilities usually become adults with disabilities and that programming must be coordinated between agencies that serve children and agencies that serve adults. Do our efforts result in the successful integration of individuals with disabilities into the adult world? Do public school programs target eventual adult status and community participation? Have agencies with programming responsibility for individuals with disabilities developed agreements that will ensure continuous service during the transition from school to work and community living? Have the community agencies developed agreements with regard to the agency that will take primary responsibility with regard to case management? Current legislation suggests some practices that can be recommended for site level program administration:

- An individualized transition plan (ITP) must be developed for each student. This plan must include descriptions of services and who will be responsible for providing the services. It is important to note that this plan will include a wide variety of activities that are other than traditional academic programming. Efforts will include cooperation with other service agencies:

- Individualized transition plans (ITP) should be carefully developed to ensure that all necessary information is included. Although service recommendations will not be needed for each individual in all areas, the ITP should include consideration of each of the following areas: income/support, including access to federal and state benefit programs; work, either an actual placement or training toward a vocational goal; living arrangements, independent or supervised; recreational and leisure activities; transportation; guardianship; medical needs; insurance; and facilitation of ongoing family relationships. Any area for which there is a recommendation must also include a statement of who will take responsibility for carrying out the action. ITPs are reviewed much like IEPs and should be fully implemented upon school exit.
- Cooperative relationships and agreements should be established with adult service agencies such as the Departments of Rehabilitation, Mental Health, and Developmental Disabilities. Collaborative programs should be initiated to ensure that the transition from school to work or postsecondary programs will be a smooth one. An individual should be appointed with specific responsibility to serve as a liaison with community service agencies.
- School curricula should be focused on the development of functional skills; those skills necessary for successful adult life. Programming for youth with disabilities should include some balance of attention to vocational, independent living and recreation and leisure activities. It must be recognized that appropriate programming for students with disabilities will not, in the vast majority of cases, be parallel to the regular academic programs. The program must be developed so that what happens to students after school graduation is an integral part of the planning process.
- Schools must make renewed efforts to involve families in the program development process. Only with family support is there any reasonable expectation that the transition process will be successful. Parents who are full participants in program planning are less likely to initiate legal challenges that are costly both in time and resources.
- Because transition is an outcome-based process, data collection is of increased importance. Follow-up studies of program graduates should be initiated. These data can be used to make any necessary program modifications.
- Transitional programming for youth with disabilities should be viewed as a proactive process. Program opportunities that

will enhance the likelihood of student success should be identified and supported. Schools need to take the initiative in developing community-based vocational programs. School programs that have the greatest potential for practical application in adulthood should be developed. Programs that have no demonstrable adult applications should be abandoned.

- Efforts to educate school personnel and the public to the fact that appropriate programs for youth with disabilities are functional rather than academic should be initiated. That the function of schooling for this group of children is to prepare for successful adulthood should be established and communicated.

References

[1] Individuals with Disabilities Education Act of 1990 (P.L. 101-476).
[2] The education of students with disabilities: Where do we stand? National Council on Disability. (1989).
[3] Individuals with Disabilities Education Act of 1990, 20 U.S.C. § 1400 et. seq.
[4] Americans with Disabilities Act, P.L. 101-336 (1990).
[5] Education of the Handicapped Amendments of 1983—Secondary Education and Transitional Services for Handicapped Youth, P.L. 99-199.
[6] Education of the Handicapped Act Amendments of 1986, P.L. 99-457.
[7] Individuals with Disabilities Education Act of 1990 supra, note 3.
[8] Carl Perkins Vocational Education Act of 1984, P.L. 98-524.
[9] Vocational Rehabilitation Amendments of 1968, P.L. 90-391.
[10] Rehabilitation Act of 1973, P.L. 93-112.
[11] See, R. M. Gargiulo, Litigation and legislation for exceptional children: An historical perspective. ICEC Q., 29(1) (1980), and G. N. WRIGHT, TOTAL REHABILITATION (1980).
[12] Rehabilitation, Comprehensive Services, and Developmental Disabilities Amendments of 1978, P.L. 95-602.
[13] L. DeStefano & D. Snauwaert. A VALUE-CRITICAL APPROACH TO TRANSITION POLICY ANALYSIS (1989).
[14] Individuals with Disabilities Education Act of 1990, supra, note 3.
[15] Rehabilitation Act Amendments of 1986, P.L. 99-506.
[16] D. Braddock & G. Fujiura, Federal foundations for transitions to adulthood. In B. LUDLOW, A. TURNBULL, & R. LUKASSON. TRANSITIONS TO ADULT LIFE FOR PEOPLE WITH MENTAL RETARDATION - PRINCIPLES AND PRACTICES (1988).
[17] Americans with Disabilities Education Act of 1990, P.L. 101-336.
[18] C. Baird. ADA - Bridges, not barriers for people with disabilities. THE SPECIAL EDGE, 5(1) (1990).
[19] Job Training Partnership Act of 1982, P.L. 97-300.
[20] Supplemental Security Income Improvement Act of 1986, P.L. 99-643.
[21] Eleventh Annual Report to Congress on the Implementation of the Education of the Handicapped Act. Dep't of Educ. (1989).
[22] Twelfth Annual Report to Congress on the Implementation of the Education of the Handicapped Act. Dep't of Educ. (1990).

11
The Individualized Education Plan

Steven S. Goldberg

Introduction

The Individuals with Disabilities Education Act (IDEA)[1] requires states to provide all "handicapped children"[2] with a Free Appropriate Public Education (FAPE) to meet their unique needs. The statute defines FAPE, in part, as those programs of "...special education and related services which...[a]re provided in conformity with an individualized education program."[3] The individualized education plan,[4] or "IEP," must be reduced to writing and be reviewed at the beginning of each school year for every child who requires special education. It can be reviewed at any time, but the statute requires that it be reexamined at least on an annual basis.[5]

Legal Issues

What type of education is "appropriate" for IEP purposes? In *Board of Education v. Rowley*,[6] the United States Supreme Court wrestled with that question. IDEA's predecessor, the Education for All Handicapped Children Act, required school districts to "identify and evaluate handicapped children, and to provide them with access to a free public education."[7] The Court concluded that Congress meant to provide access to a program of education from which handicapped children had previously been excluded; related services were to be provided if they helped a child to "benefit"[8] from an individualized program of education. The lower courts, which had held that it was the responsibility of school districts to maximize the potential for each child, had misinterpreted Congress' intent.

What are the implications of *Rowley* and its progeny for IEP development? The statute, according to the Court, means that each child should be provided with specially designed instruction and related services necessary to benefit from the program of special education. The IEP should be designed to provide a program that will allow a child to pass from grade to grade.[9] While doing little to provide a specific formula for school administrators, the Court at the very least suggested that a good effort be made to provide a program which addresses the child's basic learning difficulties.

There are several other requirements in the IDEA which school officials must take into consideration when developing an IEP. Children must be educated in the least restrictive environment appropriate to their needs.[10] They must be mainstreamed or placed in physical proximity to their nonhandicapped peers whenever appropriate.[11] The statute requires a multidisciplinary IEP team to consider the alternative placements available and to include in the IEP the least restrictive education placement possible for a particular child.[12] The placement included in the IEP must consider a child's educational, emotional, social, and physical needs.[13] The statutory requirement to place children in regular education when appropriate is not a mandate to place all so-called handicapped children in regular classrooms, but rather to place a child in contact with regular education peers when appropriate for that child. A regular or "mainstreamed" classroom placement may not always meet the requirements of least restrictive environment; in those instances, the need to place a child in the least restrictive environment will take precedence over the preference for mainstreamed placements.[14]

The statute includes the following of highly prescriptive procedural safeguards for children and their parents who wish to challenge a proposed IEP:[15] the right to obtain and review school records; the right to be involved in the initial placement decision and any subsequent changes in placement; the opportunity to request an administrative or "due process" hearing when a dispute arises, including the right to be represented by an attorney or advocate; and the opportunity to appeal the hearing officer's decision to state or federal court. Moreover, a "prevailing party" may obtain attorney's fees at the conclusion of the administrative or "due process" hearing. During the pendency of any litigation, the child remains in the current placement, unless parents and school officials agree to another placement. Because every state has accepted federal funding pursuant to IDEA, all are bound to provide these protections. While states may have different names for the statutorily prescribed procedures, all must meet IDEA's mandates in order to receive federal funding. Jurisdictions are free to provide greater procedural protections and substantive rights, but none may provide fewer rights and benefits than outlined in the federal statute and regulations.[16]

Purposes of IEP

The federal IEP provisions include two major requirements: the IEP meeting—at which parents and school officials develop and define a handicapped child's program, and the IEP report—a written record of the goals and methods for reaching them which are set forth during the meeting.[17] These provisions have several purposes. The IEP meeting allows parents (and when useful, students) to provide their input so that they and school officials may jointly consider a child's needs, goals, and the services that will be provided. In addition, the IEP process serves as a focus for resolving any differences between a parent and the school through the meeting and, when necessary, through IDEA's administrative hearing procedures. Moreover, the IEP document sets out, in writing, the resources which the participants have determined are necessary for the child to gain educational benefits from the plan. The IEP is a management tool to ensure that each child is provided the education and services appropriate to his or her special needs. It is also a monitoring device which may be used by state and federal officials to determine if handicapped children are actually receiving the free appropriate public education pursuant to IDEA.[18]

IEP Process

In all states, the state education agency is ultimately responsible for insuring that each agency which serves handicapped children complies with IDEA requirements.[19] However, a local education agency is responsible for the education of all resident handicapped children of school age, and the local education agency is responsible for drafting each child's IEP. This requirement applies even when the child's educational placement is outside of the school district of residence.[20] After the child enters an out-of-district placement, all agencies which serve a child, including the district of residence, are generally involved in any decisions made about the child's program.

A child must have a valid IEP in place before a school may offer special educational services.[21] The IEP must be developed at a meeting involving all of the required participants, be less than one calendar year old, be regarded by the family and the current school as appropriate for the child, and be implemented as written. The child's program must be implemented without delay once agreement has been reached at the IEP meeting, generally immediately after the meeting unless otherwise specified in the IEP. Some exceptions to this requirement are allowed, such as when the meeting occurs during or immediately before a vacation period or when a short delay is necessary to work out implementation arrangements. When a child has no previous IEP but is initially placed, the requirement that an IEP be "in effect" remains the same. Because an appropriate placement for a child cannot be determined until after decisions have been made about the child's needs—and these decisions are made at an IEP meeting—school officials cannot provide an appropriate placement and services until after an IEP meeting. School officials, however, are not precluded from attempting a trial placement.[22] In that event, a specific timeline must be set, and at the end of that time, a meeting must be held to finalize the child's IEP.[23]

When a child who has been receiving special education moves to another district, the new district must hold an IEP meeting before the child is placed in special education. The new district may consider the child's previous placement and school records in revising the IEP. When those records are not available, the district must develop a new IEP. The child must be provided services immediately after that meeting.[24] Every child's IEP must be reviewed at least once a year.[25] This requirement does not mean that every IEP must be reviewed at the beginning of each school year, but that it must be reviewed once during the calendar year. A child's IEP may be reviewed more often and should be reviewed as often as necessary. These meetings may be called by the school officials, the special education teacher, or a parent.[26]

The federal regulations describe the parties who must be in attendance at an IEP meeting.[27] The list includes a representative of the school, the child's teacher, the parent, the child when appropriate, and others at the discretion of the parent or the school. The school's representative must be any member of the school staff, other than the child's teacher, who is qualified to provide or supervise special education. The school representative must be able to commit the school to providing the resources agreed upon at the IEP meeting. The agency representative does not have to be the same person at every IEP meeting but may vary depending on the nature of the child's handicap and the possible resources which will have to be provided for that child.[28] Which teacher attends depends on the child and his or her handicap. For an initial placement meeting, the teacher is generally an individual who teaches in the assumed disability or the child's regular teacher. If a child receives services in both regular and special education classes, the teachers in attendance may be both the special education teacher and a regular education teacher.[29] School officials may accumulate, from several regular education teachers, information which is presented either by a regular education teacher or the child's special education teacher.[30]

Other individuals at the IEP meeting may include service providers. Related service personnel may attend IEP meetings or provide written information without appearing in person when the child has a need for specific related services. The service provider can offer information regarding the nature, frequency, and amount of services needed by the child.[31] At an IEP meeting to develop a program for the first time, someone must be present who can knowledgeably interpret the results of the instruments or procedures used to evaluate the child.[32]

One or both of the child's parents are expected to attend and actively participate in an IEP meeting. If a child has no parent available, a "surrogate parent"[33]—who is not necessarily a legal guardian—may be appointed by school officials to advocate on behalf of the child's interests. The school must take steps to gain parental participation.[34] These steps include notifying the parents early enough before the meeting to allow them to attend and scheduling the meetings at a mutually agreeable time and place. When notifying parents of an IEP meeting, school officials must delineate its purpose, time, location, and participants. A meeting may be conducted without a parent. However, in these situations the school must have a record of its attempts to arrange the meeting with the parent(s). The school should use other methods such as telephone calls to obtain information from parents when they will not be present at the IEP meeting. IDEA's intent is for parents to be active participants in the IEP process.[35] The regulations provide that the child should attend the IEP meetings when appropriate.[36] This decision is generally left up to the parent and should be based on whether the child would be helpful in developing the IEP and whether participation would benefit the child.

Once the child's program is determined, the parent must consent to it before it can be implemented.[37] An IEP is not valid without parental consent. Although signatures are not required by the federal statute or regulations, most districts have the parent sign the IEP document. Signatures are used to indicate consent to the program and provide a record of attendance at the IEP meeting. However, the parents must be informed that by participating they do not waive their right to request modifications of the program. When a parent is not in attendance at the IEP meeting, parental consent to the program must be acquired through other methods including telephone conversations, written correspondence, or personal contacts.[38]

IEP Content

Federal law prescribes in general terms the content but not the specific length or format of an IEP.[39] State and local agencies have developed standard formats of their own. The law provides that an IEP must include: a statement of the child's present levels of educational performance; a statement of annual goals, including short-term instructional objectives; a statement of the specific special education and related services to be provided to the child and the extent to which the child will be able to participate in regular educational programs; the projected dates for initiation of services and the anticipated duration of the services; and appropriate objective criteria and evaluation procedures and schedules for determining, on at least an annual basis, whether the short-term instructional objectives are being achieved.

The statement of present levels of performance is obviously different for each child depending on the child's handicapping condition and the types of special education the child will receive. Objective measures, such as test scores, should be used whenever possible. The statement should provide an accurate description of the effect of the handicap on the child's performance, including both academic and nonacademic areas when appropriate.[40] It is not necessary for the statement to cover every area of the child's education; instead it should focus on the problems resulting from the child's handicap. Each level of performance presented should be directly addressed in the IEP: annual goals, short-term objectives, and services to be rendered.[41]

The annual goals are statements which describe what the child can reasonably be expected to achieve within one calendar year.[42] This provision does not hold the school liable under contract if the child does not achieve these goals.[43] Each goal should be addressed in the other areas of the IEP; thus, there should be a statement of short-term objectives and services to be provided to help the child achieve each goal. The goals are used during a review of the IEP to help determine if the child is progressing and whether the services provided are appropriate.[44]

The short-term objectives are the intermediate steps between the present level of performance and the annual goals. They must be based on the annual goals and provide a path with objective milestones toward achievement of the goals. The objectives are not intended to be detailed instructional plans which would include specific methods, activities, and materials to be used.[45] However, the objectives should be useful to teachers in developing their instructional plans.

The IEP must include all of the services which will be provided to the child including special education, related services, physical education, and vocational education. The amount of services to be provided must be set forth so that the level of resources committed is clear to the family and the school. Once the services have been agreed to, the school district is committed to providing them.

The IEP may not be changed without following procedural requirements.[46] Revisions require a subsequent IEP meeting. Changes in the placement or amount of services require a new meeting. However, as long as there is no substantive change, some adjustment in scheduling the services may be made without an IEP revision. In some cases, it is possible to make changes in the short-term instructional objectives without an IEP revision. In order to make this change, the school must give the parents prior written notice including a statement that the school will hold an IEP meeting to discuss changes when a parent requests a meeting.

Recommendations for Practice

The following guidelines are based on federal statutes and regulations.

- A handicapped student must have a valid IEP in place before special education services are provided.
- Services must be provided as soon as possible after the IEP has been finalized.
- IEP's for students who are placed outside of the district should be monitored.
- Every IEP must be reviewed at least once a year.
- The following people must be in attendance at an IEP meeting: a representative of the school, the student's teachers, the student's parent(s), and, when appropriate, the student.
- The parent(s) must be involved in the development of the IEP.
- The IEP must include: (a) a statement of the child's present levels of educational performance; (b) a statement of annual goals, including short-term instructional objectives; (c) a statement of the specific special education and related services to be provided to the child, and the extent to which the child will be able to participate in regular educational programs; (d) a statement of the projected dates for initiation of services and the anticipated duration of services; and (e) a statement of appropriate objective criteria, evaluation procedures, and schedules for determining, on at least an annual basis, whether the short-term instructional objectives are being achieved.

- It is good practice to include a section on student discipline in every IEP.
- A student's IEP cannot be unilaterally changed by the district.
- Services must be provided according to the IEP.

References

[1] Pub. L. 101-476; 20 U.S.C. §§ 1400, *et seq.*; 34 C.F.R. Part. 300.

[2] 20 U.S.C. § 1401; 34 C.F.R. § 300.5.

[3] 20 U.S.C. § 1401; 34 C.F.R. § 300.4.

[4] 20 U.S.C. § 1401(19); 34 C.F.R. §§ 300.340 *et seq.*

[5] 20 U.S.C. § 1412(2)(b); 34 C.F.R. § 300.343.

[6] Board of Educ. of Hendrick Hudson Cent. School Dist. v. Rowley, 102 S. Ct. 3034 (1982).

[7] 458 U.S. 176, 189 (1982). 20 U.S.C. § 1412; 34 C.F.R. § 300.128.

[8] 458 U.S. at 189; 20 U.S.C. § 1401(17); 34 C.F.R. § 300.13(a).

[9] *Id.* at 189-203; Roland M. v. Concord School Committee, 910 F.2d 983 (1st Cir. 1990).

[10] 20 U.S.C. § 14121(5)(B); 1414(a)(1); 34 C.F.R. §§ 300.550, *et seq.*; Barnett v. Fairfax County School Bd., 721 F. Supp. 757 (E.D. Va. 1989).

[11] 20 U.S.C. § 1412(5)(b); 34 C.F.R. § 300.553.

[12] 20 U.S.C. § 1412 (5)(B); 34 C.F.R. § 300.552.

[13] *Id.*

[14] 20 U.S.C. § 1412; 34 C.F.R. § 300.550. *et seq.*; Chris D. v. Montgomery County Bd. of Educ., 743 F. Supp 1524 (M.D. Ala. 1990).

[15] 20 U.S.C. § 1415, 1417(C); 34 C.F.R. §§ 300.500, *et seq.*

[16] David D. v. Dartmouth School Committee, 775 F.2d 411 (3d Cir. 1985); Geis v. Bd. of Educ., 774 F.2d 575 (1st Cir. 1985).

[17] 20 U.S.C. § 1412(2)B,(4),(6); 1414(a)(5); 34 C.F.R. § 300.343; V.W. v. Favolise, 131 F.R.D. 654 (D. Conn 1990). *See generally*, S. GOLDBERG, SPECIAL EDUCATION LAW (1982); L. ROTHSTEIN, SPECIAL EDUCATION LAW (1989).

[18] 20 U.S.C. § 1412; 34 C.F.R. §§ 300. 341-342.

[19] *Id.*

[20] *Id.*; 34 C.F.R. § 300.341(b).

[21] 20 U.S.C. §§ 1412(2)(B),(4),(6); 1414(a)(5); 34 C.F.R. § 300.342.

[22] *See* U.S. Department of Education Comments to 34 C.F.R. § 300.342; 34 C.F.R. § 300.513.

[23] *Id.*

[24] 20 U.S.C. § 1412; 34 C.F.R. § 300.342.

[25] 20 U.S.C. § 1412; 34 C.F.R. § 300.343(d).

[26] 20 U.S.C. § 1412; 34 C.F.R. § 300.343.

[27] 34 C.F.R. § 300.344.

[28] *Id.*; *See also*, U.S. Department of Education comments to § 300.344.

[29] *Id.*

[30] *Id.*

[31] *Id.*

[32] 34 C.F.R. § 300.344(b).

[33] 20 U.S.C. § 1415(b)(1)(B); 34 C.F.R. § 300.514.

[34] 34 C.F.R. § 300.345; Doe v. Alabama State Dep't of Educ., 915 F.2d 651 (11th Cir. 1990.

[35] 20 U.S.C. § 1412(2)B,(4),(6); 1414(a)(5); 34 C.F.R. § 300.345.

[36] 34 C.F.R. § 300.344(a)(4).

[37] 20 U.S.C. § 1415; 34 C.F.R. §§ 300.500, 504.

[38] 34 C.F.R. § 300.345; *Cf.* Hiller by Hiller v. Board of Educ. of Brunswick Cent. School Dist., 743 F. Supp. 958 (N.D. N.Y. 1990).

[39] 20 U.S.C. §§ 1401(19); 1412(2)(B)(6); 1414(a)(5); 34 C.F.R. § 300. 346.

[40] *Id.*

[41] 34 C.F.R. § 300.346(b).

[42] 34 C.F.R. §§ 300.345, 500, 504(b)(1)(ii).

[43] 34 C.F.R. § 300.349.

[44] 34 C.F.R. § 300.346.

[45] 34 C.F.R. § 300.346(c).

[46] 20 U.S.C. § 1415; 34 C.F.R. § 300.504.

12

Discipling Students With Disabilities

Margaret Bannon Miller

Introduction

Proper discipline of students with disabilities may seem to call for a choice between unacceptable alternatives: failure to discipline in an educationally sound manner or violation of a student's federally guaranteed rights. On the contrary, both sound disciplinary principles and the rights of disabled students can be key ingredients in disciplinary decisions if administrators are aware of the basic requirements of the laws governing services to students with disabilities, especially the emphasis those laws place on the role of the "IEP team".

Consideration of and planning for disciplinary situations by the IEP team can sometimes deter serious behavioral situations which could necessitate suspension or expulsion. If such situations do arise, the case IEP team again takes a central role by deciding whether the behavior is directly related to the student's disability. Only when it determines that the disability is not causally related to the behavior does the IEP team's central importance diminish as the school's normal disciplinary processes takes over. Familiarity with the function of the IEP team and its key role in helping shape a student's behavior will safeguard against an administrative decision which could result in inappropriately punishing a student for behavior caused by the student's disability.

Legal Issues

Discipline as a Part of the Individualized Education Program (IEP)

The role of the IEP team in the education and social development of the student with disabilities cannot be overestimated. The committee, made up of persons familiar with the abilities and limitations of the student, is responsible for the formulation of the Individualized Education Program. The IEP is the cornerstone of education for every student with disabilities and includes statements regarding the child's present educational performance, annual goals, the specific special education and related services to be provided to the child, a time frame for accomplishing the goals, and appropriate objective criteria for determining the child's progress.[1]

Educators recognize that for many students with disabilities, behavior modification is essential to learning. In light of this recognition, disciplinary approaches may and often should be included in a student's IEP.[2] Further, Department of Education rules regarding students with disabilities state that in formulating an IEP, the goals and objectives must relate to the student's total education. Since discipline is recognized as a part of the total education of the disabled student, it may certainly be included in an IEP.

Suspension and Expulsion

Corporal punishment, placement in a "time out room," suspension, or even expulsion may all be appropriate forms of discipline for a student. However, suspension and expulsion of the disabled student as disciplinary tools raise issues for educators and parents because of the requirement that students with disabilities be afforded a "free appropriate public education." Suspension and expulsion necessarily mean that for a period of time the students with disabilities do not receive the services required by law. Nevertheless, both short and long-term suspension or expulsion may be appropriate methods for disciplining the disabled student, so long as due process requirements are met.

Suspension is defined as a temporary cessation of educational services. The length of a suspension, the procedures, and the reasons for which a suspension can be ordered are generally regulated by individual state statutes. The Office for Civil Rights (OCR), the Office of Special Education and Rehabilitative Services (OSERS), and courts have determined that a student with disabilities may be suspended for up to ten days before the suspension becomes a change in placement. However, the suspension or expulsion of a disabled student for more than ten consecutive school days constitutes a significant change in placement which triggers due process procedures.[3] A series of shorter suspensions totalling ten days or more in a school year may be a significant change of placement requiring evaluation if the suspensions create a pattern of exclusions.[4]

In *Hayes v. Unified School District No. 377*,[5] parents of students in a special education program brought suit against school officials.

The children, who were disruptive and violated school rules, were at times required to stay in a three-foot by five-foot room for "time out" periods and in-school suspensions.[6] The district court held, and the appellate court affirmed, that in-school suspensions of up to five days do not constitute a change in placement within the meaning of section 504 of the Rehabilitation Act of 1973.[7] The courts found that the school's use of the time-out room was clearly related to providing an appropriate public education for the plaintiffs. The students were placed in the time-out room for in-school suspension as a method of punishment and for short cool-down periods to ensure the safety of other students in the classroom from disruptive behavior.[8]

Unlike short-term suspension, the suspension or expulsion of a disabled student for more than ten consecutive school days does constitute a significant change of placement which will trigger due process procedures. Prior to making such a significant change in placement, the disabled student must be evaluated to determine whether the misconduct was caused by the student's disability. If the misconduct was a result of the student's disability, the district may not suspend or expel the student. If the misconduct is found to be unrelated to the student's handicap, the district may exclude the student. One exception to these requirements is that students who are disabled solely under section 504, i.e., not eligible for services under IDEA and who are charged with use or possession of illegal drugs or alcohol, may be expelled without an evaluation or a conference to determine whether the disability is causally related to the behavior.[9]

The first case that dealt with the issue of expulsion of students with disabilities was *S-1 v. Turlington*.[10] In *Turlington*, nine students who were classified as either educable mentally retarded, mildly mentally retarded, or dull/normal were expelled from school for the maximum time permitted by state law, approximately two years.[11] Except for one student, S-1, none were given hearings to determine whether their misconduct was a result of their disabling condition.[12] With respect to S-1, the superintendent of schools determined that since the student was not classified as seriously emotionally disturbed; his misconduct, as a matter of law, could not be a manifestation of his handicap.[13] The appellate court affirmed the trial court's ruling that before the disabled students could be expelled, a trained and knowledgeable group of persons must determine whether the student's misconduct bears a relationship to his handicapping condition.[14] Without such a determination, the students were being denied their right to a free appropriate public education.

In *Doe v. Maher*,[15] the Ninth Circuit Court of Appeals held that prior to approving a suspension that constitutes a significant change in placement, a proper determination must be made whether the misbehavior is a manifestation of the child's handicap.[16] In *Maher*, two students classified as emotionally disabled were suspended indefinitely pending expulsion proceedings. The court held that since expulsion constitutes a change in placement within the meaning of the IDEA, school officials seeking to expel a disabled student must follow procedures prescribed in the Act. These procedures include:

> (1) notifying parents in writing of the educational agency's intention to seek expulsion; (2) convening an IEP team meeting to assess the reason for the misconduct and the appropriateness of the child's current educational placement; (3) conducting an independent evaluation of the pupil's educational needs; (4) informing parents of their right to demand impartial administrative review of any IEP team decision and judicial review of the state's final administrative determination; and (5) allowing the child to remain in his then-current educational placement pending resolution of any previously mentioned review proceedings.[17]

Maher also made it clear that where the student's misbehavior was properly determined not to be a manifestation of his handicap, the student may be expelled.[18] The court found that when the student's misbehavior does not result from his or her handicapping condition, there is no justification for exempting the student from the rules which are applicable to other students, including those rules regarding expulsion.

Finally, in *Honig v. Doe*,[19] the United States Supreme Court addressed the issue of a student's placement pending the final outcome of expulsion proceedings. *Honig* was an appeal from the Ninth Circuit Court's decision in *Maher* but dealt only with the IDEA's stay-put provision and the indefinite suspensions employed by the school district in that case. The Supreme Court held that the IDEA prohibited school officials from unilaterally excluding a disabled child from class for dangerous conduct growing out of the child's disability pending review proceedings. The Court also held that school officials were permitted to suspend a disabled student temporarily for up to ten days where the student poses an immediate threat to the safety of others, but a suspension in excess of ten days constitutes a change in placement. The Court found that the language of 20 U.S.C. section 1415(e)(3) is unequivocal. It states that "during the pendency of any proceedings initiated under the Act, unless a state or local education agency and the parents or guardian of a disabled child otherwise agree, the child *shall* remain in the then-current educational placement." The only way for school officials to exclude a dangerous student from school while proceedings are pending and where parents of a truly dangerous child refuse to permit any change in placement is for school officials to invoke the court's aid under the statute, which empowers courts to grant any appropriate relief. This action can be done during the ten-day period.

Such extraordinary relief was sought by school officials in *Texas City Independent School District v. Jorstad*.[20] In *Jorstad*, school officials brought a motion for a preliminary injunction to enjoin an emotionally disturbed student from attending regular class. The student was a 13-year-old classified as emotionally disturbed and speech disabled, who had been diagnosed as exhibiting a psychotic disorder. Pursuant to his IEP, the student attended middle school. During the 1990 school year, significant behavior problems occurred, including physical aggression and frequent attacks on other students. The student twice tried to jump out of second floor windows, on several occasions threatened to kill himself and others, and caused substantial physical damage to school property. The principal considered the student to be severely dangerous to himself and to present an ongoing threat to others. In light of testimony from the principal and teachers, the district court concluded that the school district had sustained the extraordinary burden in seeking injunctive relief and ordered that the child be taken out of the general curriculum at school pending placement review.

Expulsion for Conduct Unrelated to the Disability and Cessation of Services

Recently, the question has arisen of whether a state which receives federal funds pursuant to the IDEA may cease educational services to a disabled student when the student has been properly expelled from his or her educational placement for conduct unrelated to the handicap. The courts are split on the issue of whether educational services must be continued for disabled children after expulsion. In *Maher*, the Ninth Circuit Court held that a school district may withhold educational services from a disabled child after expulsion where the misbehavior was determined not to be a manifestation of his or her handicap. However, the Fifth Circuit Court, in *S-1 v. Turlington*, stated that it would not authorize the complete cessation of educational services during expulsion.

Finally, in 1989, Robert Davila, the Assistant Secretary of Education in charge of the Office of Special Education and Rehabilitative Services (OSERS), authored a letter to Frank E. New (the "New letter")[21] of the Ohio Department of Education. In this letter, Davila asserted that educational services must continue during periods of long-term suspension or expulsion even when the misbehavior was not a manifestation of the student's handicap.

In 1990, the Metropolitan School District of Wayne Township in Indiana filed a class action lawsuit against Davila claiming that OSERS had promulgated a legislative rule, which has the force and effect of law, without complying with federal law. Legislative rules must comply with the requirements of the *Administrative Procedures Act*, including public notice and the opportunity for comment. The district court in Indiana granted the school district's motion for summary judgment holding that the New letter was a legislative rule.[22] The court found that although the New letter purported to be merely Davila's opinion as to the meaning of 20 U.S.C. section 1412(1), its effect was to change a long-standing policy of OSERS without a corresponding change in the underlying statute or regulations. Before any change could take place, the proposed rule had to be published in the Federal Register with an opportunity for comment by interested persons prior to the rule taking effect. The court found that the New letter was obviously a substantial rule or regulation in that it imposed a new and mandatory duty upon all school districts in the United States as the new duty was not expressly required by the IDEA or by *Honig v. Doe*.

The district court found that *Honig* affirmed the decision of *Doe v. Maher*; and that under *Maher*, where a student's behavior was properly determined not to be a manifestation of a disability, the disabled student may be expelled and educational services withheld. The New letter was used to enact an administrative rule in a manner contrary to the Administrative Procedures Act, and the court enjoined Davila from enforcing the New letter by withholding federal funds from Indiana. The Seventh Circuit Court of Appeals upheld the New letter.[23]

Recommendations for Practice

The following items may serve as a check list in dealing with the behavior of certain disabled students:[24]
- Include behavioral goals and objectives and disciplinary methods in the IEP of any disabled student whose behavior presents difficulty in the school setting.

- For short-term suspensions (under ten days) provide the normal due process required by state statute or regulation. As the number of days increases, convene a IEP team meeting to determine whether the student's placement is appropriate and/or whether the student's disability has any connection with the misbehavior.
- If a student is suspended for fewer than ten days, such suspension is not considered a change in placement and educational services need not continue during the period of the suspension.
- Since suspensions beyond ten days in length or suspensions which cumulatively amount to ten days in a school year constitute a change in the student's placement, such suspension should be preceded by a IEP team meeting to determine whether the student's behavior is related to the disability. If so, suspensions may continue only if the IEP team recommends such action as part of the student's behavioral program. If the behavior is not related to the handicap, the use of suspension may continue, but the parent may request a due process hearing to decide the matter.
- Both long-term suspension (more than ten days) and expulsion should be preceded by both an evaluation and a IEP team meeting to determine the relationship, if any, between the student's misbehavior and the disability. A student may not be expelled for behavior which is causally related to the student's disability.
- If the IEP team decides there is a causal relationship between the student's disability and the behavior, the committee should consider revisions in the student's IEP and/or a more restrictive placement in order to alleviate the behavior problem.
- If the IEP team decides there is no relationship between the student's disability and the behavior, the school district may proceed with its normal expulsion procedures.
- If a parent is in disagreement with the determination concerning the causal relationship, the parent may appeal that decision by asking for a special education hearing. While such hearing is proceeding, the student must remain in the current educational placement unless both the school and the parent agree to an interim change in that placement. If a student presents a real threat to himself or others, the school district may seek a change of placement through a court's injunction.
- A student who has not been determined to be handicapped, but who requests an evaluation after expulsion has been rec-

ommended by the school district, need not be evaluated prior to the expulsion. The evaluation may proceed during the period of expulsion, and if the student is found to be eligible, appropriate services must begin upon the student's return to school.

- If a student is expelled for behavior which is not related to the disability, it is questionable whether educational services may cease until the expulsion has run its course.

References

[1] 34 C.F.R. §300.346.
[2] 34 C.F.R. §300.340 *et seq.*
[3] OCR Staff Memorandum, IDELR 307:05 (1988) *cf.* 16 IDELR 491 (1989).
[4] *Id.*
[5] Hayes v. Unified School Dist. No. 377, 669 F. Supp. 1519 (D. Kan. 1987), *aff'd*, 877 F.2d 809 (10th Cir. 1989).
[6] *Id.* at 1521.
[7] *Id.* at 1524, 877 F.2d at 813.
[8] *Id.* at 813. This case is also illustrative of the close relationship between the use of discipline and in-class instruction in providing the child with a free appropriate public education.
[9] 29 U.S.C. § 706(8)(C)(iv).
[10] S-1 v. Turlington, 635 F.2d 342, 350 (5th Cir) *cert. denied*, 454 U.S. 1030 (1981).
[11] *Id.* at 344.
[12] *Id.*
[13] *Id.*
[14] *Id.* at 350.
[15] 793 F.2d 1470 (9th Cir. 1985).
[16] *Id.* at 1482.
[17] *Id.*
[18] *Id.*
[19] Honig v. Doe, 108 S. Ct. 592 (1988).
[20] Texas City Indep. School Dist. v. Jorstad, 752 F. Supp. 231 (S.D. Tex 1990).
[21] IDELR 213:258.
[22] MSD of Wayne v. Davila 770 F. Supp. 1331 (N.D. Ind. 1991).
[23] MSD of Wayne v. Davila, 969 F.2d 485 (7th Cir. 1992).
[24] Each of these recommendations should be compared to state statutes and regulations regarding services to students with disabilities since such requirements may vary from state to state.

13
Related Services

Christine M. Crawford and Perry A. Zirkel

Introduction

The provision of an appropriate education including "related services" to students with disabilities continues to challenge school administrators. Parents of these students have asked school districts to provide an array of such services including health and medical services, residential treatment, physical and occupational therapy, specialized transportation, in-home services, and special equipment use. What are the limits of the related services mandate? Over the past decade, courts and administrative agencies have established some answers for school administrators. Although state legislation or regulations may add entitlements,[1] the basic sources of related services obligations are the Individuals with Disabilities Education Act (IDEA) and section 504 of the Rehabilitation Act of 1973 (section 504).

Legal Issues

Primary Sources

The IDEA regulations specifically define "related services" as: "transportation and such developmental, corrective, and other supportive services as are required to assist a...child [with a disability] to benefit from special education."[2] The definition goes on to list as illustrative inclusions the following services: assistive technology, medical services for diagnostic or evaluative purposes, school health services, psychological and counseling services, social work services in the schools, physical and occupational therapy, speech pathology and audiology, early identification and assessment of disabilities in children, recreation, and parent counseling and training.[3] A statement of the specific related services to be provided must be included in the individualized education program (IEP) for each student with an IDEA disability.[4]

Two preliminary points about the IDEA definition need to be noted. First, the scope of related services, as illustrated by the long list of items, extends well beyond the traditional notion of formal basic education. Second, the primary limiting criterion is that the service must be necessary for the child to benefit from special education. The section 504 regulations provide for "related aids and services."[5] Although not defined as specifically as under the IDEA, these services are referred to in the Comments to the Regulations as "developmental, corrective, and other supportive services (including psychological counseling and medical diagnostic services)."[6] Although the description is similar to the definition under the IDEA,[7] section 504 provides a more extensive entitlement than does the IDEA in at least two respects: the definition of handicap is broader under section 504[8] and the related services mandate under section 504 applies not only to special, but also to regular, education.[9] The guidance added by the courts and administrative agencies starts with that provided by the Supreme Court.

Supreme Court Guidance

In *Irving Independent School District v. Tatro*,[10] the Supreme Court was asked to determine whether clean intermittent catheterization (CIC) is a related service under the IDEA. To make this determination, the Court applied the exclusion for medical services for treatment purposes, as compared to diagnostic or evaluative. Inasmuch as the IDEA regulations define "medical services" as those provided by a licensed physician[11] and CIC can be performed by any trained layperson, the Court concluded that CIC fell within the related-services inclusion for "school health services"[12] rather than the exclusion for medical treatment services. Finally, since the child could not attend school without CIC and thus required CIC to benefit from special education, the Court concluded that the child was entitled to this related service.

Anticipating the reaction of school districts, the Court noted the following limitations under the IDEA:

- To be entitled to a related services, the child must be disabled to the extent that she/he requires special education.
- A district must provide only those services necessary for the child to benefit from special education.
- Such services do not qualify when provided by a physician as compared to a nurse or other qualified person.
- The parents had not asked the district to provide equipment.[13]

The *Tatro* Court's interpretation has impacted most directly on the provisions for school health and medical services.

School Health and Medical Services

Do any in-school health services provided by a school nurse rather than by a physician, fit under the exclusion for medical treatment services? In two post-*Tatro* decisions, lower federal courts concluded that complex and constant in-school nursing care, which was required by a student with multiple disabilities in each case, closely resembled the "medical services" exclusion under the IDEA; therefore, such care did not fit within the entitlement for related services.[14] However, the line between expensive nursing services and the medical exclusion is not a clear one. For example, a recent state-level administrative review decision under the IDEA was in favor of the school district after it refused to provide a one-to-one, medically trained, full-time aide for a severely disabled student.[15] In another recent administrative decision, a hearing officer required another school district to provide tracheostomy and naso-gastric tube care and feeding to an orthopedically impaired student.[16]

Moreover, the inclusion for medical services for diagnostic or evaluative, in contrast with treatment, purposes is not inelastically limited to those specifically requested by school personnel. For example, a federal court ordered the defendant district to pay for a neurological evaluation requested by the pediatrician whom the district had previously asked to conduct a medical evaluation.[17] Similarly, in a more recent decision, a federal court ordered the defendant district to assume the cost of an in-patient psychiatric evaluation recommended by a psychologist who had conducted an independent evaluation of the plaintiff, who was a learning disabled student.[18] The key in both cases was the necessity for educational benefit, not the boundaries of the school district staff or budget.

What if the physician is needed to prescribe, monitor, and adjust medication? In a recent decision, a federal court answered that such services fit under the related-services mandate, rather than the medical-services exception, where necessary to provide meaningful access to special education.[19] Similarly, the Ninth Circuit Court of Appeals upheld a preliminary injunction against a school district to incur the costs of a psychiatrist to prescribe and monitor medication of a severely emotionally disturbed student.[20] Conversely, where they are not needed to assist the child to benefit from special education, such services are not the district's obligation.[21]

The entitlement for school health services does not end with IDEA students. For example, a Pennsylvania suit was brought under section 504 on behalf of students with physical disabilities who required health or other related services while attending regular education.[22] By way of illustration, the named plaintiff, Elizabeth S., had juvenile diabetes and required monitoring and remediation of blood sugar levels during the school day; yet, she was not covered by the IDEA because she did not need special education. The suit was dismissed by stipulation, resulting in state regulations recognizing that such students are entitled to procedural safeguards and reasonable accommodation under section 504.[23] Administrative interpretations by the Office for Civil Rights, which is responsible for enforcing section 504, suggest that administration of medication, presumably by a school nurse or other qualified staff member, is a reasonable accommodation for students such as Elizabeth S.[24]

Psychotherapy

Does psychotherapy fit under the medical services exclusion? Although not specifically included in the illustrative items in the related-services definition of the IDEA regulations, psychotherapy may fit under "counseling" or "psychological" services, depending on whether the child needs it to benefit from special education and who renders the service. As for the educational necessity criterion, a federal appeals court ruled in favor of a school district where the IEP, which did not include psychotherapy, was reasonably calculated to yield educational benefit.[25] In such circumstances, the court ruled, the school district was not required to fund the requested psychotherapy. In a recent review decision, a state education agency reached the same conclusion.[26]

As for the service provided, a federal court ordered a school district to pay for necessary psychotherapy that was provided directly by a social worker although under the supervision of a psychiatrist.[27] Similarly, another federal court upheld the provision of group and individual psychotherapy by a psychologist who had a Ph.D., where it was required to assist the child to benefit from special education.[28] Even if the psychotherapy is provided directly by a psychiatrist who is an M.D., it is not automatically disqualified by the medical services exclusion. In an Illinois case, the federal court required the defendant district to reimburse the parents for psychotherapy that had been provided by a psychiatrist because the district had failed to apprise the parents of their IDEA rights and provide the necessary therapy by its own personnel; however, the district was only liable for the amount that these services would have cost had they been provided by its own qualified personnel.[29] Somewhat similarly, a Connecticut court recently ruled that a district was liable for providing psychiatric therapy, cryptically reasoning that whether it is excluded by the medical exception "depends on the nature and purpose of the services rather than the service provider."[30]

Residential Treatment

The IDEA regulations provide that where a private residential placement is necessary for educational benefit, the various costs, including "non-medical care and room and board" must be provided free to the parent.[31] What if the medical services in such a placement are, to some extent, intertwined with the other components of the program? A New York case serves as a good illustration. The court found that the district's insistence on paying only the tuition component of an appropriate residential placement was a violation of the IDEA.[32] Citing various prior court decisions,[33] the court preserved for trial questions which portion of the charges were room/board and which were related services and whether any of the child's psychiatrist-provided psychotherapy should be compensated.

The intertwining problem is further illustrated by a cluster of California cases. The first case seems to illustrate the proposition that where the educational, behavioral, and developmental needs of the child are inextricably intertwined, the school authorities may be required to fund the residential placement as a related service.[34] However, as illustrated by two subsequent California cases, where the placement is in a psychiatric center, the answer may depend on whether the court regards the facility as a hospital or whether the court finds that the placement was primarily for the child's medical (i.e., psychiatric) or educational needs.[35] Where the hospitalization therapies were for psychiatric reasons, the costs are excluded by the medical services exception.[36]

Inasmuch as residential placement is only partially a matter of related services, the case law is complex.[37] The issue is tangential to the building-level administrator, and the remaining details are left to other available sources.[38] It is worth noting, however, that for residential placement, section 504 provides overlapping coverage.[39]

Physical and Occupational Therapy

Although the definition of related services explicitly itemizes both physical therapy and occupational therapy, disputes have arisen over the extent of this obligation. In a lead decision, the Third Circuit Court of Appeals ruled that an educational agency may not make a "blanket rule" prohibiting individual physical therapy as a related service.[40] In other cases, federal courts have ruled against school districts that refused to reimburse parents for the cost of privately arranged therapies included in the child's IEP but not provided by the district[41] or that failed to provide necessary physical or occupational therapies during summer months when lack of services would result in regression not reasonably subject to recoupment.[42] Similarly, courts have made clear that when such necessary therapies are discontinued for a significant length of time (e.g., 13 months), the school district may be liable for providing such services on a compensatory basis.[43] Again, section 504 provides overlapping coverage.[44]

Transportation

Including transportation in the definition of related services leaves for administrative and judicial proceedings the question of where the school district's obligations end. For example, the obligation does not necessarily end at the boundaries of the school district.[45] Similarly, the obligation extends, in some cases, to door-to-door for students with physical disabilities, regardless of poor road conditions, steep steps, or other such external hindrances.[46] However, a school district is not required to transport a student with a disability to a geographically distant public school when an appropriate education is available at a public school closer to the student's home.[47]

Transportation between public and private facilities has also spawned several questions. The obligation extends, for example, to private clinics for therapies not available through the district when such therapies are necessary for educational benefit.[48] However, school districts do not have to provide transportation to private schools when the district has offered an appropriate program in its own facilities.[49] Conversely, districts may be required to transport private school students with disabilities to public facilities for receipt of necessary related services.[50]

Does the IDEA transportation obligation extend to other members of the family—for example, to parental visits with a student with disabilities in a distant private placement? In a Florida case, the court ruled that the district does not have to cover unlimited parental visits to an out-of-state residential placement; the district's funding of three such visits a year fulfilled the required transportation obligation.[51]

Does the IDEA transportation obligation also include the provision of trained aides? The relevant case law suggests that districts are only required to provide specially trained transportation aides when they are necessary for the student to access, and benefit from, special education. For example, a federal court ordered a district to provide a specially trained aide to suction a student's tracheostomy while he was on the school bus.[52] Similarly, a state education agency ordered a district to provide a one-to-one attendant capable of dealing with complex physical and emotional needs as necessary for a student with multiple disabilities.[53] Again, section 504 provides overlapping coverage.[54] The Office for Civil Rights found that carrying a mobility-impaired student on and off the school bus was not an acceptable method of providing access where reasonable accommodations for providing independent access were available.[55]

Services Beyond the School Day

Does the related-services obligation extend to extracurricular activities, in-home aides, and parent training? With regard to extracurricular activities, the IDEA answer is: only where the student requires the activities for educational benefit.[56] A state-level hearing officer found against an emotionally disturbed student whose parents argued that participation in varsity football was a related service; the preponderance of the evidence did not establish that this activity was necessary for him to benefit from special education.[57] Under section 504, the hurdle is not as high for students' challenges. The regulations have an explicit nondiscrimination obligation,[58] and the case law further clarifies this obligation as providing reasonable accommodations to the broader group of covered students.[59]

With regard to in-home aides, the answer is generally adverse to the plaintiff parents when the child's special education placement is not homebound instruction. For example, a federal court ruled that a district's refusal to provide an in-home behavior management program, including aides, for an autistic, mentally retarded child was not a violation of the IDEA or section 504.[60] Similarly, a state education agency ruled that a school district was not required to provide a one-to-one attendance at the home of a student with multiple disabilities.[61]

With regard to parent training and counseling, the answer is clearly yes if it meets the necessary-benefit test for related services. For example, a federal court recently ordered a school district to develop and implement a program of parent counseling and training, finding that it was necessary for the emotionally disturbed child to benefit from his special education program.[62] Conversely, a state education agency refused to include training for parents of an emotionally disturbed student because they had not shown the requisite need.[63]

Special Equipment

Returning to where this sojourn through related services started, the *Tatro* decision mentioned, as a seeming boundary of the obligation, that the parents had not requested specialized equipment.[64] However, this boundary has several openings. First, the definition of the related service of transportation includes, "specialized equipment (such as special or adapted buses, lifts, and ramps) if required to provide special transportation for a...child [with a disability]."[65] Citing this regulation, a state court ordered a district to purchase a four-wheel drive vehicle to meet the transportation needs of two physically disabled students who lived in a very rural area which had poor road conditions.[66] This transportation obligation has been interpreted to extend to the use of wheelchairs when required to assist the child to benefit from special education.[67]

Second, school districts must provide the use of other adaptive equipment, such as FM systems,[68] computer systems with voice synthesizers,[69] and portable computers[70] to students with disabilities when necessary for educational benefit. However, a district may not have to furnish intrusive behavior management equipment when less restrictive options have not been exhausted.[71] Similarly, providing hearing aids does not generally fit under the related-services obligation.[72]

Third, "assistive technology" services and devices, which are the subject of an amendment to the IDEA, have been interpreted to be a possible part of the district's related-services obligation. In the view of the United States Department of Education, "consideration of a child's need for assistive technology must occur on a case-by-case basis in connection with the development of a child's...IEP."[73]

Fourth, the "related aids and services" requirement of section 504 may be interpreted to include special equipment.[74] Thus, providing eligible students the use of computers may be part of the reasonable accommodation obligation of section 504.[75]

Other Services

Given the elastic quality of the related-services definition and of eligible children's needs, no treatment of this subject can be entirely complete. Specialized staff, such as one-to-one aides in the classroom,[76] teachers trained in computer technology,[77] and full-time specially certified teachers,[78] is an implicit item in the related-services definitional list. Of less immediate import to public school principals is the issue of providing related services to parochial school students; the short answer is that it is constitutionally permissible to conduct such activities at public schools or other neutral sites[79] but not at the parochial school.[80] As final examples of variety and elasticity, other issues include interpreter services,[81] speech therapy,[82] related services for limited English proficient special education students,[83] and recreation therapy.[84]

Recommendations for Practice

The vast array of judicial and administrative interpretations of "related services" may be boiled down to a few relatively simple general recommendations for school principals and other administrators:

- Do not have a knee-jerk negative reaction to parental requests for related services for students with disabilities; the controlling criterion is not the narrow, traditional definition of education that pre-dated special federal and state statutes. Blanket refusals to provide related services are a blatant violation of these laws.
- Recognize that the relevant basic sources of the related-service obligation are the federal IDEA regulations and the overlapping but not identical coverage of section 504; state legislation/regulations may add to, not subtract from, this obligation.
- A determination of the related service obligation must be made on an individual case-by-case basis. The relevant questions under the IDEA are: whether the student fits within the definition of "children with disabilities;" whether the service in question is eliminated by the exclusion for medical services for treatment purposes; and, if not whether the service is necessary to assist the child to benefit from special education. The relevant questions under section 504 are similar, but the category of eligible students is broader; yet the obligation is limited to reasonable accommodations.
- Particular items that the building-level administrator may be too quick to dismiss and that need careful review to determine whether they are within the related-services entitlement of an individual child with a handicap or disability are: administration of medication, door-to-door transportation, and specialized equipment.

- Items that are less within the control of the building-level administrator but require special care are requests for residential treatment, psychotherapy, and parent counseling.

References

[1] *See, e.g.,* Krichansky v. Knox County Schools, 17 EHLR 725 (E.D. Tenn. 1991).
[2] 34 C.F.R. § 300.13(a).
[3] *Id.* The sequence of the services has been adjusted here to facilitate explanation. The attached annotation for this regulation makes clear that this list is to be interpreted as illustrative rather than exhaustive. *Id.* § 300.13 Comment.
[4] *Id.* § 300.346(c).
[5] *Id.* § 104.33(b).
[6] *Id.* § 104, Appendix A.
[7] Although less extensive, the description parallels the definition in the IDEA regulations. Similarly, although not as explicitly limited to necessary educational benefit, such services are referred to in the Comments section as "designed to meet handicapped children's individual *educational needs* to the same extent that those of nonhandicapped children are met." *Id.* (emphasis supplied).
[8] Eligibility under the IDEA is limited to each person between certain ages with one or more enumerated disabilities (e.g., mental retardation or serious emotional disturbance) "who because of these impairments need special education and related services." *Id.* § 300.5(a). In contrast, the definition under § 504 is "any person who (i) has a physical or mental impairment which substantially limits one or more major life activities, (ii) has a record of such impairment, or (iii) is regarded as having such impairment." *Id.* § 104.3(j)(1).
[9] *Id.* § 104.33(b).
[10] 468 U.S. 883 (1984).
[11] 34 C.F.R. § 300.13(b)(4).
[12] "School health services" are defined as those "provided by a qualified school nurse or other qualified person." *Id.* § 300.13(b)(10).
[13] *Tatro*, 468 U.S. at 894-95. This listing is a summary rather than quotation of the Court's statements.
[14] Detsel v. Board of Educ., 820 F.2d 587 (2d Cir. 1987), *cert. denied*, 484 U.S. 981 (1987); Bevin H. v. Wright, 666 F. Supp. 71 (W.D. Pa. 1987).
[15] Glen Rock Bd. of Educ., 16 EHLR 1102 (N.J. SEA 1990).
[16] Granite (UT) School Dist., 16 EHLR 1065 (Utah H.O. 1990); *cf.* Department of Educ. v. Katherine D., 727 F.2d 809 (9th Cir. 1984), *cert. denied*, 471 U.S. 1117 (1985); Hymes v. Harnette County Bd. of Educ., 664 F.2d 410 (4th Cir. 1981) (pre-Tatro). *See also infra* note 52 and accompanying text.
[17] Seals v. Loftis, 614 F. Supp. 302 (E.D. Tenn. 1985).
[18] Doe v. Board of Pub. Educ., EHLR 441:106 (M.D. Tenn. 1988).
[19] Brown v. Wilson County School Bd., 747 F. Supp. 436 (M.D. Tenn. 1990).
[20] Taylor v. Honig, 910 F.2d 627 (9th Cir. 1990).
[21] Palos Verdes Peninsula Unified School Dist., EHLR 507:121 (Cal. SEA 1985).
[22] Elizabeth S. v. Gilhool, EHLR 558:461 (M.D. Pa. 1987).
[23] 22 Pa. Code Ch. 15.
[24] *See, e.g.,* Pearl (MS) Pub. School Dist., 17 EHLR 1004 (OCR 1991); Fairfield-Suisun (CA) Unified School Dist., EHLR 353:205 (OCR 1989); Berlin Brothersvalley (PA) School Dist., EHLR 353:124 (OCR 1988).
[25] Tice v. Botetourt County School Bd., 908 F.2d 1200 (4th Cir. 1990).
[26] Pennsbury (PA) School Dist., 16 EHLR 778 (Pa. SEA 1990).
[27] T.G. v. Board of Educ., 576 F. Supp. 420 (D.N.J. 1983), *aff'd mem.*, 738 F.2d 425 (2d Cir. 1984), *cert. denied*, 469 U.S. 1086 (1984).
[28] Doe v. Anrig, 651 F. Supp. 424 (D. Mass. 1987).
[29] Max M. v. Illinois State Bd. of Educ., 629 F. Supp. 1504 (N.D. Ill. 1986).
[30] Board of Educ. v. Department of Educ., 17 EHLR 942 (Conn. Super. 1991).
[31] 34 C.F.R. § 300.302.

[32]Vander Malle v. Ambach, 667 F. Supp. 1015 (S.D.N.Y. 1987).

[33]See, e.g., Kruelle v. New Castle County School Dist., 642 F.2d 687 (3d Cir. 1981); Abrahamson v. Hershman, 701 F.2d 223 (1st Cir. 1983).

[34]Corbett v. Regional Cent. of the East Bay, EHLR 559:373 (N.D. Cal. 1988), vacated on other grounds, 699 F. Supp. 230 (N.D. Cal. 1988).

[35]Compare Taylor v. Honig, 910 F.2d 627 (9th Cir. 1990) (school authorities liable) with Clovis Unified School Dist. v. California, 903 F.2d 635 (9th Cir. 1990) (school authorities not liable).

[36]See, e.g., Los Gatos Unified High School Dist. v. Doe, EHLR 556:281 (N.D. Cal. 1984); Metropolitan Gov't v. Tennessee Dep't of Educ., 771 S.W.2d 427 (Tenn. App. 1989).

[37]For instance, another variation is where the residential placement is not in an approved school. See Antkowiak v. Ambach, 838 F.2d 635 (2d Cir. 1988); Schimmel v. Spillane, 819 F.2d 477 (4th Cir. 1987) (not liable). With Carter v. Florence County School Dist., 950 F2d. 156 (4th Cir. 1991).

[38]See, e.g., Huefner, Special Education Residential Placement for Students with Severe Emotional Disturbances, 67 EDUC. L. REP. 397 (1991); Huefner, Special Education Residential Placements under the Education for All Handicapped Children's Act, 18 J. LAW & EDUC. 411 (1989).

[39]34 C.F.R. § 104.33(c)(3). See, e.g., David H. v. Spring Branch Indep. School Dist., 569 F. Supp. 1324 (S.D. Tex. 1983); William S. v. Gill, 536 F. Supp. 505 (N.D. Ill. 1982).

[40]Polk v. Central Susquehanna Intermediate Unit No. 16, 853 F.2d 171 (3d Cir. 1988), cert. denied, 488 U.S. 1030 (1989).

[41]Rapid City School Dist. v. Vahle, 922 F.2d 476 (8th Cir. 1990).

[42]Holmes v. Sobol, 690 F. Supp. 154 (W.D.N.Y. 1988).

[43]Pittsburgh Bd. of Educ. v. Commonwealth Dep't of Educ., 581 A.2d 681 (Pa. Commw. 1990).

[44]See, e.g., Columbia County (GA) School Dist., EHLR 352:21 (OCR 1985).

[45]Alamo Heights Indep. School Dist. v. State Bd. of Educ., 790 F.2d 1153 (5th Cir. 1986).

[46]See Hurry v. Jones, 734 F.2d 879 (1st Cir. 1984); Kennedy v. Board of Educ., 337 S.E.2d 905 (W.V. 1985).

[47]School Bd. of Pinellas County v. Smith, 537 So. 2d 168 (Fla. App. 1989).

[48]School Dist. of Philadelphia v. Commonwealth Dep't of Educ., EHLR 441:341 (Pa. Commw. 1988).

[49]McNair v. Oak Hills Local School Dist., 872 F.2d 153 (6th Cir. 1989); Work v. McKenzie, 661 F. Supp. 225 (D.D.C. 1987).

[50]Wheatland Unified School Dist., EHLR 508:310 (Cal. H.O. 1987).

[51]Cohen v. School Bd., 450 So. 2d 1238 (Fla. App. 1984).

[52]Macomb County Intermediate School Dist. v. Joshua S., 715 F. Supp. 824 (E.D. Mich. 1989).

[53]Seattle School Dist., 16 EHLR 1091 (Wash. SEA 1990).

[54]34 C.F.R. § 104.33.

[55]Garaway (OH) Local School Dist., 17 EHLR 237 (OCR 1990).

[56]See, e.g., Rettig v. Kent School Dist., 788 F.2d 328 (6th Cir. 1986); Birmingham and Lamphere School Dists. v. Superintendent of Pub. Instruction, 328 N.W.2d 59 (Mich. App. 1982).

[57]Middletown v. Board of Educ., 17 EHLR 98 (N.J. SEA 1990).

[58]34 C.F.R. § 104. 37(a).

[59]See Cavallaro v. Ambach, 575 F. Supp. 171 (W.D.N.Y. 1983); Grube v. Bethlehem Area School Dist., 550 F. Supp. 418 (E.D. Pa. 1982); Poole v. South Plainfield Bd. of Educ., 490 F. Supp. 948 (D.N.J. 1980).

[60]Burke County Bd. of Educ. v. Denton, 895 F.2d 973 (4th Cir. 1990)

[61]Seattle School Dist., 16 EHLR 1091 (Wash. SEA 1990).

[62]Cory M. v. Montgomery County Bd. of Educ., 743 F. Supp. 1524 (M.D. Ala. 1990); see also Chris D. v. Montgomery County Bd. of Educ., 753 F. Supp. 922 (M.D. Ala. 1990).

[63]Pennsbury School Dist., 16 EHLR 778 (Pa. SEA 1990). Additionally, the parents had waived the issue by approving of the child's IEP without such service and failing to include it in the stipulated issue. Id. at 780.

[64]Tatro, 468 U.S. at 894-95.

[65]34 C.F.R. § 300.13(b)(13)(iii).

[66]Kennedy v. Board of Educ., 337 S.E.2d 905 (W. Va. 1985).

[67]Inquiry of Stohrer, EHLR 213:209 (OSEP 1989).

[68]Anthony Wayne Local School Dist., 16 EHLR 1032 (Ohio SEA 1990).

[69]San Francisco Unified School Dist., EHLR 507:416 (Cal. H.O. 1985).

[70]See, e.g., Harwich Pub. Schools, EHLR 509:306 (Mass. SEA 1988); In re Mary H., EHLR 506:325 (Mass. SEA 1984); cf. Inquiry of Hamilton, EHLR 213:269 (OSERS 1989).

[71]Northville and Wayne-Westland Pub. Schools, 16 EHLR 847 (Mich. H.O. 1990).

[72]Inquiry of Minsky, EHLR 211:19 (OSEP 1977).

[73]Inquiry of Anonymous, 18 IDELR 627 (1991). Inquiry of Goodman, 16 EHLR 1317 (OSEP 1990).

[74]Guernsey, *The Education of All Handicapped Children's Act*, § 1983, and § 504 of the Rehabilitation Act of 1973, 68 NEB. L. REV. 564, 589 (1989).

[75]*See, e.g.*, Eldon (MO) R-1 School Dist., EHLR 352:144 (OCR 1986).

[76]Seattle School Dist., 16 EHLR 1091 (Wash. SEA 1990); Thornock v. Boise Indep. School Dist. 1, 767 P2d. 1241 (Idaho 1988).

[77]San Francisco Unified School Dist., EHLR 507:416 (Cal. H.O. 1985).

[78]Kantak v. Liverpool Cent. School Dist., 16 EHLR 643 (W.D.N.Y. 1990).

[79]Board of Educ. v. Weider, 531 N.Y.S.2d 889 (1988).

[80]Goodall v. Stafford County School Bd., 930 F.2d 363 (4th Cir. 1991), *cert. denied*, 112 U.S. 188 (1991); Zobrest v. Catalina Foothills School Dist., EHLR 441:564 (D. Ark. 1989); Philadelphia School Dist., 17 EHLR 265 (Pa. SEA 1990). *But cf.* Thornock v. Boise Indep. School Dist., 767 P.2d 1241 (Idaho 1988), *cert. denied*, 109 S. Ct. 2069 (1989); Anthony Wayne Local School Dist., 16 EHLR 1032 (Ohio SEA 1990) (tuition reimbursement without Establishment Clause challenge). For more detailed analyses, *see* Wagner, *Public Responsibility for Special Education and Related Services in Private Schools*, 20 J. LAW & EDUC. 43 (1991); Mawdsley, *EHA and Parochial Schools: Legal and Policy Considerations*, 51 EDUC. L. REP. 353 (1989).

[81]*See* Cleveland (OH) Pub. School Dist., EHLR 353:307 (OCR 1987); Chattahoochee County Bd. of Educ., EHLR 508:295 (Ga. SEA 1987).

[82]*See* Johnson v. Lancaster-Lebanon Intermediate Unit, 757 F. Supp. 606 (E.D. Pa. 1991); Cleveland (OH) Pub. School Dist., EHLR 353: 307 (OCR 1989); Oakland Unified School Dist., EHLR 507:419 (Cal. SEA 1985).

[83]*See generally* Zirkel, *"SPED/LEP": Special Education for Limited English Proficient Students*, 68 EDUC. L. REP. (1991).

[84]*See In re* Christine F., EHLR 502:304 (Mass. SEA 1981); Old Rochester Regional School Dist., EHLR 502:181 (Mass. SEA 1980).

14
Infectious Diseases

Richard G. Salmon and Dee Bodkins

Introduction

A quiet revolution has occurred in recent years pursuant to public school policies that affect educational services of public school pupils and the employment status of personnel who have become infected with one of several chronic infectious diseases. Prior to the latter 1970s, pupils who contracted chronic infectious diseases often were denied access to educational services while school personnel similarly infected were either terminated or placed on indefinite furloughs. Most persons recognized that school policies that curtailed educational services to infected pupils and suspended employment of personnel were less than compassionate, but such policies were justified on the basis of protecting other children and safeguarding public health. However, federal laws specifically designed to prohibit discrimination against handicapped individuals, coupled subsequently with a series of court decisions, have restricted significantly the ability of local school boards and school administrators to alter either the educational services provided pupils or the employment status of their employees. While it is likely other diseases could be classified as both chronic and infectious, current federal case law has been limited primarily to the following diseases: Tuberculosis (TB),[1] Hepatitis B (HBV),[2] and Acquired Immune Deficiency Syndrome (AIDS).[3]

In several instances, public school pupils and school personnel suffering from one of the above chronic infectious diseases have complained that their educational services or employment status, respectively, have been discontinued or altered significantly due to their illnesses. These pupils and employees have contended that they have become handicapped as a result of their illnesses and are protected by several federal and state constitutional and statutory provisions. Specifically, plaintiffs have based their complaints upon the following: section 504 of the Vocational Rehabilitation Act of 1973;[4] Individuals with Disabilities Education Act;[5] due process and equal protection guarantees of the fourteenth amendment; and appropriate state constitutional and statutory provisions.

When determining whether the actions of local school boards and school administrators concerning pupils and school personnel with chronic infectious diseases were proper, courts have relied extensively upon section 504 of the Vocational Rehabilitation Act of 1973. The provisions of section 504 were patterned after Title VI of the Civil Rights Act of 1964[6] and were designed specifically to prohibit discrimination against handicapped individuals in programs receiving federal fiscal assistance. Detailed regulations were promulgated in 1977 by the then United States Department of Health, Education, and Welfare.[7] This act provides, in part, that, "no otherwise qualified handicapped person...shall, on the basis of handicap, be excluded from participation in, be denied the benefits of, or otherwise be subjected to discrimination under any program or activity receiving Federal financial assistance."[8] A handicapped individual is defined by the Act as a person who has the following: a physical... impairment which substantially limits one or more of [his or her] major life activities, has a record of such an impairment, or is regarded as having such an impairment.[9] The term "physical or mental impairment" is defined as:

(A) any physiological disorder or condition, cosmetic disfigurement, or anatomical loss affecting one or more of the following body systems: neurological; musculoskeletal; special sense organs; respiratory, including speech organs; cardiovascular; reproductive, digestive, genitourinary; hemic and lymphatic; skin, and endocrine; or (B) any mental or psychological disorder, such as mental retardation, organic brain syndrome, emotional or mental illness, and specific learning disabilities.[10]

Additionally, major life activities are defined as functions such as caring for one's self, performing manual tasks, walking, seeing, hearing, speaking, breathing, learning, and working.[11]

Often in conjunction with section 504 of the Vocational Rehabilitation Act of 1973, courts have relied upon the Individuals with Disabilities Education Act (IDEA) to determine the propriety of governmental actions. The primary purpose of the IDEA is to provide to the states federal fiscal assistance to partially fund educational services for the handicapped. Eligibility for federal fiscal assistance is contingent upon implementation and use of an approved state plan. An essential component of the approved state plan is that a free appropriate education, as outlined in individual education plans (IEPs), is provided all handicapped children within the geographical boundaries of the local education agencies (LEAs).[12]

Courts have been asked to determine the validity of governmental actions pursuant to the fourteenth amendment of the United States Constitution. Plaintiffs have alleged that they were deprived of certain property rights absent due process and equal protection of the laws. In at least one case, the plaintiff has asserted that the contested state action violated his right to equal protection of the laws and that strict scrutiny analysis by the court was necessary.[13]

Legal Issues

Alteration of Employee Status

The limits to which local school boards may alter the employment status of their personnel who are suffering with a chronic infectious disease were set clearly by the United States Supreme Court in the landmark case *Arline v. School Board of Nassau County*.[14] In March 1987, the Court held that a contagious disease such as tuberculosis was a handicapping condition under section 504 of the Vocational Rehabilitation Act of 1973. Gene Arline first contracted TB in 1957 at the age of fourteen. Shortly thereafter, the disease went into remission, and in 1966 she was employed as an elementary teacher in Nassau County, Florida. Arline suffered three relapses and after the third was dismissed in 1978. She brought suit in federal district court, which entered judgment for the defendants. Upon appeal, the Eleventh Circuit Court of Appeals reversed and indicated that TB was a contagious disease which constituted a "handicap" within the meaning of the Vocational Rehabilitation Act. *Arline* was remanded for further hearing as to whether risks of infection precluded Arline from being otherwise qualified for her job. The United States Supreme Court granted *certiorari* and affirmed the Eleventh Circuit Court of Appeals. *Arline* provides the following interpretation of "handicapped individual" contained within the Vocational Rehabilitation Act: "Arline...had a physical impairment as that term is defined by the [federal] regulations....This impairment was serious enough to require hospitalization, a fact more than sufficient to establish that one or more of her major life activities were substantially limited by her impairment."[15]

The defendant school district and the Solicitor General of the United States both acknowledged that Arline qualified as a handicapped individual under section 504 but justified her dismissal because of the threat that her relapses of tuberculosis posed a danger to the health of others.[16] The Court was not persuaded and indicated it would be unfair to allow an employer to seize upon the distinction between the effects of a disease on others and effects of a disease on a patient and use that distinction to justify discriminatory treatment.[17]

The Court remanded *Arline* to the district court with specific directions to determine, through individual inquiry, whether Arline was otherwise qualified for the job of elementary school teacher. The Court indicated that the inquiry should include the following:

> [Findings of fact] based on reasonable medical judgments given the state of medical knowledge, about (a) the nature of the risk (how the disease is transmitted), (b) the duration of the risk (how long is the carrier infectious), (c) the severity of the risk (what is the potential harm to third parties), and (d) the probabilities the disease will be transmitted and will cause varying degrees of harm.[18]

The Court also relied upon the *Southeastern Community College v. Davis* case which indicated that "an otherwise qualified person is one who is able to meet all of a program's requirements in spite of his handicap."[19] In the employment setting, the "otherwise qualified person is one who can perform the essential functions of the job" or a different job after "reasonable accommodation" has been made."[20] In order for the accommodation to be judged unreasonable, the Court indicated, "...it either imposes undue financial and administrative burdens...or requires a fundamental alteration in the nature of [the] program.[21]

The Court relied extensively upon expert medical opinion and recommended strongly that lower courts should "defer to the reasonable medical judgments of public health officials."[22] Although the court declined to apply broadly its ruling to those persons infected by AIDS, there is little reason to doubt that a similar ruling would prevail. Upon remand, the district court ruled that Arline was entitled to full back pay, plus benefits. In addition, the court ordered the school district to either reinstate Arline or compensate her at full salary until her scheduled retirement at age 65.[23]

Following *Arline*, the Ninth Circuit Court of Appeals, in *Chalk v. United States District Court Central District of California*,[24] addressed the alteration of the employment status of a classroom teacher who had contracted AIDS. Vincent L. Chalk brought suit against the California Department of Education, alleging that his removal from classroom teaching and his subsequent assignment to administrative duties violated section 504 of the Vocational Rehabilitation Act. Specifically, Chalk charged that he was a handicapped individual under section 504 which prohibited discrimination of otherwise qualified persons. The district court denied Chalk's motion for preliminary injunction, and he appealed. The circuit court issued an order reinstating Chalk to classroom duties holding that "the teacher was not required to disprove every theoretical possibility of harm, and the possibility that Chalk's return to teaching would produce fear and apprehension in parents and pupils was not sufficient grounds to deny preliminary injunction."[25] While the circuit court adhered to *Arline*, it also acknowledged that it was difficult for employers facing the possibility of chronic infectious diseases to reconcile the following objectives: protect other persons; continue the work mission; and accommodate the handicapped and otherwise qualified persons. In order to reconcile these objectives, the court provided the following guidelines:

> A person who poses a significant risk of communicating an infectious disease to others in the workplace will not be otherwise qualified for his or her job if reasonable accommodation will not eliminate that risk. The Act would not require a school board to place a teacher with active, contagious tuberculosis in a classroom with elementary school children.[26]

Alteration of Instructional Service

In *New York State Assoc. for Retarded Children, Inc. v. Carey*,[27] the federal district court addressed the issue of segregating within the public school certain mentally-retarded children who were classified as carriers of HBV. Immediately prior to implementation of a plan to integrate mentally retarded children in special education classes, approximately 50 of them were diagnosed as carriers of HBV and summarily excluded from their public school special education classes. In response to an injunction that prohibited the exclusion of the children identified as carriers of HBV, the school board proposed that these children be reassigned to newly created classes composed entirely of HBV carriers. Although the New York City Health Department supported the plan to isolate the carriers of HBV, the district court disagreed:

> The medical evidence upon which the proposal is based is sparse and fails to demonstrate any causal relationship between the classroom setting and transmission of the virus...the inability of the Board to offer any evidence of even one instance of actual transmission of the virus within the classroom setting, despite the fact that many of these carrier children have been attending public schools for several years.[28]

The court ruled that the segregation of children identified as carriers of HBV violated section 504 of the Vocational Rehabilitation Act, the Education of All Handicapped Children Act, the fourteenth amendment of the United States Constitution, and certain New York statutes.

In *Thomas v. Atascadero Unified School District*,[29] a federal district court held that a child infected with AIDS was both handicapped and otherwise qualified to attend regular kindergarten classes pursuant to section 504 of the Vocational Rehabilitation Act. Five-year-old Ryan Thomas became infected with the AIDS virus as an infant due to a contaminated blood transfusion. Initially, Thomas was admitted to public school kindergarten but later removed after an altercation with one of his classmates. In the skirmish, Thomas bit another child, although no skin was broken. Thomas' parents objected to the offer by the school district to provide "home tutoring" and brought action to require that he be allowed to attend regular kindergarten classes. In weighing the risk of AIDS infection to other children against the potential damage to Thomas by excluding him from school, the Court relied extensively upon the published reports by the United States Center for Disease Control and other medical documents concerning the transmission of the disease.

> The overwhelming weight of medical evidence is that the AIDS virus is not transmitted by human bites, even bites that break the skin. Based upon the abundant medical and scientific evidence before the Court, [Thomas] poses no risk of harm to his classmates and teachers. Any theoretical risk of transmission of the AIDS virus by [Thomas] in connection with his attendance in regular kindergarten class is so remote that it cannot form the basis for any exclusionary action by the School District.[30]

In the highly publicized *Ray v. School District of DeSoto County* case,[31] the federal district court issued an injunction that barred the school district from either segregating or providing homebound instruction to three pupils infected with the AIDS virus. Richard, Robert, and Randy Ray, hemophiliacs, became infected with the AIDS virus as a result of contaminated blood transfusions. Their parents voluntarily notified school authorities that the boys were infected by the AIDS virus. The school district immediately removed the three children from the regular school setting and provided homebound instruction. The parents objected and alleged violations of section 504 of the Vocational Rehabilitation Act, the fourteenth amendment of the United States Constitution, and appropriate state constitutional and statutory provisions. The court acknowledged *Arline* again, relying extensively upon expert advice from the medical profession.

> Extensive and numerous studies have consistently found no apparent risk of HIV-infection by individuals exposed through close, non-sexual contact with AIDS patients. These studies have demonstrated that contacts involving sharing of household items, such as toothbrushes, eating utensils, and baths or toilets, do not lead to HIV-infection. Similarly, there is no evidence that close personal, but non-sexual interaction, such as giving a bath, shaking hands or kissing on the lips, will cause HIV-infection.[32]

Indicating that it was obligated to accept medical science as currently available, the court said decisions cannot be based upon "speculation of what the state of medical science may be in the future, no matter how close that future may be."[33] The court held that irreparable injury was being caused the Ray children by excluding them from the regular school program. "[T]he actual, ongoing injury to [the Ray children]...clearly outweighs the potential harm to others, and the public interest in this case weighs in favor of returning these children to an integrated classroom setting."[34]

In *Kohl v. Woodhaven Learning Center*,[35] the federal district court held that an HBV carrier who had a history of biting and scratching was an otherwise qualified applicant for residential services in a life-skills and living quarters facility. Kohl, a 31-year-old, mentally-retarded and visually-impaired man with behavioral problems, applied for residential and training services in the Woodhaven Learning Center, a private, nonprofit corporation that received federal financial assistance. Kohl was denied admission because he was a carrier of HBV and funds were not available to inoculate the residential staff. The court ruled that Kohl was a handicapped individual within the meaning of section 504 of the Vocational Rehabilitation Act and used the *Arline* test to determine that he was otherwise qualified. The court found that inoculating and screening limited numbers of employees would not have imposed undue financial burden on the defendants and ordered injunctive and declaratory relief. However, upon appeal to the Eighth Circuit Court of Appeals, the case was reversed and remanded.[36] The circuit court ruled that limited inoculation of staff would not eliminate all significant risks, and Kohl could not be reasonably accommodated at Woodhaven. The United States Supreme Court denied *certiorari*.[37]

In *Parents of Child, Code No. 870901W v. Coker*,[38] the district court ruled that a pupil classified as emotionally disabled and a carrier of the HIV virus was entitled to placement in a special education class for the emotionally disturbed. The court based its decision upon the Education for All Handicapped Children Act that created a right to a Free Appropriate Public Education.[39] The placement team considered the totality of the child's condition, including the fact that he had tested HIV positive when the initial placement was made. Later, the child was removed from the emotionally-disturbed setting; subsequently, his parents filed suit. The defendants justified removal of the child on the basis of a state statute regarding contagious diseases. The court denied attempts by one defendant, the Concerned Parents Association, to admit evidence regarding the contagiousness of AIDS or error in the original placement.

> [T]he State of Oklahoma stands in the place of, for example, a group such as the Concerned Parents Association. It would render the administrative procedure established by Congress superfluous to permit such relitigation...because of his emotional disability, this Court need not address the issue of whether AIDS constitutes such a handicap.[40]

The court also noted that when a state accepts federal funds, it accepts limitations or restrictions on state statutes or regulations which conflict with the federal statutes.

In *Robertson v. Granite City Com. Unit School D. 9*,[41] the district court ruled that while a seven-year-old hemophiliac with AIDS was not handicapped within the meaning of the Education of All Handicapped Children Act, he was handicapped pursuant to the Vocational Rehabilitation Act. The court held that the placement of Jason Robertson in a modular classroom violated section 504. Initially, Robertson was enrolled in a homebound program, but upon his mother's request that he be enrolled in a regular classroom, he was transferred to a modular classroom where he was the only pupil. The court found that irreparable harm would result from the continued placement of Robertson in such a setting. "[I]t is difficult... [to] imagine anything more traumatic for a child than going to school and being placed in a classroom by himself, not being allowed to play with other children, and not even allowed to eat with his classmates...."[42]

In *Martinez v. School Board of Hillsborough County*,[43] the district court held that the placement of Eliana Martinez, a six-year-old trainable mentally-handicapped pupil infected with the AIDS virus, in a homebound program was reasonable and appropriate. Martinez, who was incontinent, was classified as TMH, but due to her infection with AIDS, she was enrolled in a homebound program. The court declined to grant an injunction and ruled that "the specific potential harm to others, [and specifically the population of the trainable mentally handicapped (TMH) classroom], outweighs the interests of the plaintiff."[44] However, after the trial, the court found that the placement of Martinez in homebound instruction violated both section 504 of the Vocational Rehabilitation Act and the Education for All Handicapped Children Act. The court acknowledged that the risk of transmittal of the AIDS virus to other children was too great to place Martinez in an unrestricted TMH classroom. The court ruled that a restricted placement "is the appropriate least restrictive environment for Martinez."[45] In an attempt to achieve a balance, the court ordered the school district to construct a separate classroom for Martinez within the confines of the TMH classroom. On appeal, the Eleventh Circuit Court of Appeals vacated the order and remanded the case to the district court.[46] Following the instructions of the circuit court, the district court held that the child with AIDS was otherwise qualified to attend class with other trainable mentally-handicapped children. The court ruled that the overall risk of transmission from all bodily substances, including blood in the saliva, did not raise significantly the risk of infection transmission. The court ordered that Martinez be readmitted to the TMH classroom in order that she may "sit at a desk alongside other mentally-disabled children her age."[47]

The issue of appropriate placement also was addressed in *Doe v. Belleville Public School District No. 118*.[48] Johnny Doe, a six-year-old hemophiliac infected with the AIDS virus, began first grade in School District No. 118. Upon notification that the child was HIV-positive, the school district developed a policy, which, in effect, resulted in his placement with a home tutor. Finding that the student did not suffer from limited strength or lack of vitality or alertness that would interfere with his educational performance, the court indicated that section 504 of the Vocational Rehabilitation Act was applicable and ordered the school district to admit Doe to the regular classroom. In a similar case, *Doe v. Dolton Elementary School District No. 148*,[49] the district court ruled that the removal of a 12-year-old pupil with AIDS from the regular classroom and his subsequent transfer to homebound instruction also violated section 504 of the Vocational Rehabilitation Act. In still another case, *Child v. Spillane*,[50] a child with AIDS was removed from kindergarten in November 1987 when the parent informed the school district that the county health department had recommended that the child be excluded from school pending a review of pertinent medical records. A medical committee was formed to review and evaluate whether the infected child would pose a risk to other students and school employees. Based upon section 504 of the Vocational Rehabilitation Act, a suit was filed requesting that the court order the school district to readmit the infected child. Subsequently, the medical committee informed the school board that the child did not pose a significant risk and recommended readmission. The child was readmitted and action was withdrawn.

Recommendations for Practice

The courts consistently have ruled that public employees and pupils infected with a chronic infectious disease fall within the meaning of "handicapped individuals" under section 504 of the Vocational Rehabilitation Act. In some instances, the IDEA has been used as the basis for litigation. However, in order for the IDEA to apply, a plaintiff would have to show that the illness adversely affects a child's educational performance.[51] Plaintiffs also have based their complaints upon the fourteenth amendment of the United States Constitution and applicable provisions of their respective state constitutions and statutes. The federal case law has been limited primarily to the following chronic infectious diseases: Tuberculosis (TB); Hepatitis B (HBV); and Acquired Immune Deficiency Syndrome (AIDS). Although the leading case, *Arline*, regarding the alteration of employment status of school personnel, dealt with TB, most of the cases concerning pupils have involved AIDS. The following recommendations for administrative practice can be made.

- Prior to the alteration of the status of either employees or pupils, the agency receiving federal financial assistance is obligated to determine whether the individual is "otherwise qualified." An otherwise qualified individual is one who is able to meet all of a program's requirements despite his or her handicap. In the context of employment, an otherwise qualified person is one who can perform "essential functions" of the job in question. When a handicapped individual is unable to perform the essential functions of the job, the court will then determine whether "reasonable accommodation" can be made by the employer. However, the employer will not be required to incur undue financial and administrative burdens or implement a fundamental alteration in the nature of the program in order to comply with reasonable accommodation. The United States Supreme Court, in the landmark *Arline* decision, outlined a procedure to be used by courts in determining whether a handicapped individual was otherwise qualified. In brief, courts are required to conduct individual inquiries based upon reasonable medical opinions concerning risk, duration of risk, severity of the disease, and the probability of transmittal of the disease.

- A series of decisions of the federal judiciary regarding the alteration or discontinuation of instructional services for disabled pupils with chronic infectious diseases consistently have required the public schools to provide a free appropriate public education in the least restrictive environment.[52] Often, the cases have occurred because the children with chronic infectious diseases have been transferred from regular or special education classroom settings to homebound instruction programs. The courts have relied primarily upon medical advice to discount the fears and apprehensions of the communities regarding the contagious nature of AIDS.

- As stated above, children with chronic infectious diseases have to be afforded a free appropriate public education, and as a consequence, must be provided procedural safeguards. This system of procedural safeguards includes notice, an opportunity for the parents or guardian of the person to examine relevant records, an impartial hearing with opportunity for participation by the person's parents or guardian and representation by counsel, and a review procedure.[53]

- Due to the volatile nature of the chronic infectious diseases issue, confidentiality of student records has to be assured. While section 504 of the Vocational Rehabilitation Act contains no provision regarding confidentiality, other federal laws, including the Family Education Rights and Privacy Act,[54] are applicable. In essence, children suffering from a chronic infectious disease have the same right to confidentiality as other children. Access to student files, including medical records, should be restricted to those persons who have a legitimate educational or medical reason to view such information.

References

[1]THE AMERICAN HERITAGE DICTIONARY OF THE ENGLISH LANGUAGE, (2d College Edition), (1985), Tuberculosis (TB) is a communicable disease...caused by a micro-organism (Mycobacterium tuberculosis) and manifesting itself in lesions of the lung, bone, and other parts of the body. See Cowley, Leonard, & Hager, Tuberculosis—A Deadly Return, CXIX(11) NEWSWEEK 52-57 (March, 16, 1992).

[2]Viral Hepatitis B (HBV) is a disease for which there is no known cure...it is of limited communicability, though an increased risk of transmission is generally associated with crowded, often unhygienic conditions found in institutions. It is transmitted primarily by blood-to-

blood contact, by means of transfusion of infected blood, or by use of a contaminated needle. *See* New York State Ass'n v. Carey, 466 F. Supp. 487 (E.D.N.Y. 1979) at 489.

[3] Acquired Immune Deficiency Syndrome (AIDS) is the clinical manifestation of a dysfunction of the human immune system caused by a recently discovered virus....To date there is not a vaccine against or cure for AIDS....The virus is transmitted from one person to another only by infected blood, semen, or vaginal fluids (and possibly, mother milk). Transmission by either semen or blood accounts for virtually all reported cases. *See* Thomas v. Atascadero Unified School Dist., 662 F. Supp. 376 (C.D. Cal. 1987) at 379-380.

[4] Public Law 93-112, 29 U.S.C. § 794.
[5] Public Law 94-142, 20 U.S.C. § 1401 *et seq.*
[6] 42 U.S.C. § 2000d.
[7] 45 C.F.R. § 84.4(a).
[8] *Id.*
[9] 29 U.S.C. § 706(8)(B).
[10] 45 C.F.R. § 84.3(j)(2)(i).
[11] 45 C.F.R. § 84.3(j)(2)(ii).
[12] *Supra.,* note 5.
[13] *See, New York State,* 466 F. Supp. 487 at 504.
[14] 480 U.S. 273 (1987).
[15] 107 S. Ct. 1123 (1984) at 1127.
[16] *Id.* at 1128.
[17] *Id.*
[18] *Id.* at 1131.
[19] 442 U.S. 397 (1979) at 406.
[20] *Arline,* 107 S. Ct. 1123 at 1131.
[21] *Id.*
[22] *Id.*
[23] 692 F. Supp. 1286 (M.D. Fl. 1988).
[24] 840 F.2d 701 (9th Cir. 1988).
[25] *Id.* at 701.
[26] *Id.* at 705.
[27] 466 F. Supp. 487 (E.D.N.Y. 1979).
[28] *Id.* at 499.
[29] 662 F. Supp. 376 (C.D. Ca. 1987).
[30] *Id.* at 380.
[31] 666 F. Supp. 1524 (M.D. Fl. 1987).
[32] *Id.* at 1530, 1531.
[33] *Id.* at 1529.
[34] *Id.* at 1535.
[35] 672 F. Supp. 1226 (W.D. Mo. 1987).
[36] 865 F.2d 930 (8th Cir. 1989).
[37] 493 U.S. 892 (1989).
[38] 676 F. Supp. 1072 (E.D. Ok. 1987).
[39] 34 C.F.R. § 104.33(a).
[40] *Parents of Child,* 676 F. Supp. at 1075.
[41] 684 F. Supp. 1002 (S.D. Ill. 1988).
[42] *Id.* at 1005.
[43] 675 F. Supp. 1574 (M.D. Fl. 1987).
[44] *Id.* at 1582.
[45] 692 F. Supp. 1293 (M.D. Fl. 1988).
[46] 861 F.2d 1502 (11th Cir. 1988).
[47] 711 F. Supp. 1066 (M.D. Fl. 1989).
[48] 672 F. Supp. 342 (S.D. Ill. 1987).
[49] 694 F. Supp. 440 (N.D. Ill. 1988).
[50] 866 F.2d 691 (4th Cir. 1989).
[51] 34 C.F.R. § 300.5(b)(7).
[52] 34 C.F.R. § 104.33(a).
[53] 34 C.F.R. § 104.36.
[54] 29 U.S.C. § 794.

15

Barrier Free Facilities

Ralph D. Mawdsley

Introduction

Establishment and maintenance of barrier free schools were, until 1991, the sole responsibilities of the United States Architectural Transportation Barriers Compliance Board (ATBCB). Created by section 502 of the Handicapped Act,[1] the ATBCB used section 504 of the Vocational Rehabilitation Act[2] to resolve violations of the Architectural Act.[3] The Architectural Barriers Act became the medium for declaring accessibility standards. Most recently, the Americans with Disabilities Act (ADA)[4] has imposed requirements on new construction (effective after January 26, 1993) and on alterations of existing facilities (effective after January 26, 1992).[5] Title II of ADA applies to public schools and Title III to private schools.[6] ADA places responsibility for enforcement of the Act on the Attorney General and the Department of Justice.[7] ADA does not invalidate other federal laws,[8] so the ATBCB can still conduct investigations, hold public hearings, and issue orders to insure compliance with the provisions of the Architectural Barriers Act.[9]

Legal Issues

Section 504 of the Vocational Rehabilitation Act requires that federally assisted programs and activities be readily accessible to and usable by individuals with handicaps; however, ADA requires alteration of existing facilities be made only if the modifications are readily achievable, that is, able to be accomplished easily and without much difficulty or expense.[10] In addition, ADA does not off-set the obligations under other federal or state laws, and state tort claims conferring greater remedies are clearly not preempted by ADA.[11] In all new construction where the first occupancy occurs after January 26, 1993, compliance with the standards in ADA "is required to the full extent that it is not structurally impracticable." If accessibility is not possible for persons with certain disabilities (e.g., those who use wheelchairs) accessibility must be assured for those with other disabilities (e.g., those with crutches and hearing and vision impairments).[12]

ADA introduces two new concepts regarding alterations of existing facilities: "primary function" and "path of travel." A primary function is a major activity for which the facility is intended; a path of travel is an unobstructed pedestrian passage from the altered area to an entrance or exit.[13]

> An alteration that affects or could affect the usability of or access to an area of a facility that contains a primary function shall be made so as to ensure that, to the maximum extent feasible, the path of travel to the altered area and the restrooms, telephones, and drinking fountains serving the altered area, are readily accessible to and usable by individuals with disabilities, including wheelchairs, unless the cost and scope of such alterations is disproportionate to the cost of the overall alteration.[14]

Where the cost of making a path of travel fully accessible to an altered area is disproportionate, ADA has established the order of priority for elements to be provided: an accessible entrance; an accessible route to the altered area; at least one accessible restroom for each sex or a single unisex restroom; accessible telephones; accessible drinking fountains; and when possible, additional accessible elements such as parking, storage, and alarms.[15]

Both ADA and the Architectural Barriers Act reference the standards published by the American National Standards Institute (ANSI). The ANSI standards are the basis for the Uniform Federal Accessibility Standards (UFAS) published in the Federal Register on August 7, 1984.[16] ANSI is a private, national organization which has published recommendations on a wide range of subjects. The most recent ANSI standards for barrier-free design are ANSI A117.1-1987 and are entitled "American National Standards for Buildings and Facilities—Providing Accessibility and Usability for Physically Handicapped People."[17] ADA has published a complete set of standards and, with only a relatively few exceptions, the ADA standards are the same as those of ANSI.[18] The exceptions deal with accessibility in new and altered construction for such items as parking places, toilets, telephones, and assembly areas.[19] To the extent that the ADA specifications are different from ANSI, ADA standards will prevail.

Specifications

Except for the new ADA regulation changes to ANSI, which do not become effective until 1992 or 1993, ANSI publication A117.1-

1986 is still the single most important and complete document of facility accessibility, in part because the ADA regulations follow ANSI and in part because ANSI minimum guidelines are referenced by most state building codes.[20] The most recent ANSI publication has essentially achieved uniformity with UFAS, although ANSI "is basically a resource for design specifications and leaves to the enforcing agency the application of criteria such as where, when, and to what extent such specifications will apply."[21] The purpose of the ANSI standards is to enable "persons with disabilities to achieve independence...[so they] can live, study, work, and participate in other community activities, fully developing their human potential...."[22] ANSI A117.1-1986 is the collaborative effort of representatives from 53 different organizations as diverse as the American Association of Retired Persons, American Foundation for the Blind, American Hotel/Motel Association, American Society of Plumbing Engineers, Builders Hardware Manufacturers Association, National Conference of States on Building Codes and Standards, National Restaurant Association and nine different agencies and cabinet-level departments.[23]

ANSI standards have been designed to deal with a wide range of physical disabilities such as, "the inability to walk, difficulty walking, reliance on walking aids, blindness and visual impairment, deafness and hearing impairment, incoordination, reaching and manipulation disabilities, lack of stamina, difficulty interpreting and reacting to sensory information and extremes of physical size."[24] The specifications remain the same "whether they are applied to new construction, remodeling alteration or rehabilitation."[25] ANSI 117.1-1986 is intended to be used in conjunction with other American National Standards: Safety Code for Elevators and Escalators,[26] Power Operated Pedestrian Doors,[27] and Power Assist and Low Energy Operated Doors.[28] A complete listing of all topics addressed in graphics and dimensions in ANSI 117.1-1986 (as well as in the ADA regulations) reveals that the concern of accessibility is one of function rather than of location such as school, hotel, or manufacturing plant.[29] Other topics include space allowances and reach ranges (e.g., wheel chair turning space, forward reach, side reach); accessible route (e.g., passing space, headroom, slope, egress); protruding objects; ground and floor surfaces; parking spaces and passenger loading zones; curb ramps; stairs; elevators; platform lifts; windows; doors; entrances; drinking fountains and water coolers; water closets; toilet stalls; urinals; lavatories; sinks and mirrors; bathtubs; shower stalls; storage; grab bars and tub and shower seats; control and operating mechanisms; alarms and detectable warnings; signage; telephones; seating, tables, and work surfaces; auditorium and assembly areas; and dwelling units.

In addition, states can and have made valuable contributions to ANSI standards.[30] Modification of the standards to suit children's dimensions is one area of interest. Specifications in ANSI A117.1-1986 "are based upon adult dimensions and anthropomorphics,"[31] but federal regulation permits modifications "concerning the age groups of the individuals who will use the buildings or equipment."[32] The areas of UFAS affected by the standards for children are: space allowance and reach range of 20 inches; parking and passenger loading zones with the loading zones protected from weather; ramps with handrails 26 to 28 inches above surface; stairs with handrails the same height as ramps; elevators with changes in the distance of hall call buttons, car controls, and emergency communications above the floor; doors with hardware 36 inches above the floor; drinking fountains and water coolers with the spout no more than 30 inches above the floor; water closets with varying distances for grab bars, toilet seats, flush controls and dispensers; urinals placed 32 inches above the floor; lavatories and mirrors including sinks and mirrors no more than 30 inches above the floor; shower stalls with modified height of seats and controls; storage including shelves and hooks placed a maximum of 36 inches above the floor; signs placed 40 inches above the floor; telephones at a 36-inch maximum above the floor; seating, tables, and work surfaces with varying heights for chairs, knee clearance and work surfaces; restaurants and cafeterias with a percentage of fixed seating or tables for handicapped and height of tray slides; libraries with a maximum reach of 36 inches for card catalogs, magazine displays, dictionary stands and reference stacks; locker rooms and gymnasium lockers with locker shelves and hooks a maximum of 26 inches above the floor and lockers with minimum 28-inch openings; classrooms including wall-mounted objects like pencil sharpeners, light switches, and blackboards having a centerline maximum height of 36 inches above the floor.[33]

Enforcement

The ADA provides a private cause of action as well as investigations by the Department of Justice and suits by the Attorney General.[34] Even with enforcement of the rights of the disabled under ADA, the most significant impact on accessibility will continue, for the near future, to come from enforcement of section 504 of the Vocational Rehabilitation Act.[35] However, since ADA is based on the Interstate Commerce power[36] while section 504 applies only to institutions, organizations, or persons receiving federal assistance,[37] ADA will eventually become a major enforcement device for private institutions that are not currently receiving federal assistance.[38] Both section 504 and ADA have broad provisions prohibiting denial of the enjoyment of benefits, goods, services, privileges, advantages, or accommodations.[39]

In program accessibility, section 504 distinguishes between existing facilities and new construction. Existing facilities can be "viewed in [their] entirety...[as to whether they are] readily accessible to and usable by handicapped persons."[40] It is not necessary for a recipient "to make each of its existing facilities or every part of a facility accessible to and usable by handicapped persons."[41] Structural changes are not required to existing facilities "where other methods are effective in achieving compliance...."[42] In new construction, "[e]ach new facility constructed by, on behalf of, or for the use of a recipient shall be designed and constructed in such a manner that the facility is readily accessible to and usable by handicapped persons...."[43] Where alterations are made to existing facilities, they shall "to the maximum extent feasible, be made in an accessible manner."[44] All design, construction, or alteration of new facilities must conform to ANSI A117.1-1986.

As indicated earlier, ADA imposes responsibilities on anyone in interstate commerce to make alterations to existing facilities that make them readily accessible to and usable by individuals with disabilities.

> Alterations include, but are not limited to, remodeling, renovation, rehabilitation, reconstruction, historic restoration, changes or rearrangement in structural parts or elements, and changes or rearrangement in the plan configuration of walls and full-height partitions. Normal maintenance, reroofing, painting or wallpapering, asbestos removal, or changes to mechanical and electrical systems are not alterations unless they affect the usability of the building or facility.[45]

Employee complaints of any form of handicap discrimination are handled by the Equal Employment Opportunity Commission (EEOC) and can result in litigation if a negotiated settlement is not possible.[46] Under ADA, the Department of Justice can also investigate discrimination.[47] In the case of discrimination in accessibility for students or employees under the Architectural Barriers Act, investigations are handled by the ATBCB which can hold administrative hearings and issue compliance orders as well as withhold or suspend federal funds.[48]

Since all states now have barrier-free legislation, the responsibility for assuring accessibility has been a state and local matter. Enforcement of handicapped accessibility can include review of all building designs by state building officials,[49] refusal to issue a certificate of occupancy,[50] and disciplinary actions against licensed architects who fail to incorporate handicapped access into building design.[51] Unfortunately, state enforcement of accessibility requirements can be erratic, inconsistent, and perhaps even non-existent.[52] More viable remedies for the disadvantaged physically disabled would be filing a complaint with the state's Human Rights Commission or filing a lawsuit seeking injunctive relief to compel compliance, damages, and attorneys' fees.[53] If the state Human Rights Commission is not effective in addressing complaints, other state remedies may be curtailed or be illusory if the Human Rights Act prohibits private causes of action to enforce the statute.[54]

In addition to state and federal standards, some larger cities may also have separate accessibility guidelines. A state may leave enforcement to local officials,[55] a practice which can create problems of enforcement by those without experience or expertise[56] or with differing interpretations of identical code sections.[57] However, if the facility has been built with federal funds, another and perhaps better option would be to file a complaint with the ATBCB.[58]

Recommendations for Practice

School officials are well advised to check their statewide building code, as well as the ADA, regarding handicap accessibility before altering existing facilities or constructing new ones. Alarmist fears of excessive escalation in building costs to achieve accessibility have largely been just that—unsubstantiated fears.[59] School officials need to examine building codes carefully for key elements to determine whether:

- the scope of renovations requires compliance with accessibility,
- the standard for accessibility has been published,
- the district has an established approval process for determining compliance with accessibility,
- a variance is necessary for intended alterations or new construction,
- employees are adequately instructed in the importance of maintaining "path of travel" under the ADA.

References

[1] 29 U.S.C. § 792(b)(1).

[2] 29 U.S.C. § 794.

[3] 42 U.S.C. §§ 4151-4171. *See* Goldman, *Architectural Barriers: A Perspective on Progress*, 5 W. NEW ENG. L. REV. 466 (1983) for a discussion of cases under the Act.

[4] 42 U.S.C. §§ 12101-12213.

[5] 56 Fed. Reg. 35599-35600, §§ 36.401, 402, (July 26, 1991).

[6] Title II (42 U.S.C §§ 12131-12150) prohibits discrimination on the basis of disability by "any department, agency, special purpose district, or other instrumentality of a State, States or local government." 42 U.S.C. § 12131 (1). title III (42 U.S.C §§ 12181-12189) prohibits discrimination on the basis of disability "in the full and equal enjoyment of the goods, services, facilities, privileges, advantages or accommodations of any place of public accommodation by any person who owns, leases (or leases to), or operates a place of public accommodation." 42 U.S.C. § 12182(a).

[7] 56 Fed. Reg. at §§ 35602-35603 (§§ 36.501-503).

[8] *Id.* at § 36.103(b).

[9] 29 U.S.C. §§ 792(d)(1) and 792(e)(2) and (3).

[10] 56 Fed. Reg. at §§ 35546-47.

[11] *Id.* at § 35547.

[12] *Id.* at 3559-3560 § 36.401(a), (c)(2) and (3)).

[13] *Id.* at 35600 § 36.403(b) and (e)).

[14] *Id.*, § 36.403(a).

[15] *Id.* at 35601 § 36.403 (g).

[16] 14 C.F.R. § 10.1-10.603.

[17] 49 Fed. Reg. 31528-31617, Aug. 7, 1984.

[18] 56 Fed. Reg. at 35607.

[19] ADA Accessibility Guidelines For Buildings and Facilities, §§ 4.1.1 through 4.1.7.

[20] *See* note, *Access to Buildings and Equal Employment Opportunities for the Disabled: A Survey of State Statutes*, 50 TENN. L.Q. 1067 (1977).

[21] American National Standard for Buildings and Facilities—Providing Accessibility and Usability for Physically Handicapped People 3 (1986).

[22] *Id.*

[23] For complete list *see id.* at 4.

[24] *Id.* at 11.

[25] *Id.* at 12.

[26] ANSI/ASME A17.1-1984.

[27] ANSI/BHMA A156.10-1985.

[28] ANSI/BHMA A156.19-1984.

[29] ADA Regulations A.5 through A.10 are different from ANSI A117.1 in their entirety and address the following areas: Restaurants and Cafeterias, Medical Care Facilities, Business and Mercantile, Libraries, Accessible Transient Lodging and Transportation Facilities. 56 Fed. Reg. at 35690 *et seq.*

[30] ADA Regulations are clear that Congress did not intend to displace any of the rights or remedies provided by federal or state law that provide greater or equal protection to individuals with disabilities. 56 Fed. Reg. 35593 (§ 36.103), July 26, 1991.

[31] Providing Accessibility, at 12.

[32] 24 C.F.R. § 304.50.

[33] OSEP-86-14, Recommendations For Accessibility to Serve Physically Handicapped Children In Elementary Schools 2-23.

[34] 56 Fed. Reg. at 35602 (§ 36.501-508).

[35] 28 C.F.R. § 41.1. Executive Order 12250, which had empowered the Justice Department to coordinate the implementation of § 504 along with Title VI and Title IX, has probably been merged into ADA.

[36] *See* 56 Fed. Reg. 35593 (§ 36.104-Definitions), July 26, 1991.

[37] 28 C.F.R. at § 41.3(d).

[38] 56 Fed. Reg. at 35554. "Private schools, including elementary and secondary schools, are covered by the rule as places of public accommodation."

[39] 28 C.F.R. § 41.3(d); 56 Fed. Reg. 35595 (§§ 36.201, 36.202), July 26, 1991.

[40] 28 C.F.R. § 45.521(a).

[41] *Id.*

[42]*Id.* at § 42.531(b). For example, in an older multi-story building it is not necessary to install an elevator if the entire program is available on the first floor. 28 C.F.R. §§ 41-56, 41.58; 45 C.F.R. § 4.23. ADA has an elevator exemption for any altered facility that has less than three stories. 56 Fed. Reg. 35601 (§ 36.404), July 26, 1991.

[43]28 C.F.R. § 45.522(a).

[44]*Id.*

[45]56 Fed. Reg. at 35600 [§ 36.402(b)].

[46]28 C.F.R. §§ 46.601-42.613. Remedies can include damages, injunctive relief, and attorneys' fees. 29 U.S.C. § 794a; 42 U.S.C. § 2000e-5(f)-(k).

[47]56 Fed. Reg. at § 36.501-505. Remedies can include injunctive relief, other equitable relief, and damages.

[48]*See* 29 U.S.C. § 792(d).

[49]*See* Ohio Rev. Code Ann. § 378.111.

[50]*See* Tex. Civ. Stat. Ann. art. 601b. *See* Granny's Cottage v. Town of Occuquan, 352 S.E.2d 10 (Va. Ct. App. 1987) (whenever a part of a building is enlarged, extended or altered in Virginia, the Uniform Statewide Building Code prohibits occupancy until a certificate of use and occupancy has been issued).

[51]*See* Goldman, *supra* note 3 at 480, citing to memorandum from Dan Wooldridge, President, California Board of Architectural Examiners, to licensed architects.

[52]*See generally*, White, *Washington State's Barrier-Free Code: Still Misunderstood After All These Years*, 20 GONZAGA L. REV. 229 (1984-85). *See also*, R. BURGDORF, THE LEGAL RIGHTS OF HANDICAPPED PERSONS, 465 (1980) (local enforcement may be in the hands of persons possessing limited or no experience in the fields of architectural barriers and with persons with handicaps).

[53]For an explanation of the State of Washington's experience, *see* White, at 243-44.

[54]*See* Code of Virginia, § 2.1-725 (prohibits private causes of action and tort actions "instituted instead of or in addition to the current statutory actions for unlawful discrimination.") *Cf.* 56 Fed. Reg. at 35602 (§ 36.501) where ADA expressly provides for private causes of action.

[55]*See* N.Y. Pub. Bldgs. Law § 52.

[56]*See* White and Burgdorf, *supra* note 52.

[57]*See* White, *supra* note 52, at 242.

[58]Architectural Barriers Act of 1968, 42 U.S.C. §§ 4151-4157 (1981); 36 C.F.R. § 1190.1-240(1980). Rehabilitation Act of 1973, 29 U.S.C. §§ 791-796 (1982); 34 C.F.R. §§ 104.21-104.30(1984).

[59]*See* Goldman, *supra* note 3 at 488-6; White, *supra* note 52 at 233.

Teachers And The Law

16

Censorship And Academic Freedom

Floyd G. Delon

Introduction

Censorship, refers to the suppression of teachers' speech and to the disciplinary action against the teachers resulting from their exercise of free speech or other constitutionally protected conduct. The extensive case law on censorship is applicable to the speech of all public employees, not just to teachers. Although the Supreme Court has rendered a series of landmark decisions on this issue over the past four decades, disputes continue to rise concerning both teacher and student first amendment protections against censorship.

The concept of academic freedom originated at the university level and is more often associated with the professor's role rather than that of the primary and secondary school teacher. While, initially, the term was used to describe the professor's right to decide what should be taught, through the years the term has taken on broader meanings. Today, even at the university level, different views exist as to its nature and even more so concerning its legal status. While some legal scholars and many academicians adhere to a position that academic freedom is an "inalienable" right of the professor or teacher to select both content and method of instruction free of any interference, others deny that academic freedom has any sort of independent existence beyond the first amendment rights possessed by all citizens.

Legal Issues

United States Supreme Court Decisions

The Court's first recognition of academic freedom came in the 1950s and 1960s cases resulting from attempts to rid the schools of suspected Communist influences.[1] It was not until 1968, in *Pickering v. Board of Education*,[2] that the Court ruled that teacher speech in the form of a letter to a newspaper was entitled to first amendment protection. The Court held that the teacher cannot be discharged or otherwise punished for speaking out on issues of "public" concern. The following year, in *Tinker v. Des Moines*, the Court proclaimed that neither students nor teachers "shed their constitutional rights to freedom of expression at the schoolhouse gate" and declared that interference with those rights could be justified only on the basis of "substantial and material" disruption.[3] In *Mt. Healthy City School District v. Doyle*,[4] the Court recognized that other legitimate reasons could exist for the disciplining of teachers who are at the same time exercising their constitutional rights. This 1977 decision established the approach for deciding such cases: the teacher has the burden of showing that constitutionally-protected conduct was involved and that this conduct was a motivating factor in the teacher's discharge or in other disciplinary action against him or her. Assuming that the teacher successfully makes that showing, the burden shifts to the school officials to prove that they would have followed the same course of action in the absence of the protected conduct. On the heels of that decision, the Court made it clear that speech of public concern is protected speech even though it may be expressed privately by the employee to the supervisor.[5] In 1983, the Court reinforced the 1968 *Pickering* standard by upholding the employer's right to dismiss an employee whose speech was of private or personal concern rather than public concern.[6]

Although the most recent Supreme Court decisions dealing with speech in public schools pertain to students' speech, they have definite implications for teachers' speech within the context most likely to be associated with academic freedom. These decisions take on added importance because of the change in philosophical orientation of the Court's majority that occurred during the last five years. In its 1986 decision, *Bethel School District No. 403 v. Fraser*,[7] the Court found no first amendment protection for obscene or vulgar speech. Two years later, the Court upheld the authority of school officials to control the curriculum in *Hazelwood School District v. Kuhlmeier*[8] when it permitted administrators to delete objectionable articles from the school newspaper.

Recent Lower Court Decisions

In light of the pattern represented by the Supreme Court decisions, one would anticipate that the lower courts have become more supportive of school officials in disputes with teachers stemming from the choice of instructional materials and methods. There are exceptions as illustrated by decisions of two federal circuit courts but these decisions predate *Bethel* and *Hazelwood*. In a 1985 case before the Sixth Circuit Court of Appeals, a teacher brought an action after being discharged because of parental complaints concerning his teaching of life sciences classes.[9] The complaints focused on the textbook and films used in the class. Although evidence indicated that the school board had approved the textbook and the principal had approved his teaching methods, he was suspended and issued a letter of reprimand. The appellate court, upholding the district court ruling, found that the board had infringed the teacher's first amendment rights and that his "exercise of 'academic freedom' had followed rather than violated his superior's instruction." The court sustained a $321,000 damage award.[10]

During this same year, the First Circuit Court of Appeals also held for a teacher who claimed that the principal and superintendent had retaliated for her exercise of first amendment rights.[11] The conduct that created the controversy consisted of the teacher's filing several grievances under the union contract, counseling two students to file appeals of discipline imposed on them, challenging the superintendent's decision to cut back the high school reading program in a heavily attended board meeting, and criticism of his conduct in the meeting in a letter to the editor published in the local newspaper. According to the teacher's complaint, the retaliation occurred in the form of an "unlawful and unjustified termination." Even though the teacher sent an untrue note to another teacher requesting that a student be excused to take a test (the student instead left school without permission), and the teacher had her certificate revoked to avoid an unwanted assignment, the court found that the evidence was sufficient to support the jury's finding of retaliation. The damages of $5,036 compensatory damages and $39,000 punitive damages against the superintendent and $5,036 compensatory and $26,000 punitive damages against the principal stood.

At the same time, teachers were unsuccessful in state courts in asserting a protected right to choose instructional materials and methods when their choices conflict with those of the administrators. The Alaska Supreme Court upheld the dismissal of a teacher who violated a school policy requiring administrative approval of supplementary materials used in classes.[12] The materials in question included a book on gay rights. The court stated that the first amendment does not "eliminate the school board's right to control the curriculum."[13]

The dispute in the other case[14] centered on a symposium arranged by a teacher following the drowning of a homosexual by three high school students. This symposium, referred to as "tolerance day," included a presentation by a lesbian. After strong negative reaction by the community and threats of disruption, the school board cancelled the meeting. The teacher who had planned the symposium brought legal action claiming that the board action violated his right to academic freedom under the first amendment. In rejecting this claim, the court stated: "However broad the protections of academic freedom may be, they do not permit a teacher to insist upon a given curriculum for the whole school where he teaches."[15]

In 1987, the Sixth Circuit Court of Appeals refused to overturn the dismissal of a teacher who had shown an "R" rated video tape to high school students.[16] The court's majority, applying the *Mt. Healthy* approach, found that the showing of the film was not "expressive or communicative" therefore unprotected by the first amendment. In an opinion concurring with the outcome, the judge relied on *Bethel*, pointing out the vulgar content of the tape which was shown to a captive audience justified the teacher's dismissal.

The Third Circuit Court of Appeals reviewed a very complicated case in which a teacher sought an injunction to prevent school officials from banning a teaching methodology she favored and barring them from retaliating against her for using and advocating the method.[17] Although the appellate court agreed with the lower court's ruling that the teacher had no academic freedom that would allow her to choose classroom management techniques, it pointed out that if the teacher were punished for her advocacy of the methodology outside the school, her first amendment rights would be violated.

The most recent decision on academic freedom and the censorship of elementary and secondary school teachers' speech was handed down by the Tenth Circuit Court of Appeals in 1991.[18] The teacher commented in a ninth grade government class that the quality of the school had declined since 1967. When asked for examples, he mentioned that today more pop cans were lying around and that discipline was better in 1967. He added: "I don't think in 1967 you would have seen two students making out on the tennis court."[19] This statement, based on a rumor the teacher had heard, resulted in complaints by the alleged participants to the principal. After investigating the incident and meeting with the teacher, the principal placed the teacher on a four-day paid administrative leave and placed a letter of reprimand in his file. The teacher filed suit charging that the punishment "chilled" his free speech rights and violated his academic freedom. Beginning with the first step of the *Mt. Healthy* analysis, the court decided that the teacher's comments were not constitutionally protected. Relying on *Hazelwood*, the court reasoned that the comments were "school sponsored expression" in a nonpublic forum;[20] therefore, school officials need only show "a legitimate pedagogical interest" in controlling the teacher's speech. The court upheld the school officials because: a teacher may not use his position to "confirm an unsubstantiated rumor," a teacher must "exhibit professionalism and sound judgment," and teachers should not "make statements about students that embarrass those students among their peers."[21] Thus, it was unnecessary for the court to go to the next step of the *Mt. Healthy* analysis. Lastly, in rejecting the teacher's other claim, the court observed: "[T]he caselaw does not support [his] position that a secondary school teacher has a constitutional right to academic freedom."[22]

Recommendations For Practice

Any attempt by principals to censor teachers' speech carries with it the risk of a lawsuit and the possibility of an assessment of damages should the principal lose. Principals should know and respect the teachers' rights. They should approach personnel problems in a spirit of fairness and attempt to resolve them by doing what is in the best interest of the students. Finally, they should recognize potential legal problems and act under the guidance of legal counsel before, not after, such problems develop.

The lessons of the cases reviewed serve as the basis for the suggestions that follow:

- Be aware that outside of the classroom a teacher has a first amendment right to voice opinions about matters of public concern even though those views may be controversial and unpopular. The only justification for interfering with or punishing the teacher for such speech is material and substantial disruption of the educational process.
- Exercise extreme caution when recommending the release of inferior or undesirable teachers who may at the same time engage in protected speech or other protected conduct. The evidence documenting the legitimate reasons for the school's action must be strong enough to convince a jury that those reasons alone would result in the action against the teacher.
- Do not base recommendations for dismissal or other disciplinary action on statements about matters of public concern that a teacher makes in a private conference because these, too, are protected speech.
- If the teacher is to be disciplined for what he or she says in the classroom or for materials or methods he or she may use,

make sure that the school has and can express some legitimate pedagogical reason, i.e., some valid educational reason for this action.

Changes in personnel on the courts from the Supreme Court down have tended to place school administrators in a stronger position with respect to their control of school operations. Furthermore, the weight of judicial opinion continues to build that academic freedom to decide the content of the curriculum and the method of instruction is not a right of elementary and secondary school teachers. Nonetheless, few would question the desirability of teacher involvement in such determinations and communication between principal and teacher about what is taught and how it is taught is essential.

References

[1] *See, e.g,* Keyishian v. Board of Regents of Univ. of State of N.Y., 385 U.S. 589 (1967).
[2] 391 U.S. 563 (1968).
[3] 393 U.S. 503 (1969).
[4] 429 U.S. 274 (1977).
[5] Givhan v. Western Line Consol. School Dist., 439 U.S. 410 (1979).
[6] Connick v. Myers, 461 U.S. 138 (1983).
[7] 478 U.S. 675 (1986).
[8] 484 U.S. 260 (1988).
[9] Stachura v. Truszkowski, 763 F.2d 211 (6th Cir. 1985).
[10] *Id.* at 215.
[11] Fishman v. Clancy, 763 F.2d 485 (1st Cir. 1985).
[12] Fisher v. Fairbanks North Star Borough School Dist., 704 P.2d 213 (Alaska 1985).
[13] *Id.* at 217.
[14] Solmitz v. Maine School Administrative Dist. No. 59, 495 A.2d 812 (Me. 1985).
[15] *Id,* at 817.
[16] Fowler v. Board of Educ. of Lincoln County, Ky., 819 F.2d 657 (6th Cir. 1987).
[17] Bradley v. Pittsburgh Bd. of Educ., 910 F.2d 1172 (3d Cir. 1990).
[18] Miles v. Denver Pub. Schools, 944 F.2d 773 (10th Cir. 1991).
[19] *Id.* at 774.
[20] *Id.* at 776. The court observed in this regard that "[a] podium before a captive audience of public school children is decisively different from a street corner soapbox."
[21] *Id.* at 778.
[22] *Id.* at 779.

17

Sexual Harassment in the Workplace

M. David Alexander and Mary F. Hughes

Introduction

Sexual harassment was raised to national prominence during the Senate confirmation hearings for United States Supreme Court nominee Clarence Thomas when Anita Hill, a law professor from the University of Oklahoma and a former employee under Thomas, testified of alleged acts of sexual harassment by Thomas.[1] Before the Thomas nomination, the law limited the damages that victims could collect in sexual harassment cases to basically equitable relief which included back pay and attorney fees. The law did not allow for punitive damages or other substantial monetary relief. On November 21, 1991, one month after the confirmation hearings, the United States Congress passed Public Law 102-166, the 1991 Civil Rights Act, which included the rights of sexual discrimination victims to sue for damages ranging from $50,000 for companies with 100 or fewer workers to $300,000 for employers with more than 500 workers.

Legal Issues

Despite the clarity of the legal language, sexual harassment is not easily defined and its incidence difficult to measure. It may range from verbal innuendo to an overt act, and the definition must be broad enough to encompass the diversity of behavior.[2] Starting in the 1970s,[3] litigation and the feminist movement prompted various studies including Catherine MacKinnon's book, *Sexual Harassment of Working Women* and because of such works sexual harassment has been recognized as a serious problem within the workplace.[4] It is uniformly cast as a gender issue, since the overwhelming majority of cases involve female workers being harassed by male colleagues and supervisors.[5] Sexual harassment or sexual contact with students in elementary and secondary education generally has been handled legally through child abuse statutes[6] and/or teacher dismissal statutes.

Title VII

Employees are protected from sexual harassment in the workplace by Title VII of the Civil Rights Act of 1964 and under the new Civil Rights Act of 1991 which amends the Civil Rights Act of 1964, strengthens the Federal Civil Rights Laws, and provides for damages in cases of intentional employment discrimination. Title VII makes it "an unlawful employment practice for an employer...to discriminate against any individual with respect to his compensation, terms, conditions or privileges of employment, because of such individual's race, color, religion, sex, or national origin."[7] Court cases concerning sex discrimination in the 1970s started recognizing sexual harassment. But it was not until 1980 that the Equal Employment Opportunity Commission (EEOC) promulgated regulations prohibiting sexual harassment. These regulations state:

> Unwelcome sexual advances, requests for sexual favors, and other verbal or physical conduct of a sexual nature constitute harassment when (1) submission to such conduct is made explicitly or implicitly a term or condition of an individual's employment, (2) submission to or rejection of such conduct by an individual is used as a basis for employment decisions affecting such individual, (3) such conduct has the purpose or effect of unreasonably interfering with an individual's work performance or creating an intimidating, hostile, or offensive working environment.[8]

Following the EEOC guidelines of 1980, there are two types of sexual harassment, *quid pro quo* and *non quid pro quo*. The United States Supreme Court in *Meritor Savings Bank, FSB v. Vinson*,[9] the leading case on sexual harassment, stated:

> [T]he guidelines provide that sexual conduct constitutes prohibited "sexual harassment," whether or not it is directly linked to the grant or denial of an economic *quid pro quo*, where such conduct has the purpose or effect of unreasonably interfering with an individual's work performance or creating an intimidating, hostile, or offensive working environment *[non quid pro quo].*[10]

The Eleventh Circuit Court of Appeals in *Henson v. Dundee* when speaking of a hostile or abusive work environment stated "[s]exual harassment which creates a hostile or offensive environment for members of one sex is every bit the arbitrary barrier to sexual equality at the workplace that racial harassment is to racial equality."[11] The EEOC guidelines further state that an employer is held responsible "for its acts and those of its agents and supervisory employees with respect to sexual harassment regardless of whether the specific acts complained of were authorized or even forbidden by the employer and regardless of whether the employer knew or should have known of their occurrence."[12] Also, an employer is held responsible for acts of sexual harassment between fellow employees where the employer "knows or should have known of the conduct, unless it can show that it took immediate and appropriate corrective action."[13]

In *Meritor Savings Bank, FSB v. Vinson*,[14] Michelle Vinson, who was an employee of the bank, was supervised by Sidney Taylor. Vinson was promoted from teller-trainee to assistant branch manager in four years with the advancements based on merit. Shortly after Vinson was employed, Taylor made sexual advances toward her and out of fear of losing her job, Vinson consented to having sexual intercourse with Taylor. They engaged in sexual intercourse approximately 40 to 50 times over the next four years. In September, Vinson told Taylor she was taking indefinite sick leave and subsequently in November was discharged for excessive use of leave.

The Supreme Court upheld the EEOC guidelines and emphasized the hostile environment concept. Taylor claimed that Vinson's participation had been voluntary, but the Court ruled that the concept of voluntary participation could not be used as a defense if the sexual advances were unwelcome. The Court said in determining whether sexual advances were unwelcome, "correct inquiry was whether the bank employee, by her conduct, indicated that sexual advances were unwelcome, not whether her actual participation in sexual intercourse was voluntary."[15]

Robinson v. Jacksonville Shipyards, Inc.[16] listed five elements which comprise a claim of sexual discrimination based on the existence of a hostile work environment. They are: plaintiff belongs to a protected category; plaintiff was subject to unwelcome sexual harassment; the harassment complained of was based on sex; the harassment complained of affected a term, condition, or privilege of employment; and *respondeat superior*, that is, defendants knew or should have known of harassment and failed to take prompt, effective remedial action. The third element imposes a requirement that Robinson [the plaintiff] "must show that but for the fact of her sex, she would not have been the object of harassment."[17] Additionally, the third element describes behavior that creates a barrier to the progress of women in the workplace because it conveys the message that they do not belong and that they are welcome in the workplace only if they will subvert their identities to the sexual stereotypes prevalent in that environment.[18]

The court also stated that individual liability attaches, if at all to the generals, not their soldiers when following policies established by their superiors and that nominal damages are available where actual loss is not proven. Lois Robinson, a female welder of Jacksonville Shipyard, Inc. (a federal contractor) was awarded court costs, attorney fees, and nominal damages of $1.00 when she complained of a sexually hostile, intimidating work environment which included pictures of women in various stages of undress and sexually suggestive or submissive poses and remarks were made by male employees and supervisors which demeaned women. The Shipyard was ordered to adopt, implement, and enforce a policy and procedures for the prevention and control of sexual harassment including education and training.

In a public school case, a high school female administrator brought action against the principal and the school district under Title VII and section 1983 alleging sexual discrimination and due process violations.[19] The judge stated in this case, "She alleges sexual discrimination and due process violations, but what she really wants is to make others pay for her mistakes. She will not succeed here."[20] The court made the following observations:

> The complaint contains allegations that, after the consensual relationship between Dr. Miller and Ms. Keppler ended, Dr. Miller subjected Ms. Keppler to "unwelcome sexual harassment, advances, and requests for sexual favors." This suggests an hostile environment claim. The complaint, however, then goes on to allege that, as a result of Ms. Keppler's refusals to comply with Dr. Miller's requests for sexual relations, Dr. Miller engaged in a campaign to have Ms. Keppler removed from her position as Director of Curriculum, a campaign that ended in success when the Board relied on his complaints about Ms. Keppler and terminated her administrative position. These allegations indicate that Ms. Keppler is seeking to recover on a *quid pro quo* theory ...[21]

Because the two had engaged in a prior consensual relationship, Ms. Keppler could establish sexual discrimination only by rebutting the presumption that Dr. Miller penalized her not because she was a woman, but instead because she was his former lover.[22]

The *Keppler* Court made it clear that once an employee engages in consensual sex with an employer, she does not forfeit her right to legal protection from that employer. A hostile environment claim remains available after a consensual sexual relationship comes to an end. A *quid pro quo* claim may be more difficult to discern. In *Trautvetter v. Quick*, an elementary school teacher, after having engaged in a sexual relationship with her principal, brought suit under Title VII for alleged sexual harassment. Her complaint was that the principal had violated her rights under Title VII by allegedly pressuring her into engaging in sexual relations with him.[23] The court concluded the relationship was consensual and did not constitute sexual harassment. The court found the school board had adequately responded to the teacher's complaint and would not have been liable under the civil rights conspiracy statute.

Title IX

Title IX of the Education Amendments of 1972 addresses sex discrimination and sexual harassment. The sexual harassment prohibition of Title IX is not clear as in Title VII. Title IX specifies: "No person in the United States shall on the basis of sex, be excluded from participation in, be denied the benefits of, or be subjected to discrimination under any education program or activity receiving federal financial assistance."[24] Since Title IX was patterned after Title VI of the Civil Rights Act of 1964 and covers students in educational institutions, some courts have ruled that Title IX does not cover school employees. But in 1982, the Supreme Court[25] stated "while section 901(a) does not expressly include [or exclude] employees within its scope...its broad directive that no person may be discriminated against on the basis of gender...includes employees as well as students."[26] The Office of Civil Rights (OCR) of the United States Department of Education is the primary administrative agency charged with enforcing Title IX. Unlike the Equal Employment Opportunity Commission (EEOC) which enforces Title VII, the OCR has failed to promulgate regulations or official guidelines regarding sexual harassment. Despite the absence of guidelines, OCR maintains that sexual harassment is prohibited by Title IX.[27] Although the issue of whether Title IX covers sexual harassment was open to debate, the Supreme Court on February 26, 1992 settled this debate once and for all. In *Franklin v. Gwinnett County Public Schools*, the Court ruled that a damage remedy is available for an action brought to enforce Title IX. Enforceability is available through an implied right of action.

In *Franklin v. Gwinnett*, a female student had been subjected to continual sexual harassment from a high school coach or teacher. School officials, after becoming aware of the harassment, discouraged the student from pressing charges against the teacher. Subsequently, the teacher resigned on the condition all matters relating to him be dropped. The school agreed and closed the investigation. In determining that Title IX allowed damages, the Court stated:

> The assertion that Title IX remedies should nevertheless be limited to back pay and prospective relief diverges from this court's traditional approach to deciding what remedies are available for violations of a federal right. Both suggested remedies are equitable in nature, and it is axiomatic that a court should determine the adequacy of damages of law before resorting to equitable relief. Moreover, both suggested remedies are clearly inadequate in that they would provide Franklin no relief: back pay because she was a student when the alleged discrimination occurred, and prospective relief because she no longer attends school in respondent system and Hill no longer teaches there.[28]

A case decided before *Franklin* appeared to indicate this liability. In *Lipsett v. University of Puerto Rico*,[29] the court stated that in a Title IX case, an educational institution is absolutely liable for *quid pro quo* sexual harassment and discriminatory discharge regardless of whether it knew, should have known, or approved of the actions of the supervisor involved. Also, the educational institution is liable for hostile environment sexual harassment, unless the educational institution can show that appropriate steps were taken to halt the hostile environment. Susan Strauss points out that if school districts do not have a sexual harassment policy and grievance procedure, they are in violation of Title IX.[30] Strauss lists specific behaviors (that are unwanted and sexual in nature) that could constitute sexual harassment especially to teens at school.[31] They are: touching, verbal comments, sexual name calling, spreading sexual rumors, gestures, jokes/cartoons/pictures, too personal a conversation, cornering/blocking movements, pulling at clothes, students "making out" in the hallway, and attempted rape and rape. Teachers who engage in these activities are usually dismissed for immorality or other just cause.[32]

Equal Protection

The Seventh Circuit Court in *Bohen v. City of East Chicago*[33] was the first federal court to recognize a sexual harassment claim under the equal protection clause of the fourteenth amendment. This action opens another legal approach for public employees.[34] To be successful, the plaintiff must show that the discrimination was intentional. This discrimination may be shown by a single event, but it is unlikely that one event will constitute denial of equal protection. In *Bohen*, the court said, "Forcing women and not men to work in an environment of sexual harassment is no different than forcing women to work in a dirtier or more hazardous environment than men simply because they were women."[35]

Recommendations For Practice

Standards for sexual harassment are the same for both public and private employers. Nolan points out that:

- Public employers, particularly educational institutions, must be careful to design their policies to conform to whatever statutory tenure or continuing contract rights exist in the state as well as to any collective bargaining agreements.[36]
- Sexual harassment in the workplace could be generalized as follows: unwarranted or unwanted sexual attention from peers, subordinates, supervisors, customers, clients, or anyone the victim must interact with in order to fulfill the duties of the job or school where the victim's responses are restrained by fear of reprisals. The range of behaviors includes but is not limited to leering, pinching, unnecessary touching or patting, verbal comments, subtle pressure for sexual activity, rape, and attempted rape.
- Employees should be aware of the EEOC sexual harassment guidelines and alert to the problem. "An employer should take all steps necessary to prevent sexual harassment from occurring, such as affirmatively raising the subject, expressing strong disapproval, developing appropriate sanctions, informing employees of their right to raise and how to raise the issue of harassment under Title VII, and developing methods to sensitize all concerned."[37]
- Most contributors to the literature are proponents of prevention. It is important to have a strong school board policy condemning sexual harassment.
- Strauss states that the school board policy should be widely disseminated, and should be included in the student and staff handbooks and should state: the district's philosophy on sex-

ual harassment; consequences to the harasser; timeline for investigation of the complaint; suggestions for possible informal resolution; clear step-by-step procedures for victims to follow without fear of retaliation; the need for confidentiality; and assignment of complaint managers must include at least one female and one male who are sensitive to the issue and able to empathize with the victim.[38]

References

[1]Testimony of Anita Hill and Clarence Thomas on nationally televised Senate confirmation hearings for United States Supreme Court nominee, Clarence Thomas, October 10-13, 1991.

[2]Schneider, *Sexual Harassment and Higher Education*, 65 Tex. L. Rev. 525 (Feb. 1987).

[3]Ingulli, *Sexual Harassment in Education*, 18 Rutgers. L. J.281, 282 (Winter 1987).

[4]*See* Mondschein and Greene, *Sexual Harassment in Employment and Educational Practices*, School Law Update 1986 (ERIC Document No. ED 272996).

[5]Gibbs, *Sex, Lies, and Politics: America's Watershed Debate on Sexual Harassment*, Time, Vol.138, No.15, October 21, 1991.

[6]*See* C. Hooker, *Teacher Dismissal for Improper Touching or Sexual Contact with Students*, 39 Educ. L. Rep. 941 (1987).

[7]42 U.S.C. § 2000e-2(a)(1).

[8]29 C.F.R. 1604.11(a)(1985).

[9]106 S. Ct. 2399 (1986).

[10]*Id.* at 2404-2405.

[11]682 F.2d 897 at 902 (11th Cir. 1982).

[12]29 C.F.R. 1604.11(c).

[13]*Id.*

[14]106 S. Ct. 2399 (1986).

[15]*Id.* at 2406.

[16]760 F. Supp. 1486 (M.D. Fla. 1991) at 1522.

[17]*Id.* at 1522 quoting *Henson*, 682 F.2d at 904 (1982).

[18]*Cf.* Price Waterhouse v. Hopkins, 490 U.S. 228, 249-51 (1989).

[19]Keppler v. Hinsdale Township High School Dist., 715 F. Supp. 862 (N.D. Ill. 1989).

[20]*Id.* at 864.

[21]*Id.* at 867.

[22]*Id.* at 869.

[23]Trautvetter v. Quick, 916 F.2d 1140 (7th Cir. 1990).

[24]20 U.S.C. § 1681.

[25]North Haven Bd. of Educ. v. Bell, 102 S. Ct. 1912 (1982).

[26]*Id.* at 1914.

[27]Schneider, *supra* note 3, at 525.

[28]Franklin v. Gwinnett County Public Schools, 112 S. Ct. 1028 (1992) at 1030-1031.

[29]864 F.2d 881, 882 (1st Cir. 1988).

[30]Strauss, *Sexual Harassment in the School: Legal Implications for Principals*, NASSP Bulletin, March 1988, pp. 93-97.

[31]*Id.* at 94.

[32]*See* Weissman v. Board of Educ. of Jefferson County School Dist. No. R-l, 547 P.2d 1267 (1976); Johnson v. Beaverhead City High School Dist., 771 P.2d 137 (1989); Fadler v. Illinois State Bd. of Educ., 506 N.E.2d 640 (5th Dist. 1987).

[33]799 F.2d. 1180 (7th Cir. 1986).

[34]In *Bohen*, the plaintiff was a fire department dispatcher. Her coworkers and supervisor subjected her to repeated acts of sexual harassment.

[35]*Id.* at 1185.

[36]Nolan, *Sexual Harassment in Public and Private Employment*, 3 Educ. L. Rep. 227, 233 (1982).

[37]29 C.F.R. 1604.11(f).

[38]Strauss, NASSP, at 97.

18
Evaluation

Joseph C. Beckham

Introduction

Whether perceived as a manager or educational leader, the principal is often charged, under provision of state statute, board rule, or negotiated agreement with the responsibility to evaluate those whom he or she supervises. The cycle of supervision typically requires that reasonable, job-related performance criteria be set and that the principal, through a process of observation, evaluation, and conferencing assist the employee to improve performance. When efforts to correct deficiencies and improve performance fail, the evaluation process may become a system for documenting inadequate performance and justifying an adverse employment decision based upon lack of competence.

Most evaluation policies require the principal to assist the employee to improve performance. These same policies compel the principal to develop the evidentiary record that will allow for identification and termination of the ineffective performer. This dual role creates unavoidable dilemmas for the school principal who, as management team and instructional leader, may feel his or her role is compromised when teachers realize that poor evaluative outcomes may lead to adverse employment decisions. When the consequences of evaluation implicate employment status, a confrontational atmosphere may develop which interferes with close working relationships and harmony in the school setting. However, the principal has no alternative but to resolve this dilemma by application of those processes and policies that are defined in the district's policy mandate for evaluation.

Legal Issues

State and federal judges have been influential in defining legal standards and professional practice guidelines relative to employee evaluation. When evaluation becomes a critical element in documenting and justifying an adverse employment decision such as de-motion or dismissal, its use may precipitate a legal challenge and force judicial review of evaluation practices. In these instances, judges have resolved employment disputes and offered guidance to principals on the proper use of evaluation. Judicially imposed standards for the evaluation of professional employees often involve the interpretation of legislative mandates, regulatory provisions, board policies, and collective bargaining agreements. As a consequence, judicial opinion is one of several sources to which the principal may turn in formulating and implementing sound practices for the evaluation of professional employees.

Elements of Appropriate Practice

The elements of a sound evaluation system may be extrapolated from a number of judicial decisions decided in the last decade. Consider the case of a North Carolina career teacher who was discharged for inadequate performance based upon a failure to maintain appropriate classroom discipline. Beginning with the 1980-81 school term, the teacher had received numerous notices of her inability to maintain classroom discipline including teacher and parental complaints and classroom evaluations by both the principal and a math-science coordinator. Throughout the 1981-82 school year, steps to improve the teacher's ability to handle discipline in her junior high school classroom were initiated, ranging from suggestions by the principal and the coordinator to week-long observations of an exemplary teacher's performance. Specific instances of her inability to control students were noted in classroom observations during the school years of 1981-82 and 1982-83. In the spring of 1983, the superintendent recommended dismissal following observations of classroom performance which indicated no improvement in the teacher's ability to maintain discipline. In a review of the dismissal, a North Carolina appeals court found no evidence of arbitrary or capricious action on the part of school authorities and concluded that the records showed a persistent but unavailing effort to get the teacher to recognize that she was not properly controlling her classes and to correct her deficiencies. The teacher's assertion, that dismissal for "inadequate performance" was vague, was rejected when the court ruled the phrase could be readily understood by people of ordinary intelligence who knew the requirements of the job and noted that evidence clearly showed that the teacher was aware that the maintenance of adequate classroom order and discipline was a relevant dimension of job performance.[1]

As another instance of judicial guidance in defining standards for evaluation, note the case of a tenured Missouri teacher who challenged her termination, contending that the dismissal was not supported by sufficient evidence of incompetence. The state appeals court reviewed the testimony of witnesses for the board, who indicated that the teacher had problems in almost every facet of teaching (grading, class motivation, class discipline) and that despite multiple efforts by several persons to assist her in learning the appropriate skills, there was no improvement in her performance. Finding that the teacher had received adequate notice of her deficiencies and reasonable time to improve her performance, the court concluded that there was substantial evidence in the record to support the board's allegation of inefficiency and incompetence and its decision to dismiss.[2]

These cases, and many others resolved in the last decade, confirm that adverse employment decisions based on unsatisfactory performance can be sustained if school officials are prepared to undertake the steps necessary to develop and implement a legally sound evaluation system. As illustrated in these decisions, repeated evaluations by multiple observers identified deficiencies related to on-the-job performance. The teacher was given regular and periodic notice of these deficiencies and an opportunity to improve performance was provided. Despite reasonable time for remediation, later evaluations confirmed that deficiencies remained.

These cases were based on conduct falling below an acceptable level of performance. While such a standard might appear to be illusive, judges have shown deference to educators in determining the appropriate standards of "competence," particularly where the behavioral standard is reasonably related to job performance. As one judicial opinion stated, public schools need not to be "married to mediocrity" in setting standards for the evaluation of professional employees.[3]

Implementing Evaluation Policies

Judges require evidence that evaluation systems are implemented in conformance with state and local district policies. The obligation to implement evaluation policies and document compliance is typically the domain of the principal. In general, judges adopt a standard of substantial compliance in order to avoid placing an undue or unreasonable burden on the school administrator. For example, the Supreme Court of Ohio refused to adopt the view that a contract clause requiring a "formal evaluation system" would require a rigorously enforced set of procedures. The court noted that the principal had developed a standardized evaluation form that included room for observations, suggestions for improvement, and space for teacher comment or rebuttal; indications that teachers were evaluated; opportunities for guidance; and opportunity to respond. Further, the teacher whose contract had not been renewed had received three classroom evaluations during the period of employment. As a consequence, the court was convinced that the procedures adopted met the requirements under the contract for employment.[4]

The standard of "substantial compliance" is also reflected in a case from Pennsylvania. The local school district appealed an order of the state education commissioner which reversed the local board's initial suspension and ultimate dismissal of a teacher for incompetence. The teacher had received two consecutive unsatisfactory ratings from the local district administrator in each of the previous two years. The unsatisfactory ratings were based on the teacher's failure to plan lessons, give directions to students, and maintain order in the classroom.

The state appeals court ruled that the suspension for cause and dismissal of the teacher was supported by substantial evidence and overruled the state commissioner of education's decision. The court found that evidence of the teacher's failure to maintain order was a significant factor justifying suspension from the classroom. Although there was evidence that rating forms were incorrectly signed by various district officials, and the district did not adopt a numerical scoring system for rating employees; the court noted that state law only required that unsatisfactory ratings be approved and signed by the district superintendent and supported by anecdotal records. The signature process used by the district resulted in errors when officials signed the wrong line on the evaluation forms or when countersignatures were not present. The court did not regard these mistakes as errors that would prejudice the teacher in a substantive manner and held such errors to be insignificant.[5]

In a case from Illinois, a tenured teacher was evaluated and found unsatisfactory with regard to discipline, classroom management, enthusiasm, and organization. The school principal developed a remediation plan, but the teacher's performance remained unsatisfactory in all four areas on quarterly evaluations. Following a report and recommendations for dismissal, the school district dismissed the teacher. The teacher sought review contending in part that the remediation plan had not been approved by the board. The state appeals court upheld the tenured teacher's discharge for failure to complete the prescribed plan of remediation and denied reinstatement. The court examined the statutory intent of the state provision requiring evaluation of teachers and concluded that it would be unreasonable to require the board to approve every remediation plan. Illinois law was interpreted to grant authority to the administrator to carry out evaluations and develop remedial plans.[6]

Complying With Due Process Standards

While courts have shown deference to school administrators in developing and implementing employee evaluation programs, failure to comply with essential elements of a sound evaluation policy can result in judicial review and reinstatement for school employees who were subjected to improperly conducted performance evaluations. Although a nontenured teacher would not normally have a right to reemployment, some state courts have ruled that failure to follow an adopted evaluation policy would create a right to renewal. In an Alabama case, a nonrenewed teacher alleged that the principal had delegated the responsibility to perform evaluations to the school's head football coach and failed to conduct follow-up evaluations required under a newly adopted board policy. The Supreme Court of Alabama recognized a claim for breach of contract on the basis of the principal's failure to comply with the district's adopted evaluation policy.[7]

In a case from West Virginia, a school psychologist, who was not renewed after appointment on three one-year contracts, won reinstatement when he established that no evaluations were conducted in his first two years of employment and termination following his third year of employment occurred only one month after his first evaluation was performed. The state court ruled that the psychologist had not been accorded his rights under the contract to annual evaluation, and, once evaluated, he was not given a satisfactory opportunity to remediate.[8]

Appropriate due process begins with predetermined, job-related criteria as a basis for identifying the employee's strengths and weaknesses. Without predetermined performance criteria, there can be no consistent and uniform standard for evaluating employees and no reasonable basis on which to predicate an adverse employment decision. By relying on evaluation criteria that are validly related to the requirements of the position, observable and properly assessed, the principal can meet the evidentiary test for relevance in the evaluation process.

Evaluation criteria should be sufficiently specific to fulfill the dual requirement of enabling the employee to guide his or her conduct and of providing a standard by which the employee's conduct can be evaluated. Evaluation forms should focus on a select number of observable behaviors which are clearly relevant to the specified criteria. Ideally, employees should have advance notice of criteria before actual evaluations or observations are initiated. Compliance with these requirements will enable the principal to conform to essential elements of due process and to rebut claims that the evaluation system is arbitrary or capricious.

Judges have consistently recognized that the teacher's ability to maintain appropriate discipline, work cooperatively with professional colleagues, and provide proper instruction and supervision are relevant competencies in evaluating teacher performance.[9] When teacher behaviors relate directly to classroom performance, the corresponding adverse impact on students is of paramount concern to the courts. Consequently, evidence that a teacher failed to construct adequate lesson plans, abused or harassed students, ineffectively used instructional materials, or failed to keep order in the classroom has been judicially accepted as an indicator of unsatisfactory performance.[10]

Principals have the responsibility to implement evaluation standards and practices that yield a documentary record which confirms the fairness and reasonableness of the process and meets the test of substantial evidence. The cumulative weight of evidence, whether drawn from classroom observations, student or parental complaints, testimony of colleagues, anecdotal memoranda, or a combination of sources must sustain the procedural integrity of the process and justify an adverse employment decision. Unsubstantiated claims of inadequate performance, conflicting appraisals of performance, or lack of uniform standards in the evaluation process may contribute to the view that there is insufficient evidence to support an adverse employment decision.

Evaluations based on classroom observations, ratings, and anecdotal records of performance can significantly contribute to the cumulative evidence necessary to justify an adverse employment decision. Where evaluations are corroborative, a strong basis for the adverse employment decision can be constructed. The use of evaluation ratings, coupled with the testimony of the principal who made the observations on which the evaluations were based was regarded as substantial evidence justifying a Nebraska board's termination decision. The principal conducted two formal evaluations using a form designed to measure teacher performance in the classroom and testified that although the teacher tried to improve her performance in relation to her fellow teachers at the school, she was below district standards. The principal's testimony was consistent with an evaluation record that detailed unsatisfactory aspects of job performance and cited specific examples to support evaluation judgments.[11] However, conflicting evidence of performance may often support a determination that there is insufficient evidence to justify an adverse employment decision.

Evidentiary records to support the stated reasons for an adverse employment decision are often essential. Observation and evaluations by several evaluators can significantly strengthen the evidentiary basis for an adverse employment decision. Consider the case of a tenured teacher of the emotionally handicapped who was terminated by a New York school board. Dismissal predicated on documented instances of the teacher's inability to control her class and inability to effectively plan and teach lessons. The decision was confirmed based on the quality and quantity of testimony offered by six witnesses. The court also held that dismissal was not an excessive or unfair penalty when there was insufficient evidence that returning the teacher to the classroom after a lesser penalty would improve her teaching.[12]

In a case from Texas, a tenured teacher who was dismissed for incompetence in the performance of duties challenged the board's use of videotape composites of her classroom teaching. The district's assessment team used classroom observations and videotapes to record teacher performance in order to assist the teacher in following the observations and criticisms of classroom performance. Both written evaluations and videotapes revealed problems in teaching performance. These deficiencies were not corrected, the teacher's performance did not improve in the second year of evaluation, and a recommendation for dismissal was made to the board. A Texas appeals court affirmed the decision that the teacher's procedural and substantive rights were not violated by the board's use of the composite videotape in the dismissal hearing, nor did the teacher have an expectation of privacy protected by law such that videotaping violated her privacy rights. The court concluded the board met the standards for substantive due process. Although the teacher had objected to videotaping her classroom performance from the beginning of the assessment process, the court concluded that the teacher did not have an expected zone of privacy in the classroom that would amount to a privacy right.[13]

Judicial opinions note several factors that contribute to a presumption of fair and reasonable evaluation processes. Reliance upon classroom observation reports completed by supervisors and persons knowledgeable in the teacher's subject matter field have considerable evidentiary value.[14] Multiple reports by different evaluators have been recognized as reducing bias and substantiating unsatisfactory performance when reports are corroborative.[15] Specifying deficiencies consistent with job-related evaluative criteria and providing reasonable opportunities for remediation and periodic re-evaluation help support the fundamental fairness of the evaluation process.[16] Post observation conferences, in which deficiencies are detailed and suggestions for remediation are offered, strengthen the view that the evaluation process is fair.[17] Anecdotal records and formal reports of complaints or reprimands contribute to the overall evidentiary weight to be accorded unsatisfactory performance evaluations.[18]

Distinguishing Remedial Behavior

An opportunity to correct remedial deficiencies is often a requirement of an evaluation policy. In these cases, notice of deficiencies will typically be accompanied by suggestions to improve performance, and a plan for remediation will be designed. The obligation to provide assistance to the teacher may be a dimension of the district's evaluation policy, but even where no assistance is mandated, the principal's good faith effort to assist the teacher to improve performance can be reflected in suggestions which are reasonably related to improving performance.

Evaluation and documentation of unsatisfactory performance may relate to a wide range of behaviors, not all of which require a remedial opportunity. A teacher's continuing refusal to comply with a principal's directive to attend PTA meetings or other conferences, including a refusal to release a student's report card after being directed to do so by the principal, might be characterized as unsatisfactory performance. The conduct, when regarded as insubordination or willful neglect of duty, would not require remedial assistance beyond a showing that the teacher had been warned to discontinue the behavior and comply with specific directives.[19] Similarly, a teacher terminated for adopting the disciplinary tactic of sharply tapping male students in the groin might argue that a remedial opportunity should be provided, but the behavior is more appropriately regarded as "unprofessional conduct" justifying dismissal rather than as a remedial deficiency.[20]

Instances of uncooperative behavior and hostility towards co-workers or supervisors may be characterized as unsatisfactory and serve as an evidentiary basis for unprofessional conduct or insubordination.[21] Evidence that a teacher failed to follow a reasonable plan of remediation designed to correct performance deficiencies might reflect neglect of duty as a basis for an adverse employment decision.[22] Refusal to follow a plan of remediation, when that plan can be shown to relate to the correction of observed deficiencies, could be construed as evidence of insubordination rather than incompetence.[23] In these cases, judges have distinguished issues of competence in which deficiencies are identified and remediation may be in order from instances in which corrective discipline is necessary. For example, a teacher's repetitive failure to follow directives for keeping her students inside her classroom and to comply with directions to keep student cumulative records up to date would be characterized as willful neglect of duty justifying dismissal without remedial assistance to improve performance.[24]

Corrective discipline, which may range from reprimand to termination, would be an appropriate response to willful neglect, insubordination, immorality or other unprofessional conduct. Incompetence typically involves job-related performance falling below an acceptable standard and often includes a reasonable opportunity to correct deficiencies if those deficiencies do not pose a significant and immediate risk of harm to students or colleagues. Still, some deficiencies related to competency may be regarded as irremedial. In considering the nature of an "irremedial deficiency" judges typically weigh the property interest of the employee while giving consideration to the length of time that may be necessary to correct the identified deficiency in relationship to the possible harm or adverse consequences for school children should the employee be permitted a period for remediation. As one court has noted, a determination of remediability must take into account the teacher's prior record, severity of the conduct, and whether the conduct resulted in actual or threatened harm to students.[25]

Avoiding Claims of Discrimination

The inherently subjective nature of performance evaluation results in close scrutiny by judges because of the potential for masking unlawful discrimination. In some instances, the evaluation process may yield evidence of overt discrimination, particularly where evaluation forms contain written observations that exhibit sexual stereotyping or where evaluation protocols single out minorities or women for rating and ranking but are not applied to all similarly situated employees.

Black teachers successfully contested nonreappointment decisions by demonstrating that the evaluation process on which nonrenewals were based was not uniformly applied to all teaching personnel in the district. The year prior to voluntary desegregation of the district, Black teachers were twice evaluated and eight of the total number of 23 Black teachers were numerically ranked. When the plan for desegregation was implemented, 17 Black teachers were not renewed, although all White teachers in the district were offered new contracts. When 17 new teachers were hired, all 17 were White. The Fifth Circuit Court of Appeals concluded the non-renewals were intentional acts of racial discrimination and noted that the separate evaluation and ranking of Black teachers was highly probative evidence of unconstitutional discrimination.[26]

Evaluations by school administrators may often influence the outcome of discrimination challenges to school board employment decisions. In one instance, an elementary school librarian of Asian origin was recommended for reassignment to the junior high level but was denied reappointment by the local board. Evaluations which accompanied the reassignment recommendations showed the librarian's performance was rated satisfactory in all respects except for deficiencies in her ability to communicate in English. The evaluations noted specifically that the librarian would do an excellent job at a school where her speech and storytelling skills would not be so critical. The school board's decision to deny renewal and reassignment to a vacant junior high school librarian position based on the employee's language skills was regarded as a subterfuge for national origin discrimination. The court noted that the librarian was being considered for a position that would not require communication with elementary students, thus the reason given was not related to actual job requirements. In this instance, the proof of discrimination was shown through evidence that the proffered explanation for nonappointment was not supported by evidence from evaluations of the employee's performance.[27]

Since litigation of employment discrimination claims is highly fact intensive, the principal must be prepared to articulate a job-related, nondiscriminatory basis for unsatisfactory performance evaluations. A principal's pre-existing intention to use the evaluation and remediation plan as a means to dismiss a teacher can be discerned from circumstantial evidence and may thwart the process of summative evaluation.[28] The most effective way for the principal to meet this obligation is to ensure that evaluation practices consist of job-related criteria uniformly applied to all employees.

Avoiding Claims of Subterfuge

The principal has an obligation to avoid using the evaluation system as a subterfuge to deny constitutionally protected rights. Consider the case of a Virginia physical education teacher who wrote a letter to the editor of the school sponsored newspaper as a response to a published allegation that physical education teachers were male chauvinists. The letter was intended to be satirical but resulted in several complaints from persons who concluded that the teacher was sexist. The principal advised the teacher that he might receive a "needs improvement" rating on professional responsibility in his next evaluation and suggested that the teacher meet with a local human relations committee and prepare an apology in a letter to the editor of the school newspaper. The teacher did meet with the committee and drafted an apology that was published by the paper. Nevertheless, the principal gave a "needs improvement" rating in annual evaluation, and the teacher filed a grievance when he was denied his step increment in pay for that year. When the school board denied the grievance, the teacher sued. The federal appeals court ruled that the teacher's letter to the school sponsored newspaper was on a matter of public concern and entitled to constitutional protection. The school board's decision to deny the grievance was overturned on the grounds that the loss of pay was predicated on an evaluation of performance directly related to the submission and publication of the letter. The fact that the letter was controversial was not a basis for denying the teacher the right to comment by punishing him with an unfavorable evaluation.[29]

As in cases involving discrimination, an evaluation system may protect the employee's constitutional rights. A nontenured teacher in a local Kentucky school district was described as an "excellent teacher" by her principal and had received good performance evaluations for the two years in which she taught. However, during the summer, the teacher and her husband of nine years divorced. Although she had been recommended for rehire by her principal, the local superintendent advised the principal and a school board member that he would not recommend rehiring because of the teacher's involvement in divorce proceedings. Because the superintendent failed to recommend her, the teacher was not rehired. The court concluded that the decision not to rehire infringed upon the teacher's right to privacy. Marital and family relationships involve privacy rights that are constitutionally protected against unwarranted governmental intrusion or interference. Although the teacher had no constitutionally protected liberty or property interest in continued employment, evidence that the superintendent refused to consider high performance evaluations and a recommendation for rehire and relied solely on the teacher's divorce as the basis for refusing to recommend rehiring, established a constitutionally impermissible basis for denying employment.[30]

In some instances, evidence that an adverse employment decision was based on an employee's exercise of free speech and association rights has been discovered within the evaluation document. Statements which indicate that the employee is not to be renewed because the employee made public remarks concerning board policy may so implicate free speech rights as to justify judicial scrutiny.[31] A negative evaluation based primarily upon the employee's activity as a union representative would be suspect.[32] Charges of "lack of cooperation," "fosters a disruptive work environment," or "fails to work effectively with peers" are often carefully scrutinized by judges because these charges are vague and an inquiry into specific incidents may uncover attempts to punish for the exercise of free speech.

For a teacher's exercise of speech to be protected, the comments must be related to a matter of public concern as opposed to a matter of private interest. An Arkansas teacher received good evaluations and was recommended for contract renewal in each of her first two years in the local district. In her third year, working with a new principal, the teacher became increasingly active in the local teacher's union and was appointed the teacher's representative in the school. Difficulties between teacher and the new principal developed initially when the teacher served as a spokesperson for the other teachers who objected to school board plans to eliminate ability grouping programs for students. Teacher complaints about the principal's personnel practices were also directed to the principal by the teacher. When the teacher was advised that general grievances would be addressed only if individual grievances were filed, she submitted an individual grievance along with two other teachers. These three teachers were then given notice of nonrenewal at the end of the year.

The federal appeals court ruled that the criticisms were not purely internal matters relevant only to employees in her school but related to matters of public concern going beyond internal policies. One of the initial disputes between the teacher and the principal involved the school district's decision to abandon ability grouping of students, a concern to every community in the nation. The court was also convinced that much of the teacher's speech directed at school personnel policies was not motivated solely by employment concerns, but was legitimate criticism of policies and administration which affected the educational function of the school. In balancing the employee's interest in commenting on matters of public concern against the employer's interest in efficiently fulfilling its responsibilities, the court could find no evidence that the teacher's criticisms introduced discord into her relations with colleagues or adversely affected her teaching performance. Neither was there evidence that the teacher's criticism reflected willful disobedience of any directive related to her teaching responsibilities. As to the suggestion that her speech disrupted her relationship with the school principal, the court found the primary source of disruption was the principal's enforcement of the personnel policies. The court concluded that the relationship between principal and teacher "is not of such a personal and intimate nature that teachers must be precluded from filing responsible grievances."[33]

Negative evaluations may have a chilling effect on the exercise of free speech even when those evaluations have no direct adverse employment consequences such as nonrenewal or dismissal. In a case from Wyoming, a federal appeals court ruled a teacher's letter to the state education association asking for an investigation of her principal was entitled to protection. The teacher's letter dealt with matters of public concern relating to high faculty turnover and sexual harassment of students and teachers and was presented by a majority of the school's teachers as a request for a public investigation. Several teachers testified that the principal's evaluations of their performance became more negative and his enforcement of school rules more restrictive after their submission of the letter calling for an investigation. Friction between the teacher and principal increased and resulted in a reprimand, a grievance by the teacher, and a recommendation by the principal that the teacher not be renewed. Although the board renewed the teacher's contract, the principal and board were held liable for damages for the negative evaluations and reprimand.[34]

Recommendations for Practice

A review of judicial opinion involving the use and misuse of evaluation in public school employment decisions suggests a number of practices that are typically linked to the principal's role. These suggested practices include the following:

- Notify employees in advance of the procedures and performance criteria that will be used in the evaluation process.
- Apply performance criteria that are job-related and sufficiently specific to inform the employee of performance deficiencies.
- Inform the employee of the outcome of the evaluation process through conference and follow-up memoranda.
- Afford the employee an opportunity to respond to unsatisfactory performance evaluations.
- Implement uniform evaluation procedures free of any implication of an invidious discriminatory intent.
- Refrain from using evaluation as a means of retaliating against the employee's exercise of free speech or other constitutional rights.

- Provide a reasonable time to correct remediable deficiencies.
- Suggest what actions the employee may take to correct deficiencies.
- Insure that recommendations for corrective action are reasonably related to identified deficiencies.
- Predicate employment recommendations on the personnel record as a whole, considering evaluations as one of several relevant aspects documenting employee performance.

References

[1] Crump v. Durham County Bd. of Educ., 327 S.E.2d 599 (N.C. Ct. App. 1985).

[2] Atherton v. Board of School Dist. of St. Joseph, 744 S.W.2d 518 (Mo. Ct. App. 1988).

[3] Briggs v. Board of Dirs., 282 N.W.2d 740, at 743 (Iowa 1979).

[4] Borman v. Gorham-Fayette Bd. of Educ., 502 N.E.2d 1031 (Ohio 1986).

[5] Board of Educ. v. Kushner, 530 A.2d 541 (Pa. Cmwlth. Ct. 1987).

[6] Powell v. Board of Educ. of Peoria, 545 N.E.2d 767 (Ill. Ct. App. 1989).

[7] Belcher v. Jefferson County Bd. of Educ., 474 So. 2d 1063 (Ala. 1985) .

[8] Wren v. McDowell Bd. of Educ., 327 S.E.2d 464 (W. Va. 1985).

[9] Mongitore v. Regan, 520 N.Y.S.2d 194 (App. Div. 1987).

[10] See Donnes v. State, 672 P.2d 617 (Mont. 1983).

[11] Eshom v. Board of Educ. of Dist. No. 54, 364 N.W.2d 7 (Neb. 1985).

[12] Mongitore, 520 N.Y.S.2d 194.

[13] Roberts v. Houston Indep. School Dist., 788 S.W.2d 107 (Tex. Ct. App. 1990).

[14] See Thompson v. School Dist. of Omaha, 623 F.2d 46 (8th Cir. 1980) (evaluations by math instructor and co-worker confirmed unsatisfactory performance evaluation by principal).

[15] Rosso v. Board of School Directors., 380 A.2d 1328 (Pa. Commw. Ct. 1977).

[16] Childers v. Indep. School Dist., 645 P.2d 992 (Okla. 1981).

[17] Jones v. Jefferson Parish School Bd., 533 F. Supp. 816 (E.D. La. 1982).

[18] See Patterson v. Masem, 594 F. Supp. 386 (E.D. Ark. 1984).

[19] Meckley v. Kanawha County Bd. of Educ., 383 S.E.2d 839 (W. Va. 1989).

[20] 713 P.2d 98 (Wash. 1986).

[21] See Grant v. Board of Educ. of School Directors of Centennial, 471 A.2d 1292 (Pa. Commw. Ct. 1984). See also, Hayes v. Phoenix-Talent School Dist., 893 F.2d 235 (9th Cir. 1990).

[22] Board of Dirs. of Sioux City Community School Dist. v. Mroz, 295 N.W.2d 447 (Iowa 1980).

[23] Thompson v. Board of Educ., 668 P.2d 954 (Colo. Ct. App. 1983).

[24] Gaulden v. Lincoln Parish School Bd., 554 So. 2d 152 (La. Ct. App. 1989).

[25] Knapp v. Whitaker, 577 F. Supp. 1265 (Ill. 1983).

[26] Harkless v. Sweeny Indep. School Dist., 554 F.2d 1353 (5th Cir. 1977).

[27] Mandhare v. S.W. LaFargue Elementary School, 605 F. Supp. 238 (E.D. La. 1985).

[28] See Forbes v. Poudre School Dist., 791 P.2d 675 (Colo. 1990).

[29] Seemuller v. Fairfax County School Bd., 878 F.2d 1578 (4th Cir. 1989).

[30] Littlejohn v. Rose, 768 F.2d 765 (6th Cir. 1985).

[31] Knapp v. Whitaker, 577 F. Supp. 1265 (Ill. 1983).

[32] See Uniondale Union Free School v. Newman, 562 N.Y.S.2d 148 (App. Div. 1990).

[33] Cox v. Dardanelle Pub. School Dist., 790 F.2d 668, at 674 (8th Cir. 1986).

[34] Wren. v. Spurlock, 798 F.2d 1313 (10th Cir. 1986).

19

Documentation for Teacher Improvement or Termination

Kelly Frels

Introduction

The primary objective of a school district's teacher evaluation system is to improve teachers' performance so they can become more successful and contribute to the objectives of the district. If the evaluation does not produce this positive result, the teacher must be replaced, either by resignation or termination. The district's evaluation system thus serves a secondary function—the removal of the unsatisfactory teacher.

Depending upon the nature of the teacher's contract with a school district, various degrees of procedural due process must be observed in relieving a person of the position if he or she does not resign. In many situations, this process culminates with a hearing before the board of education to determine whether there is cause to terminate the teacher. In teacher termination hearings, principals often are met with the claim that there is too little documentation or evidence of help being given to the teacher, therefore, the principal has not done his or her job in working with the teacher. In other cases, the claim is made that the principal has developed so much documentation that the teacher has been harassed. At other teacher termination hearings, complaints are made that the process is unfair and that the teacher did not know of these "attacks." As a result, some principals have been unwilling to bring a recommendation for termination to the board of education.

In an effort to provide support for the principal and to help ensure the fair treatment of teachers who are evaluated, a simple but effective system of documentation has been developed which can be used in conjunction with virtually any school district's evaluation system. This documentation system can be used in districts which utilize the various contractual schemes authorized by state statute.

This documentation system is founded on the concept of communication, and its goal is to humanize the evaluation and documentation process with the ultimate objective of improving a teacher's performance to an acceptable level. If a teacher's performance does not improve, the system is designed to provide an incentive for voluntary resignation or, if voluntary resignation is not received, to provide the necessary documentation for the principal to recommend the teacher's termination.

Legal Issues

This documentation system becomes an essential ingredient in preparing the district for a hearing before the board of education; and if necessary, in preparing for appeals and lawsuits filed with a state commissioner of education, an arbitrator, or a court. This system can also provide the necessary documentation to sustain the termination if the teacher files a discrimination complaint with the Equal Employment Opportunity Commission or the Department of Education. Furthermore, adherence to a system of this nature can help prevent constitutional questions from becoming significant issues. If there is a systematic documentation of poor performance before a teacher engages in a protected speech-related activity, the performance deficiency may continue to be addressed as needed and termination can be recommended. In contrast, the absence of such documentation prior to a teacher's engaging in protected speech related activity may render the termination of the teacher extremely difficult.[1]

The documentation contemplated in a teacher evaluation system involves the use of several types of written memoranda which commonly follow some informal verbal communication. First, specific incident memoranda should be used to record conferences with a teacher concerning more significant events. Second, summary memoranda should be used to record conferences with a teacher in which several incidents, problems, or deficiencies are discussed. Third, visitation memoranda should record observations made of a teacher's on-the-job performance. Fourth, an assessment instrument should be used to evaluate the teacher's overall performance.

The documentation concerning a teacher should be used for several purposes. It enables the principal to follow a teacher's actions and performance, thus enabling the principal to pinpoint weaknesses and problem areas. It also enables the teacher to understand problems he or she may have and take corrective steps if necessary. Finally, if a teacher's performance does not improve, it serves as concrete evidence to support a recommendation for termination.

Care should be taken to ensure that this process conforms with state law and school district board policies.

Memoranda to the File

Whenever a principal observes an incident or behavior which is not of a significantly serious nature to require an immediate conference with the teacher but which should be considered in the teacher's evaluation or at a general conference with the teacher, it is appropriate for the principal to prepare a short file memorandum. If possible, the principal should first mention the concern to the teacher informally. These file memoranda may be in various forms, such as notation on a calendar or in a notebook with separate pages designated for specific individuals. These file memoranda should include the name of the teacher, the name of the principal, the date of the occurrence, and the facts of the event observed. These file memoranda can be used for a conference with the teacher concerning the incident or incidents, assessment of the teacher's performance, and refreshing the memory of the principal for testimony at any proceeding or hearing relative to the teacher's performance. These file memoranda should be used sparingly and only for minor matters.

Most administrators who use the file memoranda find it helpful if the employees are aware that these memoranda are being kept and encourage the teachers to review any file memoranda concerning their performance. It is always helpful to effective communication when the principal makes informal mention of the concern as it occurs. Under most states' open records acts, copies of these file memoranda normally need not be given to the teacher unless the teacher requests them. However, if the copies are not given to the teacher, they should not be used in a subsequent hearing in an attempt to establish facts. Actually, the best practice is to incorporate the contents of these file memoranda into a summary memorandum or evaluation which is given to the teacher after a conference.

Even though it may not be the intention of the principal to use these documents as future evidence or to share the file memoranda with the teacher, the memoranda should be written with the knowledge that in a future proceeding copies may be introduced into the proceeding or made available to the teacher through a request under most states' open records acts. For example, if file memoranda are being used to refresh a principal's memory at a hearing, in most states, the attorney for the teacher is entitled to see copies of the documents. Thus, care should be taken with file memoranda, as with any other memoranda, not to write or record anything in a manner that could cause future embarrassment. A good practice is to record facts rather than conclusions in file memoranda.

Specific Incidents Memoranda

If the principal observes an incident or behavior, or has a complaint from a third party, it may be appropriate to send the teacher a memorandum concerning the incident. This memorandum should be sent only after the principal conducts any needed investigation and holds a conference with the teacher at which time the incident is discussed and the teacher's viewpoint considered. The memo should summarize the third party's complaint, response, the principal's determination, and any directives and reprimands to the teacher. If the incident is serious enough that termination is to be recommended immediately, such recommendation should be stated.

Incidents should be faced head-on, as they occur. The failure to confront problems, infractions, and deficiencies at the time they occur can weaken a later case for termination. For example, suppose several incidents occur in the fall of a school year, but they are not mentioned to the teacher by the principal. An attempt to use those incidents to support a proposed termination in the spring of that school year may prove difficult. The teacher will claim that he or she is being treated unfairly because the reasons for termination were not disclosed to the teacher during the school year. Not dealing with the problems as they occur make the principal appear to be arbitrary or devious and weakens the termination proposal.

It is wise to have the teacher acknowledge receipt of the specific incident memorandum by signing the copy. If the teacher does not agree with the facts stated in the memorandum or the action taken, the teacher should be given the opportunity to respond in writing either on the memorandum itself or through a separate document. This action can be accomplished by inviting the teacher to make a written statement concerning any differences of fact or opinion expressed by the principal in the memorandum by a certain date or within a given number of days. For example, the final paragraph of a memorandum might state, "If you disagree with the facts or conclusions stated in this memorandum, please advise me in writing no later than (date) so we can meet and work out any differences." By so doing, any disagreement can be noted, and the differences hopefully resolved, immediately. In serious situations where the employee has proven to be recalcitrant or of questionable veracity, one might consider a final sentence such as, "If you do not respond, I can only assume you agree with the facts stated in this memorandum." Statements such as the latter example should be used sparingly.

If the specific incident concerning the teacher comes from a third party such as a parent or student, care must be taken to fully examine the facts and to determine whether the third party's information is correct. It is improper and potentially disastrous to base a decision to terminate on information from a third party when the truthfulness and reliability of the allegation has not been established. Upon receiving a third party complaint, the principal should make an investigation by conducting whatever hearings are necessary to determine the accuracy of the complaint. If possible, get the complaint in writing. The third party should be advised that if adverse action is taken against the teacher based on this incident, the third party must be available to testify before the board, an arbitrator, or a court. If the third party will not agree to appear as a witness, other independent evidence must be available to establish the relevant facts at a hearing. Otherwise, action adverse to the teacher should not be taken. Next, get the teacher's side of the story; usually in a conference with the teacher. If there is a discrepancy in the third party's story and the teacher's story, the principal should attempt to determine what occurred. It may be necessary to have the teacher confront the complainant in an informal conference to determine what actually occurred.

It may not be possible for the principal to have agreement concerning what happened, so the principal must determine whose story he or she believes. If the principal has enough facts to make an accurate determination, a specific incident memorandum can be prepared. Such a memorandum should explain the findings made by the principal and the reasons for those findings. Specific directives or suggestions to the teacher might be included.[2]

Visitation and Summary Memoranda

In some school districts, it is common practice for principals to summarize a visit to a teacher's classroom. If visitation forms or checklists are used or if a visitation memorandum is prepared, the content should be reviewed with the teacher, and the teacher should be given a copy. Suggestions for improvement should be made in a conference and noted in the memorandum. A visitation memorandum may be used in a termination process, but usually the results of a visitation are reviewed in a summary memorandum or in the assessment document.

Summary memoranda are ideal ways to outline the results of conferences concerning several incidents, classroom visitations, or conferences regarding general teacher performance. Through such memoranda, the matters referred to in the file memoranda can be incorporated. Matters not reflected in other memoranda can be reduced to writing, directives can be given to the teacher, and standards can be established. Also, evidence that a conference was held and the subjects discussed can be established. A copy of each summary memorandum should be given to the teacher, and the teacher should acknowledge receipt of the memorandum. The teacher should be given an opportunity to offer in writing any differences with the facts and conclusions stated in the memorandum. If a teacher disagrees and files a response, a subsequent conference should be held to try to resolve any differences which may exist. The same comments applicable to the specific incident memoranda are applicable to summary memoranda with the major difference being that summary memoranda are designed to cover general conferences with the teacher on several matters rather than on a specific incident.

Evaluation Document and Close-Out Memorandum

The assessment or evaluation of performance document should be completed as prescribed by the policies and procedures of the district. A summary narrative or memorandum should be considered for each negative assessment noted in the document. If the assessment is such that the teacher might be terminated if no improvement is shown, the teacher should be advised that failure to improve could result in a recommendation for termination. Furthermore, it is wise to include instructions or specific directions for improvement. Such a practice not only is helpful to the teacher but also strengthens the argument that the teacher has been treated fairly if the principal's actions are correct and later questioned. Through the use of such evaluation documents, the teacher will be informed that he or she has deficiencies which could result in a proposal to terminate should those deficiencies not be remedied according to the instructions given for improvement. All identified deficiencies of the teacher and any problems which have been encountered during the assessment period should be included in the assessment document. If a deficiency from previous years has not been remedied by the teacher, it should also be noted in the assessment. In order to avoid difficulties with ratings on the evaluation, a straightforward and truthful assessment should be made. A fair system of evaluation must require the setting of standards and expectations at the beginning of the school year with the principal following through with the implementation of those standards through the evaluation process.

If the communication in the conference is effective, and it is properly reflected in the memorandum, a teacher will rarely have the occasion to respond again. However, a further response from the teacher sometimes does result, and another conference may be necessary. At some point the memorandum writing must be brought to a close, and in informal circumstances, the sending of the close-out memorandum to this conference may be appropriate. The language in the close-out memorandum inviting a response from the teacher is deleted, and the teacher is advised that the matter should be considered closed.

Recommendations For Practice

- The memorandum should be sent only after a conference with the teacher.
- In preparing any memorandum, reliance should be made on the facts. Concluding statements not supported by the facts should be avoided. For example, in a classroom visitation memorandum, the observation that the teacher's classroom was disorderly, without any explanation, is not very specific or effective. Rather, the principal should note that he or she saw three children in the classroom talking during class and saw one child playing in the back of the room. The principal should note that these acts were unnoticed by the teacher or were not corrected by the teacher.
- In preparing a memorandum, inflammatory words should not be used. For example, rather than to characterize an action as insubordination, the action might be factually described, and the teacher's action should be referred to as a failure to comply with specific official directives or school board policy.
- Directives given in a memorandum should be positive and specific, and educational jargon should be avoided. When directing a sometimes tardy teacher to arrive at school on time, state: "You are required to be at school by a specific time, and you will be expected to have signed in by that time," rather than, "You are required to be at school on time." Precise directives like these tend to avoid real or imagined confusion about what is expected.
- The specific incident memorandum, the summary memorandum, the visitation memorandum and the assessment document should be personalized as much as possible. The key to the success of this documentation system is to provide an op-

portunity for the principal and the teacher to sit down and mutually work out the problem and determine the future actions of the teacher.

- Care should be taken to treat all teachers alike, especially when dealing with absences and tardiness. It is destructive and embarrassing to have a teacher's attorney present a school's sign-in sheet at a hearing to show that other teachers have more tardies and more absences than the teacher who is being proposed for termination.
- One should never write a memorandum to a teacher when one is angry. It is much better to reflect for a day or so or to call in a third party to review a memorandum prior to sending it. By doing so, the principal can avoid statements which might be regretted later.
- In order to be effective, any memorandum must be prepared and sent to the teacher soon after the incident and the subsequent conference occur. Under no circumstances should a memorandum be prepared after the decision to terminate has been made and backdated to reflect the incident upon which the proposed termination will be based.
- The evaluator should be careful to ensure that the teacher believes he or she has been fairly treated. One should remember that if the teacher's performance does not improve and a recommendation for termination is made, the fairness of the process will be judged by the members of the board and, possibly, by the state's commissioner of education, an arbitrator, or a judge.
- Normally the only documents which would be used as documentary evidence at a termination hearing would be the summary memoranda and the evaluation or assessment instruments. Specific incident and visitation memoranda should not be used as evidence at a hearing but should be used only when necessary to refresh the principal's memory while testifying concerning the specific facts of an event.

References

[1]*See* K. FRELS AND M. SCHNEIDER-VOGEL, THE FIRST AMENDMENT AND SCHOOL EMPLOYEES: A PRACTICAL MANAGEMENT GUIDE, (Nolpe Monograph 1986).
[2]*See* R.E. BUMP, K. FRELS, and J.J. HORNER, INVESTIGATING ALLEGED WRONGDOING BY EMPLOYEES IN THE SCHOOL SETTING.

20

Marginally Effective Teachers

John Crain

Introduction

Many principals are becoming concerned about the presence of the teacher who is marginally effective. Unlike the teacher who is consistently ineffective or willfully insubordinate, the marginally effective teacher may require somewhat different professional and legal tactics on the part of the principal. The goal of the instructional leader is to either assist in improving the teacher's performance or to begin the process of an adverse employment recommendation.

Teachers may be found to be "marginally effective" for a variety of reasons: lack of experience, a smaller repertoire of skills and strategies, "burn-out," limited ability, and low commitment to students and the teaching/learning process. Observations will need to focus on both the teacher's behaviors and the outcomes of the behaviors. Those outcomes will usually be related to issues like active student participation, student success in accomplishing the day's instructional objectives, and student compliance with management and behavioral directions from the teacher. Some marginally effective teachers will respond favorably to guidance and principles of developmental supervision. Those who do not respond favorably to constructive feedback, because of their low ability or lack of commitment, should face an adverse employment decision. As the Iowa Supreme Court observed, "A school district is not married to mediocrity, but may dismiss personnel who are neither performing high quality work nor improving in performance."[1]

Legal Issues

When classroom practices are documented and joined with specific administrative directives for remediation, the courts have tended to support the school district position. The courts have upheld dismissals of teachers because students were not being properly taught,[2] instructional materials were not used effectively,[3] lesson presentations were consistently deficient,[4] and lesson plans did not meet the instructional expectations of the district.[5] The Montana Supreme Court noted a teacher's abusive and arbitrary treatment of students,[6] and an Iowa appeals court cited harassment of students and lack of rapport with students as reasonable cause for dismissal.[7]

The inability to effectively manage the classroom and control student behavior has long been recognized by the courts as valid causes for dismissal.[8] It should be noted in these cases that management of student behavior is usually not an isolated issue but is frequently linked to instruction, planning, and management.

The issue of student academic achievement as a cause for dismissal has not been fairly tested in the courts, largely because of the many uncontrolled variables attending this issue. There are, however, cases in which lack of student progress and achievement have been cited as reasons for dismissal. Lack of student progress was one of the four reasons cited in Minnesota for the termination of a tenured teacher with 19 years of experience.[9] Several other courts have viewed lack of student progress as a reasonable basis for an adverse employment decision when linked with other indications of ineffective teaching.[10]

In dealing with the marginally effective teacher, there is a professional and legal imperative to inform the teacher of the criteria that will be used to evaluate the teaching/learning process. These criteria will be the basis for judgments made about the district's instructional expectations and for the directives to improve. The United States Supreme Court has established that any criteria used to evaluate employee performance must be "demonstrably a reasonable measure of job performance."[11] Although early United States Supreme Court cases involving evaluation criteria dealt with testing,[12] the use of any evaluation criteria should be seen as related to the job the person is hired to perform. In the case of the marginally effective teacher, these criteria will be directly related to the teaching/learning process. The criteria used to evaluate and to form the basis for directives for improvement must also be clearly defined in order to avoid charges of arbitrary and capricious behavior on the part of the evaluator. A Washington appeals court overturned the decision to dismiss a principal because of the board's failure to adopt evaluative criteria. "In the absence of established criteria, the principal serves at the whim and pleasure of the superintendent. The principal has no guidelines against which to measure his/her performance and may thereby be deprived of a legitimate opportunity for improvement."[13] Other cases have found that legitimate opportunities to remediate deficiencies are seriously compromised by poorly-defined evaluation criteria.[14]

Direct Observation of Classroom Teaching

The data used in support of an adverse employment decision will be derived primarily from direct classroom observation. These observations will be based on the defined criteria. In addition, the data gathered during these observations will constitute the most significant portion of the documented evidence of the teacher's failure to meet the district's expectations for effective instruction. Multiple observations over an extended period of time by more than one qualified evaluator have been found to strengthen the district's cause of action. A Pennsylvania appeals court affirmed the dismissal of a teacher and quoted the conclusions of the Pennsylvania Secretary of Education:

> While the teacher may object to being rated so often in so short a period of time by different persons, such a procedure is clearly in the employee's best interest since it brings into the evaluation different viewpoints, thereby lessening the influence of personal bias and prejudice with respect to teaching methods.[15]

Unlike the teacher who is viewed as ineffective, multiple observations and documentation may be even more crucial for the marginally effective teacher.

Notice of Failure to Meet Expectations

Once observations have been made and documented, the teacher must be given notice that teaching performance is deficient in that it does not meet the defined criteria of the district.[16] A New York appeals court upheld the dismissal of a tenured teacher because a series of documented observations had both identified deficiencies and informed the teacher that he had not improved in the areas identified.[17]

Once the teacher has been given written notice of deficiencies, it is incumbent upon the principal to provide specific directives for improvement. These directives serve two purposes. First, the directives are based on specific alternatives to the deficiencies previously documented to the teacher. Second, they begin to establish a cause of action for insubordination if the teacher fails to act on the directives. The courts have consistently supported board action to dismiss when specific, reasonable directives were not followed.[18] When the courts support an adverse personnel action based on insubordination, the directives for change must come from an acceptable authority and the changes directed must be reasonable.[19] Accusations of arbitrary, capricious directives are best countered when the principal can demonstrate that the directives are based on defined district criteria which have a legitimate educational purpose.[20]

Adequate Time for Remediation

Failure to allow a fair and reasonable amount of time for deficiencies to be corrected may lead to reinstatement of the dismissed employee.[21] Interpretations of what constitutes "adequate time" vary. In the case of a teacher of mentally handicapped students, an Illinois court found a period of 15 days from the notice of deficiency to the final evaluation to be an unreasonable period for assessing improvement.[22] A Minnesota court found a five week period between the notice of deficiency and the final evaluation as unreasonable.[23] In another Illinois appeals court, eight weeks was seen as a reasonable period of time for a teacher to improve instruction and classroom management.[24] In a contrasting Minnesota case, eight weeks was viewed as unreasonable for a 17-year veteran teacher where practices were evaluated as deficient for the first time.[25] While there is no "magic" number for the amount of time allowed for improvement, there should be a reasonable relationship between the amount of time provided and the number of changes to be made and/or the complexity of the change.

In some cases, the courts have found that time for remediation was not important if the deficiency was irremedial or if the employee acted in a persistently insubordinate manner. Deficiencies most often cited as irremediable include immoral or insubordinate conduct, sexual misconduct with students, conviction of a felony, and repeated instances of improper discipline of students.[26] An Illinois appeals court found that "whether causes for dismissal are remediable is a question of fact and its initial determination lies within the discretion of the board."[27] Actions may be considered irremedial if behavior causes damage that cannot be undone. A series of otherwise remediable behaviors continued over a long period of time may also been seen as irremedial. A Washington court upheld the dismissal of a classroom teacher who struck male students' genitals on five different occasions because the teacher's actions were seen as so offensive that dismissal without remediation was justified.[28] In upholding a dismissal for unacceptable discipline practices, another Washington court held that "sufficient cause for discharge may be evaluated in light of the teacher's record as a whole, which may be said to demonstrate a pattern of unacceptable teaching practices."[29]

Willfulness may be another factor in determining that a deficiency is irremediable. Willfulness of the behavior presumes that there was no misunderstanding of the directive for change and that the teacher intended not to obey that directive. In a Connecticut case, a teacher was reinstated after she was absent following a denial of her request for a leave of absence. The court held that the teacher's act appeared to be an isolated one and was insufficient to be viewed as a willful, persistent behavior.[30] In another case involving absence from duty after being denied a leave of absence, a Maine court sustained a dismissal because the teacher had publicly made known her intention to disregard the board's denial of her leave request.[31] In dealing with the marginally effective teacher, the issue of persistence of behavior may be critical in establishing a pattern of ineffectiveness and a pattern of inability and/or unwillingness to comply with administrative directives. In dealing with the marginally effective teacher, directives for improvement form the basis for dismissal based on persistent and/or willful insubordination (failure to follow reasonable, job-related administrative directives). Directives must provide specific changes in classroom behavior, be based on defined and job-related criteria, and (in most circumstances) provide adequate time for improvement.

Recommendations For Practice

- Begin with well-defined criteria which all teachers are expected to meet. Avoid high-inference criteria (e.g., establishes positive learning climate; communicates information well). Instead, rely on low-inference criteria (e.g., assists students who are having difficulty; defines new content-related vocabulary).
- Observe in classrooms frequently. Use more than one qualified observer.
- Avoid the appearance of arbitrarily unequal treatment of employees. Establish procedures that identify reasons for more frequent observations (e.g., disciplinary referrals, student performance on teacher-made or standardized tests, complaints from parents/students/other teachers).
- During the observation, collect objective, observable data that relate to the defined criteria (e.g., how the teacher deals with students who are unsuccessful).
- Communicate the data to the teacher using objective, specific incident memoranda and documented conferences.

- Write specific directives for improvement. Base the directives on the defined job criteria. Directives should specify changes in behavior. Make certain directives include desired changes in both teacher and student behavior and link the two in a cause-effect relationship.
- Allow adequate time for the teacher to comply. Adequacy of time will depend on the number of changes to be made and the complexity of the changes.
- Monitor and document implementation of the directives through follow-up observations. In the case of the marginally effective teacher, numerous observations (by more than one observer) may be necessary to establish an ongoing pattern of insubordination or inability to comply with the directives.
- Avoid any judgments that will be viewed as retaliation against the teacher for exercise of constitutionally-protected rights.

References

[1]Briggs v. Board of Dirs., 282 N.W. 2d 740, at 743 (Iowa 1979).
[2]Harrison-Washington Community School Corp. v. Bales, 450 N.E. 2d 559 (Ind. Ct. App. 1983).
[3]Donnes v. State, 672 P.2d 617 (Mont. 1983).
[4]Board of Ed. of Minooka Community School Dist. No. 201 v. Ingeles, 403 N.E. 2d 277 (Ill. App. Ct. 1980).
[5]Carson City Schools v. Burnsen, 608 P.2d 507 (Nev. 1980).
[6]Donnes, 672 P.2d 617.
[7]Fay v. Board of Directors of North-Linn, 298 N.W.2d 345 (Iowa Ct. App. 1980).
[8]Merideth v. Board of Educ. of Rockwood, 513 S.W. 2d 740 (Mo. Ct. App. 1974). Mongitore v. Regan, 520 N.Y.S.2d 194 (App. Div. 1987).
[9]Whaley v. Anoka-Hennepin Indep. School Dist., 325 N.W.2d 128 (Minn. 1982).
[10]Perez v. Commission on Professional Competence, 149 Cal. App. 3d 1167 (1983).
[11]Griggs et al. v. Duke Power Company, 401 U.S. 424 (1971).
[12]Id.; See also, Albermarle Paper Company v. Moody, 422 U.S. 405 (1975).
[13]Hyde v. Wellpinit School District No. 49, 648 P.2d 892 (Wash. Ct. App. 1982).
[14]Cantrell v. Vickers, 495 F. Supp. 195 (N.D. Miss., 1980).
[15]Rosso v. Board of School Directors, 380 A.2d 1328 (Pa. Commw. Ct. 1977).
[16]Johnson v. Board of Regents, 377 F. Supp. 227 (Wis. 1974); Smith v. Board of Educ., 334 N.W.2d 150 (Iowa 1983).
[17]Clarke v. Board of Educ. of Vestal Central, 482 N.Y.S.2d 80 (1984).
[18]Merideth, 513 S.W. 740; Thompson v. Board of Educ., 668 P.2d 954 (Colo. Ct. App. 1983); Siglin v. Kayenta Unified School Dist., 655 P.2d 353 (Ariz. Ct. App. 1982).
[19]Drown v. Portsmouth School Dist., 451 F.2d 1106 (1st Cir. 1971).
[20]Potter v. Kalama Public School Dist, 644 P.2d 1229 (Wash. Ct. App. 1982).
[21]Trimboli v. Board of Educ. of Wayne County, 280 S.E.2d 686 (W. Va. 1981).
[22]Board of Educ. of Dist No. 131 v. Ill. State Bd. of Educ., 435 N.E.2d 845 (Ill. App. Ct. 1982).
[23]Ganyo v. Indep. School Dist. No. 832, 311 N.W.2d 497 (Minn. 1981).
[24]Community School Dist. No. 60 Waukegan Public Schools v. Maclin, 435 N.E.2d 845 (Ill. App. 1982).
[25]Ganyo, 311 N.W.2d 497.
[26]Maclin, 435 N.E.2d 845.
[27]Morris v. Board of Educ. of the City of Chicago, 421 N.E.2d 387, 392 (Ill. App. Ct. 1981).
[28]Mott v. Endicott School Dist. No. 308, 713 P.2d 98 (Wash. 1986).
[29]Sargent v. Selah School Dist. No. 119, 599 P.2d 25, 29 (Wash. Ct. App. 1979).
[30]Tucker v. Board of Educ. of the Town of Norfolk, 418 A.2d 933 (Conn. 1979).
[31]Fernald v. City of Ellsworth School Comm., 342 A.2d 704 (Me. 1975).

21

Dismissal Process For Classroom Teachers

R. Craig Wood and Grover H. Baldwin

Introduction

The authority to evaluate and dismiss public school employees rests in the implied and delegated authority of local boards of education.[1] These powers are derived from the state legislatures' expressed powers to maintain and operate public schools. State legislatures outline specific procedures that must be followed for certification and employment and the process of dismissing a public school employee. As part of this dismissal process, the building principal must understand and follow the procedures in making dismissal recommendations to the superintendent and subsequently to the local board of education. Failure to understand this important area, particularly the constitutional freedoms involved, places principals and boards of education in serious jeopardy.[2] Tenure does not protect an individual from examination and evaluation of his or her performance and from possible dismissal. Through statutes, rules, and regulations, states guarantee due process and safeguards within the dismissal framework.

Legal Issues

Nontenured Teacher Dismissal

A distinction is made between the rights and dismissal procedures of nontenured versus tenured teachers. Tenured teachers, those who have completed the appropriate probationary period, are granted a permanent or continuing contract and are entitled to due process in employment decisions. They are subject to reduction-in-force and may be dismissed in accordance with the tenure laws of their specific state. Typically, nontenured teachers are provided a term contract. During that time, they are not entitled to or protected by the dismissal procedures found within the tenure statutes.

They may be nonrenewed during the probationary period at the end of their contract. Both teachers and administrators are subject to the specifics of contract law.[3] The teacher is nonrenewed upon fulfillment of the current contract and when the board of education informs them that they will not be rehired.[4]

Nontenured teachers are not without rights or protections. They do retain their constitutional rights and care must be taken not to violate these rights.[5] The building principal must understand the entire process of termination of nontenured teachers and the rights these individuals possess. For dismissal of nontenured teachers, the principal must be aware of the following: the language in the employment contract that specifically addresses the nature of the position and time of service; the specific time frames under contract law including the contract renewal provisions for the teacher; and the constitutional rights of the teacher. The courts have addressed the issues of giving reasons and a hearing for the nontenured teacher.[6] The courts have also found that nontenured teachers have accrued tenure rights where they were hired for a one-half time position after the probationary period[7] and where they accrued the necessary probationary period in two districts forcing the last district to grant them tenure and dismissal proceedings.[8] In general, nontenured teachers have no right to annual reviews of their performance for the purposes of determining their future employment status.[9]

Tenured Teacher Dismissal

With its plenary powers, state legislatures provide specific reasons for dismissing tenured teachers. These may include: incompetence, immorality, insubordination, incapacity which includes neglect of duty and unprofessional conduct, and conviction of a felony. Specific reasons, tied to "just cause" clauses in collective bargaining agreements, can be used where evidence clearly supports the building principal and the district administration. The courts also apply constitutional protections to tenured teachers, as well as associational rights of union membership where provided.

The specific meaning of incompetency depends on individual state statutes. The courts have allowed broad definitions of the term. Incompetency is measured against a standard requirement for individuals performing the same or similar duties. Incompetency is defined as the "lack of ability, legal qualification, or fitness to discharge the required duty."[10] Incompetency may signify a lack of a proper teaching certificate, a lack of knowledge of subject matter, a lack of ability to establish reasonable discipline in class, a deficiency in teaching methodology, or an emotional instability that demonstrates an inability to effectively teach students.[11]

Tenured teachers may be dismissed for incompetency.[12] In the dismissal process, it is the building principal who must substantiate charges of incompetence. The aspects of dismissal are similar in all states, but specific procedures and time frames may vary according to state statutes. Two major problems arise with the use of incompetency for dismissing tenured teachers. The first is the concept that a teacher, once granted a certificate, is deemed by statute to be competent in knowledge of subject matter and pedagogy. The second is the idea that upon completing the probationary period and being granted tenure by the district, the individual is competent. With these assumptions, it falls to the district administrative personnel, and the building principal in particular, to clearly demonstrate the incompetency of the individual. It must be emphasized that incompetency is evidenced by a variety of issues, and it is vitally important that the principal maintain clear and precise documentation to substantiate any potential charges. The courts are also demanding a greater effort on the part of principals in the remediation process. Not only must such efforts be documented, but principals must take the initiative to recommend and follow through on the remediation process.[13]

Immorality is a term that often creates confusion in contemplating reasons for dismissal. It is important to note that immorality is not confined to sexual misconduct. Immorality is defined as any action which, according to the standards of the community, is deemed to be "inimical to public welfare."[14] Thus, any activity that constitutes corruption or indecency may be grounds for dismissal under a charge of immorality. The standards of immorality may never clearly articulate what is and what is not permitted in the private lives of public school teachers. The Pennsylvania Supreme Court has defined these actions as being, "[a] course of conduct as offends the morals of the community and is a bad example to the youth whose ideals a teacher is supposed to foster and to elevate."[15] In instances of alleged immorality, the district must show that a "grievous assault" on community mores has occurred.[16] This grievous assault standard is difficult to prove and great care must be exercised in developing the case.

A public school teacher serves as a role model for students. The teacher should possess and exhibit the commonly accepted social and moral standards that exist within a community. When a conflict exists between the rights of the individual and the role of an exemplar, building principals must clearly demonstrate that the private actions of a classroom teacher are directly linked to the teacher's effectiveness in the teaching and learning process. Courts will not support the dismissal of public school teachers where there is no clear connection between the immoral conduct and the teacher's classroom performance. Factors that the courts consider in weighing such decisions include: the age and maturity of the students involved; the likelihood that the teacher's conduct will have adversely affected students or other teachers; the degree of the anticipated adversity; the proximity or remoteness in time of the conduct; mitigating or aggravating circumstances surrounding the conduct; the likelihood that the conduct may be repeated; the motives underlying the conduct; and whether the conduct will have a chilling effect on the rights of the teachers involved or other teachers.[17]

The link between action and evident unfitness to teach must be clearly established. Where such a link is not made, even where the teacher was a respondent in an adulterous divorce action, the court will not sustain dismissal or revocation of a certificate.[18] Such immorality has come to include issues of neglect of duty, e.g., drinking beer with a student group one is chaperoning.[19] Where the act is considered irremediable, the courts have allowed for immediate dismissal without prior warning.[20]

A growing area of litigation based on immorality has been pregnancy of unwed public school teachers. Over the years, community and societal standards have changed. Generally, the courts have not sustained building principals and local school boards in the dismissal of unwed pregnant school teachers. The current state of the law indicates that pregnancy of an unwed teacher is not irrefutable proof of immorality.[21] If the facts show that the teacher's ability in the classroom and the teacher's respect in the community and in the school system have not been adversely affected, then the dismissal of the unwed classroom teacher will not be sustained.[22]

Insubordination by public school teachers is the willful disregard of or refusal to obey reasonable directives.[23] Dismissals for insubordination have not been upheld when: the alleged misconduct was not proven; the existence of a pertinent school rule or a superior's order was not proven; the teacher's motive for violating the rule or order was admirable; the rule or order was unreasonable; the rule or order was invalid as beyond the authority of the maker; the enforcement of the rule of order revealed possible bias or discrimination against the teacher; or the enforcement of the rule or order violated constitutional rights.[24] A building principal may issue directives to the staff for activities relating to the educational functions of the school. However, these directives must be reasonable and rational, must not be trivial, and must not infringe on the legal rights of individuals. The idea of insubordination and willful neglect must be proven and not merely assumed and may include items not directly demanded by the principal or by the contract.[25]

Incapacity encompasses issues relating to the ability and proficiency to teach in the public schools. The term is used to mean "want of legal ability to act and has been construed to include inefficiency."[26] Charges of incapacity are often coupled with claims of incompetency and neglect of duties. Absent evidence of an infringement of constitutionally protected freedoms, the courts give boards of education great latitude in determining what activities constitute nonperformance.[27] Yet the principal must be cautious not to use the knowledge of incapacity to obtain a resignation in lieu of dismissal or else the issue of coercion will arise.[28] These conditions range from lack of pupil discipline and failure to keep proper and timely records, to the inability to convey knowledge to their students.

Corporal punishment is often evidence of incapacity and unprofessional conduct where the student has been harmed excessively or where such actions are contrary to school board policy or state statute. Even with a broad interpretation, boards of education must establish a link between the teacher's alleged conduct and his or her teaching ability. However, where a charge of unprofessional conduct involves sexual contact with a student or deviant sexual actions, the board of education must only prove that the conduct existed.[29] Whatever the claim, all such charges must be clearly demonstrated and supported by the board of education.

Conduct judged to be so deficient that it seriously harms the teacher's effectiveness need not be tolerated by a school board and building principal. In these instances, dismissal can occur without attempts to remediate such behavior. Illustrative of this concept is the case where a classroom teacher repeatedly, and purposefully, struck male students in the genitals.[30] After suspension with pay, an investigation revealed that the teacher had struck at least four male students. The board of education dismissed the teacher without prior warnings nor a period of probation. In upholding the board's action, the court viewed the behavior as so offensive to warrant dismissal without remediation.

Neglect of duty is a derivative of incapacity. It is usually interwoven with other charges stemming from incapacity including unprofessional conduct. Neglect of duty may include failure to follow curriculum guides, failure to maintain adequate discipline, failure to follow prescribed teaching lessons, and similar reasons.[31] Neglect of duty usually entails carelessness on the part of the employee. This action differs from insubordination where an employee blatantly disregards specific directives of administrators or school boards. Such charges of neglect of duty must be shown to have had prior notice and a clearly established policy or directive in order to withstand judicial challenge.[32]

Occasionally, public school teachers are arrested on felony charges: a crime of a "graver or more atrocious nature than those designated as misdemeanors."[33] Such arrests may not necessarily have a direct bearing on classroom performance. However, by state statutory requirements, the conviction of a felony may be grounds for the permanent loss of a teacher's license as it demonstrates an "evident unfitness to teach" within the public schools. In general, the courts support the dismissal of teachers for felony convictions.[34]

Due Process: Procedural and Substantive

A major difference in the dismissal of tenured and nontenured faculty is the application of due process requirements for tenured faculty. These requirements include both procedural due process and substantive due process and must be followed by school administrative personnel and local boards of education. Procedural due process ensures that the "parties whose rights are to be affected are entitled to be heard, and in order that they may enjoy that right, they must be notified."[35] Substantive due process is broadly defined as "the constitutional guarantee that no person shall be arbitrarily deprived of his life, liberty or property" and shall be protected "from arbitrary and unreasonable action."[36]

Procedural due process consists of several elements. The first element is that of notification. By applicable statute, the classroom teacher must receive written notification and the specific reason cited in order for the notice of dismissal to be valid. This notification must conform with all applicable dates and manner as to its delivery. The second element is the provision for a fair and impartial hearing. The classroom teacher must be afforded an opportunity to be heard, examine and refute any evidence on which the decision is based, and have an opportunity to discredit such evidence and judgments made by cross-examination and confrontation of witnesses. Fair hearings occur at several levels. This process begins with the building principal and ends with the board of education. This process provides the assurance that the classroom teacher has multiple opportunities to be heard and avoids the charges of arbitrary, capricious, and whimsical actions[37] and thus forestalls charges of inadequate due process.

During the dismissal process, the board must show cause and follow the appropriate due process procedures.[38] In this process, the building principal has the specific responsibility to ensure that all evaluations, conferences, and remediation are documented, are related to the specific deficiencies of the teacher, and are shown to be fair and reasonable. Courts have held that dismissals are permissible as long as an individual's constitutional rights were not violated. Courts have reasoned that if terminations were for permissible reasons and were not arbitrary, capricious, or unreasonable, they are legally defensible.[39] In fact, the dismissal may stand even if the constitutional infractions were merely "incidental."[40]

Classroom teachers have a property right to the reasonable expectation of future employment with the granting of tenure.[41] A teacher's continuing contract cannot be breached by the school board without procedural and substantive due process. A liberty interest under the fourteenth amendment guarantees against invasion without due process of law. School teachers have a liberty interest in their good name and professional reputation. If administrators or school board members stigmatize a teacher's professional reputation and thus prevent the teacher from pursuing and attaining another professional position, there is a violation of this liberty interest, and due process is necessary. The United States Supreme Court addressed the issue of property rights through tenure and the liberty interests of employees.[42] The Court noted that while liberty interests are "broad and majestic," the board did not harm the teacher's "good name, reputation, honor, or integrity" in the nonrenewal of his teaching contract. If a board does not stigmatize a nontenured teacher's professional reputation, and where state statutes allow for such a procedure, a board of education may nonrenew a teacher.

Reduction-In-Force

In the face of declining enrollments and the resultant loss of financial support, boards of education are under no obligation to retain unneeded staff. Regardless of the terminology used, reduction-in-force (RIF) is the suspension of a tenured or nontenured classroom teacher for reasons unrelated to performance.[43] However, if a teacher's classroom performance led to the decline of enrollments, such dismissal or nonrenewal may be within the RIF statutes or nonperformance statutes.[44]

Fiscal insolvency is the most frequently cited reason for engaging in RIF. When fiscal insolvency is claimed, counter-claims center on determination of the validity of the fiscal data. States have their own definitions and manner for determining fiscal insolvency.[45] Whatever definition is used, when fiscal insolvency is claimed, the board of education must substantiate its actions using empirical evidence and it must be completed in good faith.[46] Numerous cases illustrate the need for clear and precise information to justify and defend the decisions that lead to the dismissal of an employee due to budgetary constraints.[47] When these data are supported, courts will uphold the decision of the board of education. In implementing RIF, the building principal, district administration, and the board of education must not engage in any activity which is or gives the appearance that the action might be arbitrary, capricious, unreasonable, or violates the constitutional rights of individuals.[48]

The complex issues of seniority and the right to "bump" are often interwoven with state statutes via local collective bargaining agreements. In general, the courts start from the position that all teachers in the district are to be treated alike, no matter what subdivision or program they work in. From that point the usage of seniority and bumping begin.[49] Some state courts have ruled that in matters of RIF, seniority extends to nontenured teachers and is the sole criteria for RIF.[50] Other courts have ruled that nontenured teachers, by virtue of their noncontinuing and nontenured status, do not possess seniority rights.[51] As a general rule, teachers may "bump" those teachers who possess less seniority within their certification areas.[52] These issues are highly dependent on state statutes and appropriate collective bargaining agreements.[53] However, the courts have held that once RIF is declared, the district must complete the process and not create positions to avoid the full effects of RIF.[54] Thus, the building principal must be familiar with the collective bargaining agreement as well as the appropriate statutory requirements. In dealing with the concerns of due process and RIF, the building principal must have a broad base knowledge of curriculum planning, enrollment projections, and potential retirements; as well as course demands, cross certifications, and the overall staff needs prior to the time of RIF.

Recommendations for Practice

For evaluation and possible dismissal of teachers, the principal must be mindful of a number of issues that may create problems in the dismissal process. To minimize risk, certain guidelines are offered:

- Maintain objectivity in all areas of the evaluation process.
- Establish standards and criteria for evaluation that are validated as accurate measures of the performance under observation.
- Maintain evidence of the teacher's failure to perform and the influence of this behavior on students, staff, and community.

- Maintain records of the specific recommendations and evidence of the degree to which the teacher has met these recommendations.
- Establish the link between the behavior or alleged incompetence and the effect on the teacher's performance.
- Be aware of the closeness between assistance offered to the teacher (as well as evaluation and follow-up) and harassment.
- Document what was done and what was expected, as well as the time frames and follow-up activities.
- Be aware of the community standards for personal and professional behavior of the teaching staff.
- Document the directives given to the teacher, the time frames for compliance, and the follow-up procedures and findings to validate the compliance of the teacher.
- Avoid any action that may be a violation of the constitutional rights of teachers.

References

[1] Graham v. Special School Dist. #1, 462 N.W.2d 78 (Minn. Ct. App. 1990).

[2] Greminger v. Seaborne, 584 F.2d 275 (8th Cir. 1984).

[3] Clark v. Mann, 562 F.2d 1104 (8th Cir. 1977).

[4] See Leola School Dist. v. McMahan, 712 S.W.2d 903 (Ark. 1986); Branch v. School Dist., 432 F. Supp. 608 (D. Mont. 1977).

[5] Harris v. Florence City Board of Educ., 568 So. 2d 827 (Ala. Civ. App. 1990).

[6] See Kharrubi v. Board of Educ. of City of New York, 519 N.Y.S.2d 671 (App. Div. 1987): Caldwell v. Blytheville, Ark. School Dist. No. 5, 746 S.W.2d 381 (Ark. Ct. App. 1988): Ford v. Caldwell Parish School Bd., 541 So. 2d 955 (La. Ct. App. 1989): Bellflower Educ. Ass'n v. Bellflower Unif. School Dist., 279 Cal. Rptr. 179 (Cal. Ct. App. 1991): Marxsen v. Board of Dir. of M.S.A.D. No. 5, 591 A.2d 867 (Me. 1991).

[7] Williams v. Hardin County Comm. School Dist. 1, 520 N.E.2d 954 (Ill. Ct. App. 1988).

[8] Six v. Job Serv. N. D., 443 N.W.2d 911 (N.D. 1989).

[9] Watson v. Eagle County School Dist. RE-50, 797 P.2d 768 (Colo. Ct. App. 1990).

[10] BLACK'S LAW DICTIONARY 688, (5th 1979).

[11] See Busker v. Board of Educ. of Elk Point, 295 N.W.2d 1 (S.D. 1980).

[12] School Dist. v. Gautier, 73 P. 954 (1903).

[13] Brown v. Wood County Board of Educ., 400 S.E.2d 213 (W. Va. 1990); and Selby v. North Callaway Bd. of Educ., 777 S.W.2d 275 (Mo. Ct. App. 1989).

[14] BLACK'S LAW DICTIONARY, at 885.

[15] Horosko v. Mt Pleasant Twp. School Dist., 6 A.2d 866 (1939), cert. denied, 308 U.S. 553 (1939).

[16] Penn-Delco School Dist. v. Urso, 382 A.2d 162 (1978).

[17] Morrison v. State Bd. of Educ., 461 P.2d 375, at 386 (Cal 1969). Specific cases involving adultery as a charge of immorality, see, Weissman v. Board of Educ. of Jefferson County School Dist., 547 P.2d 1267 (Colo. 1976); Erb v. Iowa State Board of Pub. Inst., 216 N.W.2d 339 (Iowa 1974).

[18] Id., Erb.

[19] Blaine v. Moffat County School Dist, 748 P.2d 1280 (Colo. 1988).

[20] Sauter v. Mount Vernon School Dist., 791 P.2d 549 (Wash. Ct. App. 1990); Hegener v. Chicago Bd. of Educ. 567 N.E.2d 566 (Ill. App. Ct. 1991).

[21] Avery v. Homewood City Bd. of Educ., 674 F.2d 337 (5th Cir. 1982), cert. denied, 461 U.S. 943 (1983); Andrews v. Drew Municipal Separate School Dist., 507 F.2d 611 (5th Cir. 1975), cert. granted, 423 U.S. 820 (1975), cert. dismissed, 425 U.S. 559 (1976).

[22] See generally, Acanfora v. Board of Educ. of Montgomery County, 491 F.2d 498 (4th Cir. 1974); New Mexico State Bd. of Educ. v. Stoudt, 571 P.2d 1186 (N.M. 1977).

[23]School Dist. No. 8. Pinal County v. Superior Ct., 433 P.2d 28 (1967). *See also,* Adlerstein v. Board of Educ. of New York City, 485 N.Y.S.2d 1 (N.Y. 1984).

[24]78 A.L.R.3d 83-87.

[25]Cowdery v. Philadelphia Bd. of Educ., 531 A.2d 1186 (Pa. Commw. Ct. 1987): Johnson v. School Board of Dade County, 578 So. 2d 387 (Fla. Ct. App. 1991).

[26]BLACK'S LAW DICTIONARY, at 902.

[27]Saye v. Saint Vrain Valley School Dist. RE-1J, 785 F.2d 862 (10th Cir. 1986); Kizer v. Dorchester County Vocational Educ. Bd. of Trustees, 340 S.E.2d 144 (S.C. 1986).

[28]Price v. Boulder Valley School Dist., 782 P.2d 821 (Colo. Ct. App. 1989).

[29]Tomerlin v. Dade County School Board, 318 So. 2d 159 (Fla. Ct. App. 1975); Wishart v. McDonald, 500 F.2d 1110 (1st Cir. 1974).

[30]Mott v. Endicott School Dist. No. 308, 713 P.2d 98 (Wash. 1986).

[31]*See,* Harvey v. Jefferson County School Dist. No. R-1, 710 P.2d 1103 (Colo. 1985).

[32]*Cowdery,* 531 A.2d 1186.

[33]BLACK'S LAW DICTIONARY, at 44.

[34]*See,* Bertrand v. New Mexico State Bd. of Educ., 544 P.2d 1176 (N.M. 1975); Skripchuk v. Austin, 379 A.2d 1142 (Del. Super. Ct. 1977).

[35]BLACK'S LAW DICTIONARY, at 1083.

[36]*Id.* at 1281.

[37]Belcourt v. Fort Totten Public School Dist. 454 N.W.2d 703 (N.D. 1990).

[38]*See* Nelson v. Board of Educ. of Doland School Dist., 380 N.W.2d 665 (S.D. 1986).

[39]Johnson v. Board of Regents, 377 F. Supp. 227 (W.D. Wis. 1974); *see,* Smith v. Board of Educ., 334 N.W.2d 150 (Iowa 1983).

[40]Sheets v. Stanley Community School Dist. No. 2, 413 F. Supp. 350 (D.N.D. 1975).

[41]For claims involving expectations by nontenured teachers, *see,* Sullivan v. School Bd. of Pinellas County, 773 F.2d. 1182 (11th Cir. 1985); Carmichael v. Chambers County Bd. of Educ., 581 F.2d 95 (5th Cir. 1978).

[42]*Johnson,* 377 F. Supp. 227.

[43]For a discussion of reduction-in-force and related issues, *see, Reduction in Force,* R. Craig Wood, PRINCIPLES OF SCHOOL BUSINESS MANAGEMENT, 537-557 (1986); R. Craig Wood, *Financial Exigencies and the Dismissal of Public School Teachers: A Legal Perspective,* GOVERNMENT UNION REVIEW, 1982, vol. 7, no. 3, 262-276; and R. Craig Wood, *Chapter Nine of the Federal Bankruptcy Act: A Fiscal Alternative for School Districts,* J. OF EDUC. FINANCE, 1985, 56-68.

[44]*In re* Gaetjens, 485 A.2d 1057 (N.H. 1984).

[45]*See* Frimel v. Humphrey, 555 S.W.2d 350 (Mo. 1977); California School Employees Ass'n v. Pasadena Unif. School Dist., 139 Cal. Rptr. 633 (Cal. Ct. App. 1977).

[46]Gross v. Board of Educ. of Elmsford, 571 N.Y.S.2d 200 (Ct. App. 1991).

[47]*See* Unified School Dist. v. Epperson, 583 F.2d 1118 (10th Cir. 1978); Bradfute v. Renton School Dist., 577 P.2d 157 (Wash. 1978); Freiberg v. Board of Educ. of Big Bay De Noc, 283 N.W.2d 775 (Mich. 1979).

[48]*See* Britton v. South Bend Community School Corp., 819 F.2d 766 (7th Cir. 1987), *cert. denied* 108 S. Ct. 288 (1987).

[49]Heruth v. Indep. School Dist. 434 N.W.2d 470 (Minn. Ct. App. 1989).

[50]Alexander v. Delano Joint Union High School Dist., 188 Cal. Rptr. 705 (Ct. App. 1983); Bohmann v. Board of Educ. of West Clermont, 443 N.E.2d 176 (Ohio 1983); Carmody v. Board of Directors, 453 A.2d 965 (Pa. 1982).

[51]*See* Lezette v. Bd. of Educ., 319 N.E.2d 189 (N.Y. 1974); Hill v. Dayton School Dist., 532 P.2d 1154 (Wash. 1975).

[52]*See,* McKeesport Area School Dist. v. Cicogna, 558 A.2d 116 (Pa. Commw. Ct. 1989).

[53]Fort Sumner Mun. School Bd. v. Parsons, 485 P.2d 366 (N.M. 1971); Penasco Indep. School Dist. No. 4 v. Lucero, 526 P.2d 825 (N.M. 1974); Higgins v. Bd. of Educ. of Comm. Unit School Dist. No. 303, 428 N.E.2d 1126 (Ill. 1981).

[54]*See* O'Hair v. Board of Educ., 805 P.2d 40 (Kan. Ct. App. 1990).

22

Teacher Certification

William E. Sparkman and Trudy A. Campbell

Introduction

As the instructional leader of the building, the principal has the overall responsibility for the school's program including the teaching staff. While the central office generally monitors the status of teachers' certification, principals would be well advised to check the validity of the teachers' certificates in their building on a yearly basis. This step is particularly true when a teacher on the staff is employed under a provisional endorsement or a temporary or emergency certificate valid for only one year. It can be very disrupting and disconcerting to students and parents when a teacher is dismissed during the school year for failure to have a valid certificate. What makes such situations even more frustrating is that teachers often are at fault by carelessly allowing their certificate to expire.

A teacher in Oregon was dismissed by the local school board when it was reported that she no longer had a valid teacher's certificate. What is unusual in this case was the reason that her certificate had been declared invalid by the state: a bounced check! The facts of the case are fairly straightforward and illustrate how an individual's carelessness or oversight can have tremendous personal and professional implications. The teacher received a renewal certificate from the state after her initial license had expired. She returned the renewal fee in the form of a personal check. Shortly thereafter, she was informed by the state's regulatory agency that the certificate was invalid because her check had bounced. The teacher contested her dismissal in court, which found that she was not "a teacher" within the meaning of the law since she lacked a valid teacher's certificate due to her failure to make the required payment.[1] The consequences of releasing a teacher who is not certified is profound in terms of public relations, the teacher's livelihood and career, and the disruption of the children's education program. School principals may not be directly involved in most certification issues, but it is imperative for school leaders to develop an understanding of teacher certification as a vital area of school law.

Legal Issues

There are three primary areas of concern in teacher certification: the basis of the state's authority and interest in teacher certification, the relation of certification to employment, and the reasons and processes necessary for the revocation of a certificate. Each of the 50 states has legislative statutes and administrative regulations governing teacher certification within its jurisdiction. While these statutes and regulations are state specific, there are some general principles that emerge from case law. It is advisable for principals to review the state statutes and administrative regulations governing teacher certification in their states.

A teaching certificate is a "document certifying that one has fulfilled the requirements of and may practice in the field."[2] Teaching certificates are granted by the state under its plenary power to control education. According to an Illinois judge, "the predominate purpose in licensing a trade or profession is to prevent injury to the public by assuring that the occupation will be practiced with honesty and integrity and by excluding those who are incompetent or unworthy."[3]

State's Authority in Certification

The state legislature generally delegates to the state board of education the responsibility to adopt rules and regulations governing certification. For example, a rule of the Texas State Board of Education requires, among other things, that an individual making application for a state teacher certificate must satisfy the following general requirements:

- Be a citizen of the United States or indicate intent to become a naturalized citizen;
- Be at least 18 years of age;
- Be of good moral character. The commissioner of education may refuse to issue a teaching certificate to a person who has been convicted of a felony or a misdemeanor for a crime which directly relates to the duties and responsibilities of the teaching profession;
- Be willing to support and defend the constitutions of the United States and Texas;

- Be able to speak and understand the English language sufficiently to use it easily and readily in conversation and in teaching;
- Register for and complete all appropriate examinations as prescribed by the State Board of Education...for the teacher preparation program completed.[4]

The rules must be neutral with respect to race, color, sex, religion, and national origin and must be applied in a nondiscriminatory manner. The United States Supreme Court has sustained the authority of the states to enact laws requiring resident aliens to produce evidence of their intention to become naturalized citizens of the United States before issuing a teaching certificate.[5]

The authority of the state to require teacher certification is well settled. In recent years, however, legal challenges have been mounted in several states by churches operating private, sectarian schools. Issues such as the state's authority over church schools and whether the state's interest in teacher certification is of such magnitude to allow it to burden certain individual's right to the free exercise of their religious beliefs have been questioned. In Iowa, certain individuals involved in church-sponsored schools argued unsuccessfully in court that the state certification requirements burdened their first amendment right to the free exercise of their religious beliefs. In speaking about the importance of teacher certification to the state's interest in education, a federal district court judge wrote, "[t]he importance lies, not in the piece of paper itself, but in the education a person must receive to become eligible for the certificate...[t]his kind of knowledge is essential if one is to become a good teacher."[6] Thus, Iowa's interest in requiring all teachers to be certified was sufficiently compelling to override the plaintiffs' first amendment claims.

In regard to the more general issue of the state's authority over teacher certification, the power of the state to certify teachers derives from its plenary power over education, subject only to the constraints imposed by the state or federal constitutions. This plenary power emerges from the state's police power to impose reasonable restrictions on its citizenry to promote and maintain the comfort, safety, health, and welfare of society.[7] The Washington Supreme Court stated the issue in the following manner:

> [T]here is no doubt that the state, in the exercise of such [police] power, may prescribe laws tending to promote the health, peace, morals, education, good order and welfare of the people. Police power is an attribute of sovereignty, and essential element of the power to govern, and a function that cannot be surrendered. It exists without express

declaration, and the only limitation upon it is that it must reasonably tend to correct some evil or promote some interest of the state, and not violate any direct or positive mandate of the Constitution.[8]

State teacher certification regulations also impact private schools. It is well established that the state has the authority to reasonably regulate both public and private schools.[9] Included in that general authority is the right to require teacher certification. The purpose of teacher certification is to protect the public interest so that only those qualified will be allowed to teach. The state has an interest in private schools having qualified teachers. The North Dakota Supreme Court held that teacher certification was "among the least personally intrusive methods now available to satisfy the state's prime interest in seeing that its children are taught by capable persons."[10] The Nebraska Supreme Court found that the state had a compelling interest in the certification of its teachers and concluded that the requirements were "neither arbitrary nor unreasonable" and were "a reliable indicator of the probability of success in that particular field."[11]

Teacher Certification and Employment

A teaching certificate is a license and not a contract. A license "confers no more than a mere expectancy of employment, and does not confer any claim to a specific position, or, for that matter, to any further employment."[12] Although the possession of a teaching certificate does not guarantee employment in a school district, it is required in order for the teacher to be a competent party to an employment contract and to be paid by the school board.[13] Where a state allowed waivers for credentials, a probationary employee had no statutory right to reemployment if the employee failed to make progress toward obtaining the required credential.[14] Salary benefits under an employment contract may be calculated on the basis of the type of certification held rather than the actual position of employment.[15] An individual who taught as a substitute teacher working for more than 90 school days brought action seeking damages consisting of the difference between substitute and full-time teacher's pay. The court found she could not invoke provisions of a statute entitled "Substitute Certificates" since she still held a teaching certificate.

The courts have been called upon to resolve the question of whether teachers or administrators may be employed by a school board even though they do not hold a certificate at the time they contract but can obtain one prior to assuming official duties. The answer depends upon the language of the state statute and its interpretation by the courts. In some cases, the courts have held that teachers are legally employed if they have secured a certificate prior to actually teaching;[16] but in other cases, the courts have taken the position that teachers must have a valid certificate at the time the employment contract is made.[17] Finally, the issue of timing in seeking an alternate certificate has arisen where teachers are required to obtain permanent certification to retain a position. The courts have held that time requirements must be met and backdating after the expiration of a provisional certificate is not satisfactory.[18] Furthermore, both provisional and permanent certificates must comply with the conditions set forth in the hearing panel's decision. In this case, a middle school mathematics teacher could not be reinstated on the basis of obtaining a provisional certificate in elementary education. The date of recertification can also come into question in reduction in force (RIF) agreements. The Ohio Supreme Court held that a teacher recertified in elementary education after being placed on a RIF list was entitled to recall privileges.[19]

A question that is often troubling to educators is whether or not the state can change certification requirements. This point was validated in an early Indiana case involving the revocation of a teacher's certificate. In upholding the revocation, the judge wrote that "[a] license has none of the elements of a contract, and does not confer an absolute right, but only a personal privilege to be exercised under existing restrictions, and such as may thereafter be reasonably imposed."[20] Connecticut's Supreme Court also noted that a statute providing for exchange of permanent teaching certificates for five-year certificates renewable upon completion of continuing education courses did not violate teachers' procedural or substantive due process rights nor their constitutional contract rights.[21]

A related issue is whether the state can require all currently certified teachers and administrators to take and pass a competency examination in order to retain their teaching credentials. As part of the Texas school reform package enacted in 1984, the legislature required the examination of reading and writing skills of all persons certified prior to May 1, 1986.[22] As expected, this law caused a great deal of consternation among the state's educators and resulted in several lawsuits against the state. One of the suits resulted in the Texas Supreme Court's pronouncement that the testing requirement was constitutional.[23] The court held that because a teaching certificate is not a contract, "the constitutional prohibition against impairment of contracts is not violated when the legislature imposes new conditions for the retention of the certificate."[24] In addition, the court found that state law provided adequate due process protection for teachers who failed to pass the competency test. The court rejected the contention that the law was fundamentally unfair by holding that the test had "a rational relation to the legitimate state objective of maintaining competent teachers in the public schools."[25]

On occasion, teachers may be assigned to teach a course in which they are not certified. Court opinions seem to differ on the question. A Louisiana appeals court held that teachers can only teach in the area in which they are certified.[26] On the other hand, a Missouri appeals court upheld the dismissal of a teacher who refused to teach a social studies class after she relinquished her certification in the field.[27] In this case, the teacher had been assigned to teach three social studies courses following the release of a probationary teacher due to financial exigency. Not wanting to take the new assignment, she requested the state department of education to withdraw her certification in social studies. The principal assigned her to teach the social studies courses despite the fact that she was no longer certified in that field. When the new year began, she failed to attend or teach one of the assigned social studies classes. The school board, following the required due process procedures, voted to terminate her contract on the grounds of insubordination and excessive absences. The court affirmed the termination, ruling that "the recognition by the State Board [of Education] of the practice of making such assignments clearly indicates that the absence of a particular field of study from a teacher's certificate does not invalidate a contract to teach that subject."[28] The court found that the assignment was not unreasonable given the budgetary problems, which necessitated the reduction of the teaching staff.

However, when a tenured industrial arts teacher in Kansas, who was certified to teach social science, was nonrenewed in a RIF situation the court held that the action was without good cause. The board required the social science position be filled by someone certified to teach physical education as well as to undertake some coaching. This requirement was considered an impermissible joining of primary and supplemental contracts.[29] Some states may not require certification for certain classes of teachers. In Wisconsin, for example, vocational, technical, and adult education school instructors were not required to satisfy state teacher certification requirements in order to teach limited vocational subjects to public school students.[30]

The Revocation of a Teaching Certificate

With the right to certify teachers, a state has a collateral right to revoke certificates for just cause. The suspension or revocation of a teaching certificate requires appropriate standards of due process as provided by law.[31] State statutes generally specify reasons for revocation of a certificate and provide the requisite due process procedures. Several reasons that have been accepted by the courts as valid in recent revocation cases include: wearing religious dress while performing teaching duties in contravention of state law,[32] possession of 52 marijuana plants,[33] conviction of perjury and extortion,[34] falsifying attendance records,[35] conviction of eight counts of indecent assault upon several male children,[36] mail fraud,[37] fondling female students and then attempting to persuade them to withdraw allegations,[38] and failure to obtain satisfactory evaluations.[39] Many states provide that a teacher's certificate may be suspended or canceled for abandoning an existing contract without good cause and without consent of the board of education.

All applicable standards of due process must be observed. This step would include offering proper notice and a hearing. A Florida court held that the failure by the state's Education Practices Commission to give notice that a teacher was at risk of having his license permanently revoked, even if justified by the evidence, was an error.[40]

Due process was also an issue where a nontenured teacher was placed on the New York City school board's circular distributed to principals and superintendents indicating that he could not be employed in any public school because of discontinuance of his probationary appointment. He argued this constructively revoked his teaching license without due process of law. The plaintiff prevailed on his claim that he had a property interest in his teaching license. In analyzing the claim, the court noted that property interests are created and defined with reference to state law. Prevailing New York law was framed by a Commissioner of Education decision, which held that the teaching license conferred a legitimate claim of entitlement, not to a job, but rather "to the opportunity to seek employment in all thirty-one community school districts in the New York City school system."[41] In South Carolina, when a teaching certificate was canceled by the state board on the basis of a testing company invalidating a test score, the court noted that a hearing granted to the teacher did not comport with procedural due process where the board did not disclose any evidence substantiating cancellation of the test scores.[42] In addition, Ohio's Rules of Civil Procedure are not binding upon the State Board of Education in adjudicatory proceedings nor does *res judicata* attach to teaching certificate revocation proceedings in which no determination was made on the merits.[43]

An important point is that once a teacher is certified by the state, that teacher is considered to be competent. The state bears the burden of proof in all revocation cases. A Florida court has made it clear that all forms and procedures must substantially comply with state law. The court noted that the prosecutor in revocation cases must prove a *prima facia* case, the record must substantiate the findings, and the hearing board must review contents of investigative files and actually accept such files into evidence.[44] A California appeals court overturned an order by a state commission recommending the revocation of a teacher's credentials. In a strongly worded opinion, the court stated that "it is well settled that a board commits an abuse of discretion when it revokes a license to conduct a legitimate business without competent evidence establishing just cause of revocation, and that hearsay evidence alone is insufficient to support the revocation of such a license."[45] The court further noted that hearsay evidence, unless specifically permitted by statute, is not competent evidence to support a revocation decision. Yet, trial testimony describing rape provided sufficient evidence of a teacher's immorality and misconduct for revocation even though conviction for rape was reversed.[46] Furthermore, an admission that a teacher had engaged in inappropriate sexual conduct with male students was admissible in an administrative proceeding to revoke his teaching certificate, even though the admission had been obtained following a false representation by a private investigator hired by the school.[47] On the other hand, evidence of substantive charges for distribution of drugs contained in expunged criminal records was inadmissible.[48]

Recently, a number of cases have involved the issue of authority to revoke licenses. In Rhode Island, the court ruled that the Board of Regents exceeded its authority when it canceled certificates prior to the stated expiration dates.[49] In Illinois, the appellate court held that the state superintendent lacked authority to revoke a license after the Teacher Certification Board had voted not to revoke such license;[50] and in Florida, the Education Practices Commission was not authorized to permanently revoke a teaching certificate when the administrative complaint sought only revocation with a possibility of reinstatement.[51]

Recommendations for Practice

It is clear that any person seeking state teacher certification has the responsibility to see that all requirements are met and that the appropriate paperwork is completed. It also is that person's responsibility to ensure that the certificate is current and that appropriate action is taken to renew the certificate upon its expiration.

- School principals should monitor carefully the certification status of the staff to ensure that the certificates are current and in order.

- Principals may find that they are more involved in the initial assignment of teachers or in their reassignment because of fiscal problems or changing state curriculum regulations. Whether teachers may be assigned to teach outside of their area of certification is a question to be determined by the individual state. Principals should be aware that states differ in their interpretation of this issue.

- School principals may be called upon to provide documentation in a certificate revocation case. Such documentation must provide substantial evidence of the alleged wrongdoing and be more than hearsay.

References

[1] Wagenblast v. Cook Cty. School Dist., 707 P.2d 69 (1985).
[2] WEBSTER'S NEW COLLEGIATE DICTIONARY (1981).
[3] Trigg v. Sanders, 515 N.E.2d 1367 at 1373 (Ill. App. Ct. 1987).
[4] Texas State Bd. of Educ., 19 Tex. Admin. Code § 141.3 (West April 1, 1991) (Certification of Teachers in General).
[5] Ambach v. Norwick, 441 U.S. 68 (1979).
[6] Fellowship Baptist Church v. Benton, 620 F. Supp. 308, 316 (S.D. Iowa 1985).
[7] BLACK'S LAW DICTIONARY 1317 (Rev. 4th ed. 1968). See also, Campbell v. Aldrich, 79 P.2d 257, 261 appeal dismissed, 305 U.S. 559 (1938) (where the Court held that public education and its control is a proper subject for the exercise of police power).
[8] Shea v. Olson, 53 P.2d 615, 619 (1936).
[9] Pierce v. Society of Sisters, 268 U.S. 510 (1925).
[10] State v. Patzer, 382 N.W.2d 631, 639 (N.D. 1986). See State v. Rivinius, 328 N.W.2d 220, 231 (N.D. 1982) (where state supreme court held that a statutory requirement that a church school would not be approved by the state unless the school's teachers were certified did not unduly infringe on the constitutional rights of parents in the upbringing and education of their children nor did it impinge on the free exercise rights of the defendants).
[11] State v. Faith Baptist Church, 301 N.W.2d 571, 579 (Neb. 1981). See also Sheridan Road Baptist Church v. Dept. of Educ., 396 N.W.2d 373, 395 (Mich. 1986) (where the Supreme Court of Michigan, by an equally divided court, held that teacher certification was a compelling state interest and outweighed the "indirect and minimal burden" placed upon the plaintiff's free exercise rights).
[12] Lombard v. Board of Educ., 645 F. Supp. 1574, 1577 (E.D.N.Y. 1986).
[13] Bradford Central Sch. Dist. v. Ambach, 451 N.Y.S.2d 654, 656 (N.Y. 1982).
[14] Royster v. Cushman, 261 Cal. Rptr. 458 (Cal. Ct. App. 1989).
[15] Woods v. East St. Louis School Dist., 498 N.E.2d 801 (Ill. App. Ct. 1986).

[16]Lee v. Mitchell, 156 S.W. 450 (Ark. 1913); Cottongim v. Stewart, 127 S.W.2d 149 (Ky. 1939); State ex rel. Lawson v. Cherry, 47 So. 2d 768 (Fla. 1950).

[17]O'Conner v. Francis, 59 N.Y.S. 28 (1899).

[18]Smith v. Andrews, 504 N.Y.S.2d 286 (N.Y. App. Div. 1986).

[19]Whitley v. Canton City Sch. Dist., 528 N.E.2d 167 (Ohio 1988).

[20]Stone v. Fritts, 82 N.E. 792, 794 (Ind. 1907).

[21]Connecticut Educ. Ass'n v. Tirozzi, 554 A.2d 1065 (Conn. 1989).

[22]Tex. Educ. Code Ann. § 13.047 (Vernon 1986).

[23]State v. Project Principle, Inc., 724 S.W.2d 387 (Tex. 1987). See also Texas State Teachers Ass'n v. State. 711 S.W.2d 421 (Tex. Ct. App. 1986) (state appeals court held that the required competency testing of certified teachers and administrators was not unconstitutional).

[24]State v. Project Principle, Inc., 724 S.W.2d 387 (Tex. 1987).

[25]Id. at 391.

[26]Tate v. Livingston Parish School Bd., 444 So. 2d 219 (La. Ct. App. 1983).

[27]McLaughlin v. Board of Educ., 659 S.W.2d 249 (Mo. Ct. App. 1983).

[28]Id. at 251.

[29]Bauer v. Board of Educ., 765 P.2d 1129 (Kan. 1988).

[30]Green Bay Educ. Ass'n v. State, 453 N.W.2d 915 (Wis. Ct. App. 1990).

[31]Greenwald v. Community School Bd. No. 27, 329 N.Y.S.2d 203 (N.Y. Sup. Ct. 1972).

[32]Cooper v. Eugene School Dist. No. 4J, 723 P.2d 298 (Or. 1986).

[33]Adams v. State Professional Practices Council, 406 So. 2d 1170 (Fla. Dist. Ct. App. 1981).

[34]Homer v. Commonwealth Dep't of Educ., 458 A.2d 1059 (Pa. Commw. Ct. 1983).

[35]Balentine v. Arkansas State Bd. of Educ., 684 S.W.2d 246 (Ark. 1985).

[36]Couch v. Turlington, 465 So. 2d 557 (Fla. Dist. Ct. App. 1985).

[37]Startzel v. Commonwealth Dep't of Educ., 562 A.2d 1005 (Pa. Commw. Ct. 1989).

[38]Reguero v. Teacher Standards and Practices Comm., 789 P.2d 11 (Or. Ct. App. 1990).

[39]Eiche v. Louisiana Bd. of Elementary and Secondary Educ., 582 So. 2d 186 (La. 1991).

[40]Longenecker v. Turlington, 464 So. 2d 1249 (Fla. Dist. Ct. App. 1985).

[41]Lombard v. Board of Educ., 645 F. Supp 1574 (E.D.N.Y. 1986).

[42]Brown v. South Carolina State Bd. of Educ., 391 S.E.2d 866 (S.C. 1990).

[43]Yoder v. Ohio State Bd. of Educ., 531 N.E.2d 769 (Ohio Ct. App. 1988).

[44]Fields v. Turlington, 481 So. 2d 960 (Fla. Dist. Ct. App. 1986).

[45]Carl S. v. Committee for Teacher Preparation and Licensing, 178 Cal. Rptr. 753 (Cal. Ct. App. 1991).

[46]Ulrich v. State, 555 N.E.2d 172 (Ind. Ct. App. 1990).

[47]Stedronsky v. Sobol, 572 N.Y.S.2d 445 (N.Y. App. Div. 1991).

[48]Ambus v. Utah State Bd. of Educ., 800 P.2d 811 (Utah 1990).

[49]Reback v. Rhode Island Bd. of Regents for Elementary and Secondary Educ., 560 A.2d 357 (R.I. 1989).

[50]Hunt v. Sanders, 554 N.E.2d 285 (Ill. App. Ct. 1990).

[51]Williams v. Turlington, 498 So. 2d 468 (Fla. Dist. Ct. App. 1986).

23
Student Injury

Paul Thurston and Donna Metzler

Introduction

The first obligation of a school staff is to provide a safe environment for students, an obligation which precedes even its instructional responsibility.[1] Although this obligation for school safety is understood at an abstract level, the legal underpinnings for such responsibility differ from state to state. The surest way to provide protection to students who are injured is through an insurance program where all students bear a modest cost for coverage so that those unfortunate students who do suffer injury can receive medical attention. There is a cost incentive to be vigilant about the safety of the environment since the larger the number of injuries, the higher the price of the premiums. Many school districts provide such insurance programs or make them available for parents to purchase. Beyond insurance there is an incentive for teachers and principals to provide a safe environment for students and thereby avoid liability. Since the late 1950s[2] many states have repudiated sovereign immunity, either eliminating it completely or restructuring its reach. State courts and legislatures have developed a variety of approaches in attempting to balance the need for protecting student safety in school while limiting the legal vulnerability of school employees. States differ on how they have worked out the balance of these competing interests.

The building principal desires to minimize both student injury and staff liability. Consequently, the principal needs to be knowledgeable about the legal standards which apply to situations where students are injured, and the potential district and personal liability which exists because of these injuries. Still, knowledge of the legal standards by itself does not guarantee the realization of these two objectives. As in several areas of school administration, the most effective principal is one who can take specialized knowledge, in our case the specialized legal standards of liability for student injury, and translate this in a meaningful way to teachers and staff in language they understand and support. This involves avoiding the technical legal language of torts and oversimplified rigid rules of behavior premised on fears of personal liability. Principals will likely be more successful in eliciting broad staff support and vigilance to student safety where appropriate supervision is presented as an educational responsibility rather than described as a set of threats where rigid rules are prescribed.

Liability for student injury can come from a number of torts.[3] Torts broadly refers to civil, noncontractual responsibilities that individuals in society owe to one another, which if breached, can be the basis of monetary damages awarded by a court to compensate the injured party.[4] There are a number of torts which can be the basis of liability for a range of student injuries: false imprisonments,[5] privacy,[6] and defamation.[7] This chapter will focus on the tort of negligence which is the more common legal basis upon which individual and district liability is premised when student injuries occur in school and during school related activities.

Legal Issues

For an injured party to secure monetary damages from another party for an allegedly negligent action, the injured party will need to plead and prove, at minimum, four elements.[8] Schools and their employees are not automatically responsible for every injury which may occur. For liability to be present, it must be shown that the school owes a particular duty to the injured person(s), that the behavior fell short of that required, that this breach of the duty was the proximate cause of the injury, and that there were real resultant injuries. In addition, to recover damages fully, the plaintiff normally needs to show no responsibility for causing the injury.

Duty of Care

There is a duty of care that the law recognizes one person owes to another. Usually, in the school context, it is not hard to show that the school and its employees have a duty to protect the health and safety of the students while they are in the custody of the school by virtue of statutes, contract, or common law.[9] Occasionally, a school will undertake a protective action, and injury will result at a time when the protection was not provided. Courts are then called upon to decide whether a duty of care has been assumed by the school. For example, the parents of a five year-old kindergarten student who was hit by an automobile while walking home sued the school alleging that, since the school provided crossing guards in the afternoon, the school assumed a duty to provide them in the morning when the half-day kindergarten students were walking home.[10] The Supreme Court of Colorado rejected this claim on the basis that it did not meet the elements of an assumed duty:

> [p]laintiff must first show that the defendant, either through its affirmative acts or through a promise to act, undertook to render a service that was reasonably calculated to prevent the type of harm that befell the plaintiff. Second, a plaintiff must also show either that he relied on the defendant to perform the service or that defendant's undertaking increased plaintiff's wish.[11]

Breach of Duty

A breach of the duty of care amounts to a failure of one party to conform to the standard required toward another. One has a legal duty to act as an ordinary, prudent, reasonable person for the circumstances. A child is expected to conform to the standard of care of a child of like age, education, intelligence, and experience. A breach of duty can occur either from an act or an omission.[12] The breach of the duty of care in a specific case is a question of fact. Making a showing of this breach involves both a showing of what actually happened and a showing from these facts how the defendant acted unreasonably. Failure to supervise, for example, is alleging that the teacher omitted or failed to be reasonable under the circumstances.[13] School policy is often used as evidence of reasonable actions. However, there are times when a person must violate policy in order to be reasonable. A 1986 case from Chicago provides a tragic example.[14] During a morning recess, several students were playing kickball. Two sixth-grade students collided head-on while chasing a fly ball and fell to the ground, injuring one of the students. A teacher's aide walked him from the playground to the principal's office at about 10:40 a.m. The student sat on a bench, crying, holding his head and stomach, and a red mark was noticeable on the side of his head. After about five minutes, the principal's secretary, unable to reach the mother at home, left a message for her at work. The mother called back about 11:00 a.m. and instructed the school to take the child to the hospital.

The secretary telephoned the City of Chicago's "911" emergency number and stated that an injured boy needed to be taken to the hospital. Between 10:40 a.m. and 11:30 a.m., the student's condition worsened. When the ambulance had still not arrived by 11:30 a.m., the secretary again called the "911" number and repeated the message about an injured boy needing help. At 11:45 a.m. the assistant principal called again and asked to speak directly to the fire department. The ambulance was dispatched immediately, reached the school in two minutes, and the child was at the hospital by noon. The hospital is directly across the street from the school. Because of this delay, the child's head injury severely worsened and he suffered mental and physical impairments. The court granted a $2.5 million judgment, half assessed against the school and half against the city. Even though the hospital was across the street from the school, and it was clear that the student's condition was quite serious, the secretary was conscientiously following board policy, namely, to work through the "911" emergency number system. This policy, presumably, had been made to limit the discretion of teachers and administrators. Here is a clear example of when the policy had to be violated for the people involved to be reasonable.

Causation

There needs to be a reasonably close causal connection between the alleged misconduct and the resulting injury. This involves both a cause-in-fact relationship between the behavior and injury as well as the injury being sufficiently close in time and a foreseeable consequence of the behavior. A component of both breach of duty and causation is foreseeability. Foreseeability suggests that the defendant could or should have seen the potentially dangerous consequences of the action when it was taken. This action does not mean that the defendant subjectively or personally foresaw the potential danger, but rather that a reasonable, prudent person would have foreseen the danger. The defendant is presumed to be a reasonable person. The jury then is given instructions similar to the following to determine foreseeability: "Would you, as a reasonable person, standing in the place of the defendant at the time of the injury, have foreseen the occurrence of the injury?" Under this instruction, the jury enjoys the luxury of hindsight when determining foreseeability, something which often leads to sharper vision than the defendant actually experienced. In a Florida case,[15] where a student was badly injured in a hazing incident held at night, the appellate court gave attention to the foreseeability aspect of proximate cause:

> If the harm that occurred is within the scope of the danger or risk attributable to defendant's negligent conduct, then it is deemed foreseeable. There are three ways in which the harm may fall within the scope of danger. First, the legislature may specify the type of harm. Second, if the same type of harm has occurred previously due to the same type of negligent conduct and the [individual] has actual knowledge of this, liability can be established. Third, liability can be made out if the negli-

gence complained of has resulted in harm so frequently "in the field of human experience" that harm may be expected to happen again.[16]

A similar issue of foreseeability and causation arose when a second-grade student was sent home for lunch on the first day of classes at a new school, when his mother expected the student to eat at school.[17] The student was supposed to walk home at the end of the day with his sister, but she had already had lunch. The teacher decided that it was not a long walk and asked the student if he knew how to walk home. On the way home he was attacked by a dog, whereupon he ran into the street to avoid the dog and was hit by a car. The teacher was charged with responsibility for the injury. The legal question turned on whether the teacher's action was the proximate cause of the injury. One definition of the proximate cause of an injury cited in the decision was that, "it must appear that the injury was the natural and probable consequence of such act.... To find that an injury was the natural and probable consequence of an act, it must appear that the injury complained of could have been foreseen or reasonably anticipated from the alleged negligent act."[18] As the great majority of courts do, the Ohio Court of Appeals agreed that it is not necessary for the defendant to foresee the injury in the precise form in which it resulted. But here the court considered that the teacher's conduct was not likely to have resulted in injury to the student and that those events causing the student's injury were too remotely connected, if connected at all, with the teacher's conduct to support a finding of proximate cause.

The plaintiff must show an actual loss or real damages. Nominal damages sought to indicate a technical right or the threat of future harm not yet realized are insufficient injury on which to bring a negligence action. Damages are measured in light of the particular person injured.[19]

Defenses

Even if the injured plaintiff can satisfy the *prima facie* case, the defendant still has a number of defenses available to overcome the claim. These defenses range from immunity—either common law sovereign immunity or statutory immunity—to the more usual affirmative defenses or the introduction of a different standard of liability. This area provides wide diversity among the states, and school administrators should be aware of the particular legal standards applied in their state. One should be sensitive to the divergent policy motivations underlying these defenses. Immunity, for example, limits the flow of public money to private citizens because liability payments will detract from the educational functions of the schools, whereas the affirmative defenses keep the plaintiffs from recovering for behavior for which they are responsible.

Assumption of the risk is an affirmative defense that will act as a complete bar to recovery. The concept behind assumption of the risk is that the plaintiff, either through actual knowledge or extreme recklessness, knew that the action would lead to injury. This knowledge and action in spite of it should bar recovery where the injury does in fact occur. Assumption of risk has been abandoned in many states and severely limited in others by the rise of contributory and comparative negligence.[20]

Contributory negligence is the most significant defense in negligence. The general concept of contributory negligence is that the injured plaintiff's conduct was unreasonable, given the circumstances, and led in some way to the resulting injury. The plaintiff is totally barred from recovery, since he or she should not be able to recover for something at least partially the result of his or her actions.[21] This concept is limited somewhat in applicability in the school context because students who are injured are usually minors, and minors are presumed to have only that capacity sufficient to understand danger appropriate to their age.

Comparative negligence is a refinement of the concept of contributory negligence. Whereas contributory negligence is an all or nothing proposition, comparative negligence, as the name suggests, allows the amount of the negligence between the parties to be allocated comparatively on the basis of degrees of negligence. Comparative negligence is distinguished between pure and modified forms. Pure comparative negligence allows the plaintiff to recover any amount of damages for which the defendant was negligent. For example, even if the plaintiff is found by the jury to be 95 percent negligent, the plaintiff can still recover five percent of the damages in a pure comparative negligence jurisdiction. Modified comparative negligence treats any negligence by the plaintiff over 50 percent as a total bar to recovery.[22]

Liability

A quarter of a century ago, tort liability in public schools was almost nonexistent because of sovereign immunity enjoyed by the state. The scope of such sovereign immunity is captured in a South Dakota Supreme Court quotation from a 1913 decision:

A school district officer in the performance of his duties acts in a political capacity, as much so as the governor of a state, and is not liable for negligent acts of omission occurring in the performance of such political or public duties, unless the sovereign power of the state has authorized and consented to a suit for such negligence.[23]

Sovereign immunity has eroded to a great extent, though it still exists in several states. In many states, the courts have abolished sovereign immunity,[24] or the legislatures have abolished it[25] or passed some substitute form of statutory immunity. The application of common law and statutory immunity is an important issue in many negligence claims.[26]

There are a variety of ways in which a statute can limit the liability of a school district. One is to put a monetary limit on the maximum claim that a successful plaintiff can recover.[27] A second way is to provide governmental immunity generally with specific statutory exceptions enumerated. For example, Texas school districts enjoy governmental immunity except where injuries and damages arise from the use of motor vehicles.[28] A third way is to make the employee liable only for willful and wanton misconduct.[29] Finally, some states limit claims by requiring that plaintiffs provide a notice of claim within a specified period of time, usually less than a year, if they intend to bring a suit against the district. This limit allows the district a chance to protect the evidence surrounding the incident, thereby making the district less vulnerable to frivolous suits.[30]

It is possible for a state to require that the school district assumes responsibility for indemnifying and providing a legal defense for employees who have been sued for professional misconduct. Illinois has a statute that requires:

> the school board...to indemnify and protect...employees against civil [and] constitutional rights damage claims and suits and death and bodily injury and property damage claims and suits, including defense thereof, when damages are sought for negligent or wrongful acts alleged to have been committed in the scope of employment or under the direction of the board.[31]

This requirement provides major protection for employees by making the school district responsible for providing lawyers and paying for any damage award ordered.

Recommendations for Practice

With liability for student injury being primarily a matter of state law, it is important for the principal to know the particular standards which apply. The principal should be knowledgeable about legal standards and terminology and be able to talk with faculty and staff in nontechnical terms.

- Because these liability standards are legalistic, somewhat difficult to understand, and hard to articulate, there is an inclination for principals to talk with teachers about safety in terms of absolute rules of behavior. "Never leave your room unattended because if a student is injured you and the school district will be liable for the injuries." These rules may be generally sound, but they do not completely represent an accurate description of the legal standard. There are times, for example, when failure to supervise a classroom, whether attended or not, is negligence[32] and times when it is not negligence.[33]

- The school should develop policies which provide guidelines in certain areas such as supervision and student safety. However, these policies ought not be followed blindly in all school contexts and in all circumstances. Attention should be focused on maximum student safety, not on adherence to policies.

- Student injuries are going to occur, and it is the responsibility of the whole staff to be vigilant in minimizing the injuries. Probably the best way to keep these to a minimum is being vigilant to the circumstances where potential injury might occur and communicating with one another in order to change the environment. The attention should be less on rigid rules or policies and more on actions which best protect the health and safety of the students. There should be a spirit of support among the whole school staff with an eye to providing an environment which prevents students from being in injurious situations.

References

[1]Liability exists for injuries resulting from negligent supervision. Courts have not been willing to find liability where the student has not learned because of negligent instruction by school personnel. For a detailed review and analysis of educational malpractice suits based on either a student's failure to achieve or on misclassification of a student's handicapping condition, see, O'Hara, "The Fate of Educational Malpractice," 14 EDUC. L. REP. 887 (1984).

[2]See, Molitor v. Kaneland Community Unit Dist. No. 302 163 N.E.2d 89 (Ill. 1959), cert. denied 362 U.S. 968(1960) and Carbone v. Overfield, 451 N.E.2d 1229 (Ohio 1983).

[3]The U.S. Constitution might be a source of remedy for certain specialized student injuries. Under 42 U.S.C. § 1983, where a special relationship exists between school officials and school children, an affirmative duty would be imposed upon the school officials to protect the children. *See*, DeShaney v. Winnegago County Department of Social Services, 109 S. Ct. 998 (1989). Several commentators explore the potential applicability of section 1983 liability to schools after DeShaney. *See*, William D. Valente, J.D., "School District and Official Liability for Teacher Sexual Abuse of Students under 42 U.S.C. § 1983, 57 Educ. L. Rep. 645 (1990); Steven F. Huefner, "Note, Affirmative Duties in the Public Schools after *DeShaney*" 90 Colum. L. Rev. 1940 (1990); Michah Dawn Miller, "When Teachers Sexually Abuse Children: The School District's Duty to Investigate," 43 Okla. L. Rev. 687 (1990). Courts have, to date, been reluctant to find such a special relationship in student sexual abuse by a teacher or counselor. *See*, Doe v. Douglas County School Dist. RE-1, 770 F. Supp. 591 (D.Colo. 1991) and J.O. v. Alton Community Unit School Dist. 11, 909 F.2d 267 (7th Cir. 1990). A state constitutional provision could also provide a basis for special protections for students which do not exist in common law. A Right to Safe Schools provision was added to the California Constitution in 1982: "All students and staff of public primary, elementary, junior high and senior high schools have the inalienable right to attend campuses which are safe, secure and peaceful." For a discussion of the California constitutional provision, see Stuart Biegel, The "Safe Schools Provision: Can a Nebulous Constitutional Right be a Vehicle for Change,?" 14 Hastings L.J. 789(1987).
[4]W. P. Keeton (ed.), Prosser And Keeton On Torts (5th ed. 1984), p. 2 (hereafter Prosser And Keeton On Torts); J. A. Rapp (ed.), Education Law § 12.02 [1] (Matthew Bender) (1991).
[5]Prosser And Keeton On Torts, § 11.
[6]*Id.*, § 117, p. 849; Steven R. Smith, *Privacy, Dangerousness and Counselors*, 15 J. L. & Educ. 121 (1986).
[7]Prosser And Keeton On Torts, § 111, p. 771.
[8]The exact elements necessary for carrying the plaintiff's burden in the *prima facie* case will vary from state to state. Some states, for example, will require the plaintiff to plead an absence of contributory negligence while other states do not. *See*, Prosser And Keeton On Torts, § 30, p. 164, for a more detailed description of these elements of the *prima facie* case.
[9]The exact outer limits of the duty of due care is a matter of controversy and developing law. The application of educational malpractice is, at the core, a question of whether a particular court will find a duty of due care owed by the school. For articles that discuss educational malpractice as an expanded view of duty of due care to meet changing school conditions, *see*, *Comment, Implications of Minimum Competency Legislation: A Legal Duty of Care?* 10 Pacific L.J. 947 (July 1979); *Note, Modern Concept of Duty: Hoyem v. Manhattan Beach City School District*; and *School District Liability for Injuries to Truants*, 30 Hastings L.J. 1893 (July 1979). A second example of a developing duty of care is in the area of negligent hiring of district employees. School districts have a duty to not negligently hire employees so as to ensure the safety and welfare of the students with whom they come into contact. For elaboration of this duty of care, *see*, Bruce Beezer, *School District Liability for Negligent Hiring and Retention of Unfit Employees*, 56 Educ. L. Rep. 1117 (1990).
[10]Jefferson County School Dist. R-1 v. Gilbert, 725 P.2d 774 (Colo. 1986).
[11]*Id.* at 776. *See also*, Verhel v. Independent School Dist. No. 709, 359 N.W.2d 579 (Minn. 1984) (School district held liable for injuries suffered by a student in an automobile accident which occurred when cheerleaders were bantering homes of football players. Although the accident occurred during summer, the court found the district's responsibility continued where the cheerleaders had established a summer practice schedule, adopted a constitution (read and approved by the principal) which required attendance at these practices and other summer events, and the coach kept in contact with the squad and visited some practice sessions and weekly meetings.).
[12]Bielaska v. Town of Waterford, 491 A.2d. 1071 (1985) (School liable for damages where student pushed her hand through a swinging glass door which had no crash bar, sustaining permanent injuries. Evidence showed the principal had never made any inquiries concerning prior accidents involving such doors and did not cause any warnings to be posted.).
[13]Roberts v. Robertson County Bd. of Educ., 692 S.W.2d 863 (Tenn. Ct App. 1985) (County liable for teacher's negligence where a student who was assisting another student in operating a drill press was severely injured when the drill bit deflected from the machine. The teacher, who was not in the room and was not supervising the use of the machine, was found negligent for his failure to furnish adequate instruction and supervision.).
[14]Barth v. Bd. of Educ., 490 N.E.2d 77, (1986).
[15]Bryant v. School Bd. of Duval County, 399 So. 2d 417 (Fla. Dist. Ct. App. 1981).
[16]*Id.* at 421.
[17]Person v. Gum, 455 N.E.2d 713 (Ohio Ct. App. 1983).

[18]*Id.* at 716.

[19]*See,* Swartley v. Tredyffrin Easttown School Dist., 430 A.2d 1001 (Pa. Super. Ct. 1981) (Mother who had finger crushed in school door due to negligence of school received $50,000 damages because, although the finger healed for normal use, she was an accomplished flutist and the injury limited the use of the finger for playing the flute professionally).

[20]*See,* Rutter v. Northeastern Beaver County School District, 437 A.2d 1198 (Pa. 1981) (Eye injury to football player participating in jungle football game should go to jury for consideration of extent of knowledge of potential injury and voluntariness of participation).

[21]*See,* La Fleur v. State Farm Mutual Auto. Ins. Co., 385 So. 2d 564 (La. Ct. App. 1980) (Contributory negligence found when pupil disembarked school bus in an unusual fashion and got left wrist caught in the door; School City of Gary v. Claudio, 413 N.E.2d 628 (Ind. Ct. App. 1980) (Contributory negligence denied because 10 year old student's behavior at bus stop, where he was injured, was not different than what one might expect from a 10 year old in the circumstances) and Berman v. Philadelphia Bd. of Educ., 456 A.2d 545, (Pa. Super. Ct. 1983) (Rebuttable presumption that minors between the ages of seven and fourteen are incapable of contributory negligence not overcome by any showing of superior intelligence or experience)).

[22]*See* Alvis v. Ribar 421 N.E.2d 886 (Ill. 1981) (This case provides a scholarly review of the concept of comparative negligence documenting its status in the 36 states which recognize it and distinguishes between the pure and modified forms.) and Harrison v. Montgomery County Bd. of Educ., 456 A.2d 894 (Md. 1983) (Maryland Court of Appeals traces the history of contributory and comparative negligence but concludes that it would be prudent to defer to state legislature to switch to comparative negligence.).

[23]Merrill v. Birhanzel, 310 N.W.2d 522 (S.D. 1981).

[24]*See,* Claymont School Dist. v. Beck, 424 A.2d 662 (Del. 1980).

[25]*See,* Susan C. Jacobson, *Comment, The Kansas Tort Claims Act and School Districts,* 28 U. KAN. L. REV. 619 (1980). (This article provides an overview of the Kansas Tort Claims Act-effective July 1, 1979 which replaced sovereign immunity. Like tort claims acts in other states the statute imposes liability on government units unless one of fifteen exceptions applies.).

[26]*See,* the following decisions where sovereign immunity was routinely applied to bar negligence actions against school districts: Holloway v. Dougherty County School System, 277 S.E.2d 251 (Ga. Ct. App. 1981) (Student injured when a milk crate she was standing on to get a drink turned over); Tucker v. Kershaw County School Dist. 279 S.E.2d 378 (S.C. 1981) (Student assaulted by another student during recreation class period).

[27]*See,* Espinosa v. Southern Pacific Transp. Co., 624 P.2d 162 (Or. Ct. App. 1981) (Damages limited to $100,000 by statute upheld although a $302,000 jury award was returned and the district was covered by one million dollars of insurance).

[28]*See,* Estate of Garza v. McAllen Indep. School Dist., 613 S.W.2d 526 (Tex. Civ. App. 1981) (Stabbing death of a student on a school bus held not to fall within the motor vehicle exception to governmental immunity).

[29]*See,* Pomrehn v. Crete-Monee High School Dist., 427 N.E.2d 1387 (Ill. App. 1981) (Injury to member of girl's softball team 5 minutes before practice does not amount to willful and wanton misconduct by absent coach); Holloway v. Dougherty County School Sys., 277 S.E.2d 251 (Ga. Ct. App. 1981) (An exception to the general rule of sovereign immunity exists where an individual can be liable for acts done within the scope of the official's discretionary authority when done in a willful, malicious or corrupt manner).

[30]*See,* Coonradt v. Averill Park Central School Dist., 427 N.Y.S.2d 531 (N.Y. App. Div. 1980) (Notice of late claim filed beyond 90 day statutory period allowed where district had actual knowledge of intended filing of suit and mother had sole responsibility as supporter of six children); Meli v. Dade County School Bd. 490 S.2d 120 (Fla. Dist. Ct. App. 1986) (Notice waived where responsible officials have actual knowledge of the injury and pursue a course of action which would lead claimant to believe that actual notice is unnecessary).

[31]Ill. Rev. Stat. 122; § 10-20.20 (1985).

[32]Alferoff v. Casagrande, 504 N.Y.S.2d 719 (N.Y. App. Div. 1986) (Jury verdict of negligence upheld where a student was injured by an eraser thrown while the teacher was out of the room and the teacher was aware of rowdy behavior of students in his absence).

[33]James v. Charlotte-Mecklenburg Bd. of Educ., 300 S.E.2d 21 (N.C. Ct. App. 1983) (Eye injury to sixth grader while teacher was absent from classroom was not foreseeable and teacher had no duty to remain with her class at all times).

24
Sport Law
Linda A. Sharp

Introduction

Sport law is a relatively new field which applies legal theory and precedent to issues arising from the conduct of sport and physical activity in settings ranging from professional athletics to municipal recreation programs. To say that our society is increasingly litigious is an understatement. The search is unrelenting for a "deep pocket" to foot the bill for injuries sustained. In such a climate, it is imperative that a preventive mentality be adopted regarding the physical education/athletic programs offered in schools. The strongest argument for a preventive risk management approach stems from a concern for the safety and welfare of the students. Sport law in the school setting is a critical area of concern for administrators since the possibility for personal injury is so much greater in this realm than in most school activities. It is clear that the principal cannot be disregarded as a possible defendant in litigation dealing with sport injuries.

Legal Issues

Fundamental Negligence Principles

Simply stated there are four elements of a negligence action which must be considered. The school has a *duty* to protect the students within it from unreasonable dangers. The principal has to act as a reasonable, prudent administrator would act in a particular situation. The principal is held to possess that level of expertise appropriate to his/her position. A breach of the foregoing standard of care will result in a finding of negligence assuming that the breach is the cause of the actual injury and damages result. In the area of sport law it is important to discuss the change in the defense of assumption of risk. In addition, there are three areas of concern which lead to the majority of litigation relating to school physical education/athletic programs: supervision, conduct of the activity, and equipment and facilities.

Assumption of Risk

A critical defense in sport law is the doctrine of assumption of risk. Cases in the last fifteen years have shown a marked tendency to transfer more of the responsibility to those who administer, supervise, instruct, and coach—the assumption of risk doctrine has eroded. The courts have effected this doctrinal transformation by increased emphasis on the risks involved in an activity. For the assumption of risk doctrine to be applicable, three elements must exist. First, the plaintiff must know of the danger to be encountered. Second, the participant must understand the risk involved. Third, the plaintiff must voluntarily expose himself to danger. Knowledge of risk in itself is not sufficient; it is not enough to simply inform or warn of risks. There must be an understanding and appreciation of that risk. In regard to this point, it is important to understand the effect *Thompson v. Seattle Public School District*[1] has had on the assumption of risk doctrine. In this case, Christopher Thompson, a high school football player, was seriously injured when he used his head as the primary point of contact as he was about to be tackled. He claimed that his coach failed to properly warn him of the danger of catastrophic injury connected with using his head and helmet in this fashion. A jury awarded the plaintiff, a permanent quadriplegic, a landmark $6.4 million. The jury based its award on the fact that the plaintiff had not been warned of the possibility of serious and permanent injury of this nature.

The *Thompson* case not only eviscerated the assumption of risk defense; it, in effect, created a new cause of action for "failure to warn" in a sport-related situation. Until *Thompson* it seemed clear that a participant assumed the normal risks incident to a game and that participants may be assumed to understand the basic risks inherent in an activity. An earlier decision, *Vendrell v. School District No. 26C*,[2] presented a set of facts almost identical to the *Thompson* scenario. However, the *Vendrell* court made it clear that "no prospective player need be told that a participant in the game of football may sustain injury."[3] In view of the *Thompson* decision, not only must players be warned that participation in the activity may result in injury, but more importantly, the specific risks inherent in the activity need to be addressed. The specter of catastrophic injury, if it exists in an activity, must be clearly and fully set forth in order for a participant to understand the risks involved.

The failure to warn issue is of critical importance. Coaches must convey warnings to participants. It is highly recommended that these warnings be conveyed both orally and in writing to students and parents. Films have been developed which warn students and parents of the specific risks involved in various activities. Principals should incorporate the foregoing into a risk management program developed for physical education and athletics.

Supervision

In most cases involving injury to a pupil in a physical activity setting, the principal has no direct supervisory responsibilities. In those limited situations where the principal has assumed that responsibility, he or she is obliged to act as a reasonably prudent supervisor. In one Louisiana case, the principal was serving as a playground supervisor, but in his preoccupation with "sneaking up" on the plaintiff in order to catch her in the forbidden act of rolling a volleyball standard, he neglected his supervisory duty of stopping the potentially dangerous activity as soon as possible. The plaintiff's hand was injured as the volleyball standard rolled over it. The court viewed this behavior by the principal as falling below the standard of reasonable supervision.[4]

In the majority of situations involving supervision, the negligence of the principal is discussed in terms of a failure to develop a proper supervisory plan. One important factor in the plan relates to the ratio between supervisory personnel and students.[5] The reasonable administrator must weigh the appropriate factors such as age and maturity of the students, the activity setting, any propensities the group has shown toward rowdiness,[6] and problems inherent in the area itself when developing a supervisory plan.

The case of *Dailey v. Los Angeles Unified School District*[7] illustrates the expectation that administrators will develop and implement supervisory plans. In this situation, Dailey, a high school student, was killed in a "slap boxing" fight with another student. It became clear during the trial that a comprehensive schedule of supervisory assignments had not been made. The time and manner of supervision had been left to the discretion of individual teachers with the result that there was no one supervising the area where the injury occurred. The failure to provide responsible supervision was held to be the cause of Dailey's death.

In dealing with the question of whether a duty to supervise a particular activity exists, the pivotal issue is often whether the likelihood of an accident is foreseeable. For example, an Illinois school recently argued that it had no duty as the host school for a track meet, to supervise the warm-up period. In this case, a student was hit by a classmate throwing a discus prior to the meet. The court disagreed and found a duty of supervision based on the foreseeability of injury in this hazardous type of activity.[8]

Another important responsibility for administrators is in the realm of crowd control for interscholastic competition. The courts expect adequate supervision and adherence to accepted crowd control procedures. The school administrator has a duty to protect students and patrons from reasonably foreseeable acts of third parties. The rivalry between the competing schools and the history of violence[9] or disruptive behavior in previous contests will, in large part, dictate the extent of supervision necessary.[10]

The failure to ensure that the personnel who are assigned to supervise are competent may lead to liability on the part of the school principal.[11] Where students are involved in physical activity, the assigned supervisor must be properly trained in what constitutes dangerous activity. The seminal case for this proposition is *Rivera v. Board of Education*[12] in which a non-Spanish speaking teacher who had no background in physical education was assigned to playground duty. The Spanish-speaking students persuaded the teacher to allow them to play "bombardment," a form of dodgeball. One student was struck in the eye with a ball and suffered serious injury. A qualified supervisor would have recognized the danger inherent in this situation and would not have allowed the game to take place. A similar factual situation also led to liability for a school principal when he assigned an inexperienced substitute teacher to supervise recess. While playing "kill," an elementary school student was seriously injured.[13] Further, a principal should choose a qualified replacement to supervise a physical education class if the teacher's presence is required elsewhere.[14]

Conduct of Activities

There are two cases which best illustrate the extent to which courts believe principals should take an active role in supervising physical education teachers and coaches. In the case of *Larson v. Independent School District No. 314*,[15] Steven Larson, an eighth grader, was severely injured as he performed a gymnastic exercise known as a "headspring over a rolled mat" as a required activity in his physical education class. Steven landed on his head, resulting in quadriplegia. The teacher of this class was a first year teacher who had become the instructor in mid-semester when the former teacher resigned. The teacher's alleged negligence lay in the fact that he had failed to instruct the class in the necessary progressions which are designed to lead up to the headspring. The student also alleged negligence on the part of the principal in his failure to exercise reasonable care in supervising the development, planning, and administration of the physical education curriculum. The principal did not meet with the teachers to discuss the transition. Further, he did not require the new teacher to submit any detailed plans regarding what he intended to teach. The court found that the principal had abdicated his responsibility for instructional supervision in this situation. Despite the fact that the teacher was an inexperienced teacher taking over in a difficult situation, the principal did not closely supervise his teaching. The principal's course of action was, therefore, a failure to reasonably administer the curriculum.

In the case of *Vargo v. Svitchan*,[16] a 15-year-old high school student was injured at a weightlifting training session held during the summer in preparation for football team tryouts. The plaintiff tried to lift weights well beyond his capacity at his coach's urging. He fell in his attempt and was rendered a paraplegic. In his allegations against the principal, the student asserted that the principal did not exercise close supervision over the coach even though he knew that the coach was sometimes "too rough" on his players. Also, the summer weightlifting program was purportedly in violation of high school athletic association rules. The court found that the principal had failed to reasonably exercise his supervisory powers in order to minimize injury to his students. The above two cases illustrate the necessity for principals to exert supervisory authority in regard to the physical education curriculum as well as to the interscholastic athletics.

Principals should also be cognizant of the possibility for liability relative to mismatches in the scheduling of athletic contests. In a New York case, a high school football player sustained injury allegedly because he was playing in a mismatched game in a fatigued condition. The team on which the injured student participated had a very poor record. The principal of this school had requested that his team be assigned to a less competitive division because it was clear that his football team was outclassed. However, the league supervisor denied the request. On the day of the injury, this team was playing a vastly superior opponent. The principal and the coach had discussed refusing to play the contest because of the high risk of injury. Nevertheless, the game went forward and the plaintiff, who had played virtually every down because of a lack of qualified replacements, was injured near the end of the first half. The student prevailed both at the trial court level and upon appeal to the Supreme Court Appellate Division. The school unreasonably enhanced the risk of injury to the student by playing this contest which had an evident risk of injury.[17] Although this decision was subsequently overturned on the basis that the student had assumed the risk,[18] the principle that it may be unreasonable to play contests in which the chance of injury is enhanced because of substantial skill and size disparities is an important one to consider.

The hiring of qualified personnel to teach physical education or to coach is the responsibility of the administration and the board of education. A substantial award of $385,000 resulted when an admittedly unqualified instructor was hired to teach and coach wrestling. A student became a quadriplegic as a consequence of the instructor's negligent activities and the negligence of the school district in hiring the unqualified coach.[19] Another example also emphasizes the need for competent instructors.[20] In this case, a student was killed as he was struck by a golf club swung by another student. On that day, a student teacher was supervising the class activities. Although a safe procedure had been established, the class arrangement was altered. In view of these cases it seems appropriate for the principal to assess the qualifications of any replacement instructor used. If the replacement does not possess adequate knowledge to continue the class activities as scheduled, alternate activities should be undertaken.

In terms of the provision of medical care to those students who are injured during physical education class or while participating in athletics, the school has two basic obligations: to render emergency first aid assistance until medical personnel arrive and to exercise reasonable care in procuring medical treatment for the injured student. In view of these obligations, principals have two primary responsibilities. First, they must be sure that all personnel who have teaching or coaching responsibilities in the physical education/athletics programs are competent in the administration of emergency first aid and CPR procedures.[21] It is also incumbent upon the principal to ensure that those who assist the athletic teams in the capacity of trainer or student trainer are qualified to do so.[22] The failure to do so can be costly as in *Welch v. Dunsmuir Joint Union High School District* in which a high school football player became a paraplegic when he was moved by the coaching staff without a backboard.[23]

The second responsibility of the principal in the area of medical care concerns the development of emergency procedures for timely medical assistance and adherence to those procedures. Heatstroke and shock suffered by a high school football player in *Mogabgab v. Orleans Parish School Board*[24] were compounded by the fact that he was not given access to medical treatment for over two hours after his symptoms appeared. A $2.5 million judgment was rendered in *Barth v. Board of Education*[25] in which a delay in procuring medical assistance for an 11 year-old student with a head injury allowed a blood clot to enlarge from the size of a walnut to that of an orange. Finally, a six year-old who fell at school and became unconscious died because of a delay in receiving emergency medical care. The delay, of approximately eight minutes, occurred when the principal instructed his secretary not to call an ambulance although a teacher had requested that emergency aid be summoned. The principal, after making his own assessment of the situation, eventually called for assistance but it was too late to save the student's life.[26]

Equipment and Facilities

The school has a duty to exercise reasonable care to supply equipment to physical education and athletic classes that is safe and suitable for the intended use. The equipment must be chosen appropriately based on the age and skill level of the students. The teacher/coach, based on his or her expertise in the field, is in the best position to evaluate the type of equipment necessary to protect players from injury.[27] When a reasonable recommendation for equipment is made, it is poor practice for the administrator to ignore the request. In *Berman v. Philadelphia Board of Education*,[28] a physical educator, who supervised an after-school floor hockey league, made repeated requests to the school administration to purchase protective equipment including mouth guards. The requests were denied, the program continued, and as was foreseeable, one participant suffered the loss of five teeth as he was struck by a stick. A verdict of $83,190 was returned in favor of the injured student. If necessary protective equipment cannot be afforded, the activity cannot be prudently continued.[29]

As a part of the duty to supply proper equipment, the equipment given must fit correctly.[30] Students should be given instruction in the proper fit and correct usage of the equipment. They should also be taught how to inspect their equipment and given the prerogative to return equipment which is ill-fitting or unsafe. Students should also be instructed to use protective equipment at all necessary times.[31] In conjunction with the "failure to warn" cause of action which was discussed earlier, it is critical that those pieces of equipment which come with warning labels have them affixed in a clearly visible fashion. In *Pell v. Victor J. Andrew High School*,[32] the warning label for a mini-tramp, which was assembled by the school, was placed on the underside of the trampoline bed. Thus, anyone using it was unable to read the cautionary language prepared by the manufacturer of the apparatus. This "failure to warn" resulted in a $1.6 million settlement paid by the school district to the severely injured student. In this case, the student was held not to fully understand the dangers involved. Any equipment which poses a danger to students should be securely stored when not in use.

In dealing with injuries caused by premises' defects or hazards in sport facilities, the courts determine the standard of care owed to participants in terms of their legal status as invitees, licensees, or trespassers. The student participant most often falls within the category of invitee. The school must act as a reasonable and prudent operator to make the facility reasonably safe. This duty entails three obligations: to inspect the facility to discover defects or hidden hazards; to remove or repair defects or warn users of hidden hazards; and to use reasonable precautions to protect users from foreseeable dangers.[33]

It is clear that the courts expect a regular program of preventive maintenance to be implemented. In *Woodring v. Board of Education of Manhasset Union Free School District,*[34] a missing bolt on a track railing in a gymnasium resulted in a wrongful death verdict in the amount of $1.4 million. The court stressed that the school district had no preventive maintenance program and failed to regularly inspect the gymnasium. The responsibility for the condition of the school facilities lies with the operational administrator of the physical plant. A Michigan case emphasized this point as the appellate court placed responsibility for the use and condition of the school facilities upon the principal.[35]

Once hazards/defects have been identified, remedial measures must be taken promptly. In *Van Stry v. State,*[36] a student recovered for injuries sustained when he slipped in a puddle of water in the shower room, away from the shower heads. The school had prior actual knowledge of this problem because the student had informed the instructor about the hazard on previous occasions. The school had adequate time to remedy the problem, but it did not do so. In addition, the school will be responsible for those defects of which the administration should have been aware if reasonable inspections had been undertaken. This concept of constructive knowledge emphasizes the importance of implementing a reasonable inspection and preventive maintenance program.[37] Finally, cases dealing with the installation of safety glass illustrate the concept of using reasonable precautions. There are many cases which point to the advisability of replacing nonsafety glass in doors and windows which are accessible to students as they engage in activity.[38] It should be evident to the principal, as a reasonable administrator, that non-safety glass poses a foreseeable hazard to students.

Recommendations For Practice

As mentioned at the outset of this chapter, it is highly recommended that a preventive approach by administrators be implemented. As a part of the risk management program, the following concerns should be addressed:

- Plans of supervision should be drafted which clearly specify the areas of responsibility and the expected conduct of the supervisor.
- Crowd control procedures for interscholastic contests must be established and followed.
- Supervisory assignments must be undertaken only by qualified personnel.
- Substitute instruction must be undertaken only by qualified personnel who should be provided with detailed lesson plans developed for substitute instructors by the physical education staff.
- Lesson plans by physical educators should be turned in and reviewed by the principal (particularly for inexperienced personnel) in regard to the adequacy of progressions and safety procedures in class.
- Curriculum guides and syllabi must be followed.
- Only qualified coaches, who can document their expertise, should be hired.
- Coaches should institute meetings with athletes and parents to disseminate information regarding the specific inherent risks of participation in each sport.
- Principals should be fully informed regarding the types of programs which coaches are offering, particularly if they involve special risks to students.
- Principals should ensure that all school athletic association rules are being met.
- All physical educators and coaches must possess knowledge of emergency first aid, including CPR.
- Emergency medical procedures must be developed and adhered to by all personnel ensuring that outside medical assistance is available rapidly.
- Checklists should be developed for the inspection of all equipment and facilities on a regular basis.
- The best possible safety and protective equipment which can be afforded should be provided.

- In-service workshops for personnel should be held regularly to foster a preventive environment.

References

[1]Unpublished decision.

[2]376 P.2d 406 (Wash. 1962).

[3]*Id.* at 412-13.

[4]Santee v. Orleans Parish School Bd., 430 So. 2d 254 (La. Ct. App. 1983).

[5]Gibbons v. Orleans Parish School Bd., 391 So.2d 976 (La. Ct. App. 1980); Bauer v. Board of Educ. of New York, 140 N.Y.S.2d 167 (App. Div. 1955); Chilton v. Cook County School Dist. No. 207, 325 N.E.2d 666 (Ill. App. Ct. 1975); District of Columbia v. Cassidy, 465 A.2d 395 (D.C. 1983).

[6]Kersey v. Harbin, 591 S.W.2d 745 (Mo. Ct. App. 1979); Tymkowicz v. San Jose Unified School Dist., 312 P.2d 388 (Cal. Ct. App. 1957); Cirillo v. City of Milwaukee, 150 N.W.2d 460 (Wis. 1967).

[7]470 P.2d 360 (Cal. 1970).

[8]Poelker v. Macon Community Unit School Dist. No.5, 571 N.E.2d 479 (Ill. App. Ct. 1990).

[9]St. Pierre v. Lombard, 512 So. 2d 1206 (La. Ct. App. 1987).

[10]Cook v. School Dist. UH3J, 731 P.2d 443 (Or. Ct. App. 1987).

[11]On the other hand, it is helpful to show that a teacher has extensive experience and has participated in safety courses relating to playground safety. *See* Brooks v. Orleans Parish School Bd., 560 So. 2d 633 (La. Ct. App. 1990).

[12]201 N.Y.S.2d 372 (App. Div. 1960).

[13]Cook v. Bennett, 288 N.W.2d 609 (Mich. Ct. App. 1979).

[14]Marcantel v. Allen Parish School Bd., 490 So. 2d 1162 (La. Ct. App. 1986).

[15]289 N.W.2d 112 (Minn. 1979).

[16]301 N.W.2d 1 (Mich. Ct. App. 1980).

[17]Benitez v. New York City Bd. of Educ., 530 N.Y.S.2d 825 (App. Div. 1988).

[18]543 N.Y.S.2d 29 (1989).

[19]Stehn v. Bernarr MacFadden Foundations, Inc., 434 F.2d 811 (6th Cir. 1970).

[20]Brahatcek v. Millard School Dist. No. 17, 273 N.W.2d 680 (Neb. 1979); DeMauro v. Tusculum College, 603 S.W.2d 115 (Tenn. 1980).

[21]Halper v. Vayo, 568 N.E.2d 914 (Ill. App. Ct. 1991).

[22]O'Brien v. Township High School Dist. No. 214, 392 N.E.2d 615 (Ill. App. Ct. 1979).

[23]326 P.2d 633 (Cal. Ct. App. 1958).

[24]239 So. 2d 456 (La. Ct. App. 1970).

[25]490 N.E.2d 77 (Ill. App. Ct. 1986).

[26]Czaplicki v. Gooding Joint School Dist. No. 231, 775 P.2d 640 (Idaho 1989).

[27]Everett v. Bucky Warren, Inc., 380 N.E.2d 653 (Mass. 1978).

[28]456 A.2d 545 (Pa. Super. Ct. 1983).

[29]Lynch v. Board of Educ. of Collinsville Community School Dist., 390 N.E.2d 526 (Ill. App. Ct. 1979) *aff'd* 412 N.E.2d 447 (Ill. 1980).

[30]Gerrity v. Beatty, 373 N.E.2d 1323 (Ill. 1978).

[31]Courts may look to the rules of a high school athletic association to determine when protective equipment must be worn. *See* Parisi v. Harpursville Cent. School Dist., 553 N.Y.S.2d 566 (App. Div. 1990).

[32]462 N.E.2d 858 (Ill. App. Ct. 1984).

[33]Courts continue to use the invitee/licensee distinction to ascertain the level of duty owed. Jeffers v. Olexo, 539 N.E.2d 614 (Ohio 1989). For a similar licensee/invitee distinction *see* Fuehrer v. Board of Educ. of Westerville School Dist., 574 N.E.2d 448 (Ohio 1991).

[34]435 N.Y.S.2d 52 (App. Div. 1981).

[35]*Cook*, 288 N.W.2d 609.

[36]479 N.Y.S.2d 258 (App. Div. 1984).

[37]Ardoin v. Evangeline Parish School Bd., 376 So. 2d 372 (La. Ct. App. 1979). For the proposition that lack of knowledge, either actual or constructive, may be used in favor of the school, *see* Best v. Houtz, 541 So. 2d 8 (Ala. 1989).

[38]Eddy v. Syracuse Univ., 433 N.Y.S.2d 923 (App. Div. 1980); Wilkinson v. Hartford Accident and Indemnity Co., 411 So. 2d 22 (La. 1982); Johnson v. City of Boston, 490 N.E.2d 1204 (Mass. Ct. App. 1986); Gump v. Chartiers-Houston School Dist., 558 A.2d 589 (Pa. Commw. Ct. 1989).

Schools And The Law

25
Professional Liability
Ivan B. Gluckman

Introduction

Professional liability refers to all of the kinds of liability for which a professional person can be held legally responsible. While educators can be sued for a wide variety of acts carried out in the course of their professional duties, principals are most often sued for things they allegedly failed to do. Obviously, liability for physical injury to persons using the school, whether they be parents or outsiders having business in the school, will be treated very similarly to teachers and students under the law of torts. School districts and their officials are likely to have greater exposure to legal risk in the case of students because they are minors entrusted to the school's care. Tort liability for teacher injury is often greatly diminished by worker compensation laws, but some risk can exist in this area as well. A much faster growing area of educator liability in the last two decades has been that of constitutional tort for which financial liability is provided under the Civil Rights Act of 1871 as amended and now incorporated into the United States Code as section 1983 of Title 42.[1] Finally, state legislative enactments and the provision of private insurance have an important bearing upon the degree to which educational administrators are exposed to legal liability growing out of the performance of their responsibilities.

Legal Issues

While recent years have witnessed the emergence of a number of new sources of litigation against schools and school administrators, one of the major sources continues to be the common law action for negligence. The concept of "negligence" is a broad one and can be applied in a wide variety of circumstances. As with the concept of torts itself, this breadth was intentional as a means of assuring individuals who believe themselves to be the innocent victim of another's act or omission, even if unintentional, of a legal means of being compensated for their injury. Suits based on this theory in which a plaintiff can show that the result was serious physical or emotional injury represent the kind of legal actions that can result in the largest damage awards against school defendants.

Elements of Negligence

For a plaintiff to prove a claim of negligence, he or she must present evidence of four separate elements:

- A duty of care must have existed between the plaintiff and the defendant
- The defendant must have breached that duty
- The plaintiff must have been injured
- The defendant's breach of duty must have been the proximate cause of plaintiff's injury.

Each of these elements has a long legal history, and many cases turn on whether one of them can be satisfactorily proven or not. In most cases, the issue of injury is the least questionable, especially when that injury is physical. Emotional injury, though more difficult to prove, is also allowed as a compensable form of injury. Originally, emotional harm had to be accompanied by physical injury in order to be compensable. In more recent years, such harm can form the basis of a tort action by itself and can prove as costly as many kinds of physical injury.

Duty

The success or failure of a negligence suit most commonly turns on one of the other three factors: duty, breach of that duty, and proximate cause between the breach and the injury. A duty exists between two people when the relationship between them is such that one is obligated to exercise at least ordinary care that the other person not be injured. Whether a duty exists between a plaintiff and a defendant is particularly important in a negligence case, because unless that is established, the case can proceed no further. In cases in which the plaintiff is a student or parents suing on the student's behalf, a duty is often found to exist if the injury merely occurs at school. Teachers, administrators, coaches, and activity advisers are all presumed to have a duty to exercise at least ordinary care for the health and welfare of students whose activities they are supervising though exceptions do exist.

One of the areas in which the scope of duty has often been an issue in school cases has concerned students injured on school property before or after the school day officially begins. In one well-known case, a 13-year-old student severely injured the eye of a 9-

year-old with a paper clip fired from a rubber band.[2] The accident occurred on the grounds of the elementary school where the older boy was waiting for the bus that took him to his school each morning. Evidence showed that the elementary school principal arrived at the school each morning at 8:00 a.m. and was aware that a number of students arrived there before that time, including the older ones awaiting their bus. The doors of the school opened each morning at 8:15 a.m. and students were expected to be in their seats by 8:30 a.m. The accident occurred at 8:05 a.m. In this situation, the court found that a duty to the injured plaintiff existed, but the courts made it clear that it might not have ruled the same way if the facts had been slightly different.

Other school situations in which the key issue is whether or not a duty exists involves students injured away from the school's property but exposed to the risk because of the school's program. Clearly, this situation will be the case when the student is involved in an interscholastic athletic contest at another school or on the bus going to or from school. School administrators may not be found liable where the school's duty ends. In a recent case, no duty was found to exist where the student plaintiff was struck by an automobile while away from school without permission. To hold a school and its staff responsible for such an injury merely because they failed to prevent the student from leaving school was regarded as an intolerable burden.[3]

Breach of Duty

Even more often than whether a duty exists, the key issue in school cases is whether or not the duty was breached by the defendants. It is important to note that a breach of duty can be either an act or a failure to act. In the school administration context, the breach of duty is more often an omission of an act such as the failure to provide adequate supervision. Often the defendant administrator was not even present at the time and place of the injury, and the sole basis of the claim against the administrator is the failure to have taken some earlier action that might have prevented the injury from occurring.

It is important to note that no one is automatically liable for the tortious actions of another, and school administrators are therefore not held liable for the negligent conduct of teachers or other staff members under their supervision. Some administrators misunderstand the law on this point because they have heard of a legal doctrine called *respondeat superior*, which requires employers to be responsible for some of the acts of their employees. But school administrators are not normally employers of the staff members they supervise and liability under this doctrine is typically limited to the school district. The duty of the principal is to provide adequate supervision. It is the failure to perform this duty that most often is the basis for being held liable for the tort of negligence. Whether such a breach of duty has occurred can often be a very difficult issue to determine.

The law has developed a concept known as the "reasonable person" by which to test a specific defendant's conduct. As applied to a school administrator the concept would ask: under the same circumstances that this defendant confronted, would a reasonably prudent administrator have acted as this one did? The answer requires analysis of a number of factors. Normally, it entails consideration of the physical, mental, and emotional attributes of the defendant and the minimum level of information and experience common to the community in which the person works. Obviously, the defendant cannot be expected to perform as a person of exceptional strength, intelligence, or with attributes others might possess. Defendants who are professional persons, such as school administrators will be held to a standard based on the skills and training they should have acquired in order to hold themselves out as school administrators, and this standard will be higher than that which would apply to ordinary citizens.

Consideration must not only be given to the characteristics of the defendant but also to the circumstances of the situation in which the plaintiff claims injury. These circumstances are as limitless as the number of situations that can give rise to an injury, but certainly include the following: age and maturity of the plaintiff, the nature of the risk to which the person was exposed, and the precautions that were taken by the defendant to avoid injury.

Proximate Cause

The fourth element that must be proven in a negligence claim is "proximate cause" between a defendant's conduct and the injury to the plaintiff. Often this element is very closely entwined with the issues of whether a duty itself existed and whether that duty was breached. In one case in which an elementary school teacher was held free of liability when one of her students was struck by a car while on the way home during lunch recess, the Supreme Court of Ohio based its ruling on a lack of proximate cause, and the issue of whether the teacher had breached her duty to the student was not even discussed.[4]

The court held that the principal was not liable in a case in which a student drowned while swimming in a lake at which a class picnic was held. The principal had specified certain conditions under which the trip might be made and these conditions were appropriate. While a duty was recognized as existing, the principal was regarded as fulfilling that duty. Despite the fact that the cause of the student's death was regarded as being likely to have been his own negligence in swimming in an area of the lake that was not under supervision, the Kentucky court did not discuss the possible absence of proximate cause as a basis for its finding of no negligence on the principal's part.[5]

Foreseeability

Because of the difficulty in separating the elements of negligence, the courts developed a test to determine whether or not a defendant should be held legally accountable in a suit. In addition to the "reasonable person" test, the court will ask whether such a person could have been expected to foresee the result of his or her conduct under the circumstances. If the facts lead the judge to conclude that the injury could have been foreseen and appropriate action was not taken to avoid it, the defendant will be found negligent. The test makes it unnecessary to analyze each of the four elements of negligence independently. The test's application in school cases can often place a heavy burden upon principals and other school administrators.

In a California case, a 15-year-old student was injured when she and other members of a physical education class ran from the gymnasium to a playing field. As the girl ran, she was struck by a garbage truck that was proceeding on a road on the school grounds at a speed of 25 miles per hour. Despite the fact that no other child had been injured in seven years during which students had been running from the gym to the playground, the court ruled that the administrators were negligent in that they knew of the presence of trucks on school grounds and failed "to take precautions to minimize the danger of injury to the students...other than to issue an instruction to the custodian of the grounds and to caution people to drive carefully. They failed to post a danger sign to warn students against running across the courtyard.[6]

If principals or other school administrators are expected to foresee harm in a given situation even though it has never occurred before, it should not be surprising that they will be placed in an even more precarious situation if an injury occurred previously in a similar circumstance, and the administrators either knew or should have known about it. In an Illinois case, students on a class trip to a Chicago museum were attacked and injured while visiting the museum. Though the school district and staff were not held liable for negligence because the attack was by non-students inside the building and was not reasonably foreseeable, the court made it quite clear liability would be assigned if such an incident were to occur in that museum again unless the district took greater precautions to avoid it.[7] Clearly, the doctrine of foreseeability places a heavy burden upon administrators in a community even though they are in different schools. Administrators are going to have to pay far more attention to any condition or set of circumstances that has caused injury within their own schools.

Risk Avoidance and Defense Against Liability

The best way for administrators to avoid liability for negligence is to take steps necessary to avoid injury in the first place. Such "risk-avoidance," as it is known in the insurance industry, should be the administrators first line of defense not only from the legal and financial point of view, but more importantly because it protects the health, safety, and welfare of students and others coming under the administrator's supervision. Some risks can only be avoided by eliminating activities entirely such as the use of trampolines in gym classes. This approach may be warranted in some circumstances. Administrators must be careful, however, that in the interest of safety or risk-avoidance, they do not harm the educational process that they are charged with conducting. They must remember that every profession entails some degree of risk, and that all this risk cannot be eliminated if professional duties are to be met.

Fortunately, a large part of the risks inherent in school administration can be avoided by following the basic rules that the law of negligence provides: think through any situation in advance to be aware of the risks and dangers presented and then take whatever action is appropriate and reasonable to eliminate those risks. Despite the most careful forethought and planning, accidents will occur and injury will result. When it does, lawsuits may follow. In most cases, if the administrators behaved "reasonably," the courts will not find the requisite elements for a negligence claim to exist. If they do, the law does allow a few defenses to overcome that liability.

Immunity to Suit

The primary purpose of governmental immunity is to protect the state itself and those elected and appointed officials charged with shaping and guiding its policies. The doctrine has not usually been applied to cover state employees responsible for carrying out those policies. In regard to public schools, therefore, governmental immunity will protect the school district itself and the members of its administering board. It may even be interpreted as protecting the district's chief executive, the superintendent, but employees below that level will often be subject to liability for any negligence in the conduct of their official duties. Administrators should check with their district offices to find out who may be covered by statutory immunity in their state.

Affirmative Defenses

Affirmative defenses are those that the law recognizes as excusing a defendant from liability even in those situations in which the four elements of negligence are found to be present. The two most important of these defenses are known as "contributory negligence" and "assumption of the risk." Contributory negligence means the plaintiff has contributed to his or her own injury and that action was careless enough to constitute "negligence" in itself. In school cases, however, the doctrine of contributory negligence has been considerably limited in recent years, especially where the injured plaintiff is a student. While not an absolute bar to the defense, the law recognizes the immaturity of youth as a limitation on the degree to which a student can be regarded as responsible for his or her own behavior. The younger the student, the less likely contributory negligence will be available as a defense.

Assumption of risk differs from contributory negligence in that it does not require proof that the plaintiff's conduct is reckless or irresponsible. It only requires a showing that the plaintiff knowingly and willingly placed himself in the position in which he was exposed to the risk of the injury that occurred. The most common cases in which the doctrine is invoked are those involving sports or other athletic activities. Participation in tackle football obviously entails some risk of injury and claims based on such injury may well be barred by the assumption of risk doctrine unless the plaintiff can show that the particular injury sustained was not one that the plaintiff could have reasonably anticipated or that the conduct of the defendants was so willful and wanton as to override the protection afforded them by the assumption of risk doctrine. Administrators should be aware that the burden of proving this defense is upon the defendants, and they must show the presence of three separate elements to make their case: the plaintiff should have known of the risk; the plaintiff understood the nature and quality of that risk; and the plaintiff had sufficient time, knowledge, and experience to be able to choose to avoid the danger.

Release of Liability

Many school districts employ some kind of release of liability form that students and their parents are asked to sign. These forms state that the district is released from any and all liability that might be sustained through participation of the student in some named activity. Despite the widespread use of such forms, there has long been considerable doubt among lawyers as to their effectiveness. Clearly, the parent cannot waive any right the student might have to reasonable care to which he/she is due from the district and its employees. There is equal doubt that the student, as a minor, could waive his/her own rights, at least unless he/she could be shown to have a very clear understanding of the nature of the risks involved and the effect that releasing those rights would have. Despite these concerns, there have been few reported decisions involving the issue until recently.

A state supreme court has now confronted the issue as a direct challenge by parents and students to the legality of a public school's requiring the execution of such forms as a condition of participation in interscholastic athletics. The court reviewed all the issues underlying the use of releases, including the responsibility of the schools and their personnel and the general recognition by the courts of the legality of such releases in normal contractual relationships between private parties. The court found that where public school districts conditioned participation in interscholastic athletics upon the execution of releases of liability and where the purpose of the release was to free the school district from its recognized responsibility to exercise due care in the conduct of its interscholastic athletic programs, the use of the releases was contrary to public policy and therefore null and void.

Finally, the court dealt with the issue of whether the releases could at least be regarded as express statements by students of their assumption of risk, suitable for presentation by defendants as evidence should a claim of negligence arise. The court held that the release could not operate as a total bar against possible future student claims. It left open the question as to whether a release that listed specific risks which the student assumed might not operate to bar claims arising in a case in which injury arose from those particularly listed risks.[8] Despite the weakness of release forms, most schools continue to use them because they can at least be used as evidence of knowledge and awareness of risk by students and parents. If nothing else, they may discourage suit.

Statutory Enactments

Nearly two-thirds of the states have now enacted legislation requiring school districts to defend their employees against suits alleging negligence in the conduct of their official duties and indemnifying against any damages that may be assessed against them as a result of such litigation. Most of the other states have enacted statutes that at least permit school districts to adopt such policies. Nearly all the states also permit school districts to purchase insurance to protect their employees against such claims and a few require that such insurance be provided.[9]

Administrators should ensure that they know what kind of protection is afforded them under their state statutes since most of the protections are not automatic. Legal defense by the district is often provided only if the employee requests it, often within a rather short period after notice of suit is received. Some of the statutes also have provisions excluding or excepting specific important areas of concern, such as civil rights or criminal actions.

Comparative Negligence

Another important area of legislative intervention into the common law of negligence is the creation of a doctrine called "comparative negligence." Comparative negligence statutes permit the judge or jury to assess the relative fault of plaintiff and defendants and assign damages in proportion to that degree of liability. In most cases, if the plaintiff is found to be responsible for the majority of the fault, the individual would be barred from any recovery. In at least a few states, even when the plaintiff is found to be mostly at fault, the individual may recover from the defendants that proportion of his or her legitimate damages for which those defendants are adjudged responsible.

Administrators should be aware that some states have enacted statutes that permit successful plaintiffs to recover all their damages from any defendant or defendants, regardless of the proportion of fault assigned under a comparative negligence statute if other guilty defendants are financially unable to pay their share. These "joint and several liability" laws have been strongly opposed by insurance companies and other large organizations subject to tort suit in recent years, and a number of these statutes have been withdrawn or modified.

Recent Trends in Negligence Law

Until recently, most student suits alleging negligence against schools and their administrators arose from incidents in which the students were injured as the result of some kind of accident involving the use of school-owned property or equipment. Curricular incidents often involved equipment or materials used in physical education, chemistry, or shop classes. Co-curricular activities such as interscholastic athletics and school-sponsored trips and excursions represented a fair number of suits, but in most cases they were based on allegations of failure to maintain school grounds or equipment in a safe manner, or on inadequate supervision in the use of such equipment.

Suits based on injury of one student by another have occurred, but in most cases the injury was understood by all parties to have been unavoidable by school personnel. In recent years, however, negligence actions based on injury to students have become more frequent, even though the injury sustained by the plaintiff in these cases is admittedly the result of an intentional act. In some cases, the assailant is unknown to the injured student and therefore cannot be named as a defendant in the suit. Even if the assailant is known, financial recovery against this third party may be difficult; and even if criminal prosecution is initiated against the assailant, no financial recompense is provided to the injured student.

These factors have undoubtedly led to the greatly increased number of suits of this kind against schools and school staff members. Since the attacks, whether physical or sexual, naturally occur at times and places when students are not in class or otherwise directly supervised, the individual school defendants are most likely to be administrators against whom a general allegation of inadequate supervision can be made. Broadening the scope of injuries recognized as compensable to include both emotional harm and even some more remote kinds of injury such as that to reputation, have further increased the incentives to initiating this kind of litigation.

While the courts continue to state as a general principle of law that schools are not the insurers of student safety, they seem to be becoming more willing to hold the school, if not its individual administrators, liable for these intentional assaults by third parties. Where a student is injured by an assault of another student or students, the key issue often becomes whether it can be shown that the attackers had been involved in similar incidents before or threatened such an attack, and if the school defendants knew or should have known of the attackers' dangerous propensities. Their failure to warn the plaintiff or to take action to protect the plaintiff from harm may then be found to constitute negligence on their part. This charge will most likely be made against principals since they are the school employees most likely to have knowledge of student disciplinary offenses and the responsibility for dealing with them.

Civil Rights Actions

The past two decades have witnessed an enormous explosion of litigation under a federal civil rights law, section 1983 of Title 42, U.S. Code. It is now applied in almost every area in which public agencies are involved. The statute has provided a means of legal recourse against any public official or employee who, in the administration of his or her responsibilities, is seen as depriving someone of his or her civil rights either under the constitution or any other federal law.[10] In the area of public education alone, section 1983 has been responsible for almost all of the student-oriented suits based on alleged denial of constitutional rights. The law makes it explicit by its terms that defendants found to have violated the act may be ordered to pay monetary damages to successful plaintiffs. Fortunately, the United States Supreme Court has ruled that a plaintiff must be able to demonstrate actual injury in order to receive substantial, nonpunitive damages under the Act.[11]

More recently, the Court ruled that damages under the Act can only be compensatory for actual injury or loss suffered by plaintiffs and not based on a purely speculative abstract value of a constitutional right alone.[12] Tempering this decision are holdings that damages are not limited to those capable of being proven to be actual financial losses. Damages can be awarded for mental and emotional harm, and such damages can often far exceed conventional financial losses.[13] Another element which greatly strengthens section 1983 for plaintiffs is the Civil Rights Attorney's Fees Act of 1976. This act provides for the mandatory award of attorney fees to prevailing plaintiffs in civil rights suits. The amount of these fees may very easily exceed the amount of any damages awarded by a court and are available even though the plaintiff never really incurred any cost at all because the legal services were offered on a *pro bono* basis by a law firm or civil rights organization.

Because of the broad scope of section 1983, suits initiated under this statute include not only many by students but also a large number by teachers and other employees. To a large extent, section 1983 suits by school employees have replaced contract actions as the basis of legal claims arising from employment disputes. Since teachers and other school employees are employed by the school district and not by school principals, the only basis for bringing suit against these supervisors in most employment matters is by the civil rights route.

Most often these suits allege that disciplinary or other actions taken by their superiors to which the employee objects were taken in retaliation for the proper exercise of a constitutional right, such as that of free speech or association. Many of the instances of free speech involved in these cases are statements critical of the school board or the employee's supervisor. The threat of litigation often makes boards and their administrators very cautious in initiating employee disciplinary actions, especially where the employee involved was an open and vocal critic of the administration.[14]

After a rapid increase in the number of suits under section 1983 based on alleged retaliation for the exercise of freedom of expression, the United States Supreme Court reviewed a court of appeals decision in favor of an assistant district attorney who alleged that her attempted transfer and ultimate dismissal by her supervisor, the district attorney, constituted such a violation of her civil rights.[15] The Court made clear that not all disciplinary actions, even if undertaken in response to criticism by an employee, are violative of the employee's rights to free expression. Such a violation only exists if the substance of the criticism constitutes speech about public issues.

While this Supreme Court decision has helped stem the tide of employee cases against principals and other supervisors in public agencies, it has by no means eliminated it. In a Rhode Island case, a high school teacher's criticism of the reading program in which she taught was regarded as protected by the first amendment.[16] Her reassignment to a regular English class was seen as retaliation for her criticism, and section 1983 provided an avenue of compensation for her.

Most courts have rejected suits by students based on claimed assaults, physical or sexual, by other students. In the last few years, however, growing public concern about adult sexual abuse of minor children, whether by parents or others, has resulted in a growing number of legal actions against schools and school administrators based on such allegations. Most recently, allegations of sexual harassment in the workplace have increased the level of sensitivity to any kind of sexual misconduct by persons in positions of authority. Suit is usually initiated not only against the alleged perpetrator, but also against supervisors and the employing school district. These suits have usually taken the form of civil rights actions, rather than negligence suits.

Recently, in Stoneking v. Bradford,[17] four students brought suit. All suits were based on actions by the same teacher even though the misconduct had occurred as much as seven years earlier. The claims against the school and its administrators were not found to be time-barred because the plaintiffs could not have known of the interference with their civil rights until they became aware that similar incidents were reported to the school's administrators prior to their own experience with the teacher.

School administrators must take special pains to prevent situations which can give rise to claims of this kind, and if abuses are reported, they are thoroughly investigated and appropriate action is taken. Care must be taken to assure that no information be made public about the accused employee during the investigation, lest the accused employee be provided with the basis for a defamation or similar action. The employee should be given every opportunity to clear himself/herself of charges.

Insurance: A Last Resort

School principals still are exposed to the risk of civil suit. The best way to minimize this risk is by becoming knowledgeable of the nature of the risks involved and taking proper actions in advance to avoid injury in the first place. Complete negation of such occurrences is impossible and attempts to eliminate such possibilities must necessarily interfere with the principal's performance of duties. The best answer to this dilemma is insurance protection. Most school districts have insurance policies which cover employees. Professional liability insurance providing both indemnification against damages and legal defense is also available through professional organizations and may be an automatic benefit of membership.

Recommendations for Practice

Prudent, careful school principals who are aware of their legal rights and responsibilities should be able to carry out those responsibilities by adhering to the following recommendations:

- Plan activities carefully. Make the activity fit the students, not the students fit the activity.
- Provide proper supervision. The more risky the activity, the more supervision is required. The younger or less mature the students, the more supervision is necessary.

- Repair or report all hazardous conditions to those individuals who need to know and insist that these conditions be remedied.
- All outsiders should be considered trespassers. Instruct teachers to report the presence of strangers at once.
- Keep accurate records of all incidents and accidents.
- Assign only qualified personnel to conduct or supervise an activity.
- Be aware of the constitutional rights of students and school employees.
- Try always to act as a reasonable administrator in carrying out professional responsibilities.
- Make certain that insurance coverage is provided.

References

[1] The statute reads in pertinent part: Every person who under color of any statute, ordinance, regulation, custom, or usage…subjects or causes to be subjected any citizen of the United States or other person within the jurisdiction thereof to the deprivation of any rights, privileges or immunities secured by the Constitution and laws shall be liable to the party injured in an action at law, suit in equity or other proper proceeding for redress.

[2] Titus v. Lindberg, 49 N.J. 66 (1967).

[3] Palella v. Ulmer, 518 N.Y.S.2d 91 (1987).

[4] Person v. Gum, 455 N.E.2d 713 (Ohio Ct. App. 1983).

[5] Cox v. Barnes et al., 469 S.W.2d 61 (Ky. Ct. App. 1971)

[6] Taylor v. Oakland Scavenger Co., 110 P.2d 1044 (Cal. 1941).

[7] Mancha v. Field Museum of Natural History, 283 N.E.2d 899 (Ill. 1972).

[8] Wagenblast v. Odessa School Dist. No. 105-157-166J. 758 P.2d 968 (Wash. 1988).

[9] For more detail, see NASSP LEGAL MEMORANDUM, STATUTORY PROTECTION FOR PRINCIPALS—TORT LIABILITY, (December 1986).

[10] In Maine v. Thiboutot, 448 U.S. 1 (1980).

[11] Carey v. Piphus, 435 U.S. 247 (1978).

[12] Memphis Community School Dist. v. Stachura, 477 U.S. 299 (1986).

[13] Busche v. Burkee, 649 F.2d 509 (7th Cir. 1981); cert. denied 102 S. Ct. 396.

[14] For more detail, see R. S. VACCA and H. C. HUDGINS, JR., LIABILITY OF SCHOOL OFFICIALS AND ADMINISTRATORS FOR CIVIL RIGHTS TORTS, 181-185 Michie (1982).

[15] Connick v. Myers, 461 U.S. 138 (1983).

[16] Fishman v. Clancy, 763 F.2d 485 (1st Cir. 1985).

[17] 882 F.2d 720 (3d Cir. 1988).

26
Copyright Law
Lynn Rossi Scott

Introduction

Copyright was not a concern to principals less than 20 years ago. Schools were considered part of a private audience, or their uses were considered "fair use." But the 1976 federal *Copyright Act,*[1] which took effect January 1, 1978, has changed all of that. Performances and displays in "semipublic" places such as clubs, lodges, factories, summer camps, and schools became "public performances" subject to copyright control.[2] Suddenly, it became important for school administrators to learn, understand, and follow the new copyright law.

Congress' first attempt to establish copyright law occurred in 1909. Since then, numerous technological developments forced Congress to address authors' works which, once published, could be immediately photocopied, videotaped, tape recorded, televised, or recorded onto computer software. In 1976, Congress again attempted to restate copyright law and to address the new issues raised by technology. The 1976 law merged state law with federal law and common law causing copyright issues to become exclusively a matter of federal law.[3] The 1976 law protects copyrighted material for an author's lifetime plus 50 years. It specifies the author's right and the exceptions to those rights and provides remedies for enforcement and penalties for violations.[4]

Generally, any original work of authorship set down in a suitably tangible form can be copyrighted.[5] This form includes: literary works; musical works and lyrics; dramatic works and accompanying music; pantomimes and choreographic works; pictorial, graphic and sculptural works; motion pictures and audiovisual works; sound recordings; and, now, architectural works.[6] There is no copyright protection for ideas, procedures, processes, systems, methods of operation, concepts, or principles.[7]

For a school principal, copyright law affects such diverse areas as classroom teaching, research, publishing handbooks or manuscripts, jukeboxes, school plays, band programs, dances, the student newspaper and yearbook, students' art work and sculptures, computer programs, video programs, and the school mascot.

Legal Issues

Rights of a Copyright Holder

A copyright holder has access to the following exclusive rights: reproduction of the work into copies or phonorecords; preparation of derivative works based on the copyright work; distribution of copies to the public by sale, transfer of ownership, rental, lease, or loan; public performance of literary, musical, dramatic or choreographic works, pantomimes, motion pictures and other audiovisual works; public display of literary, musical, dramatic, or choreographic works; pantomimes, and pictorial, graphic or sculptural works, including the individual images of a motion picture or audiovisual work;[8] and ownership of a work of visual art, and preventing the misuse of a name.[9] Works produced by school district employees in the course of their employment may be considered "works for hire" in absence of agreement to the contrary.[10] Should employees develop for the school district educational or instructional materials, it should be made clear to them that the district is the copyright holder and has the right to change, alter, or distribute the works as it sees fit; unless the district agrees to give up that right. Conversely, work that employees do with their own equipment, on their own time, belongs to the employee.[11]

Collaborators of a work are all joint holders of the copyright.[12] Each copyright owner has the right to change the work, with or without the other joint-holder's consent.[13] Although an author initially holds the copyright, the author may transfer the exclusive rights to others or may license others to use the work on a nonexclusive basis.[14] An author now holds a copyright as soon as he or she puts the work into tangible form, even prior to publication.[15] A copyright holder must register with the United States Copyright Office if the copyright is being infringed upon or if the work was created prior to 1978. Registration gives a copyright holder added protection in infringement lawsuits and is a prerequisite to filing a lawsuit.[16] Regardless of registration, each published work should contain the copyright symbol, "©" or the abbreviation "Copr.;" the year of first publication, public distribution; and the author or copyright holder's name, so that viewers have notice of ownership. As a result of the United States' 1988 membership in an international treaty called the Berne Convention for the Protection of Literary and Artistic Works, the copyright symbol is no longer required to protect a copyright. It is, however, still advisable.[17]

The Berne Convention also brought mandatory filing. Within three months after publication, the copyright owner must deposit two copies of the work with the U. S. Copyright Office Registration, which is separate from filing, is performed by filing copies with and paying statutory fees to the U.S. Copyright Office with a registration application. Fees begin at $20.00 for registration.[18]

Fair Use by Teachers

Copyright grants a monopoly to the copyright holder for public distribution of his or her work. "Fair Use" is a privilege owned by someone other than the copyright holder to use the copyrighted material in a reasonable manner without the copyright holder's consent.[19] The copyright law states, "the fair use of a copyrighted work, including such use...by reproduction...or by any other means...for purposes such as criticism, comment, news reporting, teaching (including multiple copies for classroom use), scholarship, or research is not an infringement of copyright."[20] This doctrine of fair use has been called an "equitable rule of reason,"[21] because its application is based on determining in each case:

- the purpose and character of the use, including nonprofit educational versus commercial intent;
- the nature of the work;
- the amount and substantiality of the portion used in relation to the work as a whole;
- the effect of the use on the potential market for the work or on the work's value.[22]

The fair use exception, like copyright protection, applies to both published and unpublished works.[23]

Relatively few cases have ever been filed against teachers based on abuse of the fair use doctrine.[24] While state universities at this point appear to be immune from liability under the eleventh amendment to the United States Constitution: school districts, teachers, and university professors do not have that same immunity.[25] Unfortunately, the fair use defense is often insufficient for teachers because one of the above four tests of purpose, nature, amount, or market effect could not be supported. A teacher may obviously copy a newspaper article for use in discussion in class and may not, just as obviously, copy verbatim a large copyrighted workbook.[26] Likewise, the copying of "anthologies", or large portions of various copyrighted works compiled into one document, violates the copyright law.[27] It is, however, the "gray areas" in between permitted and forbidden uses that cause such concern.[28]

It is for these reasons that an "Agreement on Guidelines for Classroom Copying in Not-For-Profit Educational Institutions" was published in the legislative history of the Act.[29] The agreement was reached by an *ad hoc* committee of education representatives and publishing representatives. They attempted to clarify fair use as to books, periodicals, and music. A similar agreement was later reached regarding television videotaping. The guidelines do not have the authority of federal law,[30] but several courts have considered them persuasive.[31]

In order for a teacher to be operating within the fair use classroom guidelines, he or she must act spontaneously, in good faith, copy only a small amount of a large work, make no profit, cause no significant economic loss to the copyright owner, copy material not initially published for educational use, print the notice of copyright, and have no intent to either publish the work again or display it publicly without seeking the permission of the copyright owner. Anthologies are specifically prohibited.[32] The guidelines state that a single copy made for the teacher's own use is allowed including a book chapter; a newspaper or periodical article; a short story; or a chart, graph, or diagram from a book. Using multiple copies for classroom use requires the use must be spontaneous and for only one course; limited to one poem, article, or story or two excerpts from the same author; and such copying can only occur nine times during one class term.[33]

The guidelines are very restrictive. They basically test brevity, spontaneity, and cumulative effect. If the teacher intends to use the copy only once, there is no problem. However, if the teacher intends to use the copy every year to teach a certain element in class, permission must be requested. If the article is from an older magazine from which reprints could be requested, reprints rather than copies must be used. If the copying is intended to avoid the costs of ordering reprints, a copyright infringement will occur.

The page limitations may also burden a teacher wishing to present a complete thought or idea to a class. For example, copying of poetry is limited to 250 words, prose is limited to 2,500 words for a complete article, or other works is limited to an excerpt of 1,000 words or 10 percent of the work. These page and word restrictions are designed so that the teacher cannot be allowed to copy so much material as to prevent an author from being able to sell his or her book.

Copyrighted standardized tests may never be copied by teachers.[34] Printed, copyrighted, standardized tests and data may not be transferred to computer software by anyone other than the copyright holder.[35] The factors discussed above must all be weighed on a case-by-case basis. The question that has yet to be answered succinctly is, "How much is too much?"[36] Unfortunately, there are no easy descriptions of a teacher's fair use. As one author has stated, "for educators, the Copyright Act is unacceptable not because it lacks appropriate flexibility. Rather, its various interpretations, and particularly the endorsement by Congress of the restrictive guidelines, have made its application unclear and unduly burdensome."[37] Given the severity of the Guidelines for Classroom Copying, another author has noted: "In a time of severely restricted school budgets, teachers may be tempted simply to photocopy their course materials. Although this act might appear innocent on the surface, copyright infringement, whether malicious or not, is a criminal act."[38]

Fair Use by Libraries

The copyright act further allows libraries, archives, and their employees to reproduce without permission one copy of a published or unpublished work or phonorecord and/or to distribute that copy if: there is no direct or indirect commercial advantage; the library's collections are either open to the public or available to researchers; and the reproduction includes a copyright notice.[39] The statute further differentiates between requests for copying entire works and copying portions of works. If a request is made for a portion of a copyrighted work, the copying is allowed if the library believes the requester intends to use it for private study, scholarship, and research and if the official warning of copyright printed below is displayed.[40] If an entire work is requested to be copied, the library must, in addition to the above requirements, also reasonably determine that the work cannot be obtained at a fair price elsewhere.[41] Of course, separate copies of the same work may be made on one or more separate occasions, however, systematic copying is prohibited.[42] In other words, copying cannot replace the purchasing of subscriptions by separate libraries. All unsupervised reproduction equipment and library copying centers must display the following copyright warning. If the warning is posted, the library is not liable for violations by copy machine users.[43]

NOTICE WARNING CONCERNING COPYRIGHT RESTRICTIONS

The copyright law of the United States (Title 17, United States Code) governs the making of photocopies or other reproductions of copyrighted material. Under certain conditions specified in the law, libraries and archives are authorized to furnish a photocopy or other reproduction. One of these specific conditions is that the photocopy or reproduction is not to be "used for any purpose other than private study, scholarship, or research." If a user makes a request for, or later uses, a photocopy or reproduction for purposes in excess of "fair use," that user may be liable for copyright infringement. This institution reserves the right to refuse to accept a copying order if, in its judgment, fulfillment of the order would involve violation of copyright law.[44]

Federal regulations require that the notice be printed on heavy paper in type at least 18 points in size and must be prominently displayed so as to be legible and comprehensible to a casual observer.[45] If the copy center uses an order form, the same warning must be printed either on the front side of the form or next to the requestor's signature. The type must be at least as large as the type used in the rest of the form or at least eight points in size.[46]

Compulsory Licenses

Compulsory licenses are used when there is a general use of copyrighted material in which it is difficult to determine the holder of each copyright, such as the music played at a dance. Band directors, choir directors, and drama teachers are well aware of the costs of purchasing individual musical or dramatic compositions for their students to perform. Part of the expense includes the royalty fees paid to authors. When it is impossible to determine exactly who the individual copyright holders are because so many different musical works are used, blanket or compulsory licenses are used. The American Society of Composers; Authors and Publishers (ASCAP); Broadcast Music, Inc. (BMI); and the Society of European Stage Authors and Composers, Inc. (SESAC) were formed to help music copyright owners recoup their royalty fees from copyright users.[47]

When using a compulsory license, the user need not seek permission from each copyright holder for each individual use but must pay royalty fees for the general use of music. Compulsory licenses are required for nondramatic musical compositions[48] and cable television.[49] Even educational institutions now may be required to pay these general or blanket, compulsory licenses. However, under the limitations in the Act, colleges and universities have few occasions to pay royalty fees, and public school districts have even fewer.

The Copyright Act exempts certain nonprofit performances, such as classroom performances; in-school performances; and nonprofit performances of a nondramatic literary or musical work not performed for the public, when there is no fee paid to the performers and no admission fee is charged unless the admission proceeds are used for charitable or educational purposes.[50] The exemption is not lost if regular salaries are normally paid directors or performers, such as teachers. Because of these exemptions, few public school dances, fine art productions, or talent shows should require payment of license fees. Should a planned production be outside the scope of these requirements, such as a school musical production or play to which the public is invited for a fee as a moneymaking venture, license fees should be paid.

Educational television and radio stations must pay license fees separately for their use of music.[51] In addition, it is illegal to "pipe-in" radio broadcasts through a number of speakers for the listening enjoyment of customers, clients, or patrons without paying royalty fees to the performing societies—ASCAP, BMI, or others—holding the music copyrights.[52]

Computer games and video games are copyrightable.[53] The musical selections on coin-operated jukeboxes are also copyrighted.[54] Negotiated licenses are required by vendors who install such machines in educational institutions. Those vendors are required to register their ownership of the equipment and to pay license fees.[55] That is not the school district's responsibility. However, investigators from the copyright office have been known to request permission to enter school campuses to ensure that the registration certificate is in place on the machines. Therefore, campus officials would be wise to check that installed machines do display copyright office license certificates.

Computer Software

Computer software is now protected by copyright by both case law and statutory law,[56] and at the same time, its use is becoming increasingly important in schools. The owner of a copy of a copyrighted computer program may only make copies of the program when the new copy is an essential step in using the program in conjunction with a machine and when the new copy is only for archival purposes. Archival copies of the program must be destroyed when the program itself is no longer being used. Copies made in this manner may be leased or transferred only with the copyright owner's authorization.[57]

To save money, a school district may decide to purchase one copy of a program and then "boot" that single program into the memory of all of its microcomputers. This practice allows an unlimited use of a single purchased program. While it may be less expensive for a school district to purchase fewer copies of a computer program than it has terminals, it is also illegal.[58] One author has noted that while the fair use exemption is a computer operator's best defense, it is fairly useless in this situation.[59] Further, it appears that a school district that allows its employees to use a single computer program at a number of terminals can be found to be a vicarious infringer.[60] It is not necessary for the governing body itself to know that the violation is occurring in order for liability to be found.[61] Therefore, campus administrators have a duty to their districts to ensure that such practices are not occurring on their campuses. For school districts developing their own computer software, protecting that product from someone who may use it for financial gain is appropriate. To be eligible to register a copyright on computer software, the product must exhibit original creative authorship and functional restrictions and considerations that dictate specific products are not original enough to be copyrighted.[62]

The overall microcode for a computer circuit chip involves sufficient originality to be copyrighted. So are menu command structures of computer programs, including choice of command terms, the structure and order of those terms and long prompts.[63] The Copyright Office has stated that a single copyright registration of a computer program extends copyright protection to not only the program's literal elements such as source and object codes, but also to the screen displays it creates.[64] This declaration is now being upheld in the courts.[65] Notice of a copyright should be printed on both the software packaging and on the computer display screen generated by the software.

Satellite and Cable Television

As technology becomes more and more advanced, it becomes more and more difficult for copyright law to keep abreast. For example, piracy of satellite and cable television programming becomes more and more of a problem.[66] Pay television programmers use a variety of sophisticated computer programs to "scramble" or "encrypt" the signals they broadcast so that nonsubscribers are unable to view the broadcasts. Technology designed to "unscramble" or "decrypt" those signals violates the Copyright Act.[67]

Videotapes

The advent of the videocassette recorder has caused chaos in copyright law. Not only may videocassettes containing movies or educational films be copied onto blank cassettes, but television broadcasts may be recorded for later use. The Supreme Court first looked at taping television shows in *Sony Corporation of America v. Universal City Studios.*[68] In that case, motion picture production companies sued Sony Corporation, claiming that the use of the videotape recorder allowed private individuals to tape copyrighted television shows and movies for their own private use. The two uses discussed by the Court were "time-shifting," the recording for one-time viewing at a later time, versus "library building," the retaining of recordings for repeated viewings. The Supreme Court held that home recording for the purpose of time-shifting was fair use as a nonprofit, noncommercial activity. Because most copyright holders would not object to time-shifting as it merely increases their audience, the Court reasoned that timeshifting does not harm the market, and the Congress is the proper entity to regulate the medium differently under a revision to the copyright laws.[69] So far, no revisions to the copyright law have been made to change the Court's ruling in *Sony.*

In the educational context, it has been argued that videotaping television programs to be shown as a student activity or to be used repeatedly in a library would violate the Court's holding in *Sony.*[70] In a 1982 case,[71] The Board of Cooperative Educational Services of Erie County videotaped educational television programs without permission or payment of royalty fees and then lent its tapes to schools from its vast library of 5,000 works. Schools were required to subscribe to the videotape service. The court ruled that such an organized and systematic practice of making videotapes did not constitute fair use.[72]

As one author has explained, "Whether a teacher who makes an off-the-air videotape for classroom use has violated (a) ...fair use factor is a gray area..."[73] At this point, the best advice is to follow the Guidelines for Off-Air Recording:

- a recorded broadcast may be retained for 45 days after the date of recording;
- the recording may be used once by the individual teacher, and be repeated only during the first ten days of retention;

- off air records may be made only at the request of an individual teacher, be used only by an individual teacher, not be regularly recorded in anticipation of requests, not be recorded off-air more than once at the request of the same teacher regardless of the number of times the program may be broadcast;
- a limited number of copies may be reproduced from each off-air recording to meet the legitimate needs of the teachers under these guidelines;
- off-air recordings may not be physically or electronically combined or merged to constitute teaching anthologies or compilations;
- all copies of off-air recordings must include the copyright notice on the broadcast programs as recorded.[74]

A teacher or school district renting videotapes from retail outlets and educational service centers should be able to use these tapes in the classroom. As long as the rental copy was legally made, is not copied by the teacher or anyone else, and is returned after its use; classroom use should be permitted.[75] Likewise, the purchase of videotapes, educational or otherwise, should enable a teacher to display that videotape to his or her classroom and should enable the school district to maintain a library of purchased videocassettes.

Yearbooks and Newspapers

Yearbook and newspaper advisors must be aware of copyright laws. Part of a faculty member's proper review of yearbooks and newspapers should be to confirm that no copyright laws are violated. While it may be a terrific idea to use the lyrics of a popular song as the yearbook theme or to design all layouts identical to a well established national magazine, to do so without permission and without a royalty payment may be illegal. This use may extend beyond fair use, especially when newspapers and yearbooks are sold. The most prudent measure is for the yearbook or newspaper advisor to seek permission of the copyright holder prior to production. While fair use may be a defense, it is also firmly established that copying, for example, 45 percent of a copyrighted story or a manuscript constitutes infringement in which the fair use defense is unavailable.[76]

Mascots and Emblems

In order for a pictorial or graphic work to be eligible for copyright protection, it must have a "minimum level of creativity."[77] Normally, mascots are not copyrightable—there are just too many Tigers, Yellowjackets, Longhorns and Lions around. However, a specific school's name and logo in combination with a mascot, may possess the necessary creativity to be copyrightable. Trademark protection under the Lanham Act may be available if the school can show a protectable property right and that a similar mark produced by someone else causes confusion as to the sponsorship of the product.[78] Prior to publication of any graphic work, the copyright symbol, the year of original publication, and the author's name should be placed on the work. The work must be filed and can then be registered with the United States Copyright Office if an infringement action develops.[79]

Recommendations For Practice

There are many pitfalls in copyright law for the unwary school principal. However, some basic knowledge and some basic distribution of information to students and teachers will ease a principal's mind.

- Guidelines for copying books, periodicals, music, and broadcasts should be distributed to all teachers and to students when necessary.
- Questions regarding fair use should be addressed first to the principal. Answers should be based on the Guidelines for Classroom Copying. Further questions should be addressed to the district's legal counsel.
- The printed warning must be posted near every copying machine. The warning must also be posted at any desk where copy orders are taken, and on order forms.
- Copying charges should not exceed actual reproduction costs.
- Copying should never substitute for purchase of original materials.
- Any copied materials should show the original copyright symbol.
- No copying should be done to create anthologies.
- The school district should decide if it will retain the copyrights for works created for the district by employees, or if it will allow the employees to hold the copyright.
- Works created by school district employees should contain the copyright symbol, year of publication, and name of copyright holder. Copies must be filed with the Copyright Office.
- No workbooks, standardized tests, or test booklets may be copied.
- Should use of music be outside of the copyright laws exemptions, license fees should be paid.

- Copies of computer software may only be used for archival purposes. The school may not make copies of software for concurrent use in a number of computers.
- Videotaping should be at the request of an individual teacher and must be replayed within the first ten days of the broadcast, unless permission of the copyright holder is sought.
- Yearbooks and newspapers should be reviewed prior to publication by faculty advisors for possible copyright violations.
- School mascots and emblems, if unique, may be copyrightable.[80]

References

[1]P.L. 94-553, 90 Stat. 2598, Oct. 19, 1976, codified at 17 U.S.C. § 101, et. seq.

[2]1976 United States Code Cong & Ad. News, 5677-5678, overruling Metro-Goldwyn-Mayer Distribution Co. v. Wyatt, 21 C.O. Bull. 203 (D. Md. 1932).

[3]Deni, Copyright and the Federal Government: Ghosts of Protection for Authors, COMMUNICATIONS AND THE LAW (1984).

[4]D. Johnston, COPYRIGHT HANDBOOK (1978).

[5]17 U.S.C. § 101, 102(a).

[6]17 U.S.C. § 102(a).

[7]17 U.S.C. § 102(b); Arica Institute, Inc. v. Palmer, 761 F. Supp. 1056 (S.D.N.Y. 1991).

[8]17 U.S.C. § 106.

[9]17 U.S.C. § 106A.

[10]17 U.S.C. § 201(b); Hays v. Sony Corporation, 847 F.2d 412 (7th Cir. 1988); Haslach, Isn't That Our Software?, 4 SANTA CLARA COMPUTER & HIGH TECH L. J. 307 (1988).

[11]Community for Creative Non-Violence v. Reid, 490 U.S. 730 (1989); Smith & Zirkel, Implications of CCNV v. Reid for the Educator - Author: Who Owns the Copyright?, 63 ED. L. REP. 703 (1991); Burr, A Critical Assessment of Reid's Work for Hire Framework and Its Potential Impact on the Marketplace for Scholarly Works, 24 J. MAR. L. REV. 119 (Fall 1990); VerSteeg, Copyright and the Educational Process: The Right of Teacher Inception, 75 IOWA L. REV. 381 (Jan. 1990). See also, Dodd v. Fort Smith Special School Dist. No. 100, 666 F. Supp. 1278 (W.D. Ark. 1987); Association of American Medical Colleges v. Mikaelian, 571 F. Supp. 144 (E.D. Pa. 1983), aff'd. 734 F.2d 3 (3d Cir. 1984).

[12]17 U.S.C. § 201(a).

[13]Weinstein v. University of Ill., 811 F.2d 1091, 1095 (7th Cir. 1987); Weissman v. Freeman, 868 F.2d 1313 (2d Cir. 1989).

[14]17 U.S.C. § 106, 201(d).

[15]17 U.S.C. § 102.

[16]17 U.S.C. §§ 304(a), 411, 405(a)(2).

[17]17 U.S.C. § 401; 37 C.F.R. § 202.2.

[18]17 U.S.C. §§ 407, 408, 708.

[19]Rosemont Enterprises Inc. v. Random House, Inc., 366 F.2d 303, 306 (2d Cir. 1966), cert. denied. 385 U.S. 1009 (1967).

[20]17 U.S.C. § 107.

[21]D. Johnston, at 9; Basic Books v. Kinko's Graphics Corporation, 758 F. Supp. 1522 (S.D. N.Y. 1991).

[22]17 U.S.C. § 107(1-4).

[23]Salinger v. Random House, 811 F.2d 90 (2d Cir. 1987), cert. denied. 484 U.S. 890 (1987).

[24]MacMillan Co. v. King, 223 F. 862 (D. Mass. 1914); Whitol v. Crow, 191 F. Supp. 682 (S.D. Iowa 1961), rev'd. 309 F.2d 777 (8th Cir. 1962); Marcus v. Rowley, 695 F.2d 1171 (9th Cir. 1983); Association of American Colleges v. Mikaelian, 571 F. Supp. 144; Wagner, Beware the Custom-Made Anthology, Academic Photocopying and Basic Books v. Kinko's Graphics, 68 EDUC. L. REP. 1 (1991).

[25]Lane v. First National Bank of Boston, 871 F.2d 166 (1st Cir. 1989); Kersavage v. University of Tenn., 731 F. Supp. 1327 (E. D. Tenn. 1989); BV Engineering v. University of Cal., Los Angeles, 858 F.2d 1394 (9th Cir. 1988).

[26]See also, Salinger, 811 F.2d 90; Maxtone-Graham v. Burtchaell, 803 F.2d 1253 (2d Cir. 1986).

[27]Basic Books, 758 F. Supp. 1522.

[28]Steinbach, *Photocopying Copyrighted Course Materials: Doesn't Anyone Remember the NYU Case?*, 50 ED. L. REP. 317 (1989); Dratler, To Copy or Not to Copy: The Educator's Dilemma, 19 J. L. & EDUC. 1 (1990).

[29]H. R. REP. No. 94-1476, 94th Cong., 2d Sess. 66 (1976), U.S. CODE, CONG. & ADMIN. NEWS 5659 (1976).

[30]Basic Books, 758 F. Supp. 1522; H. R. Rep. No. 94-1476; *Copyright Law and the Classroom: Photocopying, Videotaping and Fair Use*, 15 J. of L. & EDUC. 229 (1986).

[31]*Marcus*, 695 F.2d 1171; Basic Books, 758 F. Supp. 1522.

[32]H.R. REP. No. 94-1476; Smith, Classroom Use of Copyrighted Materials, 43 ED. LAW REP. 1 (1988).

[33]A full text of the guidelines is available from the U. S. Copyright Office. Request Reproduction of Copyrighted Works by Educators and Librarians: Circular R21, Copyright Office, Library of Congress, Washington, D.C., 20559.

[34]Association of American Medical Colleges v. Carey, 728 F. Supp. 873 (N.D. N.Y. 1990); Educational Testing Services v. Katzman, 793 F.2d 533 (3d Cir. 1986); Association of American Medical Colleges v. Cuomo, 928 F.2d 519 (2d Cir. 1991); Campbell, *Comment*, Testing the Copyright Clause: Copyright Protection for Educational and Psychological Tests, 69 NEB. L. REV. 791 (1990).

[35]Applied Innovations v. Regents of the University of Minn., 876 F.2d 626 (8th Cir. 1989).

[36]Harper & Row, Publishers, Inc. v. Nation Enterprises, 471 U.S. 539, (1985); Basic Books, 758 F. Supp. 1522.

[37]Sorenson, *Impact of Copyright Law on College Teaching*, 12 J. of COLLEGE & UNIV. L. 509, 537 (1986).

[38]Merickel, *The Educator's Rights to Fair Use of Copyrighted Works*, 51 ED. L. REP. 711 (1989).

[39]17 U.S.C. § 108(a)(b).

[40]17 U.S.C. § 108(d).

[41]17 U.S.C. § 108(e).

[42]17 U.S.C. § 108(g).

[43]17 U.S.C. § 108(f).

[44]37 C.F.R. § 201.14(b).

[45]37 C.F.R. § 201.14(c)(1).

[46]37 C.F.R. § 201.14(c)(2).

[47]National Cable Television Ass'n., Inc. v. Broadcast Music, Inc., 772 F. Supp. 614 (D.D.C. 1991).

[48]17 U.S.C. § 118.

[49]17 U.S.C. § 111.

[50]17 U.S.C. § 110(1-4).

[51]17 U.S.C. § 118, 37 C.F.R. § 302.

[52]*See* Broadcast Music, Inc. v. United States Shoe Corp., 678 F.2d 816 (9th Cir. 1982); Sailor Music v. Gap Stores, Inc., 516 F. Supp. 923 (S.D. N.Y. 1981), *aff'd.* 668 F.2d 84 (2d Cir. 1981), *cert. denied.*, 102 S. Ct. 2012 (1982).

[53]Williams Electronics, Inc. v. Artic International, Inc., 685 F.2d 870 (3d Cir. 1982).

[54]17 U.S.C. § 110.

[55]17 U.S.C. § 116, 116A.

[56]17 U.S.C. § 101; 102; 117; NEC Corp. v. Intel Corp., 645 F. Supp. 590 (N.D. Cal. 1986); Allen-Myland v. International Business Machines Corp, 746 F. Supp. 520 (E.D. Penn. 1990).

[57]17 U.S.C. § 117; *See also*, Apple Computer, Inc. v. Formula International, Inc. 725 F.2d 521 (9th Cir. 1984); NEC Corp., 645 F. Supp. 590.

[58]Pringle, *Computer Software in the Schools*, 28 ED. L. REP. 315 (1986).

[59]Eskew, *The Copyright Dilemma Facing Texas Educators as They Implement Computer Literacy into the Curriculum*, 22 HOUSTON L. REV. 1011 (1985).

[60]Encyclopedia Britannica Educ. Corp. v. Crooks, 542 F. Supp. 1156 (W.D. N.Y. 1982).

[61]Boz Skaggs Music v. KND Corp., 491 F. Supp. 908 (D. Conn. 1980); Chappell & Co. v. Frankel, 285 F. Supp. 798 (S.D. N.Y. 1968).

[62]Manufacturers Technologies v. CAMS, Inc., 706 F. Supp. 984 (D. Conn. 1989).

[63]NEC Corp., 10 U.S.P.Q.2d 1177.

[64]36 PAT. TRADEMARK & COPYRIGHT J. 155 (1988).

[65]Lotus Development Corp. v. Paperback Software International, 740 F. Supp. 37 (D. Mass. 1990).

[66]Litman, *Copyright Legislation and Technological Change*, 68 OR. L. REV. 275 (1989).

[67]Cable/Home Communication v. Network Productions 902 F.2d 829 (11th Cir. 1990).

[68]Sony Corp. of America v. Universal Studios, 464 U.S. 417 (1984).

[69]*Id.*

[70]Boland, Szykowny, and Flahive, *Copyright Infringement? Videocassettes on Campus*, 23 ED. LAW REP. 11 (1985).

[71]*Encyclopedia Britannica*, 542 F. Supp. 1156.

[72]*Id.*

[73]Mawdsley, *Use of Videocassettes in the Classroom*, 32 ED. L. REP. 1163, 1170 (1986).

[74]17 U.S.C. § 118(d).

[75]Mawdsley, at 1171.

[76]Quinto v. Legal Times of Washington, 506 F. Supp. 554 (D.D.C. 1981); Mitcham v. Bd. of Regents, University of Tex. Systems, 670 S.W.2d 371 (Tex. App. Ct. 1984); *Harper & Row*, 471 U.S. 539.

[77]Magic Marketing, Inc. v. Mailing Servs. of Pittsburgh, Inc., 634 F.Supp. 769 (W.D. Pa. 1986); John Muller & Co. Inc. v. New York Arrows Soccer Team, 802 F.2d 989 (8th Cir. 1986); 37 C.F.R. § 202.10(a).

[78]Lanham Act, 15 U.S.C. § 1051 *et seq.*; Board of Governors of the University of N. C. v. Helpingstine, 714 F. Supp. 167 (M.D. N.C. 1989); University of Pittsburgh v. Champion Products, 686 F.2d 1040 (3d Cir.), *cert. denied*. 459 U.S. 1087 (1982).

[79]Form TX for nondramatic literary works including computer programs; form SE for periodicals and serials; form PA for performing arts works; form VA for visual arts works; form SR for sound recordings, U.S. Copyright Office.

[80]Smith, *Classroom Use of Copyrighted Materials*, 43 ED. L. REP. 1 (Feb. 1988); *Guidelines for Classroom Copying, supra* note 29.

27

Devotional Activities in Public Schools

Martha M. McCarthy

Introduction

Religious, primarily Protestant, influences in public education were common from colonial times until the mid-twentieth century. The Bible was read and daily prayers were said in many public school classrooms until the 1960s; sectarian materials and observances reflected the dominant faith of each community. The change from heavy reliance on sectarian materials to a more secular public school curriculum was gradual and was influenced by disputes among religious sects regarding the choice of sectarian tenets to emphasize in the curriculum.[1] In communities with religious diversity, minority sects argued that religious influences should be removed from the public school program. However, only since World War II has the federal judiciary played a prominent role in resolving these disputes through interpretations of the first amendment's religion clauses. The first amendment, in part, prohibits governmental action respecting an establishment of religion (establishment clause) or interfering with the free exercise thereof (free exercise clause).[2]

Although legal controversies over religious influences in public schools have involved some free exercise claims, the decisions usually have turned on an assessment of whether specific school practices violate the establishment clause. In most establishment clause cases since 1970, the United States Supreme Court has applied a three-part test:

- Does the governmental action have a secular (nonreligious) purpose?
- Does its primary effect neither advance nor impede religion?
- Does it avoid excessive governmental entanglement with religion?

This test is often called the *Lemon* test because it was first fully developed in a 1971 education case, *Lemon v. Kurtzman*.[3] A majority of the current Supreme Court justices has voiced dissatisfaction with the *Lemon* test,[4] but the Court has not repudiated this standard. The Court continues to support a separation of church and state in education cases, even though it did not apply the stringent *Lemon* test in its most recent establishment clause decision involving public schools.[5] This chapter focuses on the evolving judicial interpretations of the establishment clause in cases pertaining to spoken prayer, silent prayer, student-initiated devotional meetings, and the distribution of religious literature in public schools.[6]

Legal Issues

Spoken Prayer

In two seminal decisions in the early 1960s, the United States Supreme Court prohibited public schools from sponsoring daily prayer and Bible reading.[7] Concluding that such activities advance religion in violation of the establishment clause, the Court reasoned that the constitutional violation was not reduced by the voluntary participation of students or the nondenominational nature of the religious activities. Public school sponsorship of daily devotionals was sufficient to abridge the establishment clause. The Court emphasized, however, that the academic study about religion was constitutionally permissible and desirable.

Federal courts have subsequently ruled that the constitutional violation is not lessened if voluntary devotional activities are initiated by individual students or teachers. In 1981, the United States Supreme Court declined to review a decision in which the Ninth Circuit Court of Appeals struck down a school's practice of allowing student-led prayers in school assemblies.[8] The following year the Court affirmed, without an opinion, a decision in which the Fifth Circuit Court of Appeals invalidated a Louisiana law allowing students to offer a prayer at the beginning of the school day or, if no students volunteered, permitting the teacher to offer a prayer.[9] In 1984, the Court affirmed without an opinion a decision of the Eleventh Circuit Court of Appeals striking down an Alabama law that allowed public school teachers to lead "willing" students in a state-composed prayer at the beginning of the school day.[10] The federal appellate courts in each of these cases reasoned that there was little constitutional distinction between the contested practices and the state-imposed devotional activities invalidated by the Supreme Court in the early 1960s.

Teachers can be dismissed for crossing the line from teaching about religion to proselytizing students.[11] While a teacher's freedom to hold religious beliefs is absolute, the practice of such beliefs in public schools is restricted by the establishment clause. In addition, a school board can be liable if it condones a teacher's proselytizing activities, even in the absence of a policy authorizing such activities.[12] In 1984, the Supreme Court declined to review a decision in which the Eleventh Circuit Court of Appeals held that classroom devotional activities initiated by teachers violated the establishment clause.[13] Noting that teachers function on behalf of the state, the appeals court rejected the argument that such activities were beyond the reach of the first amendment because they were not undertaken pursuant to board policy. The Eighth Circuit Court of Appeals voiced similar logic in finding a school board in violation of the establishment clause for condoning a band teacher's practice of holding prayer sessions before rehearsals and performances.[14]

The Supreme Court declined to address the constitutionality of graduation prayers until recently, but lower courts traditionally appeared less inclined to find an establishment clause violation in baccalaureate services and prayers during graduation ceremonies than in routine devotional activities in public education. Baccalaureate programs and graduation prayers were defended primarily because of their transient, ceremonial nature; no assertion was made that such activities were instructional rather than religious.[15]

Since the mid-1980s, however, courts have rendered conflicting rulings on this subject; some courts have continued to uphold graduation prayers whereas others have invalidated such practices under the establishment clause.[16] Several courts also have struck down prayers and other devotional activities during public school extracurricular activities, such as athletic contests.[17] Given the diversity of opinions across jurisdictions, the Supreme Court finally agreed to render an opinion in *Lee v. Weisman*, which involved a challenge to a Rhode Island school committee's practice of allowing clergy to deliver invocations and benedictions at middle and high school graduation ceremonies.[18]

It was anticipated that the Court might use its *Weisman* decision to make significant changes in establishment clause standards, but the Court did not elect to make this change. In a five-to-four decision, it affirmed the appellate court's conclusion that the graduation prayers abridged the establishment clause. While not renouncing the three-part *Lemon* test, the Court did not apply it either. Instead, the majority focused on the fact that school officials directed the performance of religious exercises at graduation ceremonies where students felt an obligation to attend.[19] The majority reasoned that the government in effect was coercing students to support religious exercises in violation of the establishment clause.

Finding a special threat of indirect coercion in the public school context, the Court majority noted the "heightened concerns with protecting freedom of conscience from subtle coercive pressure in elementary and secondary public schools."[20]

Four of the justices who joined the majority opinion in *Weisman* wrote separately, emphasizing that government coercion, while sufficient, is not required to abridge the establishment clause. However, only three of these justices voiced support for the *Lemon* test.[21] Although the *Lemon* test appears in jeopardy, the *Weisman* majority indicated that government sponsorship of religious observances still will not be tolerated in public elementary and secondary schools.

Silent Prayer

Students clearly have a free exercise right to engage in private devotional activities in public schools as long as they do not interfere with regular school activities. The constitutional controversies have focused on state laws or school board policies that condone private devotionals, thus placing the public school's imprimatur on such activities. While state laws calling for a period of silent meditation or prayer in public schools historically were assumed to be permissible under the first amendment,[22] the judiciary has become more reluctant to accept the asserted secular purpose for such laws. Since 1982, a West Virginia constitutional amendment and laws in four other states calling for a period of silent meditation or prayer in public schools have been struck down under the establishment clause.[23]

The Supreme Court rendered its first decision on this topic in 1985. In this case, *Wallace v. Jaffree*, the Court affirmed the Eleventh Circuit Court of Appeals' conclusion that a 1981 Alabama law, calling for a daily period for silent meditation or voluntary prayer, violated the establishment clause.[24] Based on an assessment of the legislative history of the law, the Supreme Court concluded that it was intended to convey a clear preference for students to engage in prayer during the moment of silence. Since a 1978 Alabama law already authorized a period of silent meditation in public schools, the Court majority concluded that the only logical reason for adding the phrase "or voluntary prayer" in the 1981 amendment was to encourage public school students to pray. The Court, however, indicated that laws calling for silent meditation or prayer in public schools without a legislative intent to impose prayer on students might withstand scrutiny under the establishment clause. Thus, the ruling left some ambiguity regarding the legality of silent prayer laws which are on the books in about half of the states.

The Supreme Court had another opportunity to clarify the legal status of silent prayer laws in 1987 when it agreed to review *Karcher v. May*, a case involving a challenge to New Jersey's silent meditation statute.[25] This law called for a moment of silence for "quiet and private contemplation or introspection" and did not actually mention "prayer." Nonetheless, the federal district court and subsequently the Third Circuit Court of Appeals ruled that the law was intended to promote religious observances in public schools. The Supreme Court, however, did not address the first amendment issue, dismissing the appeal because the plaintiffs lacked standing to challenge the appellate court's ruling. Therefore, the legality of meditation laws remains to be resolved case-by-case, based on the judiciary's interpretation of legislative intent.

Student-initiated Devotional Meetings

Requests by student groups to hold devotional meetings in public school facilities during noninstructional time raise particularly sensitive first amendment questions because such requests implicate free speech, free exercise, and association rights of students, as well as establishment clause restrictions.[26] In 1981 the Court upheld the right of college students to hold prayer meetings on state-supported campuses. In this case, *Widmar v. Vincent*, the Court ruled that any infringement on student access to the open forum for expression created on college campuses must be justified by a compelling governmental interest.[27] While recognizing that compliance with the establishment clause is a compelling state interest, the Court found no establishment clause violation in allowing all student groups equal access to campus facilities. An "equal access" policy would have the secular purpose of making campus facilities available to student organizations, and the school's endorsement of religious groups would not be implied any more than its endorsement of student political groups. Furthermore, such an "equal access" policy would not excessively entangle the government with religion because minimal supervision of student groups is required on college campuses.

From 1980 to 1985, five federal appellate courts took a different stance regarding student-initiated devotional meetings at the precollegiate level. They ruled that the establishment clause barred such devotional meetings during noninstructional time under the supervision of public school personnel,[28] reasoning that public schools must guard against giving the impression that particular religious creeds are being advanced. Distinguishing high schools from residential college campuses, these courts noted that younger students are more impressionable, schooling through at least part of high school is compulsory, faculty supervision is required for student groups at the high school level, and high school students have access to their homes for religious meetings.

Voicing displeasure with the federal judiciary's reluctance to extend the *Widmar* rationale to the precollegiate level, Congress passed the Equal Access Act (EAA) in 1984. This Act stipulates that if a federally assisted public secondary school provides a limited open forum for noncurriculum student groups to meet during noninstructional time, "equal access" to that forum cannot be denied based on the "religious, political, philosophical or other content of the speech at such meetings."[29] If the meetings have a religious orientation, school employees can attend only in a "nonparticipatory capacity" to maintain discipline.[30] Under the EAA, public high schools can decline to establish a limited forum for student expression and thus confine school access during noninstructional time to curriculum-related student groups (e.g., athletic teams, foreign language clubs, debate teams). Even if a limited open forum is created, school authorities still can curtail meetings that would disrupt educational activities.

Prior to 1990, lower courts offered conflicting opinions regarding the application and constitutionality of the EAA.[31] In 1990 the Supreme Court resolved some of the legal questions when it rendered a significant decision, *Board of Education of the Westside Community Schools v. Mergens*.[32] The controversy that eventually led to the Supreme Court's decision arose after a group of students at a Nebraska high school sought permission to form a club that would meet at the public school and engage in Bible discussions, prayer, and fellowship. The federal district court upheld school authorities' denial of the request, concluding that the EAA did not apply because all thirty student groups that met in the school were curriculum related and part of the student activities program designed to advance educational objectives. Thus, the high school had not created a limited open forum subject to the EAA.[33]

However, the Eighth Circuit Court of Appeals and ultimately the Supreme Court disagreed, ruling that the school could not bar the religious club from the limited forum it had created for noncurriculum student groups to hold meetings. The Supreme Court declared that "even if a public secondary school allows only one noncurriculum-related student group to meet, the Act's obligations are triggered and the school may not deny other clubs, on the basis of the content of their speech, equal access to meet on school premises during noninstructional time."[34] Acknowledging the law's ambiguity as to the definition of "curriculum related," the majority concluded that student groups would be exempt from the Act's coverage only if they relate to subject matter that is currently, or soon would be, taught in the curriculum, if they relate to the body of courses as a whole, or if participation in the group is required as part of a course or awarded credit.[35]

Because the Court granted relief on statutory grounds, it was not necessary to address the students' claims that the denial of school access for religious meetings violated their free speech and free exercise rights. However, the Court did address the school district's contention that the EAA violates the establishment clause. Concluding that it does not, the justices were not of a single mind as to their reasoning. Only four justices concluded that the EAA satisfies the three-part test under the establishment clause since "the logic of *Widmar* applies with equal force to the Equal Access Act."[36] The plurality emphasized that "there is a crucial difference between government speech endorsing religion, which the establishment clause forbids, and private speech endorsing religion, which the free speech and free exercise clauses protect."[37] For more than two decades prior to the *Mergens* decision, the federal judiciary struck down practices under the establishment clause regardless of whether school authorities actually organized religious activities or simply permitted students to do so.[38] But the *Mergens* ruling marked a departure in allowing devotional meetings as long as they are not initiated or led by school personnel.[39]

The EAA was championed by the religious right, but the law protects student expression far beyond religious meetings. Fearing that controversial student groups at odds with school objectives (e.g., hate groups) will be granted school access under the EAA, some school boards have opted to eliminate any forum for student groups that are not an extension of the curriculum. But such efforts will not go unchallenged, as the definition of "curriculum related" remains open to multiple interpretations. Also, the Supreme Court in *Mergens* did not address the potential conflict between the EAA and state constitutional provisions. If a state constitution imposes greater separation of church and state than required by the Federal Constitution, should the EAA or the state constitution prevail? Two federal district courts have rendered conflicting decisions on this question,[40] and it seems likely that the Supreme Court eventually will have to resolve the matter.

Distribution of Religious Literature

The Supreme Court has not addressed the distribution of religious literature in public schools, but a number of lower courts have prohibited religious sects from distributing materials to captive student audiences. For example, several courts have struck down school board policies allowing the Gideon Society to visit schools and present Bibles to students who wish to accept them.[41] Departing from the prevailing view, an Indiana federal district court upheld a school district's policy allowing religious organizations, such as the Gideon Society, to distribute religious literature in public school classrooms.[42] An Illinois federal district court held that school authorities could not prohibit the distribution of Gideon Bibles on the sidewalk in front of a high school, reasoning that the sidewalk was a public forum for use by the general public.[43]

More controversial have been requests by students to distribute religious publications. Like meetings of student-initiated religious groups, these requests pit free speech protections against establishment clause restrictions. Some courts have applied the same legal principles to students' distribution of religious and nonreligious literature. A Colorado federal district court held that high school students had a free expression right to distribute a religious newsletter as long as the activity did not create a disturbance.[44] Also finding the distribution of religious literature to be protected speech, a Pennsylvania federal district court held that students were entitled to distribute sectarian material during noninstructional time.[45]

In contrast, a California appeals court held that a student religious club was not entitled to distribute its materials on the high school campus or advertise in the school's yearbook, and the United States Supreme Court declined to review this decision.[46] The state appeals court determined that the school did not maintain a limited forum for student clubs as only recognized school-related student groups were granted access to school facilities during noninstructional time. The court further concluded that even if the school had created a limited forum for noncurriculum student groups, the establishment clause would preclude using the prestige and authority of the school to advance religious causes. An Illinois federal district court also concluded that adherence to the establishment clause is a compelling state interest that would justify restrictions on the distribution of religious literature in public elementary and junior high schools if the materials might be viewed as representing the schools.[47] The court upheld the school district's revised policy prohibiting students from distributing more than ten copies of religious materials that are not primarily prepared by students or that concern activities of nonschool-sponsored organizations. However, enforcement of the board's original policy that placed a total ban on students' distribution of any religious literature was permanently enjoined. Until the Supreme Court addresses the first amendment issues involved in the distribution of religious literature in public schools, standards seem likely to vary across jurisdictions.

Recommendations for Practice

The Bill of Rights was intended to remove certain subjects from political debate,[48] but all three branches of government have become involved in disputes over the role of religion in public education. School prayer has become a volatile political issue with candidates for public office being pressed to take a stand. Viewed in isolation, the controversy over devotional activities in public education may appear to be much ado about nothing. A daily prayer or moment for devotionals may pose little threat of influencing students' religious beliefs or eroding the wall of separation between church and state. However, controversies over devotional activities in public schools are simply part of a larger controversy over the place of religious doctrine in public education and over the definition of what constitutes a "religion" for first amendment purposes.[49]

While the federal judiciary has not mandated a strict separation between church and state, courts have been less supportive of governmental accommodation toward religion in the public school context than they have in other settings. For example, the United States Supreme Court has upheld the use of public funds to support legislative prayer[50] and to erect a Christmas display with the nativity scene.[51] But federal courts have not condoned such religious accommodations in public schools.[52] The Court has indicated on several occasions that governmental accommodations toward religion that may be permissible in other settings are unconstitutional in public schools.[53] The impressionability of children and compulsory nature of schooling have been offered as justifications for special sensitivity to establishment clause restrictions where precollegiate children are involved.

The principle of governmental neutrality, however, is easier to state than to apply. Courts will continue to be called on to interpret the first amendment's religion clauses as a fine line often exists between neutrality and hostility and between accommodation and advancement. Some of the most sensitive controversies will likely involve the delicate balance between separation and accommodation in connection with religious influences in public schools. Although the law governing devotional activities in public education is still evolving, the following principles can be gleaned from litigation to date:

- School sanctioned prayer during the public school day violates the establishment clause, regardless of whether participation is voluntary.
- Public school teachers can be discharged for proselytizing activities, and school boards can be held liable for condoning such activities.
- The academic study of religion in public schools is permissible, but such instruction cannot be a guise to advance sectarian tenets.
- Religious observances in public school graduation exercises that are directed by the public school violate the establishment clause.
- Students can engage in silent prayer in public schools, but school authorities cannot promote such silent devotionals.
- If a federally assisted high school has created a limited forum for noncurriculum student groups to meet during noninstructional time, all student groups including religious groups, must be allowed school access.
- School authorities would be wise to bar religious organizations from distributing their sectarian literature in public schools; individual students may have a free expression right to distribute such literature as long as they comply with reasonable school regulations.

References

[1] W. BERNS THE FIRST AMENDMENT AND THE FUTURE OF AMERICNAN DEMOCRACY, 66-67 (1976); L. PFEFFER, CHURCH, STATE, AND FREEDOM, 335-338 (1967).

[2] Although the first amendment was specifically directed toward Congress, its restrictions have been applied to state action through judicial interpretations of the fourteenth amendment's protection of individual liberties against state interference. See Everson v. Board of Educ., 330 U.S. 1, 15-16 (1947); Cantwell v. Connecticut, 310 U.S. 296, 303 (1940); Gitlow v. New York, 268 U.S. 652, 666 (1925).

[3] 403 U.S. 602 (1971). The test was first announced in Walz v. Tax Comm'n of the City of New York, 397 U.S. 664, 668-669 (1970).

[4] See County of Allegheny v. American Civil Liberties Union, 492 U.S. 573 at 655-656 (1989) (Kennedy, J., concurring in part, dissenting in part); Edwards v. Aguillard, 482 U.S. 578, 636-640 (1987) (Scalia, J., dissenting); Aguilar v. Felton, 473 U.S. 402, 426-430 (1985) (O'Connor, J., dissenting); Wallace, 472 U.S. at 108-113 (1985) (Rehnquist, J., dissenting); Roemer v. Maryland Bd. of Pub. Works, 426 U.S. 736, 768-769 (1976) (White, J., concurring in judgment).

[5] Lee v. Weisman, 60 U.S.L.W. 4723 (1992). See text with note 18, infra.

[6] This chapter builds in part on M. MCCARTHY and N. CAMBRON-MCCABE, PUBLIC SCHOOL LAW: TEACHERS' AND STUDENTS' RIGHTS, 3d ed., 25-34 (1992).

[7] School Dist. of Abington Township v. Schempp, 374 U.S. 203 (1963); Engel v. Vitale, 370 U.S. 421 (1962).

[8] Collins v. Chandler Unified School Dist., 644 F.2d 759 (9th Cir. 1981), cert. denied, 454 U.S. 863 (1981).

[9] Karen B. v. Treen, 653 F.2d 897 (5th Cir. 1981), aff'd mem., 455 U.S. 913 (1982).

[10] Jaffree v. Board of School Comm'rs of Mobile County, 705 F.2d 1526 (11th Cir. 1983), aff'd mem. in part sub. nom.; Wallace v. Jaffree, 466 U.S. 924 (1984).

[11] Fink v. Board of Educ. of the Warren County School Dist., 442 A.2d 837 (Pa. Commw. Ct. 1982), appeal dismissed, 460 U.S.1048 (1983); LaRocca v. Board of Educ. of Rye City School Dist., 406 N.Y.S.2d 348 (App. Div. 1978), appeal dismissed, 386 N.E.2d 266 (N.Y. 1978).

[12] In Bell v. Little Axe Indep. School Dist. No. 70, 766 F.2d 1391, 1412 (10th Cir. 1985), the appeals court held that school authorities could be liable for damages to compensate individuals for the "inherent value" of their rights under the establishment clause. However, the United Supreme Court subsequently ruled that compensatory damages must be based on actual injury suffered rather than on the perceived value of constitutional rights, Memphis Community School Dist. v. Stachura, 477 U.S. 299 (1986).

[13] Jaffree v. Board of School Comm'rs of Mobile County, 705 F.2d 1526 (11th Cir. 1983), cert. denied, 466 U.S. 926 (1984).

[14] Steele v. Van Buren Pub. School Dist., 845 F.2d 1492 (8th Cir. 1988).

[15] Upholding invocations and benedictions during the graduation ceremony, see Grossberg v. Deusebio, 380 F. Supp. 285 (E.D. Va. 1974); Wiest v. Mt. Lebanon School Dist., 320 A.2d 362 (Pa. 1974), cert. denied, 419 U.S. 967 (1974). Upholding public school sponsorship of baccalaureate programs, see Chamberlin v. Dade County Bd. of Pub. Instruction, 160 So. 2d 97 (Fla. 1964), rev'd, 377 U.S. 402 (1964); Goodwin v. Cross County School Dist. No. 7, 394 F. Supp. 417 (E.D. Ark. 1973).

[16] Upholding graduation prayers or baccalaureate services, see Jones v. Clear Creek Indep. School Dist., 930 F.2d 416 (5th Cir. 1991), vacated and remanded for reconsideration in light of Lee v. Weisman, 1992 WL 143639 (1992); Albright v. Board of Educ. of Granite School Dist., 765 F. Supp. 682 (D. Utah 1991); Randall v. Pegan, 765 F. Supp. 793 (W.D. N.Y. 1991). See also Stein v. Plainwell Community Schools, 822 F.2d 1406 (6th Cir. 1987) (while voicing general approval of invocations and benedictions in graduation ceremonies, the appeals court held that the observances at issue endorsed one religious view, Christianity, in violation of the establishment clause). Striking down graduation prayers under the establishment clause, see Lundberg v. West Monona Community School Dist., 731 F. Supp. 331 (ND Iowa 1989); Graham v. Central Community School Dist., 608 F. Supp. 531 (S.D. Iowa 1985); Sands v. Morongo Unified School Dist. 809 P2d 809 (Cal. 1991); Kay v. David Douglas School Dist. No. 40, 719 P.2d 875 (Or. Ct. App. 1986), vacated, 738 P.2d 1389 (Or. 1987), cert. denied 484 U.S. 1032 (1988); Bennett v. Livermore, 238 Cal. Rptr. 819 (Cal. Ct. App. 1987). See also, Guidry v. Broussard, 897 F.2d 181 (5th Cir. 1990) (school authorities' rejection of a student's valedictory speech because it would have the primary effect of advancing religion did not violate the student's free speech rights).

[17] See Jager v. Douglas County School Dist., 862 F.2d 824 (11th Cir. 1989), cert. denied, 490 U.S. 1090 (1989); Doe v. Aldine Indep. School Dist., 563 F. Supp. 883 (S.D. Tex. 1982).

[18] 728 F. Supp. 68, 71 (D.R.I. 1990), aff'd, 908 F.2d 1090 (1st Cir. 1990), aff'd, 60 U.S.L.W. 4723 (1992).

[19] The majority distinguished the situation in Marsh v. Chambers, 463 U.S. 783 (1983), where the Court upheld the use of state funds to support a chaplain to open legislative sessions with a prayer, noting that legislatures feel no obligation to remain in the room during the opening devotionals. In contrast, graduates who object to the prayers "are induced to conform" to the religious exercises during the graduation ceremony, 112 S. Ct. 2649 (1992).

[20] 112 S. Ct. at 2651.

[21] Id. at 4728 (Blackmun, J, concurring) (supporting the Lemon test); id. at 4731 (Souter, J., concurring). Justices Stevens and O'Connor joined both concurring opinions as well as the majority opinion written by Justice Kennedy.

[22] See Gaines v. Anderson, 421 F. Supp. 337 (D. Mass. 1976); Opinion of the Justices, 307 A.2d 558 (N.H. 1973).

[23] May v. Cooperman, 780 F.2d 240 (3d Cir. 1985), appeal dismissed sub nom. Jaffree v. Board of School Comm'rs of Mobile County, 554 F. Supp. 1104 (S.D. Ala. 1983), rev'd sub nom. Jaffree v. Wallace, 705 F.2d 1526, 1535-1536 (11th Cir. 1983), aff'd in part, 472 U.S. 38 (1985); Beck v. McElrath, 548 F. Supp. 1161 (M.D. Tenn. 1982), appeal dismissed, vacated and remanded, 718 F.2d 1098 (6th Cir. 1983); Walter v. West Virginia Bd. of Educ., 610 F. Supp. 1169 (S.D. W.V. 1985); Duffy v. Las Cruces Pub. Schools, 557 F. Supp. 1013 (N.M. 1983); Karcher v. May, 484 U.S. 72 (1987).

[24] 705 F.2d 1526 (11th Cir. 1983), aff'd in part, 472 U.S. 38 (1985).

[25] 780 F.2d 240 (3d Cir. 1983), appeal dismissed, 484 U.S. 72 (1987).

[26] Some recent controversies have also focused on requests by religious groups to use public school facilities, and a range of judicial opinions have been offered. Several courts have relied on the first amendment's free speech clause in enjoining public schools from barring religious

meetings where a forum for community meetings has been established. *See* Gregoire v. Centennial School Dist., 907 F.2d 1366 (3d Cir. 1990), *cert. denied*, 111 S. Ct. 253 (1990); .

[27] 454 U.S. 263 (1981).

[28] Bender v. Williamsport Area School Dist., 741 F.2d 538 (3d Cir. 1984), *vacated*, 475 U.S. 534 (1986); Bell v. Little Axe Indep. School Dist. No. 70, 766 F.2d 1391 (10th Cir. 1985); Nartowicz v. Clayton County School Dist., 736 F.2d 646 (11th Cir. 1984).

[29] 20 U.S.C. 4071 (1988). The EAA was a compromise measure; critics of school prayer proposals viewed the EAA as a vehicle to defuse the congressional momentum to enact a law sanctioning some type of daily prayer during the school day.

[30] 20 U.S.C. § 4071(c)(3) (1988).

[31] *See* Garnett v. Renton School Dist. No. 403, 874 F.2d 608 (9th Cir. 1989), *cert. granted and judgment vacated*, 110 S. Ct. 2608 (1990), *on remand*, 772 F. Supp. 531 (W.D. Wash. 1991); Student Coalition for Peace v. Lower Merion School Dist., 776 F.2d 431 (3d Cir. 1985), *on remand*, 633 F. Supp. 1040 (E.D. Pa. 1986); Clark v. Dallas Indep. School Dist., 671 F. Supp. 1119 (N.D. Tex. 1987), *modified*, 701 F. Supp. 594 (N.D. Tex. 1988); Thompson v. Waynesboro Area School Dist., 673 F. Supp. 1379 (M.D. Pa. 1987).

[32] 110 S. Ct. 2356 (1990).

[33] *Mergens, id.*, No. CV 85-0-426 (D. Neb. 1988). The student clubs were allowed access to the school's bulletin boards, newspaper, public address system, and club fair.

[34] *Mergens, id.*, 110 S. Ct. at 2364.

[35] *Id.* at 2366.

[36] *Id.* at 2371 (O'Connor, J., joined by Rehnquist, C.J., White, and Blackmun, J.J.).

[37] *Id.* at 2372. It appears that different standards are applied in evaluating curriculum-related activities under the EAA versus the free speech clause of the first amendment. *See* Hazelwood School Dist. v. Kuhlmeier, 484 U.S. 260 (1988); McCarthy and Cambron-McCabe, Public School Law, chapter 4.

[38] *See*, e.g., Collins v. Chandler Unified School Dist., 644 F.2d 759, 761 (9th Cir. 1981), *cert. denied*, 454 U.S. 863 (1981).

[39] According to Justice Stevens, who wrote the sole dissenting opinion in Mergens, the majority came "perilously close to an outright command to allow organized prayer...on school premises," 110 S. Ct. at 2391 (Stevens, J., dissenting).

[40] Hoppock v. Twin Falls School Dist., 772 F. Supp. 1160 (D. Idaho 1991) (the EAA prevails over the state constitutional prohibition on the use of public funds for any religious purpose); Garnett v. Renton School Dist., 772 F. Supp. 531 (W.D. Wash. 1991) (the state constitutional prohibition on any sectarian influences in public schools precludes using public school property for student religious meetings).

[41] *See* Meltzer v. Board of Pub. Instruction of Orange County, Fla., 548 F.2d 559 (5th Cir. 1977), rehearing, 577 F.2d 311 (5th Cir. 1978), *cert. denied*, 439 U.S. 1089 (1979) (although the appeals court indicated that a policy allowing the distribution of Gideon Bibles in public schools would violate the establishment clause, the final order did not provide a declaration to this effect as the school board had tabled its policy authorizing such distribution); Hernandez v. Hanson, 430 F. Supp. 1154 (D. Neb. 1977); Goodwin v. Cross County School Dist., 394 F. Supp. 417 (E.D. Ark. 1973); Tudor v. Board of Educ., 100 A.2d 857 (N.J. 1953), *cert. denied*, 348 U.S. 816 (1954); Miller v. Cooper, 244 P.2d 520 (N.M. 1952).

[42] Berger v. Rensselaer Cent. School Corp., 766 F. Supp. 696 (N.D. Ind. 1991).

[43] Bacon v. Bradley-Bourbonnais High School Dist. No. 307, 707 F. Supp. 1005 (C.D. Ill. 1989).

[44] Rivera v. East Otero School Dist. R-1, 721 F. Supp. 1189 (D. Colo. 1989).

[45] Thompson v. Waynesboro Area School Dist., 673 F. Supp. 1379 (M.D. Pa. 1987).

[46] Perumal v. Saddleback Valley Unified School Dist., 243 Cal. Rptr. 545 (Cal. Ct. App. 1988), *cert. denied*, 488 U.S. 933 (1988).

[47] Hedges v. Wauconda Community Unit School Dist. No. 118, No. 90C 6604 (N.D. Ill. 1991).

[48] *See* West Virginia State Bd. of Educ. v. Barnette, 319 U.S. 624, 638 (1943).

[49] *For example*, some public school materials and offerings are being challenged as unconstitutionally advancing "secular humanism" or "new age theology," which are alleged to be antithetic creeds subject to establishment clause restrictions.

[50] Marsh v. Chambers, 463 U.S. 783 (1983).

[51] Lynch v. Donnelly, 465 U.S. 668 (1984).

[52] *See* Edwards v. Aguillard, 482 U.S. 578 (1987) (invalidating Louisiana's law requiring instruction in the Biblical account of creation whenever evolution is introduced); Stone v. Graham, 449 U.S. 39 (1980) (invalidating a law requiring public schools to post copies of the Ten Commandments); McCarthy and Cambron-McCabe Public School Law, 28-34.

[53] *See* Lee v. Weisman, 60 U.S.L.W. 4726 (1992); Wallace v. Jaffree, 472 U.S. 38, 60 (1985).

28
Religion In The School Curriculum

Frank R. Kemerer

Introduction

The role of religion in the public school curriculum is a confusing and controversial area of education law. It is also a volatile issue in the community. Part of the reason for the volatility is that the United States Constitution has two religion clauses, and both are to some extent in a state of dynamic tension, one with the other. The first is the establishment clause: "Congress shall make no law respecting an establishment of religion." The second is the free exercise clause: "or prohibiting the free exercise thereof." By virtue of the fourteenth amendment, both apply to states and their political subdivisions, including public schools.

Legal Issues

The Establishment Clause

When analyzing a case under the establishment clause, courts traditionally have used a three-part set of guidelines announced in a 1971 United States Supreme Court decision, *Lemon v. Kurtzman.*[1] The so-called *"Lemon* test" requires that a statute or governmental activity satisfy the following three criteria: there must be a secular purpose, there must be a primary effect which neither advances nor inhibits religion, there must not be excessive governmental entanglement with religion. If governmental action violates any of these criteria, the action is unconstitutional.

In the past, the Supreme Court has been zealous in applying the *Lemon* test to the public schools. As Justice William J. Brennan, Jr., noted in the 1987 creation-science case, *Edwards v. Aguillard,* "[f]amilies entrust public schools with the education of their children, but condition their trust on the understanding that the classroom will not purposely be used to advance religious views.... Students in such institutions are impressionable and their attendance is involuntary."[2] Because of this attitude, the Court often has applied a higher level of scrutiny to establishment clause cases involving public elementary and secondary schools than to those involving higher education.[3]

It is important to note, however, that the Court membership has changed in recent years. Those Justices who staunchly maintained the wall of separation between church and state have been replaced by more conservative Justices who seem willing to accommodate greater expressions of religion in public life. Yet, in the recent decision of the high court in *Lee v. Weisman*[4], significant changes were not made in the role of religion in public schools. Instead, by a narrow five-to-four ruling, the Court struck down the use of invocations and benedictions at school commencement ceremonies. However, at least four Justices appear prepared to modify significantly the *Lemon* guidelines or abandon them altogether.

Teaching Creation-Science

Edwards v. Aguillard, a 1987 United States Supreme Court decision, involved a challenge to a Louisiana statute requiring that the public schools give equal treatment to creation-science.[5] The statute, entitled the *Balanced Treatment for Creation-Science and Evolution-Science Act*, defined creation science as scientific evidence for the theory that life appeared on earth relatively recently (in geological terms) and has changed little since its appearance. The law required that if either evolution or creation-science is taught, the other theory must also be taught. The law also provided that each school board prepare curriculum guides and make available teaching aids and resource materials on creation science. Finally, the law prohibited school boards from discriminating against someone who teaches creation-science.

By a strong seven-to-two majority, the Court found the act's primary purpose to be sectarian: to "restructure the science curriculum to conform to a particular religious viewpoint."[6] The Court rejected the state's argument that it was promoting academic freedom. On the contrary, the Justices noted that teachers had ample freedom before the law was enacted to add other scientific theories about the origin of man to the curriculum. By limiting them to only two views and requiring that both be taught, the Louisiana statute resulted in inhibiting, not promoting, academic freedom.

The decision is important because it adds the United States Supreme Court's imprimatur to earlier lower court decisions rejecting the teaching of creation-science in public schools. At the same time, it is important to note that a school district is not left with the option of teaching only evolution. As Justice Brennan noted in a key sentence, "teaching a variety of scientific theories about the origins of humankind to schoolchildren might be validly done with the clear secular intent of enhancing the effectiveness of science instruction."[7]

In some jurisdictions, teachers have a court-sanctioned academic freedom right to lead classroom discussion on controversial topics.[8] Elsewhere, the "teacher empowerment" movement has increased teacher autonomy in the classroom. It is important for school principals to be sure that teachers do not violate the *Edwards* decision in class discussions, since teachers are considered state actors when performing their duties.[9] While a teacher cannot teach the religious theory of creation-science, it might be possible to discuss the scientific evidence associated with it as part of a secular program of instruction about the origin of man. However, if the teacher is a strong believer in the religious view of creation and grants an inordinate amount of time to discussing this view, it is likely to be viewed as a breach of the establishment clause. In a recent case, the United States Court of Appeals for the Seventh Circuit was unsympathetic to a teacher's claim that he had a right under the first amendment to introduce creation-science into his social studies classes.[10] It is also possible that a teacher who attempts to teach just the scientific elements of creation-science may be drawn into discussions of the religious underpinnings of the theory, which might impermissibly entangle the state and religion contrary to another of the *Lemon* guidelines.[11] Principals need to monitor what teachers are saying about creation-science in their classrooms to be sure that the *Edwards v. Aguillard* ruling is being followed.

Teaching About Religion

In several decisions, the United States Supreme Court has commented that nothing precludes public schools from teaching about religion. For example, in an early school prayer decision, the Court stated, "one's education is not complete without a study of comparative religion or the history of religion and its relationship to the advancement of civilization. It certainly may be said that the Bible is worthy of study for its literary and historic qualities."[12] Thus, the curriculum need not be sanitized of any mention of religion. In fact, if this were to occur, a strong argument could be made that the school has violated the second *Lemon* guideline by being hostile toward religion. There are strong pedagogical reasons for including

religion in the curriculum, so long as it is done without proselytizing on behalf of a particular religion or religion in general.

Aside from creation-science, the most sensitive area involves Bible study classes. While it is theoretically possible to offer such
courses, a review of lower court decisions indicates that most do
not pass judicial muster. A case-in-point is *Hall v. Board of School
Commissioners*, a decision of the Fifth Circuit Court of Appeals.[13]
The Bible Literature course at issue in the case utilized a state-
approved textbook entitled *The Bible for Youthful Patriots, Parts I
and II*, which was found to approach the subject from a fundamentalist Christian perspective. Bibles were distributed to students who
did not have them. The course was taught by an ordained Baptist
minister who also was a teacher at the high school and who, according to expert testimony, taught essentially a fundamentalist,
evangelical doctrine. The appeals court concluded that even assuming an intent to restrict the course to secular study, the primary
effect was the advancement of religion. The court ordered a prohibition of the state-approved textbook. It ordered the district court
to fashion an appropriate remedy "to ensure that any future course
is taught within a secular framework focusing on the literary or
historical aspects of the Bible, not the religious aspects."[14]

In *Wiley v. Franklin* a federal district court in Tennessee observed that the issue was not use of the Bible as an instructional
vehicle but rather "the selectivity, emphasis, objectivity, and inter-
pretative manner, or lack thereof, with which the Bible is taught."[15]
The case involved the teaching of Bible study courses to elementary
age children. The intent of the school boards was to use the Bible
"in relation to its place in the origin of the republic, the establishment and development of public education, the emphasis on
public worth, and its pervading influences in the country's government, history, and the very fabric of American society."[16] Upon scrutiny, however, the court found that the volunteer Bible Study Committee, which administered and funded the study program, was
operating from a predominately Christian, Protestant orientation.
The court found that the program violated all three *Lemon* guidelines. The school boards were ordered to revise the program by establishing minimum standards for employing teachers of the
courses, to exclude any religious test or profession of faith, to release teachers teaching the courses who do not meet these standards, to place responsibility for the administration of the program
in the hands of the school board or school staff person, and to revise
Bible study curriculum to reflect only secular purposes.[17]

Holiday Observance Programs

The leading case supporting the observances of holidays with religious overtones continues to be *Florey v. Sioux Falls School District*, a decision of the Eighth Circuit Court of Appeals.[18] *Florey* involved a school policy allowing teachers to observe holidays which have both a religious and secular basis. Included among them were Christmas, Easter, Passover, Hanukkah, St. Valentine's Day, St. Patrick's Day, and Halloween. The school policy allowed explanation of the nature of the holidays in an unbiased and objective manner without sectarian indoctrination together with references to music, art, literature, and the use of religious symbols. The policy had been developed by a special committee representing various constituencies and faiths in the community. The committee had been set up after complaints about religious favoritism in the school had arisen. The court concluded that the program passed muster under the Supreme Court's *Lemon* decision.

Secular Humanism

Upon occasion, school administrators are accused of fostering a religion of secular humanism by not incorporating religion into the curriculum. The first question to be asked is whether secular humanism is a religion under the establishment clause. If so, can the school unconstitutionally promote it through its curriculum? The issue is highly controversial. To date, the United States Supreme Court has not decided a case dealing with the question. However, the Eleventh Circuit Court of Appeals faced this question in 1987.

In *Smith v. Board of School Commissioners of Mobile County, Alabama,* [19] fundamentalist Christians alleged that textbooks used in the public schools unconstitutionally established the religion of secular humanism. In an extraordinary decision, the trial judge found that secular humanism constitutes a religion for establishment clause purposes. This case was the first time any court had so ruled. The judge found that 44 of the 45 textbooks at issue in the case did unconstitutionally establish the religion of secular humanism in the public schools of Alabama since the textbooks had the primary effect of advancing this religion, thus failing the second *Lemon* guideline. The books involved were 30 elementary school social studies texts, ten high school history texts, and five high school home economics texts. The trial judge issued an injunction forbidding the public schools from using the 44 books for any purpose other than as a resource in a comparative religion class.

Given the novelty of the trial judge's thinking, most legal commentators were not surprised when the Eleventh Circuit Court of

Appeals reversed the decision.[20] The court refused to consider the question of whether secular humanism is a religion or the related and equally difficult question of what constitutes a religion for establishment clause analysis. The court merely noted that the issue need not be resolved because the case could be decided even assuming, for the sake of argument, that secular humanism is a religion. The school district had not breached the establishment clause, the appeals court reasoned, merely because some of the content of the books happened to coincide with secular humanist views. "In order for government conduct to constitute an impermissible advancement of religion, the government action must amount to an endorsement of religion."[21] Nor were the books considered hostile to organized religion. "The message conveyed by these textbooks... is one of neutrality: the textbooks neither endorse theistic religion as a system of belief, nor discredit it."[22]

An important question left unresolved by the Eleventh Circuit Court of Appeals opinion is whether secular humanism is a religion under the establishment clause. To date, the word "religion" in the establishment clause has been confined, by virtue of United States Supreme Court rulings, to theistic religions. However, in cases involving the free exercise clause, the Supreme Court has interpreted the clause more broadly. Indeed, in one free exercise clause case, the Court in a footnote acknowledged that secular humanism is a religion.[23] Since secular humanism is not a theistic religion, it is not possible for the school to promote it contrary to the establishment clause under current United States Supreme Court rulings. However, it would be a violation of that clause for the school to be hostile to theistic religion.

The Free Exercise Clause

Do public schools unconstitutionally infringe on the religious rights of school children when they refuse to exempt the students from classes using objectionable textbooks? In *Grove v. Mead School District No. 354*, the Ninth Circuit Court of Appeals was confronted with a case involving the use of the book, *The Learning Tree*, in a public school.[24] The plaintiff argued that the book established secular humanism in the schools contrary to the establishment clause and that compelling her to read it violated her religious beliefs. The court rejected her claim that the book established secular humanism as a religion and noted that, because the school exempted her from reading the book and from class discussions regarding the book, her free exercise claim could not be considered.

The Supreme Court refused to hear the *Grove* case in October of 1985.

A group in Tennessee brought a free exercise clause complaint regarding textbooks used in the Tennessee public schools in *Mozert v. Hawkins County Board of Education.*[25] The specific complaint was that the reading books used by the school district contained stories dealing with topics the parents and some of the students found objectionable on religious grounds. The complaint was first brought to school officials. For several weeks, any student who objected to the material was excused from reading class. The students went to the library or available office areas and worked on materials from an older reading series to which their parents did not object. In November 1983, the school board voted to end all alternative reading programs and to require all students to use the Holt, Rinehart and Winston series the students and parents found objectionable. After this action, the students who had been accommodated refused to read from the Holt series or attend the reading classes where the books were being used. Several children were suspended for this behavior, and most were eventually removed from public schools and taught at home or attended private schools. In December, 14 parents and 17 students filed a lawsuit in federal court asking that the Hawkins County School Board be required to accommodate the religious beliefs of the plaintiffs. The trial court eventually ruled in favor of the plaintiffs and ordered the school board to excuse the objecting students from any classes that used the Holt readers.

The Sixth Circuit Court of Appeals reversed the decision.[26] Under prior United States Supreme Court holdings, the court noted, it must be shown that the state applied some form of coercion in order to prove a violation of the free exercise clause. Mere exposure to religiously objectionable material does not constitute an infringement on the right to freely exercise one's religion:

> There was no evidence that the conduct required of the students was forbidden by their religion. Rather, the witnesses testified that reading the Holt series "could" or "might" lead the students to come to conclusions that were contrary to teachings of their and their parents' religious beliefs. This is not sufficient to establish an unconstitutional burden.[27]

Additionally, the court noted the state's interest in having a uniform curriculum and the administrative problems inherent in exempting students from parts of it. In March 1988, the United States Supreme Court refused to hear the *Mozert* appeal.[28] In the absence of a definitive ruling from the Supreme Court, these decisions indicate that refusal to accommodate the religious objections of a student to a curricular requirement is not a violation of the free exercise clause.

Recommendations for Practice

Taken together, the rulings to date involving the establishment clause and the free exercise clause as applied to the public school curriculum indicate that local authorities continue to have broad discretion, so long as they are essentially neutral with regard to religion. Neutrality does not mean hostility to religion.

- Under the *Edwards* ruling, it is legal for a school district to include in its curriculum the scientific evidence supporting creation-science if the scientific evidence is associated with a variety of other theories about the origin of man and the material is presented objectively.
- Studying about religion is most commonly done in social studies classes. Works of religious literature are often studied in English classes. Involvement of religion in the curriculum, in this manner, raises few legal questions.
- It is apparent that Bible study courses, particularly at the elementary level, must be carefully constructed to withstand legal challenge. If the intent is to teach religion, rather than teach about religion, the courses are best taught off school grounds and without school sponsorship or involvement.
- The *Florey* case provides a good rationale to follow regarding including religion in holiday programs. So long as the religious elements are one part of an otherwise secular holiday observance policy and, so long as they are presented objectively and without indoctrination, the program has a good chance of withstanding legal challenge.
- Several years ago, a coalition of 14 organizations advanced the following six guidelines on teaching about religion in the public school: the school's approach to religion is academic, not devotional; the school may strive for student awareness of religion but should not press for student acceptance of any one religion; the school may sponsor study about religion but may not sponsor the practice of religion; the school may expose students to a diversity of religious views but may not impose any particular view; the school may educate about all religions but may not promote or denigrate any religion; and the school may inform the student about various beliefs but

should not seek to confirm the student to any particular belief.[29]

- In the free exercise arena, so long as textbooks do not contain material explicitly prohibited by a student's faith, the federal courts will not interfere with the choices made by local authorities in setting the curriculum and requiring students to participate. The school may wish to accommodate the student as in *Grove*, but there is no constitutional requirement that this action be done. Note, however, that state law or school board policy may require that somewhat greater deference be given to parental requests for exemptions.

- Principals should be aware that with the changing membership of the United States Supreme Court, interpretations of both the establishment and free exercise clauses may change in the future. Such changes would likely allow greater accommodation of religion in the public school program.

References

[1] Lemon v. Kurtzman, 403 U.S. 602 (1971).

[2] Edwards v. Aguillard, 107 S. Ct. 2573, 2577 (1987).

[3] A prime example is Widmar v. Vincent, 454 U.S. 263 (1981), in which the Court ruled that public colleges and universities must allow their campus facilities to be used for student religious discussion and exercise. The justices observed that in their view, college students are less impressionable than younger students and thus more able to view such a policy as one of neutrality toward religion. The Widmar v. Vincent precedent has been followed in Westside Community Schools v. Mergens, 110 S. Ct. 2356 (1990) (Upholding access of non-school sponsored student groups, including those which are religious, to the secondary school campus before and after school under the federal Equal Access Act).

[4] Lee v. Weisman, 112 S. Ct. 2649 (1992).

[5] *Edwards*, 107 S. Ct. 2573.

[6] *Id.* at 2582.

[7] *Id.* at 2583.

[8] *See* Keefe v. Geanakos, 418 F.2d 359 (1st Cir. 1969); Kingsville I.S.D. v. Cooper, 611 F.2d 1109 (5th Cir. 1980).

[9] The claim that when teachers are acting in their capacity as classroom teacher, they are acting as private individuals has been uniformly rejected. *See*, for example, Breen v. Runkel, 614 F. Supp. 355 (W.D. Mich 1985).

[10] Webster v. New Lenox School District No. 122, 917 F.2d 1004 (7th Cir. 1990).

[11] In Aguilar v. Felton, 105 S. Ct. 3232 (1985), the Supreme Court invalidated a program where public school teachers taught underprivileged, underachieving children in private inner-city schools of New York City. The Court held that since the instruction took place in private schools, public school teachers might be drawn into discussions on the subject of religion, thus excessively entangling the teachers, who are representatives of the state, with religion.

[12] School Dist. of Abington v. Schempp, 374 U.S. 222, 225 (1963).

[13] 656 F.2d 999 (5th Cir. 1981), *modified*, 707 F.2d 464 (11th Cir. 1983).

[14] *Id.* at 1003.

[15] Wiley v. Franklin, 468 F. Supp. 133, *supplemented*, 474 F. Supp. 525 (E.D. Tenn. 1979), *supplemented*, 497 F. Supp. 390 (E.D. Tenn. 1980). *See also* Doe v. Human, 725 F. Supp. 1499 (W.D. Ark. 1989) (preliminary injunction granted against Bible classes taught to elementary students from a sectarian perspective), *aff'd* 923 F.2d 857 (8th Cir. 1990) (without opinion), *cert. denied*, 111 S.Ct. 1315 (1991).

[16] *Wiley*, 468 F. Supp. at 137.

[17]For a similar set of guidelines for Bible study courses, *see* Crockett v. Sorenson, 568 F. Supp. 1422 (W.D. Va. 1983).

[18]Florey v. Sioux Falls School Dist. 619 F.2d 1311 (8th Cir. 1980), *cert. denied*, 449 U.S. 987 (1980).

[19]Smith v. Board of Comm'rs of Mobile County, Ala., 655 F. Supp. 939 (S.D. Ala. 1987).

[20]827 F.2d 684 (11th Cir. 1987).

[21]*Id.* at 692.

[22]*Id.*

[23]Torcaso v. Watkins, 367 U.S. 488, 495 (1961). "Among religions in this country which do not teach what would generally be considered a belief in the existence of God are Buddhism, Taoism, Ethical Culture, Secular Humanism, and others."

[24]Grove v. Mead School Dist. No. 354, 753 F.2d 1528 (9th Cir. 1985), *cert. denied*, 474 U.S. 826 (1985).

[25]Mozert v. Hawkins County Pub. Schools, 579 F. Supp. 1051 (E.D. Tenn. 1984).

[26]Mozert v. Hawkins County Bd. of Educ., 827 F.2d 1058 (6th Cir. 1987).

[27]*Id.* at 1070.

[28]108 S. Ct. 1029 (1988).

[29]This account is taken from School Board News (June 22, 1988). The coalition's brochure, Religion in the Public School Curriculum: Questions and Answers, has been widely disseminated.

29
Educational Curriculum and Legal Issues
Billie Goode Blair

Introduction

Curriculum is a method of providing a framework of study for the promotion of well-informed and responsible citizens of the future. While some curriculum components are specified or suggested at the state level, implementation of the curriculum and its content continues to be left largely up to local boards of education. There are three instances, however, in which states tend to be directly involved in curricular processes: graduation requirements; curriculum guidelines and frameworks; and textbook selection.[1] Courts generally acknowledge state and local power over education and are reluctant to interfere with curriculum decisions. Curriculum issues most frequently contested in courts of law include:
- sectarian interests and beliefs reflected in the curriculum,
- removal of material from instructional programs,
- removal of library books,
- the study of evolution and creationism,
- sex education programs,
- bilingual education programs.

Legal Issues

Removal of Materials from the Instructional Program

Throughout the history of public schooling, content which promoted sectarian interests and beliefs has been challenged in the courts. Religious groups have attempted to impose their views on public education and to have their beliefs adopted as official school policy. The courts have adopted a stance opposing the casting of a "pall of orthodoxy"[2] over public school classrooms. In *McCollum v. Board of Education*,[3] *Board of Education Island Trees Union Free*

School v. Pico,[4] and *Pratt v. Independent School District No. 831,*[5] the courts resisted attempts by religious groups to compel schools to remove offending materials citing that, should this take place, very little curricular substance would remain.

In more recent rulings, the courts have been more inclined to find in favor of some administrative discretion in removal or exclusion of materials. Two cases, in particular, can give insight into recent trends. In *Hazelwood School District v. Kuhlmeier,*[6] the United States Supreme Court upheld excision of two pages from the student newspaper by the principal. In deleting the two pages, one of which dealt with teen pregnancy and a second with divorce and its effects on students, the Court agreed with the principal that the articles were not protective enough of the identities of the students and that, in the instance of teen pregnancy, some of the descriptions of sexual involvement were inappropriate for the younger students to read.

In the case of *Virgil v. School Board of Columbia County, Florida,*[7] parents objected to a textbook which contained both required and optional readings for a course in humanities. The objection centered on two optional readings, Chaucer's *The Miller's Tale* and Aristophanes' *Lysistrata.* Both contained sexually explicit material. Upon review of the material by a school board advisory committee, the committee recommended continued use of the textbook in the instructional program but advised against use of the readings in question. When the committee's report was brought before the board of education, the superintendent disagreed and proposed that the two readings either be deleted from the texts or that use of the texts be discontinued. As a result of the superintendent's proposal, the board voted to discontinue use of the texts. In response to this decision, parents at the school filed an action against the school board charging that they had violated the students' first amendment rights. The court ruled that the school board may take such action as is "reasonably related to legitimate pedagogical concerns."

Removal of Library Books

Two additional cases highlight the court's proclivity to support the prerogative of school boards in selecting and discontinuing instructional materials. In two instances, *Bicknell*[8] and *President's Council,*[9] the Second Circuit Court of Appeals upheld a school board's actions in removing books from public school libraries. The court noted that there are no stipulations that once books are on the shelves they will remain there forever. According to the court's decision, removal of obscene materials does not threaten suppression of ideas. In the *President's Council* ruling, the court stated that oversight of a school library "involves a constant process of selection and winnowing based not only on educational needs but financial and architectural realities."

In 1980, the Seventh Circuit Court of Appeals held that:

> [I]t is legitimate for school officials to develop an opinion about what type of citizens are good citizens, to determine what curriculum and material will best develop good citizens, and to prohibit the use of texts, remove library books, and delete courses from the curriculum as a part of the effort to shape students into good citizens.[10]

However, in *Board of Education v. Pico*,[11] the Supreme Court did not support a board of education when they excluded books based on seemingly theistic beliefs, or dislike of the ideas contained in the books.

Evolution Science Versus Creation Science

In a 1968 Arkansas case, *Epperson v. State of Arkansas*,[12] the Court found that a state statute violated the first amendment by disallowing scientific theory to be taught because it conflicted with Biblical doctrine. A more recent case dealt with Louisiana's "Creationism Act."[13] The act forbade the teaching of evolution in public schools unless accompanied by instruction in creation science. In responding to the legal challenge, the Court cited the Establishment Clause which forbids enactment of a law "respecting an establishment of religion." In applying the three-prong *Lemon* test,[14] the Court determined that no clear secular purpose was found in the action of the legislature. It was clear from the legislative history that the intent of the bill's sponsor was to narrow the science curriculum. Further, the Court found that the Creationism Act required that curriculum guides be developed for creation science but not for evolution; that research services were supplied for creation science but not for evolution; that only creation scientists would be allowed to serve on a panel of resource services; and that discrimination was forbidden against anyone choosing to teach creation science while no similar protection was offered for those who taught evolution or other noncreation theories. Thus, the act did not preserve academic freedom but, rather, served to discredit evolution.

Recently, fundamentalists have charged that the theory of evolution actually constitutes a religion called secular humanism which portrays life in nonmoral and nontheistic terms. In *Mozert v. Hawkins County Board of Education*,[15] a group of public school parents objected to the texts adopted by the board of education and the teaching of "critical reading." Parents stated that the values taught in the texts were contrary to their religious beliefs. They further charged that the texts presented the theory of evolution and propounded a religion of secular humanism and ideas of "futuristic supernaturalism" which portrayed "Man as God." Testimony by the plaintiffs indicated that they did not want their children attempting critical judgments. The Sixth Circuit Court of Appeals found no evidence that the schools required students to believe or say they believed that "all religions are merely different roads to God," but rather that the schools sought to provide tolerance of divergent religious views. The curriculum was designed to present a wide range of ideas and concepts.

In a similar case in the Eleventh Circuit Court of Appeals concerning allegations by fundamentalist Christians, the court ruled that textbooks used in the public schools of Mobile County, Alabama, unconstitutionally established secular humanism as a religion.[16] The court ruled that the district had not breached the Establishment Clause but was utilizing books whose content happened to coincide with the views of secular humanism. The court found no endorsement of religion on the part of the schools, a nonpermissible advancement of religion. The court also ruled that the message of the texts was a neutral one, neither endorsing theistic religion nor discrediting it.

Sex Education Programs

Several cases concerning sex education in the curriculum have been heard by the courts. Religious bodies have challenged sex education course offerings based on encroachment of religious liberty and privacy. The courts have consistently found that the courses present public health information that furthers educational objectives. In *Cornwell v. State Board of Education*,[17] Baltimore County taxpayers sought to prevent implementation of a program of sex education in the Baltimore County Schools. Plaintiffs stated that parents had the exclusive constitutional right to instruction in sexual matters under the first amendment. The court ruled that the state's interest in the health of its children outweighed the claims of the plaintiffs.

In similar cases, a New Jersey court upheld the state's comprehensive sex education mandate, stating that the curriculum guidelines did not suggest antagonism toward Christianity.[18] In a Pennsylvania case, the state's interest in the health and welfare of its children was cited as a significant finding.[19] In two cases, concessions to opponents of sex education classes have been granted. In *Valent v. New Jersey Board of Education*,[20] the court acknowledged that students should be free to be excused from classes if it is deemed that such instruction is in opposition to sectarian beliefs. The Supreme Court of Hawaii registered approval for the state agency's sex education program because it was optional.[21]

Programs of Language: Bilingual Education

Perhaps the most famous language education case was *Lau v. Nichols*, decided in 1974.[22] Plaintiffs cited the Civil Rights Act of 1964 which bans discrimination in any federally-funded program on the basis of race, color, or national origin. The San Francisco School District, which received federal funds, was charged with failure to provide non-English speaking Chinese students with instruction to bridge the language gap. The Court ruled that where students from minority groups lacked the ability to speak and understand English, the district must provide programs to respond to the language deficiency. The Court's ruling contended that since English skills are prerequisite to participation in public school programs, the failure to provide instruction constituted inequality of treatment. In later rulings, the courts have tended to give discretion to school districts in meeting requirements of language instruction. The Ninth Circuit Court of Appeals ruled in 1978 that not all programs were required to be bilingual according to the United States Constitution and civil rights laws.[23]

The enactment of the Equal Educational Opportunities Act was used in a 1981 case. The Fifth Circuit Court of Appeals found that, while required to offer remedial programs, school districts could enjoy some latitude in meeting the requirements.[24] Therefore, the court found the district's bilingual program to be nondiscriminatory. Later charges that the district's practice was racially and ethnically discriminatory brought a similar finding of nondiscrimination by the court.[25] The Bilingual Act of 1974 does specify that language instruction be offered in a child's native language to allow for effective progress.

Recommendations for Practice

A review of court cases on curriculum and curricular offerings in public schools has given rise to legal challenges based on theistic versus nontheistic study, removal of textual materials from school programs, removal of books from school libraries, and programs of sex education and bilingual study. The administrator needs to be aware of the following points:

- Offensive materials of a sexually explicit nature can be removed or excluded from the school program when appropriate.
- Removal of books from libraries should not be based on dislike of the ideas contained in them or specific theistic beliefs.
- School districts may not offer special protections for programs promoting creationism nor prohibit the teaching of evolution theory.
- Sex education programs have been upheld by the courts on the basis of their contribution to public health.
- While language instruction programs for non-English speaking students have been required by the courts, specific implementation is the prerogative of individual school districts.

References

[1] *Academic Freedom in the Public Schools; The Right to Teach*, 48 N.Y.U.L. REV. 1183 (1973).

[2] Keyishian v. Board of Regents, 385 U.S. 589, 87 S. Ct. 675 (1967).

[3] People ex. rel. McCollum v. Board of Educ., 333 U.S. 203, 68 S. Ct. 461 (1948).

[4] Board of Educ., Island Trees Union Free School Dist. No. 26 v. Pico, 457 U.S. 853, 102 S. Ct. 2799 (1982).

[5] Pratt v. Indep. School Dist. No. 831, Forest Lake, Minn., 670 F.2d 771 (8th Cir. 1982).

[6] Hazelwood School Dist. v. Kuhlmeier, 484 U.S. 260, 108 S. Ct. 562 (1988).

[7] Virgil v. School Bd. of Columbia County, Fla., 862 F.2d 1517 (11th Cir. 1989).

[8] Bicknell v. Vergennes Union High School Bd. of Directors, 638 F.2d 438 (2d Cir. 1980).

[9] President's Council, Dist. 25 v. Community School Bd. No. 25, 457 F.2d 289 (2d Cir. 1972), cert. denied, 409 U.S. 998 (1972).

[10] Zykan v. Warsaw Community School Corp., 631 F.2d 1300, 1303 (7th Cir. 1980).

[11] McCollum, 333 U.S. 203.

[12] Epperson v. State of Ark., 393 U.S. 97, 89 S. Ct. 266 (1968).

[13] Edwards v. Aguillard, 482 U.S. 578 (1987).

[14] Lemon v. Kurtzman, 403 U.S. 602 (1971).

[15] Mozert v. Hawkins County Bd. of Educ., 827 F.2d 1058 (6th Cir., 1987).

[16] Smith v. Board of School Comm'rs. of Mobile County, 827 F.2d 684 (11th Cir. 1987).

[17] Cornwell v. State Bd. of Educ., 314 F. Supp. 340 (D. Md. 1969), affirmed 428 F.2d 471 (4th Cir. 1970), cert. denied, 400 U.S. 942, 91 S. Ct. 240 (1970).

[18] Smith v. Ricci, 446 A.2d 501 (N.J. 1982), appeal dismissed sub nom. Smith v. Brandt, 459 U.S. 962 (1982).

[19] Aubrey v. School Dist. of Philadelphia, 63 Pa. Cmwlth. Ct. 330, 437 A.2d 1306 (1981).

[20] Valent v. New Jersey State Bd. of Educ., 274 A.2d 832, 840-841 (N.J. Super. Ct. Ch. Div. 1971).

[21] Medeiros v. Kiyosaki, 478 P.2d 314 (Haw. 1970).

[22] Lau v. Nichols, 414 U.S. 563, 94 S. Ct. 786 (1974).

[23] Guadalupe Org., Inc. v. Tempe Elementary School Dist. No. 3, 587 F.2d 1022 (9th Cir. 1978).

[24] Castaneda v. Pickard, 648 F.2d 989 (5th Cir. 1981).

[25] Castaneda v. Pickard, 781 F.2d 456 (5th Cir. 1986).

30
Home Instruction

Henry S. Lufler, Jr.

Introduction

Home instruction is an educational alternative selected by parents espousing a variety of educational, religious, or philosophical reservations about enrolling their children in public schools. The debate about the educational effectiveness of home instruction is vigorous. Some educators argue that parents cannot replace the expertise and resources of a school system. Schools, they argue, teach important interpersonal skills necessary for students if they are to function effectively in the larger American society as adults.[1] Home instruction advocates respond that the education received by children at home can be superior to that received in the public schools. Some go further, arguing that public schools expose children to values and attitudes that are destructive to their individual growth.[2]

School principals frequently find themselves in the middle of legal disputes involving claims made by home instruction parents, on the one hand, and compulsory attendance statutes on the other. State compulsory attendance statutes, grounded on the assumption that states have an obligation to ensure that all children receive a basic education, have been challenged by home instruction parents on a variety of constitutional grounds, most commonly that they are in conflict with parents' first amendment religious rights.

Legal Issues

State Regulation of Home Instruction

The legal issues surrounding home instruction present a clash between two strong interests: the right of parents to select educational alternatives for their children and the state's constitutional or statutory mandate to regulate the choices that parents make, at least to the extent of ensuring that children are educated.[3] The United States Supreme Court addressed this clash of competing interests in 1925, ruling that parents could send their children to private schools without violating state compulsory attendance laws.[4] In the same decision, however, the Court upheld the right of states to adopt reasonable regulations for the operation of private schools in such areas as the supervision of teachers and students.[5] The state's interest in education is reflected in state constitutional provisions that guarantee a free education to all children and state statutory provisions that require students to attend schools until attaining a specified age.

State statutes regulating public and private schools and home instruction vary widely. Some states virtually preclude home instruction or the operation of small private schools by requiring that all instruction be provided by certified teachers. Others have virtually no requirements other than requiring home instruction parents to register with a state education department or local school district.

State regulation of home instruction falls into three general categories: regulating the credentials of those offering the instruction; requiring parents to show they are providing "equivalent instruction" to that offered in the public schools; or measuring student progress through the use of nationally normed tests. Among the three approaches, "equivalent instruction" statutes have been the most susceptible to legal challenge, especially in states where there were no administrative rules defining how equivalency is to be measured.[6] Equivalency statutes also have been attacked on the ground that local school officials were biased when deciding if home instruction was equivalent. Such claims have been universally unsuccessful.[7]

While courts give wide latitude to states to enforce compulsory attendance statutes and to regulate home instruction, numerous challenges continue to be filed. These challenges almost always are based on three interrelated constitutional claims: that the first amendment religious rights of parents have been violated; that the enforcement of compulsory attendance laws has violated the parents fourteenth amendment procedural or substantive due process rights; and that there is a constitutional right to educate children at home, presented with reference to a scattering of precedents that give individuals a right to privacy or the right to make family choices.

Religious Claims

The first amendment's free exercise of religion clause and compulsory attendance statutes often conflict. In resolving such conflicts, courts consider the extent to which religious freedom is impinged by the governmental regulation. As a general rule, state regulation of home instruction has been found to involve a minimal loss of free exercise rights, a loss justified by the need of the state to ensure that children are educated to become productive adults.

The case most frequently cited by plaintiffs in home instruction cases is *Wisconsin v. Yoder*.[8] *Yoder* gave Amish parents the right to end their children's public-school education after the eighth grade. The plaintiffs successfully argued that their religious freedom would be violated if their children were exposed to the "worldly" and "competitive" values that they saw as being present in public secondary schools.

In deciding *Yoder*, however, the Supreme Court used an analysis that focused so intensely on the special nature of the Amish sect that it offers little value as a precedent for religious claims advanced by non-Amish groups. The Court looked at the 300 year-old history of the group, observing that the community was self-contained and self-sufficient. For the Amish, then, the Court found that the state's traditional arguments for compulsory education, such as the need to prepare children to function in a larger society, did not apply. But the Court cautioned, "[i]t cannot be overemphasized that we are not dealing with a way of life and mode of education by a group claiming to have recently discovered some 'progressive' or more enlightened process for rearing children for modern life."[9] Plaintiffs in home instruction cases have been unsuccessful in convincing courts that the "*Yoder* exception" to compulsory attendance laws should be expanded to other groups. Courts also have not extended the decision to other cases where the plaintiff was not a member of an organized sect but held personal religious views similar to those of the Amish.

Home instruction parents also have advanced the claims that their religious rights were violated by laws in some states requiring them to report the curriculum they were following. Similar arguments have been used to attack state regulations regarding the credentials of those providing home instruction. Courts have held, however, that these requirements make little or no intrusion on religious freedom.[10] The judicial reasoning used in these cases relies on the fact that parents remain free to base their educational decisions on religious grounds. They can, for example, use a religion based home instruction curriculum. Therefore, state requirements mandating reporting, testing, or instructor credentials do not intrude on the basic religious rights of parents. At the same time, courts have reasoned that the requirements preserve the state's interest in ensuring that all children receive a basic education. As the North Dakota Supreme Court put it, "[t]he freedom to hold religious beliefs is absolute...[but] the freedom to act, even if the action is in accord with religious convictions, is not totally free from legislative restrictions."[11]

Due Process Claims

The failure of parents to send their children to school can result in prosecution for a violation of compulsory attendance statutes. Because a criminal violation is alleged, due process standards must be met. Attendance laws therefore cannot be so vague as to invite different interpretations in different jurisdictions. Parents facing prosecution for some violation of compulsory attendance laws frequently allege that their due process rights have been violated because the attendance statutes are overly broad or the terms within them are ill defined. For example, several states have or had private school regulations but no statutory definition of what constitutes a "private school." Several lawsuits were filed by parents in these states claiming that their homes were private schools. These suits enjoyed mixed success. Some state supreme courts struck down statutes without a definition[12] while others were satisfied that no definition was needed to permit the conclusion that a home was not a school.[13]

Some state statutes contain provisions that small private school or home instruction programs must be "equivalent" to those offered in public schools. Statutes that place the burden of proof on parents to show that their home instruction curriculum is equivalent to that of the public schools are difficult for parents to satisfy. If the burden of proof falls on school systems, school personnel probably will lack the data about the student necessary to satisfy a court. The term "equivalent" itself invites varying definitions and has been struck down as overly broad in some jurisdictions.[14] On the other hand, the broadest of these statutes, the Massachusetts law requiring local public school administrators to determine if private schools in the district had programs "equal in thoroughness and efficiency" to public school offerings, has been upheld.[15] Different interpretations of equivalency within a state also have led to due process challenges. Courts have concluded that the fourteenth amendment rights of plaintiffs were violated because a statute requiring equivalence had been interpreted variously by different school districts in a state.[16]

The legal vulnerability of equivalence statutes is altered where administrative rules provide definitions of terms and standards for reviewing home instruction or private schools. In fact, a federal appeals court remanded a home instruction case arguing equivalency, concluding that it should be reconsidered in light of recently promulgated program review standards developed by a state department of education.[17] Rules also afford plaintiffs an administrative appeals process for reviewing unfavorable school district decisions, making judicial intervention less likely.

School officials cannot go to extreme lengths in regulating home instruction programs without providing fodder for due process challenges. A Massachusetts district court rejected an attempt by public school officials to monitor private school offerings through extensive classroom visits, holding that there were less restrictive ways of protecting the state's interest.[18] In another case, a federal appeals court ruled that a lower court could not order the padlocking of a church school to prevent the operation of a school not meeting standards.[19] Finally, Kentucky officials were found to have been overzealous in prosecuting parents who did not send their children to a school to which they were "conscientiously opposed."[20]

School officials must exercise caution when proceeding in home instruction cases, as state statutes that vary in content regulate the nature of attendance law prosecutions. All states provide a course of action against parents for failing to send their children to school. Juvenile court proceedings to have a child adjudged to be in need of court supervision also may be possible, but parents must be the focus of legal actions. Courts have rejected attempts by school officials who sought to prosecute private school personnel for "inducing children to be truant"[21] and attempts to prosecute children for being "unruly" under delinquency statutes when it was parents who were keeping them at home.[22]

Home Instruction as a Constitutional Right

Home instruction advocates frequently assert that there is a constitutional right to educate children at home.[23] Home instruction litigation, however, offers scant support for this proposition. Courts have decided these cases on narrower grounds, without creating a new constitutional right and in most instances without spending significant time addressing the question. The United States Supreme Court has never decided the question of whether the states have an obligation to permit some form of home instruction. In fact, in 1984 the Court refused to hear a federal court of appeals decision upholding a state law that totally banned home instruction.[24] Nevertheless, the constitutional right to home instruction continues to be raised using fourteenth amendment liberty or privacy claims as the justification. The advancing of these claims involves reference to cases well outside education law. For example, the Supreme

Court's controversial decision that a woman's right to privacy included the right to have an abortion contained language about the right of individuals to make basic life decisions including "education and the upbringing of children."[25]

In a variety of education cases where parents have raised the possibility of similar privacy rights, courts have not agreed. For example, plaintiffs have failed in challenges asserting that family rights were impinged by state athletic association transfer rules[26] or by a school decision not to admit a child to an accelerated curriculum.[27] Similarly, family rights cannot be used as justification for avoiding state child vaccination requirements.[28] In summary, the argument that there is a constitutional right to educate a child at home relies mostly on a smattering of unpublished decisions from local courts and selective passages from published decisions addressing other issues.

Recommendations for Practice

Parents who decide to educate their children at home, or who start a school with like-minded parents, have firm ideas about the shortcomings of the public schools. While their criticism varies depending on their philosophical and religious views, home instruction parents are likely to be suspicious of public school administrators and to be well informed about attendance laws. In dealing with home instruction parents, then, administrators will likewise need to be well versed in state administrative policies and statutes. These laws vary substantially from state to state and are likely to be updated frequently. Many school attendance laws recently have been modified as states wrestle with the issues of truancy and dropout prevention.

While courts generally have upheld the reasonable regulation of home instruction, administrators must be cautious not to provide *ad hoc* interpretations of rules or to make requirements of parents on a case-by-case basis. State departments of education generally have a home instruction expert on staff who can provide advice. Here are some further comments that apply to districts in all the states.

- Local school administrators have a clear obligation to enforce compulsory attendance laws, and the mere assertion by parents that they are educating their children at home requires investigation to ensure that there is compliance with state statutes.
- Special problems may be presented by home instruction students who are returning to the public schools. Neither court

decisions nor administrative rules will answer all the questions that will occur when this happens since many parents educate their children at home during a child's elementary school years, following the commonly held home instruction tenet that children should not be taken from the home when younger. Far fewer parents seek to provide a high school education. School systems, then, must decide how to credit the years of home instruction and should have a uniform policy on this matter to avoid allegations that individual students have been mistreated.

- As a safe rule of thumb, given the blurred distinction between home instruction and private schools, it probably is safe to assume that any assistance mandated by state law for private schools also must be given to home instruction parents. School systems should avoid providing services not mandated by law.

- Home instruction will be an alternative selected by some parents in most school districts and need not be characterized as a "problem" if school boards approve reasonable policies conforming with state laws and rules to deal with individual cases. As is the case with all educational issues that involve strongly held parental beliefs and an uncertain legal terrain, seeking advice from counsel before proceeding with individual cases is recommended.

References

[1] See Note, *Education and the Law: State Interests and Individual Rights*, 74 MICH. L. REV. 1373 (1976).

[2] See Moore, *Research and Common Sense: Therapies for our Homes and Schools*, 84 TCHRS. C. REC. 2 (1982).

[3] The legal basis for compulsory attendance laws is the common law doctrine of *parens patriae* which provides that the state has the authority to pass laws for the well-being of its citizens. See Project, *Education and the Law: State Interests and Individual Rights*, 74 MICH. L. REV. 1371 (1976). The classic *parens patriae* school attendance case is Prince v. Massachusetts, 321 U.S. 158 (1944) which upheld a Massachusetts child labor law over the objections of parents.

[4] Pierce v. Society of the Sisters of the Holy Names of Jesus and Mary, 268 U.S. 510 (1925).

[5] See also, Runyon v. McCrary, 427 U.S. 160 (1976) (parents do not have a right to send their children to a racially segregated private school).

[6] See Blackwelder v. Safnauer, 689 F. Supp. 106 (N.D. N.Y. 1988) (state curriculum standards provided an adequate basis for equivalency review).

[7] See State v. Anderson, 427 N.W.2d 316 (N.D. 1988).

[8] 406 U.S. 205 (1972).

[9] *Id.* at 235.

[10] See State *ex rel.* Douglas v. Faith Baptist Church, 301 N.W.2d 571 (Neb. 1981), *appeal dismissed*, 454 U.S. 803 (1981) (submission of courses of study; case dismissed for want of a federal question); State *ex rel.* Douglas v. Morrow, 343 N.W.2d 903 (Neb. 1984) (certified teacher requirement upheld); Grigg v. Virginia, 297 S.E.2d 799 (Va. 1982) (state-approved tutors for home instruction); Pruessner v. Benton, 368 N.W.2d 74 (Iowa 1985), *cert. denied*, 474 U.S. 1033 (1985) (reporting requirements upheld); Sheridan Road Baptist Church v. Department of Educ., 396 N.W.2d 373 (Mich. 1986), *cert. denied*, 481 U.S. 1050

(1987) (certified teacher requirement); Murphy v. Arkansas, 852 F.2d 1039 (8th Cir. 1988) (requirement of standardized testing upheld).

[11] North Dakota v. Rivinius, 328 N.W.2d 220, 223 (N.D. 1982). *See also*, State v. Patzer, 382 N.W.2d 631 (N.D. 1986) (certification is one of the least intrusive means of ensuring that children receive an education).

[12] State v. Popanz, 332 N.W.2d 750 (Wis. 1983); Roemhild v. State, 308 S.E.2d 154 (Ga. 1983).

[13] Burrow v. State, 669 S.W.2d 441 (Ark. 1984); Delconte v. State, 308 S.E.2d 898 (N.C. Ct. App. 1983), *rev'd*, 329 S.E.2d 636 (N.C. 1985).

[14] Ellis v. O'Hara, 612 F. Supp. 379 (E.D. Mo. 1985) ("substantially equivalent" violates substantive due process rights); *see* Mazanec v. North Judson-San Pierre School Corp., 763 F.2d 845 (7th Cir. 1985).

[15] Braintree Baptist Temple v. Holbrook Pub. Schools, 616 F. Supp. 81 (D. Mass. 1984). *See also*, State v. Schmidt, 505 N.E.2d 627 (Ohio 1987).

[16] State v. Newstrom, 371 N.W.2d 525 (Minn. 1985); State v. Budke, 371 N.W.2d 533 (Minn. 1985).

[17] Fellowship Baptist Church v. Benton, 815 F.2d 485 (8th Cir. 1987).

[18] New Life Baptist Church Academy v. East Longmeadow, 666 F. Supp. 293 (D. Mass. 1987). The court used Lemon v. Kurtzman, 403 U.S. 602 (1971) to determine constitutionality under an establishment clause challenge. The district court concluded that the extensive visits violated the "excessive government entanglement" test in *Lemon*.

[19] McCurry v. Tesch, 738 F.2d 271 (8th Cir. 1984).

[20] Kentucky State Bd. v. Rudasill, 589 S.W.2d 877 (Ky. 1979), *cert denied*, 446 U.S. 938 (1980).

[21] Bangor Baptist Church v. Maine Dep't of Educ., 576 F. Supp 1299 (D. Me. 1983).

[22] *In re* C.S., 382 N.W.2d 381 (N.D. 1986).

[23] *See* Stocklin-Enright, *The Constitutionality of Home Education: The Role of the Parent, the State, and the Child*, 18 WILLAMETTE L. J. 563 (1982) and Devins, *A Constitutional Right to Home Instruction*, 62 WASH. U.L.Q. 435 (1984). For the perspective that home instruction is a legislative prerogative and not a constitutional right, *see* Comment, *Parental Rights: Educational Alternatives and Curriculum Control*, 26 WASH. & LEE LAW REV. 277 (1979).

[24] Duro v. District Attorney, 712 F.2d 96 (4th Cir. 1983).

[25] Roe v. Wade, 410 U.S. 113 (1973).

[26] Walsh v. Louisiana High School Athletic Ass'n, 616 F.2d 152 (5th Cir. 1980), *cert. denied*, 449 U.S. 1124 (1981).

[27] Student Doe v. Pennsylvania, 593 F. Supp 54 (E.D. Pa. 1984).

[28] Sherr v. Northport-East Northport Union Free School Dist., 672 F. Supp. 81 (E.D. N.Y. 1987).

31
Reform And Equality of Education

Linda L. Hale

Introduction

The most liberal element in the American political system during the conservative 1950s may have been the Supreme Court. After President Dwight Eisenhower named Earl Warren as Chief Justice in 1953, the Court embarked on a period of judicial activism unique in history.[1] To credit or blame Warren for this activism, or even to label it a "Warren Court," is somewhat misleading. Warren was far from the most liberal member of the Court, and followed the majority as often as he led it until his retirement in 1969. In short, the Warren Court was a product of its time. Its roots lay in the "Roosevelt revolution" of 1937 and 1941, when deaths and retirements allowed President Franklin D. Roosevelt to restructure the Court, replacing the conservative justices who in the previous fifteen years had overturned some 200 state and federal laws because they interfered with free enterprise.[2]

The best remembered of Roosevelt's appointees were Felix Frankfurter, William O. Douglas, Hugo Black, and Robert Jackson. One of their main worries was the effect of government power on the liberties of the citizens. The rise of totalitarianism in Europe sharpened their concern. As Justice Frankfurter expressed it in 1943, "All members of the Court...are equally zealous to enforce the constitutional protection of the free play of human spirit."[3] This concern necessarily entailed judicial activism, because the field of civil liberties law rested somewhere between the primitive and nonexistent in 1940. Black rights were subject to the "separate but equal" concept. At the same time, the public temper of that era made it certain that a judicial excursion into the arena of civil liberties would be controversial. The mood of the forties and early fifties was shaped by hot war, cold war, and McCarthyism. It was difficult enough to elaborate a philosophy of civil rights in tranquil times because the people whose rights needed protecting included minorities and mavericks. In a society at war, on the brink of war, and rent with suspicion, the defenders of civil liberties themselves often came under attack.[4] As a result, it is scarcely surprising that the Court's first steps into the field during the late 1940s were hesitant ones. In the years after the war, the Court declared that the white primary system was unconstitutional, and that separate educational facilities were inherently unequal at the graduate school level.[5] No one foresaw that Chief Justice Warren would quicken the pace and lead the Court into a bold affirmation of individual rights and freedom. By the time he retired as Chief Justice in 1969, the Bill of Rights had a very different meaning from what it had in 1940. His niche in history was not won without personal cost, however. A small but noisy band of conservatives cried for his impeachment throughout the 1960s. Eisenhower came to regret his appointment, saying it was "the biggest damn-fool thing I ever did."[6] Posterity may not agree.

Legal Issues

As the Warren Court began its work, black Americans pushed steadily at the social barriers to equality. They entered professions such as law, medicine, and education that had previously been closed to them.[7] Greater wealth, more education, and improved status, in turn, made the legal barriers to equality even more intolerable. By the mid-1950s, black Americans were prepared to take the initiative in the fight against discrimination. During Earl Warren's first term in 1954, the Supreme Court handed down a landmark decision in *Brown v. Board of Education*.[8] The Chief Justice, writing for a unanimous Court, held that racially separate school facilities are "inherently unequal" and thus contrary to the fourteenth amendment.[9] As a result, the separate but equal doctrine was struck down. In a second decision a year later, the Court directed local school boards to take the responsibility for drawing up plans for desegregation and required that it be done with "all deliberate speed."[10] The Court declined, however, to set a deadline, giving an opportunity for delay. All over the South, citizen councils and other voluntary associations were formed to resist desegregation.[11] President Eisenhower encouraged the resistance with a public statement that he would enforce the Court's decision regardless of his own beliefs, which implied that he privately disagreed with the decision.[12] By the time Eisenhower left office six years later, some progress had been made in the upper South and in such border states as Kansas and Delaware, but not a single school district in the lower South had yielded.[13] In Prince Edward County, Virginia, the district even abolished its public school system altogether, rather than permit racial mixing.[14]

In such an atmosphere, it is scarcely surprising that southern blacks took matters into their own hands. On December 1, 1955, a black seamstress by the name of Rosa Parks refused to yield her seat to a white person on a city bus in Montgomery Alabama.[15] Her action violated both city ordinance and southern custom. She was forcibly ejected, but four days later, Montgomery blacks began a boycott of city buses under the leadership of Reverend Martin Luther King, Jr.[16] Eleven months later, the United States Supreme Court struck down ordinances such as Montgomery's and the city capitulated to the boycott.[17]

The focus of school desegregation activities during the next twenty years remained fixed on the South, where desegregation efforts took a number of different forms.[18] Court approved public placement laws involved the initial placement of students in a school designated for their race. Transfers to other schools were then considered on an individual basis. However, many courts went on to consider other factors, including the possibility of disruption within a school or the prospect of protest or economic retaliation by whites against blacks. Needless to say, very little desegregation was accomplished by these laws, and they were declared unconstitutional in the 1960s.[19]

Court approved choice plans were then introduced in an attempt to eliminate discrimination.[20] By requiring every student to choose a school at the beginning of the year, they eliminated the earlier method of assigning pupils to schools based on race. A student's choice of school could only be denied if the institution was overcrowded.[21] However, only a few black children took part in the choice plan.[22] Many applicants were threatened by local citizens. Others were rejected because they had improperly registered or had "bad character."[23] The caveat of overcrowding was also used by local school boards to deny them admission. As a result of these tactics, ninety-four percent of southern black students were still studying in all-black schools in 1965.[24]

Affirmative action remedies were initiated by the Supreme Court under Earl Warren in 1968 in the *Green v. County School Board of New Kent County* decision.[25] A Virginia school district had adopted a choice plan "in order to remain eligible for federal financial aid."[26] The plan allowed all students except those in the first and eighth grades to choose each year between two schools, one of which was dominated by white students and the other by black students. Any pupil that did not make a choice was assigned to the school they had previously attended. The school board lawyers argued that the district had fully complied with its duties to desegregate according to the provisions set out in *Brown v. Board of Education*.[27] But the Supreme Court unanimously declared that the school district had not properly complied with the law. After noting that it took the district eleven years to implement its program, the Court charged:

> This deliberate perpetration of the unconstitutional dual system can only have compounded the harm of such a system. Such delays are no longer tolerable, for the "governing constitutional principles no longer bear the imprint of newly enunciated doctrine." Moreover, a plan that at this late date fails to provide meaningful assurance of prompt and effective disestablishment of a dual system is also intolerable. The time for mere "deliberate speed" has run out.[28]

After three years of operation, not a single white child had chosen to attend the black school in the New Kent County School District, and only fifteen percent of the black students had chosen the white school.[29] The Court decided that a dual system remained in place, so that "[t]he Board must be required to formulate a new plan and...fashion steps which promise realistically to convert promptly to a system without a white school, but just schools."[30]

The administration of President Richard M. Nixon reversed the government's civil rights priorities.[31] Wooing southern conservatives who had thrown their support to George Wallace in the 1968 election, Nixon named two southerners to vacancies on the Supreme Court, only to have them rejected by the Senate because of their dubious judicial qualifications and segregationist background. The retirement of Earl Warren and other justices, however, gave Nixon five appointments to the Court during his first two years in office, enabling him to restructure it on more conservative lines. Although Nixon's appointees did not always vote as the president anticipated, the Court under Chief Justice Warren Burger was much different from the liberal, activist "Warren Court."

Yet the Supreme Court continued its attempt to end the tactics being used to keep school districts segregated in the *Alexander v. Holmes*[32] case by requiring all districts that were still engaging in discrimination to "immediately" end the practice. The ruling also prohibited incremental desegregation plans that only gradually implemented desegregation a grade at a time.[33] The Court then attempted in the *Swann v. Charlotte-Mecklenberg Board of Education*[34] case of 1971 to define more precisely the duties of school authorities and district courts in implementing the *Brown v. Board of Education*[35]decision. Chief Justice Warren Burger announced that every school was not required to reflect the racial composition of the school system as a whole.[36] He insisted that single race schools are not unconstitutional *per se*, although it is the burden of the districts to prove that "such school assignments are genuinely nondiscriminatory."[37] Burger went on to assert that when schools used techniques like altering attendance zones to accomplish desegregation, the courts should judge the methods by their results.[38] If the techniques served the purpose of desegregating schools, the courts should verify their constitutionality.[39] Finally, the Chief Justice proclaimed that school busing plans were permissible for "dismantling a dual system where it was feasible,"[40] although plans should be avoided that would "either risk the health of the children or significantly impinge on the educational process."[41]

In contrast to the federal efforts to combat segregation in the south, desegregation was "largely token and voluntary" in the northern and western parts of the country between 1954 and 1970.[42] The first major court decision involving a dispute outside the South was the *Keyes v. School District No. 1*, Denver, Colorado[43] case of 1973. The Denver school district had attempted to separate the races by gerrymandering attendance zones and manipulating student assignments. As a result, an elementary school opened in 1960 which had an enrollment that was ninety-three percent black and seven percent Hispanic.[44] The trial court decided that the school board's actions created de jure segregation in one section of Denver, and a remedial order was issued.[45] The Burger Court stressed that the facts in the Keyes case amounted to de jure segregation and emphasized that "the differentiating factor between *de jure* segregation and so-called *de facto* segregation...is purpose or intent to segregate."[46]

During its 1971 term, the Supreme Court in *Milliken v. Bradley*[47] examined the power of federal courts to order remedies for segregation that would directly affect school districts. More specifically, the Court was asked to decide whether the constitution required school districts near Detroit to participate in remedying discrimination even though a formerly *de jure* segregated district in the city contained a high percentage of blacks and meaningful racial mixing was impossible to achieve because of the low percentage of whites. In a five to four vote, the Court decided that outlying districts should not be required to participate in remediation as long as they were not practicing discriminatory acts.[48] However, the Supreme Court affirmed a lower court's decision that Detroit was practicing *de jure* segregation and the lower courts were instructed to formulate a decree to eliminate the practice within the school district.[49]

The Supreme Court was asked to consider the remedial powers of the federal courts in school desegregation cases during 1977 in the second *Milliken v. Bradley*[50] case, when the City of Detroit challenged four elements of the desegregation plan ordered by the lower courts. The Supreme Court unanimously agreed with the goal to develop remedial reading and communication skills programs, inservice education programs to assist teachers in coping with problems that might evolve in the desegregation process, new testing programs that might evolve in the desegregation process, new testing programs free from racial, ethnic, or cultural bias, and expanded counselling and career guidance programs.[51] It emphasized that:

> [t]hese specific educational remedies, although normally left to the discretion of the elected school board and professional educators, were deemed necessary to restore the victims of discriminatory conduct to the position they would have enjoyed in terms of education had these four components been provided in a nondiscriminatory manner in a school system free from pervasive *de jure* racial segregation.[52]

Courts have attempted to secure compliance with the *Brown v. Board of Education* decision since *Milliken* and have endeavored to offer equal educational opportunity to the races by exercising broad control over the organization, administration, and programs of the public schools.[53] Justices have been involved in reopening schools that were closed by local districts to avoid desegregation and have prohibited the closing of schools for the same reason.[54] They have drawn up orders requiring state taxation to support schools, have ordered that pupils and teachers be assigned to specific schools to achieve racial balance, and have required busing programs to remedy desegregation and ensure racial balance.[55]

The desegregation plans that have been implemented by the courts are generally classified as voluntary or involuntary, depending on whether students are allowed to choose the school they will attend.[56] Voluntary desegregation plans usually involve three techniques. First, freedom of choice methods allow students to transfer to the school of their choice.[57] Their decision cannot be overturned unless the school is overcrowded. A second voluntary desegregation plan includes a broad array of educational alternatives that are offered as part of a standard curriculum.[58] The third voluntary desegregation plan allows a person to transfer from a school where the student is a member of the majority racial population to a school where the student is a member of a minority community.[59]

Involuntary desegregation plans include neighborhood attendance zones that assign students to outlying schools because nearby schools are not designated for their race.[60] This strategy was developed primarily to end the dual system practice of sending students to outlying schools because nearby schools were not designated for their race.[61] Another involuntary plan embodies rezoning, which is usually required when a school is closed or a magnet school is opened.[62] In both situations, students must be assigned elsewhere. Finally, pairing and clustering desegregation plans involve reassigning students between a pair or group of schools by grade restructuring.[63] For example, one school where the majority of students are white and another where the majority are black that educate children in grades kindergarten through six might be paired by converting the former into an elementary school for grades kindergarten through third and the latter into an upper elementary school for grades four through six.[64]

Educational Reforms for the Nineties

Despite voluntary and involuntary plans for desegregation, racial problems continue to plague the public school systems of the nation. A 1989 report prepared by ten federally funded Desegregation Assistance Centers indicates that the difficulties include school policies and procedures that result in racially or sexually identifiable outcomes; program counseling or assignment by school staffs that create classes that are racially, ethnically, or sexually identifiable; grouping practices between or within classes that create racially, ethnically, or sexually identifiable groups for extended periods of time; and extracurricular activities that evolve into groups identifiable by race, ethnicity, or sex.[65] The report went on to reveal that black students are 2.3 times as likely as white students to be classified as emotionally disturbed, mentally retarded, or trainable.[66] Black students are suspended from school at nearly three times the rate of their white counterparts. The average performance of black and Hispanic students on the Scholastic Aptitude Test, the National Assessment of Educational Progress, and the American College Testing Program is more than fifty points lower than the average performance of white students.[67] Finally, the report indicates that physical desegregation during the 1980s remained fairly constant, although some of the southern states have eased up on enforcement procedures and thereby encouraged resegregation.[68] A study of school integration in Milwaukee since 1976 was published by the

Wisconsin Policy Research Institute.[69] The report summarized the integration process in the Milwaukee school system.

- It has failed to develop a strategy for increasing academic achievement of black students.
- It has created a system of racial segregation to replace one based on economic class.
- It has prevented strategies from being used that might have increased academic achievement by minority students. These include programs based on increased parental or community involvement, school-based autonomy, and higher expectations for students.
- It has placed an inequitable and discriminatory transportation burden on black families, reflecting a conscious policy to minimize white opposition to busing.
- The overall result of Milwaukee's policies is a dual system with traditional schools on the one hand and specialty and suburban schools on the other. Many students in the traditional schools are confronted by a difficult environment at home and low expectations at school that are not conducive to high achievement.[70]

Parental Choice

After the National Commission on Excellence in Education published *A Nation At Risk*,[71] in order to highlight the decline in the quality of elementary and secondary education in the United States, the administration of President Ronald Reagan proposed compensatory education vouchers, tuition tax credits, and public school choice programs in order to reform the system.[72] Public concern about the structure of the nation's schools increased as a result of these actions. At the forefront of the debate is the issue of parental choice. Milton Friedman, one of the originators of the concept, advocates learning procedures which would expand achievement and quality.[73]

The opponents of school choice argue that the program exacerbates social, economic, racial, religious, and ethnic divisions within American society, and that it will reverse any progress that has been made in desegregating education.[74] They believe that poor and minority students in the inner cities will be forced to attend neighborhood schools, while middle class white students will enroll in elite, private schools. Housing patterns, transportation difficulties, and racial discrimination will make it much harder for inner city minority students to enroll in suburban or outlying middle class schools.[75] Increased financial aid will be provided to the private and elite schools populated by middle class students.[76]

Black Immersion Schools.

The effort to reform the educational system has also involved the concept of "black male immersion" schools.[77] Two Baltimore elementary schools have attracted attention by offering two classes exclusively for black males.[78] Although the classes are held in integrated schools, they are taught by black males who serve as role models and offer academic guidance. The Dade County Public School System is implementing a three-year pilot program that targets first, second, and third grade students and is designed around an Afrocentric perspective.[79] The program's goal is to improve the achievement of African American male children by focusing on cultural pride, self-confidence, respect, and academic success. The proponents of black immersion schools insist that behavioral problems have disappeared, test scores have increased, and student attitudes toward life have improved.[80] They also argue that radical measures are necessary to defeat the cycle of academic underachievement among black men.[81] Other supporters of these programs believe that black and white students learn differently.[82] Therefore, traditional methods for teaching and testing them are inappropriate.

Opponents of black immersion schools think they simply represent new forms of racism and sexism that are unconstitutional.[83] They ask why special programs should be offered to black males when the educational needs of black females, whites, or other minorities are not being met.[84] As Leonard Stevens put it, "black parents have a right to expect schools to succeed with their children."[85] As a result, "all children deserve *bona fide* school reform, not showy acts of desperation that test the law and defy common educational sense."[86] Stevens reasons that when schools do not work, the "schools" need to be fixed.

Busing

The effort to achieve racial balance by busing students has been controversial since the policy was instituted. The Supreme Court began to eliminate school busing and other court ordered desegregation remedies as early as 1971 in the *Swann v. Charlotte-Mecklenburg Board of Education* case.[87] The Court concluded that, "at some point, these school authorities and others like them should have achieved full compliance with this Court's decision in *Brown I*. The systems would then be unitary in the sense required by our decisions in *Green* and *Alexander*."[88]

The United States Supreme Court decided in *Board of Education of Oklahoma City v. Dowell*[89] to allow previously segregated school districts to be released from court-ordered busing even if some segregation remained in tact, although it stipulated that the school district must have taken "practicable" steps to eliminate segregation. After reviewing the case, the Court concluded that the "necessary concern for the important values of local control of public school systems dictates that a Federal Court's regulatory control of such systems not extend beyond the time required to remedy the effect of past intentional discrimination."[90]

The Justices explained that when the decree is terminated, the school district can change the desegregation plan as long as it does not commit any new intentional act of discrimination.[91] The Court defined three general standards for determining how to declare a school district unitary: the school district must demonstrate that it has complied with all court orders for a reasonable period of time; it must prove that it will not reinstate segregation policies; and it must have eliminated any trace of prior segregation from all aspects of school operations to the extent practicable.[92] The Court underscored that in some circumstances, the existence of racially identifiable schools may be solely the result of residential segregation caused by the decisions of private individuals or economics.[93] Thus single race schools whose racial composition cannot be attributed to prior school segregation are permissible.

Recommendations for Practice

The struggle to bring into operation the mandate of *Brown* has taught the nation that the road between moral precept and public policy is a rough one. Nevertheless, people must not be immobilized by equality's limitations but rather energized by its substantive force. As a result, schools must:

- Develop strategies for increasing academic achievement of black students including programs based on increased parental or community involvement, school-based autonomy, and higher expectations for students.
- Address the issue that many students in traditional schools are confronted by a difficult environment at home and low expectations at school that are not conducive to high achievement.
- Understand that black parents have a right to expect schools to succeed with their children.

References

[1] *See* A. RICE, THE WARREN COURT 1959-1969, 210-23 (1987); J. POLLACK EARL WARREN: THE JUDGE WHO CHANGED AMERICA (1979); L. FRIEDMAN, THE HISTORY OF AMERICAN LAW, 567-83 (1973); H. HUDGINS THE WARREN COURT AND THE PUBLIC SCHOOLS: AN ANALYSIS OF SUPREME COURT DECISIONS (1970).

[2] *See* POLLACK, at 55-96.

[3] J. BURNS THE SOLDIER OF FREEDOM, 257 (1970).

[4] FRIEDMAN, at 580.

[5] Sipuel v. Board of Regents of Univ. of Okla., 332 U.S. 631 (1948); McLaurin v. Oklahoma State Regents for Higher Educ., 339 U.S. 637 (1950); Sweatt v. Painter, 339 U.S. 629 (1950).

[6] S. AMBROSE, EISENHOWER: SOLDIER AND PRESIDENT, 420 (1990).

[7] A. STRICKMAN and J. REICH, THE BLACK AMERICAN EXPERIENCE, 209-227 (1974).

[8] 347 U.S. 483 (1954).

[9] *Id.* at 495.

[10] Brown v. Board of Educ. (*Brown II*), 349 U.S. 294, 301 (1955).

[11] D. Goldfield, BLACK, WHITE AND SOUTHERN: RACE RELATIONS AND SOUTHERN CULTURE 1940 TO THE PRESENT, 81-84 (1990).

[12] J. DURAN A MODERATE AMONG EXTRMISTS: DWIGHT D. EISENHOWER AND THE SCHOOL DEGREGATION CRISIS, 274-79 (1981).

[13] *Id.*

[14] *Id.*

[15] *See* J. WILLIAMS, EYES ON THE PRIZE: AMERICA'S CIVIL RIGHTS YEARS 1954-1965, 66-69 (1987).

[16] D. GOLDFIELD, at 96-102.

[17] J. WILLIAMS, at 70-89.

[18] *See* Gordon, *School Desegregation: A Look at the 70's and 80's*, J.L. & EDUC. 189, 194 (1989).

[19] *See* Blush v. Orleans Parish School Bd., 308 F.2d 491 (1962) (where the school board applied the Louisiana Pupil Placement Act discriminatorily when it was applied to black first graders only after they had already been assigned to segregated schools in a dual school system); Northcross v. Board of Educ., 302 F.2d 818 (1962) (where the court held that school authorities have the burden to initiate desegregation and black children cannot be required to apply for that which they are entitled to as a matter of right).

[20] C. ROSSELL, THE CARROT OR THE STICK FOR SCHOOL DESEGREGATION POLICY, 4 (1990).

[21] *Id.* at 5.

[22] *Id.*

[23] *Id.*

[24] *Id.* at 116.

[25] 391 U.S. 430 (1968).

[26] *Id.* at 433.

[27] 347 U.S. 483.

[28] *Green*, 391 U.S. at 438.

[29] D. GOLDFIELD, at 257.

[30] *Green*, 391 U.S. 430, 442.

[31] J. POLLACK, at 286-333.

[32] 396 U.S. 19 (1970).

[33] *Id.* at 20.

[34] 402 U.S. 1 (1971).

[35] 347 U.S. 483.

[36] 396 U.S. at 25.

[37] *Id.* at 26.

[38] *Id.* at 28.

[39] *Id.*

[40] *Id.* at 29.

[41] *Id.* at 30-31.

[42] C. ROSSELL, at 3.

[43] 413 U.S. 189 (1973).

[44] *Id.* at 200 n.10.

[45] *Id.* at 193, 196.

[46] *Id.* at 208.

[47] 418 U.S. 717 (1974).

[48] *Id.* at 753.

[49] *Id.*.

[50] 433 U.S. 267 (1977).

[51] *Id.* at 274.

[52] *Id.* at 282.

[53] *See* J. HOGAN, THE SCHOOLS, THE COURTS, AND THE PUBLIC INTEREST 31 (1987).

[54] *Id.*

[55] *Id.*

[56] F. WELCH & A. LIGHT, NEW EVIDENCE ON SCHOOL DESEGREGATION, 23-28 (1987).

[57] *Id.* at 24. *See* DIRECTIONS—MILWAUKEE PUBLIC SCHOOLS: SCHOOL SELECTION CATALOG (1991-92). (Available from the Milwaukee Public School System in Milwaukee, Wisconsin)

[58] F. WELCH & A. LIGHT NEW EVIDENCE ON SCHOOL DESEGREGATION, 23-28 (1987).

[59] *Id.* One example of this type of program is the Milwaukee/Suburban School Transfer Program, or Chapter 220.

[60] *Id.* at 26.

[61] *Id.*

[62] *Id.* at 27.

[63] *Id.*

[64] The Madison Public School District employs a pairing program that receives financial aid through Wisconsin Statute § 121.85. *See* Madison Metropolitan School District Integration Plan 1 (June 1984).

[65] E. SIMON-MCWILLIAMS, RESEGREGATION OF PUBLIC SCHOOLS: THE THIRD GENERATION 13-14 (1989).

[66] *Id.* at 15.

[67] *Id.*

[68] *Id.* at 17.

[69] G. Mitchell, WISCONSIN POLICY RESEARCH INSTITUTE REPORT: AN EVALUATION OF STATE-FINANCED SCHOOL INTEGRATION IN METROPOLITAN MILWAUKEE (1989).

[70] *Id.* at 4.

[71] *See* National Commission on Excellence In Education, A NATION AT RISK (1983).

[72] *Address to the National Association of Independent Schools*, EDUCATION WEEK, Feb. 28, 1985 at 30.

[73] *See* M. FRIEDMAN & R. FRIEDMAN, FREE TO CHOOSE (1980).

[74] J. WITTE, CHOICE IN AMERICAN EDUCATION 12-15 (1990). *But see*, Davis v. Grover, 480 N.W.2d 460 (1992). The Wisconsin Supreme Court concluded that a state statute which provides state subsidy for certain "low-income city children" to attend private schools was constitutional.

[75] J. WITTE, at 5.

[76] *Id.*

[77] *See* Whitaker, *Do Black Males Need Special Schools?* 46 EBONY, March 1991; Farber, *"Africa Centered" School Plan is Rooted in 60's Struggle*, THE NEW YORK TIMES, Feb. 5, 1991, § 1, at l, col. 2; Howell, *Fighting a Cycle of Failure*, NEWSDAY, Nov. 4, 1990, at 7.

[78] Cooper, *Three Rs and Role Model In Baltimore Third Grade: Single-Sex Class Harnesses Boys' Instincts*, THE WASHINGTON POST, Dec. 5, 1990, at Al.

[79] *See Afrocentric/Enhancement Self-Esteem Opportunity Program A.E.S.O.P.* June 1991 (available from the Division of Multicultural Programs, Dade County Public Schools, Miami, Florida).

[80] Ramsey, The Gannett New Service, Jan. 8, 1991; Howell, at 7.

[81] African American Male Task Force, Educating American Males: A Dream Deferred, May 1990.

[82] *See* J. IRVINE, BLACK STUDENTS AND SCHOOL FAILURE, 21-42 (1990).

[83] *See* Fein & Reynolds, *Milwaukee's Racist School Experiment, Legal Times*, Nov. 12, 1990, at 4; Stevens, *Separate But Equal Has No Place*, 10 EDUCATION WEEK, Oct. 31, 1990, at 14; Innerst, *Schools Segregate Black Male Pupils*, The WASHINGTON TIMES, Oct. 19, 1990, § A, at A1.

[84] *Id.*

[85] STEVENS, at 15.

[86] *Id.*

[87] 402 U.S. 1 (1971).

[88] *Id.* at 31.

[89] 111 S. Ct. 630 (1991). *See also*, Tatel & Borkowski, *Dowell Upheld Basic Principles, Left Hard Issues for Later Case*, NATL. L. J., March 18, 1991 at 18.

[90] *Id.* at 637 (quoting Spangler v. Pasadena City Bd. of Educ., 611 F.2d 1239, 1245 n.5 (Kennedy, J. concurring) (9th Cir. 1979).

[91] *Id.* at 638.

[92] *Id.* at 636. For a discussion of unitary status *see* Chandler, *The End of School Busing?, School Desegregation and the Findings of Unitary Status*, 40 OKLA. L. REV. 519, 533 (1987).

[93] *Id.*

32
Legal Issues for School Reform

James Gordon Ward

Introduction

American public schools always seem to be in the process of reform. Education reform has been at the forefront of the public policy agenda at least since the 1983 publication of *A Nation at Risk*, which was the Reagan Administration's contribution to improving education for America's children. Since 1983, hundreds of education reform reports have been issued, most every state has experienced education reform legislation, and countless articles and books have been written about education reform in the United States. The most recent reform initiative has been President Bush's "America 2000" proposal. Yet, in spite of numerous well-publicized reform proposals in most American schools, it has been business as usual.

Education reform in the United States since 1983 has been through three major stages:

- Stage 1 in the early part of the 1980s was characterized by a top down approach to reform, with heavy state mandates and regulation, which imposed new legal requirements on schools.
- Stage 2 took place during the later part of the decade of the 1980s and focused on teacher and administrator preparation. This reform stage did not so much create new legal requirements for schools as much as they had an impact on institutions of higher education and state policymakers.
- Stage 3 emerged at the end of the decade and emphasized restructuring schools to meet the demands of the information age and a global economy. The legal implications are less clear here, but this reform stage has the potential to raise significant legal issues.

A common element in most of the stage 3 reform initiatives is some approach to restructuring American schools to better achieve their purposes. Phillip C. Schlechty defined restructuring as "altering systems of rules, roles, and relationships so that schools can serve existing purposes more effectively or serve new purposes altogether."[1] Discussion of "rules, roles, and relationships" has clear legal implications, but the issue of the purposes of education is even more fundamental. Schlechty's emphasis on the role of the school leader in school restructuring involves principals in this process in a key way. Therefore, school restructuring as part of the third stage in education reform has legal implications for principals. Social psychologist Seymour B. Sarason sees this stage of reform as altering power relationships in schools.[2] Power relationships within schools involve rules, regulations, and administrative procedures, all encompassing questions of law.

Legal Issues

The purpose of this chapter is not so much to review the legal aspects of new rules, roles, and relationships as much as it is to review recent trends in school reform and to identify the significant issues which may have legal implications for school administrators. A critical political issue which has great legal meaning is what is the state's responsibility for providing an adequate education for all children. For the purposes of this discussion, "the state" refers to the state and local systems of public education that have developed in the United States.[3] This issue involves critical questions of school purpose as well as related issues.

The State's Responsibility

The basis for this line of analysis involving the question of the state's duty to provide an adequate education for all children is explored by Hubsch who argues that "the 1980s have witnessed an outcry against a perceived decline in the academic performance of elementary and secondary schools in this country....The public outcry has arisen because citizens are dissatisfied with the quality of performance in our public schools."[4] One avenue for redress of this perceived decline in academic performance is through the legislative process, but another avenue is through the courts.

Hubsch distinguishes between two grand traditions in American political philosophy and demonstrates how each suggest a different legal strategy for redress for the failure of schools to provide an adequate education. The liberal political tradition stresses equal educational opportunity and the instruments for attaining and protecting equal opportunity are the equal protection and due process guarantees against discriminatory action against individuals. A problem with the liberal approach, Hubsch argues, is that "the state courts have agreed with the decision of the Supreme Court in *Rodriguez* that equal protection provides only a negative prohibition against disparities in minimal access to educational opportunity."[5] In the current dissatisfaction with public education it is not the violation of minimal standards of education that concern the public, but the lack of provision of high quality education for all children. Hubsch posits that a better strategy is to move to guarantee high quality education through enforcement of state education articles according to the traditions of a republican political philosophy. A republican philosophy holds that the creation of the state requires individuals to join together in public life for the preservation and advancement of the community.

The skills necessary for full participation in the political life of the community, the skills necessary for full citizenship, are those provided by education. As Hubsch says, "In sum, education is essential to self-government."[6] This republican approach does not focus on state deprivation of individual rights and liberties, but on the argument that the state is responsible for advancing good citizenship through the high quality education of all individuals. Government has a clear and explicit duty to educate its citizens well. A reading of state constitutional provisions on education shows that states have accepted this republican theory of government and "have in fact recognized an affirmative obligation of government to educate its citizens."[7] Hubsch documents how the words *shall*, *ought*, and *duty* are contained in state constitution education articles. These words all impose an obligation.

One area of education where the distinction between the liberal theory of the state and the republican theory of the state can be readily seen is in the area of school finance. The early school finance litigation focused on alleged violations of equal protection and by the late 1970s, these suits were not meeting with much success. Since 1989, a new group of school finance reform cases have come forth arguing violations of state constitution education clauses and these have been based on the republican ideal of high quality education for all citizens.[8]

However, this same approach can be applied to provision of education for the handicapped and the limited English proficient, for children in poverty, or for any other educational program. The strategy employed in such cases and the defenses against legal action depend, in part, on the way one views public education and which political theory one subscribes to. Is the affirmative duty of the state to provide education for all children primarily to the individual to guarantee equal educational opportunity, or primarily to the state itself to ensure good citizenship? A number of other questions are also raised in this analysis.

Critical Educational Questions

An analysis of commentary on recent case law relating to the question of the state's responsibility for providing education for all children leads to a number of critical issues. They include:

- Should the focus be on equality or quality?
- Should the focus be on school inputs or school outputs and outcomes?
- What should be the form and locus of accountability to the public?
- Is the fundamental purpose of education citizenship or economic well-being?

The remainder of this chapter will explore these critical questions and discuss their implications for public school building and program administrators.

Equality of Quality?

Hubsch points out that equal protection claims "do not impose an affirmative duty upon any state to provide its students with an assured quality education."[9] Equal protection clauses, whether federal or state, only require that the state provide education equally to all children at whatever quality level has been selected through the public policy process. However, recent school finance reform cases have taken a different approach emphasizing constitutional language in education articles which speak to the education quality issue. Hubsch observes that:

> More creative litigants and courts have applied the educational clauses in a more powerful fashion, mandating positive standards of quality education. These standards have indirectly encouraged equalization, by establishing a minimum threshold of quality that may exceed the minimum level required by the dictum of *Rodriguez*. More importantly, enforcement of quality standards by these state courts effects the republican principles that the framers of the education articles of the state constitution originally intended.[10]

These standards impose a new responsibility on school administrators. Instead of merely being concerned about the equity issues in programs, school administrators must now also be as concerned about issues of quality. This raises questions of who sets quality standards, how will quality be measured, what reward or sanctions will be developed to ensure quality compliance, and the like. In the past, schools could get away with offering substandard education as long as the system could reasonably argue that all children receive the same level of education. Now the emphasis has shifted to examining quality questions. It is interesting to note in the Hubsch commentary how the new emphasis on quality seems to subsume issues of equality since equality is reached through high quality standards.

Measure of Inputs or Outputs?

If quality is to become the new standard, how do you measure quality? Hubsch points out that the state supreme courts in West Virginia, New Jersey, and Washington have not prescribed the standards to be used to measure quality, but left it to the respective state legislatures to specify the proper remedy.[11] It would seem that if a basic premise is that education reform is spawned by a concern about the academic performance of schools, then the emphasis would be on the outputs or outcomes of education. However, with the shift in emphasis from equality to quality, there has not been a parallel shift from considering outputs. As Levine has shown in her insightful analysis of the legislative and judicial entanglements in Texas in the aftermath of a successful school finance reform suit there in 1989, the courts and the legislatures are still measuring quality in terms of inputs.[12] The common metric for judging quality still seems to be the revenues available per pupil. When more sophisticated quality measures are used, they are still input measures like pupil-teacher ratios, instructional resources available, computers available, and curricular offerings.

While many schools have moved toward developing quality measures that focus on school outputs or school outcomes, the courts still measure inputs. This measure raises a dilemma for school officials who embrace the quality concept and attempt to discuss quality in terms of student performance. There is a tendency in education, perhaps because of our past narrow view of equating study in education with education psychology, to believe that if something exists, it must be measurable. Consequently, if it is not measurable, it does not exist. Yet, much of what represents quality in education is not easily and directly measurable. The issue of quality measurement is not an easy one to address, but it is emerging as a major issue for schools and school administrators. Courts have been hesitant to impose their views in this area, although legislatures have been less reluctant. Nonetheless, it may be in the best interests of school administrators to assume leadership in quality measurement before standards are imposed from outside the school system.

Form and Locus of Accountability for Quality?

The dilemma is that the public is demanding improvements in student performance, which focuses on school outputs and the courts discuss quality in terms of resource inputs. This view raises questions of how accountability should be approached and certainly raises questions involving the relationship of inputs and outputs. Hanushek, an economist, argues that there is no demonstrated relationship between school resource inputs and student performance.[13] Murnane counters Hanushek's analysis by discussing the limitations of the production function research approach used in the studies Hanushek analyzes and suggests that production function studies might show a stronger relationship between inputs and performance if schools attended more to reforms relating to the selection and hiring of teachers, how instruction is organized, and time spent on instruction.[14]

Economist James K. Galbraith supports this view with his argument, based on an analysis of American economic productivity data, that perceived declines in productivity may not result so much from declines in unmeasured inputs, but from increases in unmeasured quality improvements in outputs.[15] While Galbraith does not apply this concept of unmeasured quality improvements to education, it can be applied to schools. Many of the improvements in public education in terms of increased services for special needs children, more comprehensive social services for children, increased emphasis on affective curricular areas, and recent attention to critical thinking and problem solving skills may have greatly improved the quality of education without showing up as gains in student performance on traditional assessment and accountability measures. An important issue in public education is how to measure these quality gains in a meaningful and understandable manner.

Not only are measures of accountability important, but an equally important issue is the locus of accountability. When states are adding new educational mandates and cutting state budgets for education, is it reasonable to hold school officials solely responsible for student performance and school outcomes? Is the principal to be held responsible for school performance when the imposition of a site-based management system turns significant school policy making authority over to teachers and parents? These are important issues of the locus of accountability. With the system of mixed governance and shared decisionmaking authority that characterizes American public schools, it is difficult to ascertain who is legally as well as morally responsible for school performance. The locus of accountability issues must be addressed in educational policy so that there is a reasonable relationship between accountability and discretionary authority for education decisionmaking.

What Is the Fundamental Purpose of Public Schooling?

It has become fashionable to discuss school improvement in terms of providing a better work force, in terms of education for economic development, and in terms of business satisfaction with school performance. In Galbraith's examination of American economic productivity, he confronts this approach:

> As an examination of the industries where the U.S. is most successful reveals, the well-springs of competitive success simply are not to be found in the public schools. Rather, they lie in blunter and more sweeping instruments: development of agriculture and energy resources, technology-forcing mechanisms, and wholesale subsidy of industrial research and development.[16]

His argument is that there are important social and political rationales for supporting public investment in high quality education, but that the economic rationale is weak.

It makes a big difference in how a school administrator fashions educational programs depending on whether one accepts the premise of business that the purpose of education is economic success or whether one embraces the more classic view that education is for citizenship. The economic rationale for education more closely parallels the liberal view of equal educational opportunity and individual rights, where the citizenship view is compatible with the republican theory of education for the well being of the community. These questions are not merely philosophical, but the answer one accepts makes a big difference in how one views school quality, school performance, and accountability.

Recommendations for Practice

This discussion of educational reform and the directions it may be taking involve a number of key questions. These include:

- Should the emphasis in school administration be on ensuring equality among individual students or in developing programs of high quality for all students?
- In considering quality, should we emphasize the quality of program resource inputs?
- How can we assess what we are doing for purposes of accountability?
- At what level should the public education system be accountable and who should be accountable for what?
- Is our fundamental purpose the economic well being of students (education for the work force) or is it the good citizenship of students?

The movement toward quality as a major goal of education and the tendency in recent years to base school finance law suits on the state constitution education articles make these very pertinent questions. To answer these questions involves restructuring schools in many cases and altering power relationships within schools and school systems. They are questions that not only the courts and legislatures must struggle with, but also questions that confront school administrators in their daily lives.

References

[1]P. SCHLECHTY, SCHOOLS FOR THE TWENTY-FIRST CENTURY, xvi (1990).
[2]S. SARASON, THE PREDICTABLE FAILURE OF EDUCATIONAL REFORM, 49 (1991).
[3]M. CARNOY, THE STATE AND POLITICAL THEORY. 3 (1984).
[4]Hubsch, Education and Self-Government: *The Right to Education Under State Constitutional Law*, 18 J. OF LAW AND EDUC. 93 (1989).
[5]*Id.* at 115.
[6]*Id.* at 96.
[7]*Id.* at 96-97.
[8]Hubsch, *The Third Wave: The Impact of Montana, Kentucky, and Texas Decisions on the Future of Public School Finance Reform Litigation*, 19 J. OF LAW AND EDUC. (1990).
[9]Hubsch, at 106.
[10]*Id.* at 127-128.
[11]*Id.* at 133.
[12]Levine, *Meeting the Third Wave: Legislative Approaches to Recent Judicial School Finance Rulings*, 28 HARV. J. ON LEGISLATION 507 (1991).
[13]Hanushek, *When School Finance "Reform" May Not Be Good Policy*, 28 HARV. J. ON LEGISLATION 423 (1991).
[14]Murnane, *Interpreting the Evidence on "Does Money Matter"?* 28 HARV. J. ON LEGISLATION 457 (1991).
[15]Galbraith, *A New Picture of the American Economy*, THE AMERICAN PROSPECT 26 (Fall 1991).
[16]*Id.* at 35.

33

School Finance

William E. Camp

Introduction

School finance is increasingly becoming a high priority issue in both the political and legal spheres of education. The competition for money to finance both public and private education will force changes in the way educational programs are delivered and will have a real impact at the school site level. As money becomes scarce, more groups are looking to the courts to allow or force the redistribution of funds between recipients. Legal decisions concerning school finance may mean there will be winners and losers in the competition for limited funds. The impact at the individual school site will be immense as funds are shifted between wealthy and poor school districts or between public and private schools. It is important for the principal to stay abreast of these legal battles as changes may bring alterations in funding that impact the individual school sites.

Legal Issues

School Funding Equity

The era of school finance reform began in the late 1960s with *McInnis v. Shapiro*[1] and has led to more than 100 cases litigated within the courts with 25 of these decisions being determined in the states' highest courts. The successful cases have pursued relief under state constitutions but initial efforts were first tested in the federal courts. Early federal decisions uniformly have denied a federal responsibility for education. In *Rodriguez v. San Antonio Independent School District,*[2] the Court refused to use a heightened level of judicial review by finding neither a fundamental right to education or a suspect class of individuals whose rights were being denied. The Court went on to find a rational relationship between the state's efforts to establish local control of schools and the Texas school finance system. The impact of *Rodriguez* in the federal courts has continued as later cases upheld the inappropriateness of federal judicial interference.

Failing to force federal responsibility for education or to require more than a rational basis for funding schools, litigation turned to the states. *Serrano v. Priest*[3] was the first successful challenge to school finance reform at the state level. The California Supreme Court ruled that education was a fundamental right under the state's constitution, that the system of funding schools in California violated the state equal protection clause, and that education funding could not be conditioned on residence but should consider the wealth of the state as a whole. *Serrano* demonstrated that change could be forced through the courts as state constitutions may afford greater protections than those available under the United States Constitution.[4]

The efforts for reform continued when the New Jersey Supreme Court overturned that state's funding scheme in *Robinson v. Cahill*.[5] The state plan for funding schools in New Jersey was found unconstitutional based on the state's education article since the New Jersey constitution required a "thorough and efficient" system of schools. The effect of *Robinson* was especially significant for reform because it utilized language in the education article of the state constitution and has become the primary technique in recent challenges since 34 states currently utilize similar constitutional language referring to a common, uniform, or thorough and/or efficient system of free public schools. In a recent case in Montana, the court ruled the method of financing schools violated the requirement of equality of educational opportunity for each student as stated in the education clause.[6] In Kentucky, the court ruled in *Rose v. The Council for Better Education*,[7] that the entire state system of schools was unconstitutional based on a thorough review of the meaning of an efficient system of public schools. In Texas, the state supreme court ruled that procedures for financing public schools violated the state's constitutional requirement that an "efficient" system of public schools be created for the "general diffusion of knowledge."[8] In *Abbott v. Burke*,[9] the school funding system in New Jersey was again declared unconstitutional as applied to the poorer urban school districts in the state because it failed to meet the requirements of the education clause calling for "thorough and efficient" education. The court used a narrowly defined decision that applied primarily to poorer urban school districts. All four recent decisions led to a demand for a thorough revamping of the school finance systems in the respective states.

While victories for the proponents of reform of school funding changes are becoming more consistent, the cases still must be decided on a state by state basis depending on the specific language in the state's constitution. In the case *Coalition for Equitable School Funding v. State*,[10] plaintiffs alleged that the current method of funding public schools in Oregon violated the constitutional requirements that the state provide sufficient funds to school districts to satisfy all educational standards imposed by state law, guarantee that all students receive equal educational resources, and equalize the property tax burden on all property owners. The Oregon Supreme Court disagreed ruling that Oregon's method of funding public schools did not violate the state's constitution.

The decisions in *Rodriguez, Serrano, Robinson,* and the cases which followed made it clear that responsibility for education has largely fallen to the states. The extent of that responsibility has depended on language embraced by individual state constitutions. The results vary, with the courts in fourteen cases ruling that the state funding system is constitutional and eleven ruling the state system is unconstitutional. Where states have constitutional language inducing heightened scrutiny, challenges have generally been successful. In those states where plaintiffs have failed to successfully challenge the school funding, failure appears to have largely been the consequence of insufficient language to force more than the minimal rational relationship between the funding formula and state interests.[11]

School Funding Adequacy

The success of school equity cases has led to new efforts to force states to provide an adequate education to all students within a state. While equity decisions may force a state to revise the method of distribution of funds between districts, the legislatures in many states have chosen to reallocate existing funds rather than bring poorer districts funding to the level of more affluent districts. Not only does this action mean that wealthier districts with higher property value and the expectations by citizens within the district for a higher level level of education are now receiving less funding, but the poorer districts within the state are only being brought to a minimum level of funding. These districts are now combining their efforts to bring legal challenges attempting to force the states' legislatures to raise the school funding levels for all districts.

The Texas case *Andrews v. Edgewood*[12] takes the issue one step further by attempting to define an adequate education for all districts in the state. Following the successful equity challenge concerning the constitutional requirements to provide an "efficient" system of education in Texas as determined in *Edgewood I* and

Edgewood II,[13] districts within the state are now challenging the adequacy of funding in *Andrews* based on constitutional language calling for "suitable" funding of education in Texas. The case addresses two major issues: the lack of adequate funding from the state and the provision of state funds to cover new state mandates for educational reform. As stated by the plaintiffs, "In its quest to meet its constitutional duty to provide state funding, the legislature cannot sacrifice the quality of public education in Texas. To comply with the 'suitable provision' mandate, education programs and funding must at least be adequate."[14]

The results in this case will have important implications for other states in future challenges to educational funding. The issue of adequacy is one of the newer legal challenges to states' methods of providing education and is a legal effort to force legislators to recognize and provide more than a basic, minimum level of education. The issue of adequacy strikes at the heart of educational reform since it demands that legislators fund a quality education for all students within a state.

Funding Church-affiliated Schools

Another issue that continues to gain attention is the continued efforts to use public funds to support private schools, especially church-affiliated schools. These efforts currently have minimum impact on the redistribution of funds as the use of public funds to support church-affiliated schools has long been constrained by the "tests" established in *Lemon v. Kurtzman.*[15] In the *Lemon* case, the Supreme Court held that aid in the form of direct reimbursement for teachers' salaries or purchase of service contracts was unconstitutional as a violation of the establishment clause. Even more important was the three-pronged test used by the court to review church-state conflicts for funding going to sectarian schools. The *Lemon* test stated that governmental action must have a valid secular purpose, its primary effect can neither advance nor inhibit religion, and it cannot excessively entangle the state in religion.[16] As a result, legislative action to provide funds to support church-affiliated schools has been narrowly defined and very limited.

Public aid is typically allowed to students of parochial schools when the benefits are available to the general student population and can be provided in a neutral environment that does not require excessive monitoring by the state. The first example of this type of support was the public subsidy of student bus fares to attend parochial schools. In *Everson v. Board of Education,*[17] the Court equated transportation with other public services and stated the benefit was provided to the students as a result of their citizenry and not to the church-affiliated school.[18] In 1983, the Court upheld a Rhode Island statute requiring local schools to provide transportation to all students who meet the state school transportation requirement even when it involved the parochial school students being transported outside their district.[19]

The "child benefit standard" has been the basis for other limited support for parochial students. The constitutionality of a New York statute permitting the loan of secular textbooks to parochial school students was upheld. Supporting the "child benefit theory," the Court noted in *Board of Education v. Allen*[20] that the benefit of a state loan of textbooks was to the students and parents and not to the schools. The courts have also allowed the provision of diagnostic services for speech, hearing, and psychological disorders;[21] cash reimbursements for costs attached to a state-mandated testing program; and the expenses for complying with state-mandated reporting procedures.[22] Recently, courts have supported the use of vans or mobile classrooms to provide Chapter I services to students who attend parochial schools as long as the services were provided adjacent to but not on the sectarian school grounds.[23]

In this manner, the use of public funds for church-affiliated schools has been limited and has been directed at the student and not the school. The courts have denied the support where there is an excessive entanglement of the parochial school and the state or where the funding is directed to the school. Examples in which the courts have denied funding include the loan of instructional material to private schools,[24] the provision of public funds for maintenance and repair of church-affiliated schools,[25] reimbursing costs to the school for teacher prepared tests mandated by the state,[26] providing for speech or hearing therapy and counseling at the church-affiliated school,[27] the use of public school buses for parochial school field trips,[28] and the use of public funds for programs operating in the parochial schools.[29]

One of the most important issues facing schools is the development of programs for school choice. The school choice options could redistribute tremendous levels of funds between public and private schools, especially church-affiliated schools. The Supreme Court provided the legal basis in *Mueller v. Allen*[30] for allowing this action when it approved a Minnesota statute granting tax deductions for tuition, textbooks, and school transportation. The law provided for the reimbursement through tax tuition credits to the parents of elementary or secondary students attending either private, parochial, or public schools. These efforts to provide public support for children attending private schools continues. The Supreme

Court of Wisconsin recently upheld the use of a choice program in *Davis v. Grover.*[31] The Parental Choice Program permitted children from low-income families to attend nonsectarian private schools.

Recommendations for Practice

School finance has taken on new importance in the past decade with many new legal challenges gaining momentum in redistributing funds between schools. Since these efforts mean that some schools may receive greater funding while others lose valuable resources to support programs, principals should be aware of the implications for their school sites. Principals should be proactive in addressing these changes by:

- planning for the changes in funding in instructional plans
- taking an active part in lobbying through professional organizations for favorable political resolution of the issues.

References

[1] 293 F. Supp. 327 (N.D. Ill. 1968), *aff'd sub. nom.*, McInnis v. Ogilvie, 394 U.S. 322 (1969).

[2] 411 U.S. 1 (1973).

[3] 487 P.2d 1241 (Cal. 1971). These principles were upheld in subsequent review under Serrano II, 557 P.2d 929 (Cal. 1976).

[4] D. Thompson. *School Finance Litigation: A Rising Concern.* NOLPE NOTES, 1990.

[5] 287 A.2d 187 (N.J. Super. Ct. 1972), *aff'd*, 303 A.2d 273 (N.J. 1973).

[6] Helena Elementary School Dist. v. State, 769 P.2d 684 (Mont. 1989).

[7] 790 S.W.2d 186 (Ky 1989).

[8] Edgewood Indep. School Dist. v. Kirby, 777 S.W.2d 391 (Tex. 1989), and Edgewood II, 804 S.W.2d 491 (Tex. 1991).

[9] Abbott v. Burke, 575 A.2d 359 (N.J. 1990).

[10] 811 P.2d 116 (Or. 1991).

[11] D. Thompson, *Supra* note 4.

[12] Nos. D-1477 (Supreme Ct. of Tex. 1991).

[13] Edgewood Indep. School Dist. v. Kirby, 777 S.W.2d 391 (Tex. 1989), and Edgewood II, 804 S.W.2d 491 (Tex. 1991).

[14] Nos. D-1477 (Supreme Ct. of Tex. 1991).

[15] 403 U.S. 602 (1970)

[16] *Id.*

[17] 330 U.S. 1 (1947).

[18] P. Anthony, *Public Funding for Religious Schools*, PRINCIPAL'S HANDBOOK: CURRENT ISSUES IN SCHOOL LAW, 241-248 (W. E. CAMP, et. al., eds., 1989).

[19] Members of the Jamestown School Committee v. Schmidt, 699 F.2d 1 (1983).

[20] 392 U.S. 236 (1968).

[21] Wolman v. Walter, 433 U.S. 229 (1977).

[22] Committee for Public Educ. and Religious Liberty v. Regan, 444 U.S. 646 (1980).

[23] Walker v. San Francisco Unified Sch. Dist., 761 F. Supp. 1463 (N.D. Cal. 1991).

[24] Meek v. Pittinger, 421 U.S. 350 (1973).

[25] Committee for Public Educ. and Religious Liberty v. Nyquist, 413 U.S. 756 (1973).

[26] *Levitt*, 413 U.S. 472 (1973).

[27] Wolman v. Walter, 433 U.S. 229 (1977).

[28] *Id..*

[29] Aguilar v. Felton, 473 U.S. 402 (1985).

[30] 463 U.S. 388 (1983).

[31] 480 N.W.2d 460 (Wis. 1992).

34

Legal Ramifications In the Coming Decade

Mary Jane Connelly

Introduction

This book, written by experts in the field of school law, addresses those legal issues that confront school administrators and, in particular, school principals. It is not exhaustive in its coverage, and principals are cautioned that the law is subject to change as new federal and state constitutional and statutory laws, rules, and regulations are added or amended. Interpretation of the law by federal and state courts may also impact and cause changes in the law.

What may the school principal expect in the future? Litigation is likely to continue on many of the issues already identified in the text. Emphases are likely to change with the prevailing conservative mood of the country. For example, more conservative decisions are expected to be handed down by the Supreme Court. Significant changes in the membership of the Supreme Court, the highest Court in the land, made by the Reagan and Bush administrations have shifted the balance to a more conservative Court. The Reagan administration appointed the first female Associate Justice, conservative Sandra Day O'Connor to replace Potter Stewart. Conservative Associate Justice William Rehnquist, originally appointed to the highest Court by Mr. Nixon, replaced Chief Justice Warren Burger. Antonin Scalia and Anthony Kennedy were also appointed during Mr. Reagan's Presidency replacing Associate Justices William Rehnquist and Lewis Powell. Mr. Bush's appointments include conservative David Souter and Clarence Thomas, a conservative Black, replacing liberal Associate Justices William Brennan and Thurgood Marshall. Still, the election of President Clinton may provide the opportunity to appoint judges that will shift the Court in a more moderate direction.

Legal Issues

Free Speech Issues

In 1986, the United States Supreme Court addressed the limits of free speech in *Bethel School District No. 403 v. Fraser.*[1] A student delivered a lewd and indecent speech in support of a candidate for elective office. He was suspended for two days and his name was removed from the list of candidates for commencement speaker. The Court upheld the school's actions citing *New Jersey v. T.L.O.*[2]

> Given the school's need to be able to impose disciplinary sanctions for a wide range of unanticipated conduct disruptive of the educational process, the school disciplinary rules need not be as detailed as a criminal code which imposes criminal sanctions.... The school disciplinary rule proscribing "obscene" language...gave adequate warning to Fraser that his lewd speech could subject him to sanctions.[3]

In *Hazelwood School District v. Kulhmeier,*[4] the United States Supreme Court upheld the right of a school principal to remove material from a school sponsored, student newspaper if the principal had sound, pedagogical reasons to do so. The two articles removed from the paper dealt with such sensitive issues as divorce and abortion. The principal's actions were supported because of the age of the audience and the subjects of the reports were identifiable.

Since that decision, a federal district court in Florida has upheld the right of a school board to remove materials from the curriculum that they felt were sexually explicit and vulgar. In *Virgil v. School Board of Columbia County, Florida,*[5] a high school had designed a humanities course for eleventh and twelfth graders. The course used a text which included Aristophanes' *Lysistrata* and Chaucer's *The Miller's Tale.* Neither of these were required readings; however, a portion of *Lysistrata* had been read aloud in class. An angry parent filed a complaint with the school board. The school board responded by ratifying a decision of the superintendent to remove the offending text from the curriculum. Plaintiffs, represented by the American Civil Liberties Union, challenged the action of the school board and claimed that the removal of the textbook violated their first amendment rights. Basing its decision on the *Hazelwood School District v. Kulhmeier*[6] decision, the federal district court disagreed with plaintiffs' claim and ruled in favor of the school board. The court noted that educators have discretion over the curriculum, and although the works were of literary value, they were sexually explicit and vulgar, and it was reasonable to exclude the materials from the curriculum.

In the same vein, a California court addressed the issue of prior restraint over a student newspaper. In *Leeb v. DeLong*,[7] the school principal prevented the distribution of a student paper that contained features on fictitious items including one that stated *Playboy Magazine* would publish photographs of nude high school girls. A photo of several girls from the school standing in line to be photographed accompanied the item. The California court noted that high school newspapers are a limited forum, and school officials should have a concern for the educational purpose served. The California Education Code and the school district's regulations provided for censorship to avoid potential liability. The court ruled that the free press provisions of the California Constitution should not be construed to require publication of potentially libelous material concerning one student to protect the free speech rights of another student. As long as there are student elections and newspapers, litigation on matters of free speech and freedom of the press are likely to continue. Given the present conservative mood of the country, the courts will support principals if they are able to articulate their pedagogical concerns when addressing first amendment issues.

Equal Access Act Issues

In 1990, the United States Supreme Court upheld the right of students to organize a Bible club on school grounds during an activity period. In *Board of Education of Westside Community School v. Mergens*,[8] the Court ruled that the school established a limited open forum when some club activities, not directly related to the curriculum, were approved by the school. The Court upheld the Equal Access Act of 1984 allowing secondary students the right to form clubs for religious, political, and philosophic study. The club must be voluntary, conducted by students, and must not be perceived as a school sponsored activity.

Earlier, in 1987, four Washington State high school students formed a Bible study group which met at a church adjacent to the school. The school district refused to grant the students permission to meet on school grounds during nonschool time. The students claimed the school violated their rights under the United States Constitution, the Equal Access Act, and the Washington State Constitution because the school had created a limited open forum. In denying plaintiffs' claims, the federal district court noted that other groups who were permitted to meet on campus were sponsored by the school and the activities were related to the curriculum. The strictures of the Washington State Constitution were far greater than the United States Constitution, and allowing the Bible group to meet on school grounds would appear to create an atmosphere of religious partisanship.[9]

In light of the *Mergens* decisions, the case was vacated and remanded by the United States Supreme Court.[10] The Supreme Court held that the school was a limited open forum and religious clubs should be allowed access to the school. However, on remand, the federal district held that the Equal Access Act violated the Washington State Constitution and the school district did not have to allow access to student religious groups.[11] Litigation on issues involving the Equal Access Act are likely to continue to further clarify the scope of the federal statute and its application to the various states. Although *Mergens* was an 8-1 decision, many of the Justices expressed individual thoughts and concerns.

Invocations and Benedictions

The Eleventh Circuit Court of Appeals addressed the subject of invocations prior to high school football games in *Jager v. Douglas County School District*.[12] The court determined that the *Lemon*[13] test controlled and even though the practice had ceased, invocations prior to football games were unconstitutional.

The Fifth Circuit Court of Appeals had held that graduation prayers that solemnize the ceremony are constitutional. In *Jones v. Clear Creek Independent School District*,[14] the court approved the school district's resolution requiring that invocations be nonsectarian and nonproselytizing and presented by student volunteers. The case was vacated and remanded to the lower court.[15] However, the Supreme Court of the United States in *Lee v. Weisman*,[16] upheld yet another case dealing with invocations at graduation. The First Circuit Court of Appeals had ruled that a benediction invoking a deity and delivered by a member of the clergy at a high school graduation violated the Establishment Clause of the United States Constitution. The five-to-four decision handed down by the Court did not overturn the *Lemon* decision as many expected.[17] The Court ruled that prayer at a high school graduation was unconstitutional.

In California, two taxpayers brought suit objecting to the inclusion of religious invocations and benedictions conducted by a protestant minister and a catholic priest at graduation ceremonies.[18] The California Supreme Court concluded that the practice impermissibly conveyed a message that the district favored the religious beliefs of the speakers, violating the principles of religious freedom and official neutrality.[19]

In yet another recent case, a federal district court in New York approved the leasing of a high school's auditorium to conduct a baccalaureate service.[20] A graduating senior and the New York Civil Liberty Union successfully requested the principal cancel the baccalaureate service traditionally arranged by the principal and officers of the senior class and sponsoring local ministers and pastors as speakers. A nondenominational study group expressed their interest in sponsoring the service and their request was approved. The event was to take place in the auditorium as originally planned. The graduating senior and her father brought suit challenging the school district and its superintendent. The court determined that the first amendment was not violated because the school board had formally and publicly disassociated itself from the service. The court noted that an equal access policy did not convey a message of affiliation or endorsement.

Other Legal Issues and Future Litigation

School finance issues continue to fill many state court dockets and principals will need to be mindful of what is happening in their own states. Kern Alexander has made a strong case to Congress to make education a fundamental right which could be the basis for reversing the 1973 Supreme Court decision, *San Antonio Independent School District v. Rodriguez.*[21]

A number of states and localities have banned the use of corporal punishment. When the *Ingraham v. Wright*[22] decision was handed down, only a handful of states had banned the practice. A number of states provide for home schooling and principals must be aware of their state's laws regarding the provision for home schooling. There is heightened awareness and sensitivity toward sexual harassment brought about by the public attention given the William Kennedy Smith rape trial, the confirmation hearings of Supreme Court Associate Justice Clarence Thomas, and the trial of heavyweight boxing champion Mike Tyson.

Special education litigation issues are focusing attention on the needs of the handicapped. Recent federal legislation has increased the awareness on the lack of barrier free environments. Principals need to take this seriously and remedy situations prohibiting a free, appropriate, public education for the handicapped.

Recommendations for Practice

The principal is faced with a myriad of legal issues on a daily basis and this text was developed as a reference to be used when confronted with legal questions. Courts will support the thoughtful, conscientious, and careful administrator who has acted in a fair and reasonable manner. Ignorance is not a defense and it is imperative that school officials keep abreast with developing legal issues.

- It is possible with the present composition of a conservative Supreme Court that there will be a shift in sentiment. Court watchers may see a move toward more narrowly defined decisions as courts struggle with such issues as student discipline, prayer in schools, affirmative action mandates, and the provision of special education services.
- Principals should take an active stance in staying abreast of the developments in school law. Sources of information for updates include legal newsletters and books published by the **National Organization on Legal Problems of Education (NOLPE)**. Other sources include appropriate legal journals and monographs.
- Principals should offer regular staff development sessions to their faculty and staff on school law. Inservice offered through attorneys and university faculty provides recent information on changes in laws and their impact on school operations.

References

[1] 106 S. Ct. 3159 (1986).
[2] 105 S. Ct. 733 (1985).
[3] *Id.*
[4] 108 S. Ct. 562 (1988).
[5] 677 F. Supp. 1547 (M.D. Fla. 1988).
[6] *Hazelwood,* 108 S. Ct. 562.
[7] 243 Cal. Rptr. 494 (Ct. App. 1988).
[8] 110 S. Ct. 2356 (1990).
[9] Garnett v. Renton School District No. 403, 675 F. Supp. 1268 (W. D. Wash. 1987).
[10] 110 S. Ct. 2608 (1990).
[11] Garnett v. Renton School Dist. 772 F. Supp. 531 (W.D. Wash. 1991).
[12] 862 F.2d 824 (11th Cir. 1989).
[13] 91 S. Ct. 2105 (1971).
[14] 930 F.2d 416 (5th Cir. 1991).
[15] 112 S. Ct. 3020 (1992).
[16] No. 90-1014. Lee v. Weisman, 59 U.S.L.W. 2095 (1st Cir. 1990).
[17] 112 S. Ct. 2649 (1992).
[18] Sands v. Morongo Unif. School Dist., 809 P.2d 809 (Cal. 1991).
[19] *Cert. denied,* 112 S. Ct. 3026 (1992)..
[20] Randall v. Pegan, 765 F. Supp. 793 (W.D.N.Y. 1991).
[21] 93 S. Ct. 1278, *rehearing denied,* 93 S. Ct. 1919 (1973).
[22] 97 S. Ct. 1401 (1977).

Index

Authors

M. David Alexander is Director, Division of Administrative and Educational Services, College of Education, Virginia Polytechnic Institute and State University. He is co-author of nine books including *American Public School Law* (1992).

Grover H. Baldwin is Professor and Department Chair in Educational Administration at the University of Toledo. He is an active writer in the area of school law, politics, finance, and policy.

Joseph C. Beckham is Professor and Chair of the Department of Educational Leadership at Florida State University. He is active in the Florida Bar Association and is a former President of the National Organization on Legal Problems of Education.

Billie Goode Blair is Professor of Education and Department Chair of Elementary Education at California State University, San Bernardino. She is the author of *Curriculum: The Strategic Key To Success* (1992).

Dee Botkins is Supervisor of Special Education in Warren County, Virginia.

Nelda H. Cambron-McCabe is Professor and Chair of the Department of Educational Leadership at Miami University in Oxford, Ohio. She is co-author of *Public School Law: Teachers' and Students' Rights* (1992).

William E. Camp is Professor of Education at California State University, San Bernardino. He is a former principal and assistant superintendent and is co-editor of *Principal's Handbook: Current Issues in School Law* (1989).

Trudy A. Campbell is Assistant Professor of Education at Texas Tech University. She has been a school administrator and foreign language teacher in the public schools of Illinois.

John Crain is an Associate Professor of Education at the University of North Texas. He is a former Assistant Superintendent of Dallas Independent School District.

Christine M. Crawford is a liaison counselor with Lehigh University's Centennial School, an approved private school for students with serious emotion disturbances.

Mary Jane Connelly is an Associate Professor and Department Head of Educational Leadership at The University of Tennessee, Knoxville. She was editor of the *Journal of Education Finance* and co-editor for *Principal's Handbook: Current Issues in School Law* (1989).

Joan L. Curcio is an Associate Professor at the University of Florida. She has been a school principal and assistant superintendent of schools and was nationally recognized in 1984 as one of the 100 top administrators for her work as a principal.

Floyd G. Delon is the Executive Director of the National Organization on Legal Problems of Education.

Carol A. Denzinger is a graduate assistant at Kent State University.

Patricia F. First is a Professor in the Department of Educational Leadership and Policy Studies at the University of Oklahoma. She is the author of *Educational Policy for School Administrators* (1992) and co-editor of *School Boards: Changing Local Control* (1992).

Kelly Frels is a Partner with Bracewell and Patterson of Houston, Texas. He has chaired the State Bar of Texas' School Law Section, served as President of the Council of School Attorneys of both the Texas Association of School Boards and the National School Boards Association, and served as President of the National Organization on Legal Problems of Education.

Ivan B. Gluckman is Legal Counsel and Director of Legal Services for the National Association of Secondary School Principals (NASSP). He is a member of the Editorial Advisory Committee of *West's Education Law Reporter*.

Steven S. Goldberg is Associate Professor of Education at Beaver College. He specializes in school law with an emphasis in special education.

Linda L. Hale is an attorney at the law firm of Michael, Best & Friedrich in Milwaukee, Wisconsin. She was an editor of the *Marquette Law Review* and a judicial law clerk for the Honorable Donald Steinmetz of the Wisconsin Supreme Court.

Jeffrey J. Horner is an attorney at the Houston law firm of Bracewell and Patterson. He works in the school law section and specializes in the representation of school districts and colleges.

Mary F. Hughes is an education research specialist with the West Virginia Education Fund. She has worked as a research and development specialist with the Appalachia Laboratory and her primary areas of research are legal and fiscal policy in public schools.

Frank R. Kemerer is Regents Professor of Education Law and Administration in the College of Education at the University of North Texas. He is the author of ten books and monographs, including a legal textbook, a book on Texas school law, and a biography of an activist Texas federal judge.

Kenneth E. Lane is Associate Professor of Education and Assistant to the Dean at California State University, San Bernardino. He teaches school law and has numerous publications relating to school law, facilities, and administration.

Henry S. Lufler, Jr. is Associate Dean of the School of Education of the University of Wisconsin-Madison. He is co-author of *School Discipline* and author of a handbook on school law for teachers and administrators in Wisconsin.

Ralph D. Mawdsley is a Professor of Educational Administration at Cleveland State University. He received his J.D. from the University of Illinois and is on the Board of Directors for NOLPE and the Editorial Advisory Committee for *West's Education Law Reporter*.

Martha M. McCarthy is Professor of Education at Indiana University. She has written extensively in the area of school law, is co-author of *Public School Law: Teachers' and Students' Rights* (1992), and is former President of the National Organization on Legal Problems of Education.

Jeff L. McNair is Associate Professor of Education at California State University, San Bernardino. He is Program Coordinator for Special Education.

Donna K. Metzler is an attorney with the Law Offices of Stuart, White, and Associates in Aurora, Illinois. She specializes in school and municipal law.

Amy C. Milford is a doctoral student at the University of Florida in the Department of Educational Leadership. She is a graduate of the University of Florida Law School and a member of the Florida Bar Association.

Margaret Bannon Miller is a partner with the law firm of Bose, McKinney & Evans in Indianapolis, Indiana. She was director of legal services and chief negotiator for the Evansville-Vanderburgh School Corporation.

Richard G. Salmon is Professor in Educational Administration in the College of Education, Virginia Polytechnic Institute and State University. He has written extensively in the areas of school law and finance.

David Schimmel is a Professor of Education at the University of Massachusetts at Amherst. He has written numerous articles and is co-author of several books, the most recent of which are *Parents, Schools and the Law* and *Teachers and the Law*.

Lynn Rossi Scott is an attorney with Rohne, Hoodenpyle, Lobert, and Myers. She specializes in school law and has written articles and given numerous presentations to school boards.

Linda A. Sharp is an Assistant Professor in Sport Management at Indiana University. She is an attorney and consultant in the area of sport law and is author of the monograph *Sport Law* (1990).

Gail Paulus Sorenson is Professor at the University of North Carolina at Charlotte. She has written extensively and is co-author of *School Law for Counselors, Psychologists, and Social Workers* (1991).

William E. Sparkman is Professor of Education and Associate Dean for Graduate Education and Research at Texas Tech University. He served as President of the American Education Finance Association and has written numerous articles and chapters on school finance and school law.

David O. Stine is an Associate Professor of Education and Coordinator of Administrative Interns at California State University, San Bernardino. He is a former principal and assistant superintendent of schools in California and currently serves as Board President for San Bernardino County Schools.

Stanley L. Swartz is Professor of Education at California State University, San Bernardino. He is a member of the educational administration and special education faculties and has research interests in public policy in special services and in school governance.

Stephen B. Thomas is Professor and Coordinator for Educational Administration at Kent State University. He is a former President of the National Association on Legal Problems of Education, and he has over 100 publications including 16 books.

Paul W. Thurston is an Associate Professor, Department Head in Educational Administration, and Director of the National Center of School Leadership at the University of Illinois. He holds a Ph.D in educational administration and a J.D. from the University of Iowa and has broad interests in the law as it relates to educational policy and to administrative responsibilities.

Joseph Turpin is Associate Professor of Education at California State University, San Bernardino. He is Program Coordinator for Rehabilitation Counseling.

Julie K. Underwood is an Associate Professor and Department Chair at the University of Wisconsin-Madison. She is an attorney specializing in students' rights and special education and is co-editor of *Principal's Handbook: Current Issues in School Law* (1989).

Richard S. Vacca is a Professor of Education at Virginia Commonwealth University. He has co-authored five textbooks and has served as the Scholar-In-Residence for the American Association of School Administrators (1991).

James Gordon Ward is Associate Dean for Administration and School Relations at the University of Illinois at Urbana-Champaign. He is an elected member of the Urbana Board of Education, past president of the American Education Finance Association, and former Director of Research for the American Federation of Teachers (AFL-CIO).

R. Craig Wood is Professor and Chair for the Department of Educational Leadership at the University of Florida. He is a former assistant superintendent of schools and has written extensively in the areas of school finance, business management, and law.

Perry A. Zirkel is University Professor of Education and Law at Lehigh University, where he formerly was Dean of the College of Education. He has written over 400 publications on various aspects of school law and writes a regular column jointly published in *Principal* and *NASSP Bulletin*.